GETTYSBURG'S *MOST HELLISH* BATTLEGROUND

GETTYSBURG'S *MOST HELLISH* BATTLEGROUND

★★★

The Devil's Den, July 2, 1863

PHILLIP THOMAS TUCKER

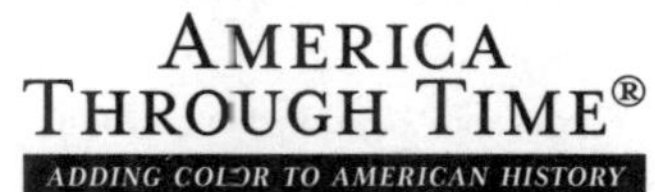

To the young men and boys on both sides who fought and died at the Devil's Den and Houck's Ridge on the afternoon of July 2, 1863.

America Through Time is an imprint of Fonthill Media LLC
www.through-time.com
office@through-time.com

Published by Arcadia Publishing by arrangement with Fonthill Media LLC
For all general information, please contact Arcadia Publishing:
Telephone: 843-853-2070
Fax: 843-853-0044
E-mail: sales@arcadiapublishing.com
For customer service and orders:
Toll-Free 1-888-313-2665

www.arcadiapublishing.com

First published 2019

ISBN 978-1-63499-123-0

Typeset in 10pt on 13pt Sabon
Printed and bound in England

Contents

Introduction

By the summer of 1863, the overly-ambitious Southern experiment in nationhood was on shaky ground and the most flimsy of foundations, because time and manpower were fast running out for the Army of Northern Virginia to achieve a decisive victory. President Abraham Lincoln had already issued the Emancipation Proclamation to bestow the war-weary Union with the moral high ground and a new motivation to wage a righteous war to destroy the anachronism known as the Confederacy, which had been left far behind by the most progressive nations of the western world. A new birth of freedom had been bestowed to America, and the Confederacy and its defenders found themselves entirely on the wrong side of history.

Quite simply, in an increasingly brutal war of attrition against a vastly more powerful opponent, the clock was ticking on the Confederacy's short lifetime. If decisive victory was not achieved by his Army of Northern Virginia during his second invasion of the North in the summer of 1863, then General Robert Edward Lee sensed almost instinctively that the opportunity to vanquish the Army of the Potomac would never come again. Therefore, on the second day during the dramatic showdown at Gettysburg in Adams County, southeastern Pennsylvania, Lee was going for broke as never before on July 2, 1863. Once again, he was placing his faith in the combat capabilities of his seasoned fighting men and the almost always-reliable formula of unleashing the tactical offensive to win the decisive victory in the hope of breathing new life into his beleaguered Southern nation, which had been totally unprepared for the first modern war and a lengthy conflict of attrition.

Long the most winning of all generals on either side in America's most cruel war, Lee realized that July 2 presented his best chance to destroy the hard-hit Army of the Potomac, which had taken a severe beating on the first day's fighting, July 1. On the second day, therefore, he knew that it was now or never, despite the fact that Spain-born Major General George Gordon Meade, who had been appointed to command the Army of the Potomac only days before, had skillfully aligned his troops on the best available high ground in the area: Cemetery Ridge and Culp's Hill on the north, and Cemetery Ridge that spanned south from Cemetery Hill.

For a host of reasons, consequently, Lee relied on the power of hard-hitting assaults, most famously against the defenders of Little Round Top at the southern end of the lengthy battle-line in a desperate bid to turn the vulnerable Union left flank, on the afternoon of July 2. These attacks were delivered from his best combat troops in a desperate bid to achieve the sparkling success that his war-weary nation so badly needed to survive America's bloodiest war.

Indeed, Lee depended largely upon his finest combat troops to win it all on the decisive afternoon of July 2: two brigades that consisted of crack Alabama (five regiments), Arkansas (one regiment), and Texas (three regiments) soldiers of Major General John Bell Hood's Division, Lieutenant General James Longstreet's First Corps, Army of Northern Virginia. Young Hood, a hard-fighting native Kentuckian and proud West Pointer, was the army's most aggressive division commander, and the performance of his battle-hardened command might well reap the decisive victory that his manpower-short nation and army had dreamed about achieving for more than two years, because they were trapped in a brutal war of attrition against a vastly more powerful opponent.

However, General Hood's sterling leadership qualities and aggressiveness were early negated on the afternoon of July 2 when he was badly-wounded in leading the assault on the high ground. Therefore, it would be largely left to the common Alabama and Texas soldiers to win decisive victory mostly on their own, while the defenders in blue benefitted far more from highly-capable leadership at all levels, especially by the ever-reliable General Meade, in the dramatic struggle on the southern flank. In total and in a far greater representation than the number of Lone Star State men in Hood's three Texas regiments, around 6,000 Alabama men in seventeen infantry regiments and two batteries fought at Gettysburg. But none of these troops played more distinguished roles during the three-day showdown than Hood's fighters of the 4th, 15th, 44th 47th, and 48th Alabama of Brigadier General Evander McIver Law's Brigade.

Unlike the earlier struggles for possession of the Devil's Den, a massive concentration of enormous boulders, and Jacob Houck's Ridge (the Devil's Den was situated at the ridge's southern end), the later fight for possession of nearby Little Round Top has been popularized by many historians, writers, novelists (especially Michael Sharra with his 1974 *The Killer Angels*), journalists, and filmmakers as the turning point to the epic three-day contest in which nearly 50,000 men on both sides fell. Because of this intense focus on Little Round Top's story, the equally crucial struggle for the possession of Houck's Ridge, immediately before, or west of, Little Round Top, and the Devil's Den has been long largely overlooked in regard to its strategic importance as a major turning point of the largest battle ever fought on the North American continent. All in all, this omission has been a most ironic development because Houck's Ridge (its southern end was the boulder-strewn top of the Devil's Den) was the true left of the Army of the Potomac at the beginning of the bloody struggle on the second day.

Therefore, the dramatic story of the bitter contest for the possession of Devil's Den and Houck's Ridge was all about the first effort (a successful one at that) to turn Army of the Potomac's left, which set the stage for the showdown at Little Round Top. Hence, this generally overlooked earlier fight immediately on the west side of Plum Rum that erupted before a shot was fired in anger on Little Round Top, immediately on Plum Run's east side, was of supreme importance and needs to be greater appreciated for its significance in the overall struggle to turn the Union left flank.

The capture of strategic Houck's Ridge and the Devil's Den—the first Union left flank before Little Round Top was occupied by Union troops to become the new left flank—were outstanding Confederate successes that captured the strategic high ground on Meade's southern flank. Nevertheless, despite this significant achievement before Little Round Top, rising around 150 feet from the valley of Plum Run just to the east, the struggle for the higher elevation of Little Round Top has been long popularized as the Battle of Gettysburg's decisive turning point that was unsuccessful for Confederate fortunes, while obscuring the earlier contest to turn the Union left flank at Houck's Ridge and the Devil's Den that was successful for Hood's attackers.

Here, just west of Plum Run that flowed south along the foot of Little Round Top, a golden opportunity was first and early presented to Hood's troops because Major General Daniel Edgar Sickles, a hardheaded political general who thought he was smarter than the army's commander in regard to the complexities of the soldier's art, had advanced his entire Third Corps without orders around two-thirds of a mile west to the high ground of the Peach Orchard and the Emmitsburg Road Ridge from General George Gordon Meade's main defensive line on Cemetery Ridge. Sickles' authorized advance and deployment so far before Cemetery Ridge meant he had was now forced to defend a far more lengthy line that was stretched much thinner out of necessity just before Lieutenant General James Longstreet, Lee's top lieutenant, launched his offensive effort to turn Meade's left with his powerful First Corps: an unforeseen (created by the irascible Dan Sickles on his own) tactical reality that left far too few Federals to defend the far left flank on the south at Houck's Ridge and the Devil's Den (the left flank of Sickles' Third Corps and the Army of the Potomac), which resulted in a recipe for disaster as General Meade fully realized.

This golden tactical opportunity that was presented to "Old Bulldog" Longstreet, a West Pointer and Mexican-American War veteran, and his seasoned First Corps veterans, including Hood's Division, existed for an extended period, before Union troops of Colonel Strong Vincent's Brigade, Fifth Corps, took possession of Little Round Top at the last minute.

The generally-overlooked struggle, before the famous contest for Little Round Top erupted in full fury, at the Devil's Den was most distinguished by a surreal landscape for which so many young men on both sides fought and died with a remarkable degree of courage. No single feature on America's most visited battlefield—that consisted of around 25 square miles in total—during the three days of intense combat can quite compare (then and today) to the most hellish and surreal landscape than this eerie-looking place called the Devil's Den. Located around 500 yards west of the higher

Little Round Top, this promiscuous jumble of granite-like boulders, crevices, and ledges of solidified igneous rock—the Devil's Den—stood at the southern end of Jacob Houck's Ridge to present a most formidable objective for Hood's attackers.

Initially and appropriately called "Stoney Point" by local residents and the citizens of Gettysburg before the war, the around 10 acres of the Devil's Den was the most famous geological anomaly—once molten rock (magma) that had violently thrust up from the earth's core to break through the earth's surface and then gradually cooled 180 million years ago to leave behind what was Adam County's strangest landscape that consisted of a massive pile of elephantine boulders—on the Gettysburg battlefield.

Today's popular name of Devil's Den entered into common usage months after the battle, emerging in 1864 when the war was waged with renewed fury during the struggle to capture the Confederacy's capital of Richmond, Virginia. Regardless of its different unique names at different times in America's past, the folly of man in waging the horrors of civil war and fighting tenaciously for possession of this unique geological feature of solidified igneous rock combined to create what truly became a hell on earth for the young men and boys who fought there. Quite simply, there was no place more eerie and surreal-like to the soldiers of both sides on the hot afternoon of July 2 than the Devil's Den, and this strange-looking place seemingly in the middle of nowhere was the last sight on earth for many young men.

As mentioned, the vicious struggle for possession of the Devil's Den and Houck's Ridge (Devil's Den was its southernmost and lower appendage) was more strategically important to the ultimate possession of the Union left than has been generally realized by many historians, because this crucial fight has been overlooked and so thoroughly overshadowed by the more famous chapters of the Battle of Gettysburg: Little Round Top on July 2 and the Pickett's Charge on July 3.

After all, the Confederate assaults directed at the first Union left flank at the Devil's Den and Houck's Ridge was Lee's desperate attempt turn the Union Army's left flank, before the struggle at Little Round Top which was the final round of intense combat on the southern end of the battle-line. Therefore, these two contests on opposite sides of Plum Run were more closely intertwined and connected than generally assumed. During the most important confrontation during the four years of war, the key to winning this crucial battle on the second day was Lee's attempt to turn Meade's left flank on the strategic high ground of Houck's Ridge and the Devil's Den, because these two high ground defensive positions anchored General Sickles' vulnerable left flank.

For such reasons, some of the most desperate combat on the decisive day of July 2 bestowed a grim immortality and the most appropriate sobriquet of the Devil's Den to this blood-soaked ground at the southern end of the battle-line. Here, the best fighting men of Hood's Division—the crack soldiers of the Texas Brigade—spearheaded the offensive effort that overwhelmed Houck's Ridge and the Devil's Den, leading the way as on past battlefields.

Most importantly, this tactical gain achieved by Lee's attackers was a significant accomplishment because Houck's Ridge anchored the left of not only General Sickles'

Third Corps, but also the Army of the Potomac to fulfill General Lee's ambitious plan on the second day: to turn the Union left flank. One lucky survivor of the carnage, Private James O. Bradfield, Company "E," 1st Texas Infantry Regiment, Hood's Division, explained how without a measure of exaggeration or hyperbole: "Here in a little cove called the Devil's Den occurred one of the wildest, fiercest struggles of the war." In this regard, the Devil's Den was certainly Satan's bloody playground on the all-important afternoon of July 2, 1862.

Indeed, this often overlooked struggle played a key role in the final outcome of the three-day Battle of Gettysburg, and to an extent not fully recognized by historians, who have mostly ignored this crucial contest. In fact, the savage combat that swirled through and around the giant boulders, ledges, and crevices of Devil's Den and along the barren, rocky length of Houck's Ridge was some of the most tenacious fighting at Gettysburg, because the stakes were so high.

Located at the ridge's southern end and easily in sight the barren, rocky slope of Little Round Top on Plum Run's other side, the Devil's Den presented one of the war's most formidable challenges to the attackers, who had never previously fought in such a hellish region. Here and contrary to popular perceptions, the bitter fighting for possession of the strategic high ground was even was more severe and heavier (and hence resulted in higher casualties, especially, of course, among the attackers) than during the celebrated struggle for Little Round Top, which later erupted at the new Union left flank.

Ironically, the overall negligence and obscurity of the struggle for the Devil's Den has developed despite the popularity of perhaps the most famous photograph of the Civil War—the photo of the dead Confederate soldier, who was long misidentified as a Rebel "sharpshooter," lying behind the rock wall, or barricade, situated between two large boulders at the Devil's Den. The body of the young man lies beside a nearby musket—probably not his own—that the photographer (Timothy H. O'Sullivan, who had been born in either Ireland or New York City around 1840 and served as an apprentice to famed photographer Mathew Brady) had carefully orchestrated. On July 6, 1863, O'Sullivan was a member of the Alexander Gardner team of photographers, who took photographs of some of the last Confederate dead before they were buried by Union details.

To create this famous photograph, the body of the so-called "sharpshooter" was placed against the stone barricade by the photographers for a more dramatic visual effect. But in truth, this unfortunate young soldier had actually originally fallen in the attack on the western side of the Devil's Den. To obtain their photograph, the body—the soldier, perhaps only a teenager, had been dead for four days by this time—was then moved by these photographers to the well-known site situated between the two boulders and behind the rock barricade.

This young, dark-haired soldier was an attacker who fell on the western side of the Devil's Den on the afternoon of July 2 and most likely a member of the 1st Texas Infantry Regiment, Hood's Texas Brigade. Quite simply, he played no part in the sharpshooting on

Little Round Top that began after the assault that resulted in the capture of the Devil's Den and then continued the next day. The famous O'Sullivan photograph was entirely staged, but with an artistic touch that resulted in Gettysburg's most memorable photograph.

This legendary photograph, taken by O'Sullivan on July 6, 1863, and the most well-known of all Gettysburg photographs, has played a part in promoting the mistaken impression and popular misconception that the Devil's Den was nothing more than an insignificant and obscure position for Rebel sharpshooters, and, therefore, it was not important in the battle's overall outcome. Ironically, to this day, popular writers have continued to speculate about the identity of the young Rebel soldier lying behind the stone barricade in this most recognizable part of the Devil's Den—the sharpshooters' position situated between two large boulders and behind the hand-made rock wall. The rock barricade had been created by Hood's men after the July 2 assaults by soldiers-*cum*-sharpshooters for protection for firing across the valley of Plum Run upon the Federal artillerymen, who manned the guns on the crest of Little Round Top.

Of course, although the exact identity of this deceased soldier will probably never be known with any degree of certainty, it is the opinion of this author that this young man was very likely a soldier of the 1st Texas Infantry Regiment, whose right charged up the western side of the Devil's Den, where this soldier fell and met his Maker. Ironically, historians have attributed the identity of this fallen soldier to a number of regiments, but not a Texas regiment: speculations and guesswork that have revealed their lack of knowledge about the exact details of the central role played by the 1st Texas in capturing the Devil's Den.

Unfortunately and as noted, the popular and famous photo has helped to create the mistaken impression that the Devil's Den played only a minor and fringe role in the struggle for possession of the Union left flank—a mere insignificant sharpshooter position that faced Little Round Top. Unfortunately, this mistaken impression has lingered to this day. Because the Devil's Den was well-defended by Federals at the southern end of the battle-line and located in a strategic position at the southern base of Houck's Ridge, it served as an extremely important anchor of the left flank of the Army of the Potomac, before Little Round Top was occupied by Union troops of the Fifth Corps, Army of the Potomac.

Clearly, the location of the Devil's Den made it one of the most strategic and important positions on the Gettysburg battlefield, and even more significant than Little Round Top at the time, because the most famous elevation to the east had not yet become a bone of contention. Nevertheless, the myth has persisted to this day that the Devil's Den was an isolated and remote place where only Confederate sharpshooters fought as part of the better-known struggle for possession of Little Round Top, because of the popularity of this famous photograph of the dead Rebel "sharpshooter" and the giant shadow cast by the popularity of the struggle for the high ground on Plum Run's east side.

This development of an undeserved obscurity and general misunderstanding of the importance of the earlier fight for the Devil's Den has also occurred because it has been generally forgotten that this truly strategic point—along with Houck's Ridge, of course—was the crucial location of the vulnerable left flank of the Army of the Potomac, before the arrival of Union reinforcements on Little Round Top. But in truth, the Devil's Den lay at the heart of the struggle for the first Union left flank on the high ground of Houck's Ridge, before the more famous fight for the second, or last, Union left flank on Little Round Top.

Significantly, this extremely popular photograph (please see the cover of this current book) of the body of the alleged "sharpshooter" has fully captured the spirit, essence, and horror of the Devil's Den. Indeed, to this day, no place on any battlefield in North America is quite like the Devil's Den. Strange and ominous because of its seemingly unearthly and eerie landscape that looks entirely out-of-place among the lush rolling farmlands of Adams County, Pennsylvania, the Devil's Den has become a very popular site for large numbers of tourists because of the sensational qualities of this enormous maze of huge boulders and rocky outcroppings: a massive concentration of feldspar, pyroxene, and plagioclase rock that seemingly have been placed here by an ancient deity for entirely unknown reasons. Consequently, the appropriately-named Devil's Den became not only the most hellish and surreal terrain on the entire battlefield of Gettysburg, but also one of the most grim killing fields of the largest battle ever fought in the western hemisphere.

Quite simply, no single spot on America's most revered battlefield can quite compare to the Devil's Den on multiple levels. In a strange paradox, no place on any eastern theater battlefield seemed (then and today) more truly bizarre-looking and out-of-place than the Devil's Den, appearing more like a typical geological feature of the boulder-strewn mountains of America's rugged southwestern deserts or in the heavily-wooded foothills of the Rocky Mountains. Colonel William F. Perry, who commanded an excellent Alabama regiment of Hood's Division and was long traumatized by the searing memory of the savage combat that had raged among the boulders, crevices, and ledges, described Gettysburg's most hellish battleground, the Devil's Den: "Large rocks, from six to fifteen feet high, are thrown together in confusion over a considerable area, and yet so disposed as to leave everywhere among them winding passages carpeted with moss. Many of the recesses are never visited by sunshine, and a cavernous coolness pervades the air within it." Indeed, this was Gettysburg's most surreal battleground of the three days of combat and place of death for some of the best and brightest of the Army of Northern Virginia and the Army of the Potomac in a dramatic showdown in which everything was at stake for two nations.

Wide expanses of open ground (farmer's broad fields of summer and grassy meadows that seemed to flow to the horizon) were relatively rare on Civil War battlefields, especially in Virginia and the even more heavily-wooded and less cultivated landscapes of the western theater compared to the eastern theater. But in general, the intense combat that raged around Gettysburg was fought in more open areas than on most of the war's brutal killing grounds, which made Devil's Den still another kind of anomaly not found on any other battlefield in America.

Therefore, precisely because of the mostly open terrain that appeared like a thick carpet of green (expansive pasture lands, including wide clover fields) and yellow (broad fields of wheat that stood high and near harvesting), which covered the fertile ground of Adams County, Gettysburg, the scene of one of the war's most conventional battles was fought primarily on a lengthy expanse of open ground that was reminiscent of a Napoleonic battlefield in a more romantic age. Almost as if on a drill field or parade ground, well-organized alignments, maneuvers, and sweeping assaults (almost all Confederate during the entire three days because General Meade remained on the defensive with his hard-pressed infantry unlike his powerful Cavalry Corps that became more aggressive on the afternoon July 3) of traditional linear tactics of the tactical offensive dominated the fighting across wide expanses of Gettysburg's open fields, especially between Seminary and Cemetery Ridges: very nearly a replay of the great conventional battles that had long raged across central Europe when Napoleon Bonaparte became the master of Europe.

But, as noted, this situation was certainly not the case at the Devil's Den. Among the giant boulders of the Devil's Den and along the barren heights of Houck's Ridge, the vicious combat, including hand-to-hand fighting, was more eerie than at any other part of the Gettysburg battlefield, because it was less conventional and more asymmetrical in this unique environment. In this sense, before the dramatic showdown for possession of Little Round Top, the initial struggle on the Union Army's first left flank was quite unlike any other clash during the first three days of July. This close-range combat was of an especially savage nature that swirled through the most unique and distinctive geological feature found anywhere on the Gettysburg battlefield.

Even more than the combat that raged in the wide open fields that dominated the Gettysburg battlefield from July 1 to July 3, the fighting in and around the Devil's Den was especially nightmarish, raging with an unbridled fury and at exceptionally close range amid the maze of boulders and rocks. Bayonets, musket-butts, and fists were used by powder-stained antagonists when they battled for survival in a primeval struggle among the boulders, ledges, and crevices: a true Darwinian struggle of survival of the fittest.

Lee's westernmost and most frontier warriors from the Lone Star State of General Hood's Texas Brigade and the Alabama Brigade rose splendidly to the challenge on the afternoon of July 2. Here, a greater measure of frontier-style combat, as long witnessed by the people of Texas through the course of the republic's history, raged in and around the Devil's Den than anywhere else during the bloodiest three days in American history.

One veteran Texas soldier said in best in describing the nightmarish combat that roared in and around the Devil's Den, which consisted of "more than Indian fighting than anything I [ever] experienced during the war." Therefore, it was most appropriate that Lee's toughest combat troops, the seasoned soldiers of the crack Texas Brigade, engaged in this vicious kind of close-quarter combat that was so reminiscent of western frontier fighting, especially Indian warfare. Both the Texans and Alabamians of Hood's Division were roughhewn westerners so unlike the generally more refined Virginians, and these determined soldiers not only maintained their elite status as fighting men, but also took it to a loftier height on the afternoon of July 2.

Indeed, it took exceptionally hardy and resilient American fighting men, who embodied sterling western frontier traits (self-reliance, resilience, and a host of other specialized skills—especially marksmanship—and the hard-learned lessons stemming from Indian warfare and Texas Revolutionary War experience from 1835–1836) to overcome one of Gettysburg's most formidable defensive challenges at the far southern end of the battle-line. These well-honed skills were more diversified among Hood's Texas soldiers than any other fighting men in the Army of Northern Virginia, because of their unique backgrounds and experiences in America's most frontier state in 1861. Against the odds and in successfully overcoming one obstacle after another, Hood's Texas Rebels played the key role in leading the way in capturing not only Houck's Ridge, but also the Devil's Den.

Most of all, the bloody struggle that swirled around the boulder-studded terrain of the Devil's Den was dominated by the common soldiers' survival of the fittest instincts in the western frontier tradition, because so much was at stake for both armies. The close-quarter combat among the giant boulders and rocks raged out-of-control on Gettysburg's most unusual battleground that forever became known as the Devil's Den because of the extent of the carnage and bloodletting.

The nightmarish combat of the Devil's Den was never forgotten by survivors, who thanked God that they had survived the killing among the immense boulders at the southern end of Houck's Ridge. As seemingly the most inappropriate part of a pristine Adams County landscape that gradually dipped eastward from the South Mountain Range (the northern extension of the Blue Ridge Mountain Range) to the fertile lowlands along the Susquehanna River, this surreal-looking battlefield of giant rocks, that appeared entirely out-of-place, had been created when a glacier carved out a shallow valley between the two parallel north–south running ridges, Seminary Ridge, to the west, and Cemetery Ridge—Meade's primary defensive line—to the northeast that extended south to Little Round Top.

When the glacier ice had receded at the Ice Age's end, the mammoth glacier left behind the jumble of massive granite-like boulders strewn in random fashion just northwest of heavily-forested Big Round Top, which towered above Little Round Top—around 120 lower than its more heavily-timbered twin—located just to the north of one of the highest elevations, Big Round Top, in Adams County at around 270 feet above the floor of the valley of Plum Run. This small, clear watercourse flowed between the Devil's Den and Little Round Top, and trickled gently south at the foot of the higher elevation with a barren western face from recent timber cutting. General Hood's seasoned men from the east Texas lowlands—the plain of the Gulf of Mexico—had never seen such a stranger-looking landscape before July 2, 1863.

Perfectly befitting its name and for plenty of valid reasons, the Devil's Den, which was a name that would have disturbed the most devout fighting men in the ranks of both armies, was a nightmarish battleground never forgotten by anyone who fought there. Many soldiers met their Maker and came of age at this strange-looking place that consisted of a labyrinth of rocky passages, ledges, and crevices among the giant boulders, which were situated amid the pastoral landscape of the surrounding rich farmlands made productive by a rich, limestone soil and industrious farmers of mostly German descent. To the combatants on both sides, the Devil's Den appeared to be an almost ghostly apparition that was oddly situated, almost as if dropped from the sky to land among the picturesque fields of plenty and an agricultural paradise that lay south of Gettysburg. For good reason, the Devil's Den and its strange environs had been long shunned by generations of farmers and woodcutters, almost as if some intangible evil lurked among the eerie-looking boulders that seemed so out-of-place.

On the bloody afternoon of July 2, 1863, to leave an enduring legacy, the savage combat that raged through the Devil's Den and Houck's Ridge resulted in a transcendental experience for the Texas Brigade's soldiers. In overall tactical terms, the Devil's Den was much more of a surreal and nightmarish battlefield than Houck's Ridge or Little Round Top.

The Devil's Den, located around 500 yards west of Little Round Top, became one of the attackers' top priorities, because this jumble of piled-up rocks and boulders had to be captured by Hood's troops to fulfill Lee's ambitious vision of turning Meade's left flank to unhinge the entire Cemetery Ridge defensive line. Therefore, the bitter contest for the Devil's Den and Houck's Ridge, situated on the northwest side of the Plum Run Valley through which marshy Plum Run flowed lazily southward and eventually into the Potomac River, was all important during the crucial period, before Union troops gained possession of Little Round Top to create a new and even more formidable left flank. Most importantly, this initial, or westernmost, high ground Union defensive position that loomed before the wide, open ground of farmers' lush fields (primarily the so-called "Triangular Field") first had to be captured for any realistic hope of securing possession of Little Round Top, which became the solid anchor of the Union left, after the fall of Houck's Ridge and the Devil's Den.

However, almost the entire focus of the second day's fighting on the far south has emphasized the well-known story of what happened on Little Round Top from the narrow perspective and one-sided focus by generations of historians, including to this day. But this decidedly narrow and distorted focus has been inevitable largely because many historians have become so completely enamored with the much-embellished and popular story of Colonel Joshua Lawrence Chamberlain and his 20th Maine Volunteer Infantry's romanticized defensive stand on the left flank of Colonel Vincent Strong's Brigade, First Division, Third Brigade, Fifth Corps, on Little Round Top, while equally important earlier contests have been ignored or minimized, especially the bloody struggle for Meade's (Dan Sickles' Third Corps) original left flank.

On the bloodiest day of the brutal slugfest at Gettysburg, the men of the 1st Texas, Hood's Division, encountered their greatest challenge in overrunning Houck's Ridge and the Devil's Den. Like their outgunned agrarian nation after decisive defeat at

Gettysburg, these Texans were never quite the same and their hopes for the future were never as bright, after losing so many of their comrades during Hood's attacks to overrun the strategic high ground at any cost. Indeed, a transformation of sorts among Hood's fighters took place during the fierce combat that raged for a lengthy period around the jumble of massive array of stacked-up boulders. Here, these hardened veterans realized that they no longer faced the same kind of bluecoat opponent, who they had systemically routed at Gaines's Mill and Second Manassas in spearheading hard-hitting assaults: an ominous sign for the future.

These crack Texan troops, flying their red, white, and blue Lone Star flag that reminded them of a successful people's 1835–1836 revolution against the Republic of Mexico confidently entered into the maelstrom of the Devil's Den with a heightened *esprit de corps* and fighting spirit that was well-known throughout the Army of Northern Virginia. In the surreal combat that swirled over Houck's Ridge and the Devil's Den for what seemed like an eternity and with a fury seldom seen, the surviving Texans had literally gone to hell and back on the bloody afternoon of July 2 and they would never be the same afterward. Indeed, as the Texas soldiers discovered to their horror, no single spot on America's largest battlefield quite compared to the truly nightmarish qualities of the fighting in the Devil's Den.

However and as mentioned, the supreme importance of the struggle for the Devil's Den has been overshadowed by the unparalleled popularity of the nearby and later fight for possession of Little Round Top. Little Round Top was later occupied by Union troops, Colonel Vincent's Brigade, which included Colonel Joshua Lawrence Chamberlain and his 20th Maine Volunteer Infantry, just in the nick of time, after the capture of Houck's Ridge. The arrival of Vincent's troops on Little Round Top set the stage for the most dramatic showdown at Gettysburg, after Pickett's Charge. But as mentioned, the excessive focus on Little Round Top's story has thoroughly overshadowed the importance of the earlier capture of the Devil's Den and Houck's Ridge—the first struggle for the Union left flank. This longtime almost routine and casual ignoring of this crucial contest on Plum Run's other side (west) has lately reached all-time highs in the annals of Civil War historiography, because of the increased popularity of the Little Round Top story.

The excessive popularity of the Little Round Top story that still exists today can be easily explained by the following closely-connected developments that laid the primary foundation for today's accepted version of events: John Pullen's 1957 classic regimental history of the 20th Maine; Michael Shaara's even more popular 1974 Pulitzer Prize-winning novel *The Killer Angels*; and then Ted Turner's 1994 Gettysburg movie, based upon *The Killer Angels* and its excessive romantic portrayal of leading characters, especially wearing the blue, in traditional novelist form.

Faithfully following the established pattern, Shaara's popular novel overly-glorified the fight of the 20th Maine on Little Round Top and its saint-like (ironically, the same divine qualities of ancient Greek mythological heroes—partly to fulfill the modern public's psychological and emotional need for romantic myth in a non-heroic age—

that had earlier elevated General Robert E. Lee into a God on the Confederate Mount Olympus by "Lost Cause" mythology during the post-Civil War period) regimental commander from Bowdoin College, Maine, Colonel Chamberlain.

This popular interpretation that has been long accepted as gospel represented a classic case of a deliberately manufactured mythology of a victor culture. Meanwhile, the equally significant story of the all-important struggle for possession of Houck's Ridge and the Devil's Den and the notable accomplishments of Hood's troops—especially in capturing the original left of the Union line before Little Round Top was occupied by Union troops of the Fifth Corps—have been relatively ignored by leading historians and buffs alike for more than a century and a half.

In a case of history coming full circle, the Texas Revolution's enduring legacies, including the famous defense of the old Franciscan mission (the Alamo) located just outside San Antonio de Bexar on the cold early morning, before sunrise, of March 6, 1836, were alive in the hearts and minds of Hood's Texans on Gettysburg's gory field, where they battled against the odds more than a 1,000 miles from their homes. A large percentage of the younger soldiers were the sons and grandsons of the revolutionary Texians. The fact that their fathers had won their independence from Mexico when General Sam Houston's attackers reaped their one-sided victory at San Jacinto on April 21, 1836, was never forgotten by Hood's Texans.

Like General Lee, the Confederacy's president, Jefferson Davis, a fellow West Pointer and Mexican-American War hero of the Battle of Buena Vista when he had led a Mississippi regiment of soldiers uniformed in red shirts, fully appreciated how the inspirational Texas Revolutionary legacies served as a key factor that explained why the Texans so early evolved into Lee's best fighting men. President Davis had early emphasized to the Texas Brigade soldiers how Southern troops from the twelve "other states [of the Confederacy] have their reputations to gain [but] the sons of the defenders of the Alamo have theirs to maintain!" In this sense, the Texas Revolution and its legacies had come to Adams County, Pennsylvania, on the bloody afternoon of July 2.

Even the boys in blue understood how the Texans were perpetuating a most distinguished historical and military legacy that stemmed from the Texas Revolution, when a new frontier republic in the southwest had been created in the fiery forge of violent revolution. The historical legacies of these crack Texas soldiers had preceded them by the time that they faced their greatest challenge at Gettysburg, when they excelled beyond even what they had performed to wide acclaim on the field of Antietam on September 17, 1862.

Therefore, the heroic memory of the Alamo, whose defenders mostly hailed from the Deep South, was still vibrant to the Texas Brigade's soldiers when they marched with Enfield rifled muskets on shoulders during the invasion of Pennsylvania, where a number of Alamo defenders had been born. On July 2, the elite Texas soldiers fully maintained this distinctive historical legacy of the Texas Revolution, while proving to be entirely worthy as successors during the bitter struggle for possession of Houck's

Ridge and the Devil's Den, those "awful rocks," strewn with bodies and the debris of battle, in one dying Confederate's words, during the climactic battle that ultimately determined the destiny of America.

Filling in a long-existing gap in regard to the most written about and famous battle in American history, this current book will present the dramatic story about the all-important capture of Houck's Ridge and the Devil's Den (the first Union left flank held by Third Corps troops under General Sickles), which represented a sparkling success: quite unlike the equally valiant later attempts of the other Texans (the 4th and 5th Texas Infantry Regiments) and Alabamians of Brigadier General Evander McIver Law's Alabama Brigade, Hood's Division, who failed to achieve their vital tactical objective in capturing Little Round Top (the second Union left flank). By overrunning the dominant crest of Houck's Ridge, the 1st Texas captured and permanently retained possession of more Union artillery pieces than any other Army of Northern Virginia troops during the three days of fighting at Gettysburg.

Even though the Texans played the leading role in overwhelming Houck's Ridge, capturing four field pieces of a veteran New York Battery that were positioned on the barren crest, and overrunning the great mass of boulders known as the Devil's Den, the resistance of brave Third Corps defenders was so staunch that precious time was bought for sizeable Union reinforcements—first Colonel Strong Vincent's Brigade and later other Fifth Corps units—to arrive and occupy Little Round Top: a tight strategic grip that the tenacious defenders in blue never lost, despite the best efforts of Hood's troops (hard-fighting Alabama and Texas veterans) to push them off their all-important perches during repeated desperate assaults, when the life of the Army of the Potomac hung precariously in the balance.

Therefore, initially unknown to them in the beginning of the assault, Hood's attackers on July 2 were actually destined to face a defense in depth of two successive formidable elevations, which presented the ultimate challenge for the tactical offensive: first, Houck's Ridge and the diabase boulders of the Devil's Den of around 10 acres, and then Little Round Top. Ironically, as fate would have it, General Meade had made no plans or gave no orders to defend either Houck's Ridge or the Devil's Den, which became the eye of the storm.

Unfortunately and as noted, the full story of this true early turning point has been long ignored and minimized by historians, who have repeatedly focused on the most popular aspects of Gettysburg's story, especially the struggle for possession of Little Round Top. Nevertheless, a great deal was at stake during this climactic showdown before the fight for possession of Little Round Top: quite simply, whoever held the strategic crest of Houck's Ridge and the Devil's Den dominated and controlled the Army of the Potomac's left flank, which might have well ultimately determined the final outcome of the most important battle of the Civil War. For General James "Old Pete" Longstreet's soldiers of Hood's Division, this boulder-strewn place that was located seemingly in the middle of nowhere was most appropriately named, because it became a hell on earth for them and the Third Corps defenders at the southern end of the battle-line.

Nevertheless, these young men and boys of Hood's Division somehow overcame the odds and excelled in capturing the highest ground position on the Union Army's left flank at the time, despite their heroic efforts of the equally heroic defenders. Symbolically, the Devil's Den and Houck's Ridge remained in Rebel hands and flew Southern battle-flags in triumph unlike in the case of Little Round Top that was never overwhelmed by the attackers, after some of the most savage combat waged at any sector on the Gettysburg battlefield.

Besides breaking new ground in the field of Gettysburg historiography, this book has been written to honor the bravery and sacrifice of the common soldiers, whose personal stories have been most often neglected, on both sides during this long-ignored crucial phase of the most decisive battle of the Civil War. But most of all, the primary purpose of this book has been to reemphasize the long-overlooked and generally-forgotten importance of the bloody struggle for the first left flank of the Army of the Potomac that has been long relegated to the dark shadows by the famous contest for the army's second left flank at Little Round Top, because of the excessive glorification and romance. Therefore, it is time to shine a new light and fresh focus on the bitter struggle for possession of the Devil's Den, including a detailed look at the common soldiers on both sides who fought there with great distinction.

Even more, another primary thesis of this current book has been to demonstrate that top Confederate leadership, including General Lee, doomed the best efforts of the common soldiers on July 2, 1863. Indeed, the plethora of mistakes committed by a badly-fumbling and incompetent Confederate leadership at the highest levels was one of the most overlooked reasons for defeat on the second day. The sense of desperation that dominated Lee's mood—both desperate and reckless—and stubborn tactical thinking at Gettysburg sabotaged the excellent fighting of the common soldiers in the ranks, and this was especially the case of Hood's men, who attempted in vain to turn the left flank at Little Round Top.

In this sense, the superior fighting capabilities demonstrated by Hood's troops in attempting to turn Meade's left were entirely wasted and they died in vain because of the folly of Southern leadership, including General Lee. Consequently, this book will take a close look at the army's elite fighting men and how their determined efforts were in vain on a bloody afternoon of decision, when everything was at stake.

It is the view of this historian that the best way to truly understand the essence of a battle, especially a decisive one, and its most subtle ebbs and currents can be better deciphered by closely analyzing the backgrounds of the men in the ranks and the histories of their units, especially if elite commands. Most importantly, it is necessary to understand in detail the motivations, idealism, and belief systems that shaped and defined the actions of the common soldiers at Gettysburg. Therefore, one thesis of this book will be to explore the overlooked factors that made these American fighting men truly elite warriors, and how this eliteness translated into superior combat performances on the second day at Gettysburg.

The brave men who fought at the Devil's Den died for what they believed was right, and this, of course, was the case of the soldiers on both sides. Hood's men earned a well-deserved compliment for what they accomplished against almost insurmountable odds on the afternoon of July 2, which was quite simply the "best three hours' fighting ever done by any troops on any battlefield." But most importantly, the Union defenders of the Devil's Den and Houck's Ridge sacrificed themselves to buy precious time to not only save the hard-pressed Army of the Potomac, but also the Union in the end. These courageous boys in blue persevered and won the day by splendid fighting, because they truly rose to the occasion quite unlike on any previous battlefield of this war.

The young soldiers who died in the struggle for possession of the Devil's Den have been forgotten compared to the fighting men of Little Round Top on July 2, and especially Pickett's Charge on the final day, July 3. But they fought and died for what they believed was right with an unparalleled tenacity at the Devil's Den, and they were no less heroic than the attackers of Pickett's Charge and the defenders of Cemetery Ridge. Here, at the Devil's Den, the young men and boys on both sides seemed not only to be fighting on the Devil's own home ground, but also against the Devil himself during one of the most nightmarish struggles of the Civil War.

In his famous Gettysburg Address that he presented on historic November 19, 1863 to pay a glowing tribute to the multitude of fallen Americans, which included the brave men who fought like devils to the bitter end during the tenacious defense of the jumbled pile of boulders and ledges of the Devil's Den, President Abraham Lincoln emphasized in his dedication of Gettysburg's "hallowed ground" that memorialized the thousands of courageous Americans (both fought in the hope that their respective republics would survive and live a long life), who were buried in the national cemetery on Cemetery Hill that served as "a final resting place for those who died here, that the nation might live."

Phillip Thomas Tucker, Ph.D.
Washington, D.C.
December 10, 2018

1

Hard-Fighting Men from the West

In the end, top Confederate leadership, including General Robert E. Lee, his top lieutenants, and division and brigade commanders, doomed the determined efforts—some of the best fighting seen in the war—of the common soldiers in the ranks at the Battle of Gettysburg, and this was especially the case on the decisive second day: July 2, 1863. Quite simply, a truly capable and competent Confederate leadership would have won the most decisive victory of the war on the second day at Gettysburg, and there would have never been any reason to launch the ill-fated Pickett's Charge on the afternoon of July 3.

To verify this central thesis of how the combat prowess and remarkable battlefield achievements, including the capture of the Devil's Den and Houck's Ridge, on the second day at Gettysburg were misused and wasted by Confederate leadership, it is first necessary to explore in detail the story of the elite troops of the Army of Northern Virginia, the Texans of Major General John Bell Hood's Division.

By the time of the decisive showdown at Gettysburg, southeastern Pennsylvania, the battle-tested troops of Lieutenant General James Longstreet's First Corps were considered to be the finest fighting men of the Army of Northern Virginia, and for good reason. Hood commanded the elite division of this hard-hitting corps of tried soldiers, who had achieved one success after another. They had won impressive victories across Virginia, and were determined to repeat their success north of the Potomac River during the summer of 1863.

Appropriately, despite his relative youth and before becoming division commander, Hood had previously served as the leader of the crack brigade, which consisted of three Texas infantry regiments and one Arkansas infantry regiment by the time of the Gettysburg Campaign. General Hood and his men faced their greatest challenge on the afternoon of July 2, including in regard to overwhelming the tenacious defenders of the Devil's Den.

But another brigade of Hood's Division fully demonstrated that it also consisted of crack troops during the dramatic showdown at Gettysburg during the first three days of July 1863: Brigadier General Evander McIver's five seasoned Alabama regiments. Two of these Alabama regiments fought with distinction at the Devil's Den, and then at Little Round Top in conjunction with the Texas men. But it was the Texas soldiers who had long demonstrated that they were the army's best fighting soldiers, and this legacy continued at Gettysburg. Therefore, these dependable fighting men from the Lone Star State need to be analyzed in greater detail today to reveal how and why they emerged as the best fighters of an army known for its combat prowess, especially in regard to the tactical offensive during the dramatic showdown at Gettysburg.

When the 1st, 4th, and 5th Texas Regiments were brigaded together for the first time at the small town of Dumfries, Virginia, located about halfway between Washington, D.C., and the Confederacy's capital at Richmond, Virginia, on a chilly November 13, 1861, the Texas Brigade's central foundation was laid firmly in place. But more importantly, what also was set in place was the creation of the hardest fighting and most lethal combat unit of General Lee's Army of Northern Virginia. Even more to guarantee a most distinguished place in the historical record, the Texas Brigade evolved into one of the most effective and deadly fighting machines in the history of the annals of American military history: a fact that was fully demonstrated not only across Virginia, but also during the two major battles fought north of the Potomac River, Antietam, Maryland, on September 17, 1862, and Gettysburg.

In the war's early days, a confident Texan, who knew of his command's immense potential and promise, of Brigadier General John Bell Hood's Texas Brigade made a bold prediction in a letter that had proved prophetic on the gory battlefields of Virginia, Maryland, and Pennsylvania, especially in the bloodletting at Gettysburg: "that when 'the fight' takes place the Texas Brigade will kill more Yankees, storm more batteries, and capture fewer prisoners than any brigade in the service."[1]

These revealing words about the men who served under the Kentucky-born Hood, who began his career as the popular commander of the 4th Texas, represented no idle boast or exaggeration. Instead, and as its combat record demonstrated year after year, this glowing statement was not at all an example of hyperbole, but a most accurate assessment of the superior fighting qualities and future battlefield achievements of perhaps the finest combat brigade of the Civil War. More than any other Army of Northern Virginia troops, General Lee came to rely with complete confidence upon the Texas Brigade's combat prowess, especially in offensive operations, during the most severe crisis situations year after year. And no contest was more severe than the offensive effort calculated to overwhelm the defenders of the Devil's Den, Houck's Ridge, and Little Round Top on the second day at Gettysburg.

In one major eastern campaign after another, the Texas Brigade (the only combat unit in the entire Army of Northern Virginia to represent the seventh state that departed the Union with much fanfare) performed beyond expectations. The command served as General Lee's hard-hitting shock troops second to none. Repeatedly employed in crucial no-win and emergency situations, where the Texans often snatched victory from the jaws of defeat, stemmed a serious crisis situation, or delivered a lethal offensive blow to save the day, Hood's Texas Brigade always arose to the supreme challenge, despite the odds and slim chances for success. At Gettysburg, the hard-fighting men of the Texas Brigade assaulted not only one, but two high ground positions that presented formidable obstacles: first, the high ground of Houck's Ridge, including the boulder-strewn Devil's Den, and then Little Round Top on the other side, east, of Plum Run that flowed south along the foot of Little Round Top.

From beginning to end, the fact that these Texas Rebels from the distant western frontier were the hardest fighting combat troops of Lee's Army engendered fear in the ranks of the Army of the Potomac. Consequently, Lee's well-placed faith in the Texas Brigade's capabilities on the battlefield was unmatched in any other of his brigades. Like the tough westerners of the famous Iron Brigade, Army of the Potomac, these hardy Texas Rebels—a comparable contingent of dependable western fighting men—fought their best whenever the odds of success were the least likely, and where the danger was greatest, including in both the western and eastern theaters.

To truly appreciate the Texas Brigade, the commonplace views of non-Texans, both during the war and including modern historians, not tainted by regional or state bias were significant when it came to analyzing this distinctive command. With ample justification, Douglas Southall Freeman, whose Virginia bias and "Lost Cause" Virginia-first inclinations were negated by the Texas Brigade's elite qualities, described the Texas Brigade as "the most renowned Brigade of the entire Army" of Northern Virginia.[2]

Indeed, the crack "Texas Brigade, with Hood as its leader, stands out among Civil War combat units. Whenever Robert E. Lee needed decisive action to tip the scales of battle, Hood's men were often employed as shock troops [including at] Gaines's Mill, Second Manassas, Sharpsburg, and Gettysburg."[3]

Joseph B. Mitchell, a West Pointer, summarized how Hood's Texas Brigade "acquired a remarkable reputation for hard fighting and dauntless courage, second to none."[4] Gaining a well-deserved respect for these unsurpassed western fighting men and representing the common views of so many of Lee's top officers, Major Robert Augustus Stiles, an aristocratic Virginian of the Richmond Howitzers and a Yale graduate (Class of 1859), marveled at the long list of achievements of, "those greatest of all soldiers, the Texas Brigade."[5]

Such lofty opinions of the Texas Brigade's superior quality were common during the war years and, significantly, from an early date. Although such glowing tributes read like gross exaggerations dominated by romantic flourishes, the realities of what the Texas Brigade men accomplished on one battlefield after another were firmly rooted in the undeniable facts. Like people across the South, John H. Reagan, the postmaster general of the Confederacy, admired the Texas Brigade's superior fighting prowess of these roughhewn soldiers from the "Lone Star State." He wrote: "I doubt if there has even been a brigade, or other military organization in the history of the world, that equaled it in the heroic valor and self-sacrificing conduct of its members, and in the brilliancy of its services" across the Confederacy.[6]

These Texas Brigade soldiers early acquired a widespread reputation for ferocity on the battlefield, excelling against the odds regardless of the combat situation as if mere numbers did not count for much during a climactic showdown. This early reputation as an elite combat unit was a significant development because most other famous Civil War combat commands (North and South) only came close to acquiring that coveted reputation after much longer periods of service. Not so with the Texans. In a remarkable development rare in the annals of Civil War historiography, the Texans fought with the same skill of hardened veterans from the beginning of their service. Consequently, to the surprise of friend and especially foe, they early fought like seasoned troops quite unlike any other men of the Army of Northern Virginia.[7]

Like so many other high-ranking officers of Lee's Army, South Carolina-born General Daniel Harvey Hill, an intellectual West Pointer (Class of 1842) and Mexican-American War veteran, was awed by the Texas soldiers, who always fought with a fanatical desperation that astounded easterners on both sides, seemingly as if possessed, with a fanatical conviction to "do or die" on the battlefield. By the time of the Antietam campaign in the late summer of 1862, Hill fully recognized the Texans' combat superiority. Even though a proud product of the Tar Heel State noted for its provincial attitudes and homes state bias that ensured a rivalry with neighboring Virginia, Hill paid a glowing tribute to the combat prowess of the Texas Brigade. He expounded upon a widespread opinion of the overall superior quality of the Texas Rebels by admitting with a sense of admiration how General "Hood's men [from Texas] always fight well…"[8]

Even General William Dorsey Pender, a promising, young North Carolinian who was fated to be mortally wounded on the second day at Gettysburg, bestowed a lofty compliment upon the Texans when he penned in a letter: "I have North Carolina troops and am determined that if any effort of mine can do it, this [North Carolina] Brigade shall be second to none but Hood's Texas boys." Indeed, the unparalleled combat performances of the Texas Brigade was what other Army of Northern Virginia soldiers aspired to emulate, but seldom, if ever, matched during the four years of war.[9]

What was truly significant about these glowing tributes across the South about the Texans' combat superiority was the fact that these compliments were forthcoming from so many leading generals and officials from the East. After all, this was a time when state pride and provincial prejudices across the South usually ensured that such lofty praise and recognition for another state's soldiers, especially those troops who hailed from the Confederacy's most remote corner and farthest from the capital of Richmond, were almost never forthcoming.

During some of the greatest Confederate assaults of the war, it was generally acknowledged, especially in regard to a vital combat situation of extreme importance, throughout the Confederacy that "nobody would be so far in front but a Texan." Lee called upon his battle-hardened Texans to save the day in one emergency situation because "The Texas Brigade always has driven the enemy, and I want them to do it now."[10]

The lethal fighting qualities and superior battlefield performances of the Texas Brigade not only gave confidence to Confederate top leaders, but also to the entire army. Like other non-Texas units that served briefly (during the summer and fall of 1862 during the army's first invasion of the North that ended at the Battle of Antietam) in the so-called Texas Brigade, the overall quality of the infantry of the famed Wade Hampton Legion, composed of "the flower of the old Palmetto [South Carolina] State," was considerably enhanced, when fighting beside the Texans, because of an indescribable osmosis.

During this well-known process of osmosis, the elite qualities and confidence of the Texas Rebels literally wore off on nearby troops, regardless of from what state they hailed. A South Carolinian of the Hampton Legion and a respected company commander, Captain E. Scott Carson, wrote: "We placed great confidence in our Texas brothers that lasted through the war. On more than one occasion I heard the question, 'What troops [are] on our right or left?' and when the reply would come, 'The Texans!' a feeling of delight and confidence would thrill the breasts of the entire regiment."[11]

One rejuvenated Virginian never forgot the dramatic moment at Second Manassas, where the 5th Texas (along with the Texas Brigade's remainder) was part of the spearhead of the First Corps's assault and won the well-deserved sobriquet "the Bloody Fifth," in late August 1862: "When our reserve, led by Hood's Texas Brigade, the pride and glory of the Army of Northern Virginia, came on a run, gathering all the fragments of the other commands in their front and [then] dashed straight at the enemy."[12]

Far more than the better publicized Stonewall Brigade of Virginians because of their close connection with Lieutenant General Thomas Jonathan "Stonewall" Jackson, who emerged as second only to Lee on the pantheon of popular Confederate leaders atop the South's Mount Olympus, Hood's Texas Brigade proved itself by its hard fighting qualities alone (entirely without the advantages of the usual provincial and biased press—Texas newspapers were located too far away—or high-level politicians promoting their unmatched accomplishments on the battlefield unlike in the case of Jackson's overly-acclaimed Virginians and the powerful Richmond, Virginia, press that dominated the South's news media) to be Lee's finest combat brigade.

In striking contrast and unlike the legendary Iron Brigade, Army of the Potomac, the Stonewall Brigade's lofty reputation was largely founded upon a plethora of other non-combat related factors: a combat unit primarily famous because of its close relationship to "Stonewall" Jackson, the famed Virginian who long promoted his Old Dominion command; Lee's own Virginia bias and excessive Virginia-first priorities; romantic-minded, popular novelists, such as John E. Cooke, of the nineteenth and twentieth century; popular Victorian Era and "Lost Cause" romanticism that created enduring fiction and popular myths; the influential Richmond wartime press whose gross exaggerations of significant Virginia contributions became codified in some of the most respected history books to this day; the persistence of "Lost Cause" mythologies and an excessive Virginia-first focus that has long dominated Southern history; and influential historians, such as Douglas Southall Freeman, who excessively glorified the Stonewall Brigade and Virginia's contributions to continue the traditional distortion of the historical record first began by the influential wartime Virginia press (newspapers) of the Confederate capital.[13]

As repeatedly demonstrated on numerous battlefields in compiling the most distinguished combat record in the Confederacy's premier army, the Texas Brigade earned its record the old fashioned and hardest way of all: literally with blood, sweat, and tears from a long list of unsurpassed battlefield accomplishments over an extended period of time and on both sides of the Potomac River. The Texas Brigade was especially lethal when unleashed on the tactical offensive, a certain guarantee to secure victory often against all expectations. Few, if any, other units on either side were as lethal and absolutely devastating in an offensive role as the Texas Brigade. Quite simply, in an inversion of the usual situation, the Texas Brigade was an elite fighting machine more on the battlefield than off the field of strife.

But much more than simply the superior fighting qualities and distinguished combat record of Hood's Texas Rebels distinguished them from their peers. This situation was especially the case with the much-emphasized Virginians, who have been long viewed as ideal representatives (the antithesis of the rowdy, uncouth Texians from the southwest frontier) of the so-called higher and nobler traits of antebellum Southern society, fitting romantic stereotypes and myths in the popular mind. The unorthodox and ever-individualistic soldiers of the crack Texas regiments of Hood's Division were most distinctive in overall appearance and style that revealed the much less refined and genteel influences of the westernmost frontier.

Indeed, the Texans manifested the very essence and spirit of the western frontier, and this continued until the war's end. Presenting an enigma and paradox to a professional, textbook West Pointer's vision of professional fighting men, Hood's Texans were not elite troops in the traditional sense. These soldiers, generally taller and longer-limbed men compared to most easterners, never marched in order or in perfect step, while wearing neat, clean uniforms with shiny brass buttons. Quite simply, they were not known for possessing an outward military bearing and soldiery look in accordance with strict army regulations and rules, which were simply ignored by the Texans.

In many ways, these often unruly Texans were not only the most unorthodox but also the most democratic of all soldiers of an already excessively democratic Army of Northern Virginia. West Pointers, especially the strict, unbending martinets, who visited the Texas Brigade's untidy camps, were horrified by the casual nature and informal manner of the common soldiers, especially toward officers. In general, the average Texas Brigade soldier did not care much for officers, because they were seen as unnecessary when it came to hard fighting and winning victory on the battlefield.

What was most apparent to any officer was an overall general lack of discipline and a carefree attitude that existed among these unorthodox Texas men when off the battlefield. Only on the battlefield (where, of course, it counted the most) were the Texas Rebels concerned about the meticulous precision of maneuvering and obeying officers' orders to the letter, especially during the attack. Quite unlike any other troops and seemingly contradicting their lofty reputations for combat prowess, the usual boring routine of mundane inspections, rules, regulations, and drill field maneuvers meant nothing to these self-reliant Texas frontiersmen. Most of all, they still thought for themselves and acted accordingly to their free-thinking ways of the southwest frontier tradition to ensure a greater flexibility on the battlefield. More than anything else and especially in regard to outward appearances, what counted to Hood's Texans was to emerge victorious on the field of strife at any cost, which led to a frightfully high cost on battlefields across the eastern theater.

Either in spearheading an attack or in covering the army's withdrawal to safety in an emergency situation, these highly-motivated Lone Star State men earned a reputation for an unmatched combat prowess. In this way and instead of neat appearances to impress high-ranking officers or pretty ladies in a crowd of onlookers, the seasoned Texas Rebels allowed their unparalleled battlefield accomplishments to speak eloquently for themselves. As ever-individualist frontiersmen, ranchers, and yeoman farmers from the lands west of the Mississippi, they despised the mindless discipline, red tape, and protocol of the strict military world that made little sense to Lee's most commonsense fighting men.

Most of all, Hood's Texans especially disliked haughty, aristocratic officers, when it came to puffed-up pretensions or artificial notions of superiority stemming from the usual lofty amount of respect accorded to rank, politics, and privilege that were much too arbitrary and eastern-based to their ultra-egalitarian frame of mind. In short, the young men and boys from Texas did not play the game of soldiering like other troops, especially showy types like the army's most famed cavalryman General James Ewell Brown (Jeb) Stuart, for outward show or to impress the ladies. Instead, they were focused on a single pursuit that was extremely serious business to these no-nonsense fighting men: the winning of decisive victory on the battlefield at any cost. And this was especially the case in regard to the bloody struggle at the Devil's Den and Houck's Ridge.[14]

Achieving a Rare Eliteness

In America's citizen-soldier tradition that extended back before the French and Indian War (known as the Seven Years' War in Europe), the Texas Brigade was not originally established as an elite unit like in the case of the most famous elite combat units in world military history: the famed Theban Sacred Band of ancient Greece, Rome's Praetorian Guard, Caesar's Tenth Legion, and Napoleon Bonaparte's famed Imperial Guard, especially the Old Guard.

Most importantly, that much-coveted eliteness had to be earned by the Texas Rebels by a large amount of blood expended during some of the hardest fought battles of the Civil War.[15] Utilizing a most appropriate historical analogy to one of the most elite units in the annals of ancient history, Corporal Joseph Benjamin Polley, 4th Texas, compared one Lone Star State color bearer to "the standard bearer of the Tenth Legion."[16]

As part of a central mystery and enduring riddle, why exactly had Hood's Texans become the best combat troops of the Army of Northern Virginia and what made them so from the beginning to the end? Why were the soldiers of the 1st Texas and the Texas Brigade able to compile an unparalleled combat record of seemingly endless battlefield accomplishments beyond what was achieved by other troops, including the much-celebrated Virginians? Year after year, how and why were the Texans able to accomplish what other troops could not achieve on the battlefield?

What forgotten and overlooked factors enabled these Texas Rebels to repeatedly excel exceptionally well and far beyond the typical battlefield performances of other Confederate troops? How and why were these Texans able to repeatedly rise to even the most severe challenge under the greatest disadvantages and in repeated no-win situations against the odds in Virginia, Maryland, and Pennsylvania? Quite simply, what were the hidden, long-ignored factors that made the Texans the army's best combat troops by the time of the dramatic showdown at Gettysburg? Ironically, such questions have seldom been asked and explored in detail.

More than in previous works, this book will attempt to find the elusive answers to these seldom-asked questions in the search for the long-elusive answers in an attempt to explain the sources of the distinguished performances of the Texas Brigade during the most important battle of the Civil War, Gettysburg. The answers to such questions will certainly help to explain what happened and why during the struggle for possession of the Devil's Den on the bloody afternoon of July 2, 1863. Most of all, this requires an in-depth and close analysis of the average common soldiers in the ranks of Hood's finest combat brigade.

Shaped by the Stern Challenges of the Frontier Experience

First and foremost as the Army of Northern Virginia's only men from the most westernmost part of the Confederacy, the western and frontier experiences significantly shaped the character and quality of the Texas Brigade. In the early 1820s, American settlement on the southwest frontier, known as Tejas (Texas), was allowed by the government of the Republic of Mexico to counter the mounted Native American menace (especially the wide-ranging Comanche who dominated the southern plains) that had long impeded Mexico's economic development of its northeastern province and to serve as a buffer from foreign encroachment. From the beginning, life for the American settlers of the Stephen Fuller Austin Colony, nestled on the fertile lands on the lower Brazos and Colorado Rivers of the Gulf of Mexico's coastal plain, was a unique frontier experience. This overall experience in an untamed borderland nestled between two neighboring republics and vastly-different cultures created an entirely new man on the remote southwest frontier, the Texian.

Although an untamed vastness of a pristine Texas, blessed with boundless potential and promise, was owned by a neighboring republic located on the opposite side of the Sabine and Red Rivers, this virgin land of plenty had been first won by the American settlers against the forces of nature and war-like Native Americans, Comanche, Kiowa, and Apache. First and foremost, this sprawling land had to be conquered by mostly Protestant settlers (the Texians) without assistance from the far-away central government in Mexico City: a distant and largely apathetic government representing a nation of a vastly different race, culture, and religion. Descendants of the Anglo-Celtic pioneers who had led the relentless advance of America's western frontier since the colonial period, the men and women who tamed the Texas frontier were a hardy breed of pioneers, who had undergone and survived a searing process that was the forge of the harsh southwest frontier experience: in essence, a most challenging Darwinian survival of the fittest experience that created the Texian.[17]

Indeed, of "all the Americans who went west in the 19th Century, none held a stronger claim to singularity than the pioneers who boldly planted their roots in the soil of Texas. They were the first Americans ever to settle the immense land west of Missouri [and] They were the only Americans ever to settle in force in a land ruled by a large and unfriendly power," whose culture was Latino and strongly anti-Protestant because of its strict Catholicism.[18]

First and foremost, the first Texian settlers had to literally conquer this land of so much promise with not only the ax and plow, but also with the musket, shotgun, and rifle: dual civilian and military requirements that forged a new people on the southwest frontier. These resourceful and resilient pioneers from the United States, primarily from the South, were just the type of hard-working individuals needed by Mexico, which had failed—like Spain—to develop the region, to tame a land that had long defied conquest on multiple levels. After all, the ancestors of the Anglo-Celtic settlers had already thrown off the shackles of a European imperial power—the mother country which had attempted to rule a New World Empire from London, England—in the American Revolution.

In the citizen-soldier tradition, the Texians also possessed experience in various Southern militias, including service under General Andrew, "Irish Andy," Jackson, the son of an Irish immigrant from Ulster Province, north Ireland, during the Creek War and the War of 1812, before migrating to Texas. Some of these settlers had fought in the January 1815 Battle of New Orleans that had saved Louisiana from British conquest during the so-called Second American Revolution. Also while serving under the consummate Scotch-Irish warrior Jackson whose toughness guaranteed success over any opponent who stood in this way, they also possessed experience in Indian warfare, especially the Creek War of 1814 that had been waged in today's Alabama and the First and Second Seminole Wars in the subtropical wilderness of today's Florida.

Consequently, the early Texians "were no strangers to war; they were born to it."[19] Early Texian settler Noah Smithwick, born in North Carolina, described the existence of a distinguished military legacy and a well-armed populace at the time of the beginning of the Texas Revolution in early October 1835: "... our only arms were Bowie knives and long single-barreled muzzle-loading flintlock rifles, the same that our fathers won their independence with, and that the famous Kentucky brigade used with such telling effect in the battle of New Orleans."[20] A knowledgeable journalist of the day correctly described with some amazement how most of all "the Texians

[were] entirely a military people, not only fought, but drank in platoons," which was a feature of the frontier experience.[21]

More than a century ago, historian Frederick Jackson Turner formulated his famous frontier thesis in attempting to explain how the frontier experience and the West's egalitarian environment created a new man in a profound shaping process that forged not only the American character, but also a true blue Republican. He theorized how the frontier experience transformed the European immigrant into an American who loved his new nation, while creating a democratic society that prospered on the western frontier. Perhaps no such Turner-like transformation in the entire course of United States history was better exemplified than the experience of the settlers on the Texas frontier of the southwest: America's most remote and wildest frontier region by the start of the Civil War, which was the antithesis of the world of the refined, aristocratic Virginians.

Indeed, even by 1861, Texas was still very a remote and isolated region, and the men in Hood's ranks still personified the spirit of the frontier experience. Spanning endlessly to the western horizon, the Lone Star State seemed to have no end like its seemingly unlimited promise. This wild land swarmed with Indians, Mexicans, Tejanos, and Anglo bandits, and renegades of all colors, creeds, and nationalities. Mounted on lithe horses first brought to the North American continent by the Spanish Conquistadors, Native Americans, especially the fierce Comanche, had long raided northern and western Texas, and south along the Mexican border. In the process of merely surviving life on the raw Texas frontier located at the isolated southern end of the Great Plains, where the Southern woodlands faded away and into sprawling western prairies, American settlers were transformed into a new type of person by the harsh conditions and a host of stern challenges on the southwest frontier.

An entirely unique product of not only the southwestern frontier but also the northern borderlands with Mexico, the Texians possessed not only a special, but also a most distinguished history. Indeed, "alone among the American states it was once its own nation [the Republic of Texas], born like most historic nations in blood and iron." Like the people of the thirteen colonies during the eighteenth century and despite disastrous military setbacks in early 1836, the Texians won their own revolution in April 1836, thanks to decisive victory at San Jacinto, to gain their independence from Mexico in a war of liberation unlike any other Americans of the nineteenth century.

The Texians won their brutal struggle against a more powerful Mexico that the Texians early equated to the forefathers' fight for liberty in the American Revolution. Before annexation by the United States in 1845, the Republic of Texas survived for a decade as an independent nation that represented an entirely unique and "singular" experience in the history of the United States. From the beginning of Anglo-Celtic settlement in Texas in the 1820s, the revered word of Texian identified the earliest settlers, representing a new breed that was extraordinarily tough and resilient. After becoming part of the United States in 1845, the usage of the word "Texan" was still widespread. The popular term of Texian continued to be widely used during the Civil War years by Southerners and the Texans themselves, including Texas

Brigade members who basked in this special terminology like a badge of honor and holy shroud.

Exactly what manner of men were these hardened products of the old Spanish borderlands and southwest frontier who proudly called themselves a Texian with a good deal of confidence and cockiness? What exactly did the word Texian mean and represent to the Texas Brigade soldiers by the time of the showdown at Gettysburg? One Texas Confederate explained how the Texian was an independent individual characterized by "energy, bravery, a practical view of all matters, self-reliance, moderation, and a disposition to act in concert with their fellow citizens [and these] were the characteristics of the early settlers. Danger menaced them unceasingly, rendered them cautious, and molded them into soldiers."[22]

In a Darwinian-like experiment, the southwestern environment created not only a new culture and distinctive identity that was alive and well among the Civil War generation, but also a vibrant sense of nationalism that was far more western than Southern and closer to the Republic of Texas than a typical state in the Union. In the insightful words of respected historian T. R. Fehrenbach, like in regard to the Texas Brigade soldiers: "The Texan mystique was created by the chemistry of the frontier in the crucible of history and forged into an enduring state of heart and mind."[23]

Even among America's historic frontiers and western borderlands throughout its history of westward expansion all the way to the Pacific's shores for more than a century, the Texas frontier stood out as the most unique one of all. Fehrenbach's revealing words captured the essence of the Texas frontier experience: "Texas had the bloodiest and longest running frontiers in American history," leaving the hardy survivors who were the most distinctive frontier types in America by 1861. It was not only the wildest and most unruly frontier, but also the most sprawling land in America by the time of the Civil War. The vast expanses of Texas—stretching from gulf coastal lands in the east that looked identical to those of western Louisiana to the more parched lands of the Rio Grande River in the south bordering northeast Mexico—played a leading role in molding this new man who rose splendidly to the challenge of the Civil War years. All in all, the beautiful land of Texas itself most of all "dominates [everything and everyone for successive generations] in an almost Russian sense."[24]

This seemingly boundless land and searing historical experience that tempered body and soul resulted in the formation of a new type of man, known for toughness, resiliency, and resourcefulness, the Texian. This southwest frontier environment and experience instilled unique characteristics among the Texians of the revolutionary period, and then later the Texans of the Civil War generation: a process that made them entirely unique (in general as both citizens in peacetime and fighting men) and altogether different from their fellow Southerners, especially Virginians. The southwest frontier and borderland experience combined to bestow a unique set of characteristics among the Texans in this unforgiving environment, including a heightened sense of individualism and ultra-democratic proclivities to verify the validity of the Turner Frontier Thesis.

By way of the wilderness (prairie and woodlands), revolutionary war (1835–1836) and frontier experiences, the Texian evolved into a hardened "soldier" out of necessity merely to survive his harsh frontier and wartime-like environment, while struggling far from government support, family, and friends. Quite literally, the Texian had been early placed on his own in an untamed land, to live or die. But it was more than simple survival of the fittest that had forged the unique personal qualities of the Texian, especially sterling personal characteristics (initiative, resourcefulness, never-say-die attitude, resiliency, etc.), which rose to the fore on July 2 at Gettysburg. Out of urgent necessity, the Texian not only defended his home and family from the wrath of nature and rampaging Native Americans, but also the hard-earned independence won by defeating an invader who represented centralized power (much like the American colonists against the British from 1775–1783) that led to the establishment of their own independent republic in early March 1836.

Clearly, the Texian was very much of a product of natural selection on the southwestern frontier that led to the creation a distinctive individual with a host of specialized characteristics that had been created out of the forge of adversity by the frontier and Texas Revolutionary War experience. In purely evolutionary terms, the Texian (basically the Anglo-Celtic settler who were the vast majority) represented "the final extension of several immigrant Scots-Irish generations, each more assertive than its predecessor, each more willing to take chances, each more prone to violence, each more certain of its place in the world."[25]

Southern descendants of the resourceful Scotch-Irish, who were war-like and resilient from generations of difficult lives and in struggling in vain against the hated English interlopers in defending their native homelands of north Ireland and Scotland, had first brought the warrior tradition with them when they migrated to Texas. Most importantly, the Scotch-Irish, who hailed from Ulster Province in north Ireland, also carried distinctive qualities: an acute sense of autonomy, an independent streak, and a passionate love of freedom and democracy, an egalitarian spirit that could not be suppressed, and a militant defiance of authority, especially toward a far-away central power, either located in London or Mexico City. These pioneers, both men and women, of Celtic descent were not only natural revolutionaries when confronted by arbitrary and abusive central authority, but also ideal rebels, like their forefathers before them on both sides of the Atlantic. It was these distinctive character traits and legacies of distinguished revolutionary experiences from both sides of the Atlantic that rose to the fore among the men of Hood's Texas Brigade on one Civil War battlefield after another.[26]

The descendants of the Celts (from Ireland and Scotland) of Texas hailed primarily from either their native ancient land or the Deep South, where their ancestors had first journeyed across the Atlantic to such Southern ports as Charleston, South Carolina, New Orleans, Louisiana, and Mobile, Alabama. In general, the Irish who had migrated from New Orleans and American migrants from Louisiana tended to settle along the Gulf of Mexico in southeast Texas, Georgians along the Louisiana border in east Texas, Alabamians in east central Texas, and Tennesseans just west of the Alabama settlers.[27]

For the most part, the average Texan Rebel in a gray and butternut uniform was a highly-specialized product of a distinctive Scots-Irish heritage and cultural tradition, the frontier experience, longtime warfare with Native Americans, and a distinctive people's uprising on the southwest frontier: all in all, historical, revolutionary, and evolutionary experiences quite unlike any other Army of Northern Virginia soldiers. Indeed, from the crucible of the dual frontier and revolutionary experiences and "out of a chemistry of culture and struggle, Texans emerged very much a people" in a nationalist sense that was entirely distinctive from any other region in the United States. Therefore, the Texan brought an entire set of unique characteristics and distinctive qualities with him on the battlefields of Virginia, Maryland, and Pennsylvania, especially to the grim killing fields of Gettysburg on the crucial second day.

Consequently, Texas Brigade's followers were quite unlike any other Confederate soldiers in the eastern theater in regard to manner, culture, and heritage, which were all inordinately pronounced and distinctive. Quite simply, Hood's men were literally a breed apart and they acted accordingly, because they had more in common with the Texian antecedents, especially those of 1835–1836, than contemporary Southerners, especially the more refined areas of the eastern Tidewater and the aristocratic planter class of Virginia and South Carolina. Most significantly, the western frontier legacy and experience were forgotten factors that helped to explain the remarkable success story of the most distinctive and unique fighting men in the Army of Northern Virginia.

For such reasons, the Texas Brigade soldiers warmly embraced the enduring term of Texian with great pride and wore it like a badge of honor. In essence, they were paying tribute to their revolutionary ancestors, who won full possession of Texas with combat prowess and sheer determination against the odds. In the hearts and minds of the Texas troops from 1861 to 1865, they were still very much the stereotypical Texians to the core. After all, Hood's Lone Star State men remained defiantly independent-minded and outrageously egalitarian to an extreme degree, while battling for still another republic's independence against another central government located far away. Most appropriately, consequently, these soldiers fought under not only the Confederacy's war banners, but, significantly, also under the Long Star State flag.

By 1863, even the provincial journalists of the *Richmond Enquirer*, Virginia, which almost always excessively promoted the battlefield achievements of Virginia troops at the expense of western soldiers, was forced to admit that "No troops in the service have more distinguished themselves than those from Texas." Shaped by an unique history of decades of conflict against Native Americans and Mexicans, both regulars and guerrillas, literally a training ground of adversity unseen anywhere else in America, and the unforgiving environment on the Texas frontier, the Texas Brigade soldiers were in essence the very embodiment of the traditional Texians in body, mind, and spirit: a guarantee that they were destined to carry the legacies of the frontier experiences, legacies, and revolutionary war traditions with them on battlefields across America.[28]

A young soldier of Company "F," 5th Texas, described one of his comrades, who still retained the very essence of the western frontier experience. His "name was

Pemberton, but was nicknamed 'Wild Bill.' He was a West Texas product and a fine, noble young fellow, and was well up on cowboy lore, therefore originated his nickname."[29]

A 4th Texas soldier who read the pages of the Holy Bible with supreme devotion and loved his attractive wife, Mary Eliza West, who had been born to privilege in South Carolina, Private John Camden West, Company "E" (Lone Star Guards), 4th Texas, described an especially fearsome officer of the 1st Texas, Captain David K. Rice from Houston. As West, who had migrated to Texas from South Carolina in 1855, explained, Rice was "a very rough looking customer, reminding me of descriptions I have read of pirates in yellow covered novels; he was weather-beaten and fierce looking [and he] was about twenty years of age, with a beardless face as smooth as a woman's."[30] Captain Rice was as combative as he appeared at first glance, performing well during the Battle of Gettysburg.[31]

Texas's existence as an independent republic had been sufficiently long (a decade) before annexation by the United States in 1845 to form a distinct separate identity and nationalism. For ample good reason, consequently, the Texas Brigade soldiers took great pride in this vibrant sense of nationalism, embracing a distinctive historical tradition and legacy that made them so different from the non-Texans other Army of Northern Virginia soldiers. Indeed, the Texas soldier in gray and butternut was much closer to the frontier and revolutionary experiences than any other men in service (North or South) during the four years of the Civil War.

But, in overall terms, the southwester frontier experience had the greatest impact on molding these yeoman farmers and frontiersmen into a reliable and resourceful soldiery, because they brought the unique characteristics of the western frontier with them to the eastern theater and to the small market and college town known as Gettysburg, and a strange place called the Devil's Den.

A perceptive New Orleans, Louisiana, journalist early understood as much about the Texas Rebels. Therefore, he made a bold prediction in regard to the fighting qualities of the Texas Brigade soldiers: "… such men as these will make quick work of the Yankee racers when they get a chance [because the art of war] was to them [but] a pastime; its hardships are every day events, for they have been brought upon [*sic.*] the frontier, and have been cradled amid dangers."[32]

This was, most of all, a most challenging life-or-death environment where hardships and difficulties were just a part of daily life unlike elsewhere in America. Wars, battles, and skirmishes were fought for generations against the two ancient enemies of the Texians: the hostile southern Great Plains tribes, especially the best light cavalry in North America (the Comanche), and Mexican military, irregulars, and banditos. Battling these ancient foes over this lengthy period was simply a way-of-life for the rugged Texians, who had been literally born to adversity.

Quite simply, life on the Texas frontier was a classic case of survival of the fittest in its purist form. Here, in a Darwinian-like struggle that included a methodical and often brutal process of natural selection, only the strong, most intelligent, and resourceful individual lived to see the next day's sunrise. Meanwhile, the weak and not quickly adaptable died alone, losing their Darwinian struggle like an ancient extinct species that had failed to successfully adapt to new changes. The Texas frontier, where simple survival was the foremost and primary concern of men, animals and even in regard to the growth of natural vegetation, was the most warlike environment of the United States.

In fact, this Texian homeland of Texas Brigade members had long been far bloodier than the much-publicized arena of "Bloody Kansas" of the 1850s, although this grim fact was not recognized or publicized. Whereas "Bloody Kansas" was a sobriquet earned from a relatively brief period of sectional strife between pro-slavery Missourians and anti-slavery Kansans, the dark, blood-stained annals of Texas history consisted of decades of constant bitter warfare, ethnic and racial conflict, and to a degree of adversity and suffering unseen elsewhere in America during this turbulent period.

Rugged Texian settlers had long struggled to ensure survival not only against extreme weather and harsh environmental conditions, but also merely to exist to see the next sunrise. No-quarter warfare had long existed between Native Americans and settlers of Tejas that exacted a high price for these settlers, who had fallen in love with its natural beauty and promise, while overlooking its many perils.[33] Perhaps Noah Smithwick, a settler who had been born in North Carolina, said it best, concluding: "It was a terrible baptism, that of the Lone Star republic; but, we had triumphed" in the end.[34]

As nowhere else in the United States, warfare was a way-of-life on the Texas frontier: brutal conflicts against the Karankawas, Tonkawas, Apaches, Wacos, Comanches, Kiowa, and Mexican regular forces and guerrillas noted for their ruthlessness toward soldiers and civilians, especially if captured. Fighting raged on both sides of the shallow Rio Grande River, with Mexicans invading Texas and Texans invading Mexico long after the Texas Revolution, because Mexico refused to recognize Texas independence and sought to regain its lost province of boundless promise. Some Texas Brigade soldiers, therefore, possessed years of prior military experience in combating Indian raids, before volunteering to fight against the boys in blue during the spring of 1861.

Such survival experiences and a challenging environment of almost constant warfare on the isolated Texas frontier combined to create an entirely new type of Civil War soldier, who was known for his superior combat prowess and frontier ways of fighting. In the heat of combat, this more resilient and resourceful kind of fighting man, who reflected both the virtues and vices of the frontier experience. Not surprisingly, consequently, these modern Texians in gray and butternut early earned a widespread reputation in the North and South for an unparalleled ferocity in combat and unmatched lethality. In addition, this inherent combativeness of the Texian soldier provided their brigade with a legendary reputation that was second to none, including at Gettysburg.

Clearly, one of the principal secrets of the remarkable battlefield successes of the Texas Brigade was the toughening process on the southwestern frontier and Texas Revolutionary experiences, which rose to the fore on July 2, 1863. For the most part, northern people grew up under no such comparable unforgiving conditions in which survival of the fittest was the primary order of the day.

Therefore, Texans early became experts at the use of shotguns, rifles, and six-shooter revolvers and knowledgeable about the art of war out of absolute necessity, because survival depended upon it. Corporal Joseph Benjamin Polley, 4th Texas Infantry, wrote how "armed as most of the Texans were with Minnie and Enfield rifles, and accustomed as they were to the use of fire-arms from their earliest boyhood, their marksmanship proved [far] superior to that of the Federals" on battlefields across the eastern theater.[35]

Corporal Joe Polley's words were right on target like his well-aimed shots from his musket. His father, Joseph H. Polley and a New York native, migrated to Texas in 1819 with Missourian Moses Austin, who was the father of the ambitious colonizing dream of Texas. He then returned in 1821 with Moses's son, Stephen Fuller Austin, who took up the colonization project after his father's death, as one of the original "Old Three Hundred" colonists of the Austin Colony. Joseph Benjamin Polley was born near Bailey's Prairie (later Brazoria County) in the Brazos River country in the Austin Colony in October 1840. Then, at age seven, the family moved around 30 miles east of San Antonio to settle on the sprawling grasslands of the central plains at a small farm on Cibolo (an Indian name for buffalo) Creek. Fueled by a desire to serve the Lone Star State, Joe Polly departed Wesleyan College at Florence, Alabama, and returned to Texas to enlist in the 5th Texas, which played a distinguished role at Gettysburg on the second day.[36]

Born of the long-existing martial traditions of the frontier and Texas Revolutionary experiences, a high level of superior marksmanship made the Texas Brigade members ideal attackers in key battlefield situation, especially at close range: well-honed qualities that led to the capture of Houck's Ridge and the Devil's Den. Clearly, a diverse variety of factors explained why the Texas Brigade fought so well at Gettysburg. One typical Texas Brigade soldier was described by an admiring comrade who emphasized the environmental qualities that led to the creation of a lethal soldiery who successfully carried the high ground at the Devil's Den, Houck's Ridge, and Little Round Top:

> His acquaintance with the habits and haunts of deer, turkeys and smaller game, his unerring aim, and his trusty rifle, kept his father's table well supplied with fresh meat. The same qualities that made him a successful hunter in the wilds of Texas, stood him in good stead when, as a soldier in battle, or as a scout or skirmishers, his marksmanship was employed against human beings.[37]

As printed in the pages of the *Richmond Enquirer*, an Austin, Texas, correspondent early wrote prophetically about the Confederacy's best fighting troops:

> I have seen the [future Texas Brigade] men destined for the battlefields of Virginia and a finer set of men I never beheld. Of lithe and vigorous frames, they are the best fighters and marksmen in the state [of Texas and] Some of them had a great deal of sport at Eagle Lake [in southeastern Colorado County in the Colorado River country of East Texas] killing

alligators. It was a most interesting occasion. They could shoot them in the eye at 200 yards and hit them every time.[38]

Combating the threat of alligators, including large-sized man-eaters, on the cypress-lined rivers and dark bayous of East Texas, including the Trinity River, which flowed southeast into the Gulf of Mexico, was part of the early Texas experience. These volunteers continued the frontier tradition of killing alligators with well-placed shots to the head, while improving their marksmanship skills during the excitement-filled journey to Virginia.[39]

Far more than their legions of admirers or romantic prose-writing journalists, those people who bestowed the most praise were individuals who learned first-hand the Texans' combat prowess at close range, the boys in blue. A good many Federals never survived to tell the tale. But Yankee survivors gained awe for the superior fighting qualities of Hood's Texas Rebels. After first meeting with the Texans, one Yankee marveled at their frontier-like combat qualities: "The firing of the Texans was so accurate and their movements so cunning and Indian like, that [the Union soldiers] never wish to make their acquaintance again."[40]

From an early date because of their lofty reputations that preceded them, Northern troops, especially easterners in blue, were fearful of engaging the Texas Rebels, because they fought more like Native Americans than conventional troops. Such pervasive fears among even veteran Federal troops were widespread "because they knew the Texans were the rear-guard, and feared to attack such desperadoes," known for their combat prowess, especially in crisis situations.[41]

More abundant experience in irregular or asymmetrical warfare, which had been gained by Hood's men before the conflict's beginning, paid high dividends for the Texas Brigade on one battlefield after another, especially at Gettysburg. Omnipresent threats from two ancient foe (Mexicans and Native Americans) and decades of bitter conflict gave the Texas Brigade soldiers a decided advantage and sharpened edge in the ways of warfare. The time-honored motto that also motivated Lee's Texans was the frontier equation of to "do or die." This never-say-die axiom and war-cry of Texas Brigade soldiers from 1861–1865 exemplified the requirements of battling Native Americans and Mexicans.[42]

Indeed, the almost constant wars against the Indians and Mexicans up to the time of the Civil War had transformed the Texans into the most militarized and warlike people in the newly-created Southern nation. Under multiple threats from virtually every direction and seemingly without end, the Texans had been early forced to defend themselves on their own as best they could under the most challenging circumstances. Without government support in a remote region and relatively few in numbers, the early Texians had formed their own paramilitary units of mounted soldiers to protect their isolated communities, the first Texas Rangers. In this way, the Texas Rangers first emerged as an effective protective force on the Texas frontier, riding forth from remote frontier settlements to confront "the real people"—the Comanche. In the tradition of New England's "Minute Men" of Massachusetts during the initial armed clashes in April 1775 at Lexington and Concord, the American Revolution, the first Texian settlers of Stephen Fuller Austin's Colony, located in the fertile lands of the lower Brazos and Colorado River country near the Gulf of Mexico, banded together to strike back at Native American tormentors as early as 1821.

During the Texas Revolution after their official creation in 1835, Texas Rangers units became more formalized in organized units. These frontier units evolved into permanent defense organizations to protect homes, families, and the newly-declared Texas Republic, after independence was finally won in April 1836. During the course of the Texas Revolution, the most famous ranger command in Texas was the famed Gonzales Mounted Ranger Company, whose members hailed from the small town of Gonzales, Texas. To meet the urgent, desperate appeals of South Carolina-born Lieutenant Colonel William Barret Travis for assistance, almost all of the young men and boys of Gonzales, located just east of San Antonio de Bexar, grabbed their horses, muskets and rifles, and powder horns to reinforce the diminutive Alamo garrison under siege of thousands of Mexican fighting men. Led by Lieutenant George C. Kimbell, these thirty-two rangers rode through the Mexican lines to enter the Alamo in the cold, predawn darkness of March 1. These brave volunteers never returned to Gonzales. Instead, they earned their revered places in Texas history as the "Immortal Thirty-Two," falling to rise no more on the bloody morning of March 6, 1836.[43]

Even though lacking prestigious training at the United States Military Academy at West Point, New York, or leading Southern military academies, such as the Virginia Military Institute, Lexington, Virginia, where so many upper-class Virginians were educated in the military sciences, the rawboned Texas Brigade soldiers learned about and gained considerable tactical flexibility and initiative long before the firing of Confederate guns on Fort Sumter.

At its November 1861 formation among the rolling hills just north of Fredericksburg, Virginia, the Texas Brigade consisted of a unique mix of Indian fighters, former Texas Rangers, United States Army scouts and veterans, western frontier plainsmen, former Republic of Texas soldiers, Buffalo hunters, woodsman, trappers, ranchers, cowboys, and Texas Revolutionary and Mexican War veterans. Among the Mexican War veterans of the Texas Brigade were men who had marched triumphantly into Mexico City, including a young engineer officer named Robert Edward Lee, George Edward Pickett, and James Longstreet (who commanded the First Corps, Army of Northern Virginia, and of which the Texas Brigade was a part at Gettysburg), of General Winfield Scott's Army in September 1847.

In a January 1862 letter from Virginia, consequently, teenage Corporal Joseph Benjamin Polley, 4th Texas, described how the wartime environment of Virginia was nothing new to the Texans, who only too well knew of the perils of warfare as a way-of-life, since their earliest childhood experiences: "The roll, I must inform you, is not the spasmodic rat-a-tat you are accustomed to hear when a company of home guards are drilling in the vicinity of your prairie home [on the western frontier] but is [more] continuous."[44]

This environmental and wartime conditioning before the momentous year of 1861 made the Texas Brigade's members entirely different from Lee's other soldiers, who were much farther removed (usually generations and often many decades as in the case of Virginia) from the frontier experiences. For the vast majority of Army of Northern Virginia soldiers and especially for Confederates from the eastern seaboard, the western frontier legacies lingered back to the misty tales from grandfather's and great-grandfather's stories heard by them in early childhood. But the average Texan of the Civil War generation was altogether different and an enigma compared to other members of the Army of Northern Virginia. Most of all, the harrowing forge of the western and frontier experiences had significantly tempered the Texas Brigade men to an unmatched degree and quite unlike any other combat command of the Army of Northern Virginia.

Impressed by the sight of these hardened young men from the far distant Texas frontier, one Virginian early viewed the rambunctious Lone Star State men with a great deal of amazement. He described how "these men are a stalwart set of soldiers, [who] will do fine service" for the Confederacy. As their battlefield performances verified, especially at Gettysburg, these Texas soldiers were extremely resilient and resourceful combat troops. They repeatedly demonstrated an uncanny ability to adapt to crisis situations on the battlefield: byproducts of the heightened individualism, personal initiative, and self-reliance born out of the frontier and western experiences. Since the war's beginning, the Texas Rebels also possessed a superior *élan* and *esprit de corps*, which also arose to the fore in hard-hitting offensive roles, such as on the bloody afternoon of July 2, 1862.[45]

Because of their frontier isolation and lack of support from government (first Mexico, then the Texas Republic, and afterward the State of Texas), the Texans early developed a penchant for unorthodoxy and unconventionality, which were natural byproducts derived from the harsh land from where they hailed. These distinctive characteristics were early noted by the observers of these long-legged and long-haired Texas Rebels, who marched forth with an easy confident stride.

But more importantly, such distinctive traits and sterling qualities bestowed the Texas Confederates with an unprecedented and unmatched degree of tactical initiative, resiliency, and flexibility that rose to the fore at Gettysburg. For them, therefore, the overall challenge of the Civil War was no different or nothing new, presenting yet another serious threat that had to be met head-on and aggressively like on the southwest frontier: the tactical wisdom of the unleashing of a preemptive strike which ensured that Texas Brigade troops early journeyed to the eastern theater and the war's epicenter with the firm conviction of teaching the Federals a lesson that they would never forget.

Consequently, in 1861, hundreds of zealous Texas Rebels had marched off to war to protect their homes and families. Except now the brewing threat emanated from a perceived antagonistic centralized government in Washington, D.C. In one Texas soldier's words that revealed his motivation in idealistic terms: "I now shoulder my musket and go to defend our Southern soil from the base impositions of Northern fanatics." The frontier experience, warlike conditions, and a host of enemies on all sides (Native Americans to the north, east, and west and Mexicans to the south) had early produced high-motivated and resourceful soldiers, who knew how to take care of themselves on the field of strife. This almost never-ending war-like environment of the southwest frontier had "molded them into soldiers" of steely determination.[46] Northern periodicals, therefore, early warned the people and soldiers of the North about what to expect from this new breed of soldier, who was viewed as not only a super warrior but also as "half wolf, half hyena and man."[47]

Clearly, from the beginning and for a wide variety of reasons, the average Texas Brigade soldier proved to be the consummate warrior of an almost fanatical nature. Like a fiery crucible that forged a new kind of soldiery never seen before in the East, the harsh Texas environment, extreme adversity on multiple levels, and the frontier experience all created a unique soldiery well adapted to the challenge of attacking the high ground at Gettysburg. After all, this was the kind of fighting man who possessed the well-honed capabilities to not only reverse the tide on the battlefield, but also to achieve a decisive success. A common view expressed by Southerners across the Confederacy was that "No army on earth can whip these men [of the Texas Brigade because] they may be cut to pieces and killed, but routed and whipped, never!"[48]

As their battlefield performances demonstrated at Gettysburg, the Texas soldiers proved that they indeed were the toughest, hardest-fighting, and most resilient soldiers of the army: a remarkable achievement by any measure. Although other famed combat units, especially the Stonewall Brigade of Virginians, have garnered far more recognition because of the excessive focus and embellishments of the Richmond and eastern press, the Texas Brigade early evolved into the hardest-hitting combat unit of the Army of Northern Virginia, compiling a lengthy record of dramatic battlefield accomplishments second to none.[49]

For ample good reason in the first campaign of the Texas Brigade on the Virginia Peninsula, Thomas Jonathan "Stonewall" Jackson, although biased toward his fellow Virginians that revealed his own Old Dominion background, marveled at the Texans' battlefield achievements in their sweeping attack that swept everything before it at Gaines's Mill, declaring with astonishment: "These men that carried this place were soldiers indeed."[50]

But this battlefield feat was destined to be greatly exceeded by Hood's Texas during the assault on the Devil's Den on the critical second day at Gettysburg, when everything was at stake. All in all, the earlier battles of 1861 and 1862 were just the training ground in preparation for the ultimate showdown at Gettysburg on July 2, 1863.

Lee's Tough Common Soldiers from the Southwest Frontier

But what were some other forgotten factors that also led to the making of an elite combat brigade? Providing a representative example that revealed one elusive answer to this intriguing question, when an advanced group of nine Texas soldiers were surrounded by Union cavalry, "they had no thought of surrender." Instead, they gamely took shelter in a house and fought back, keeping the Yankees at bay for an extended period of time: a mini-Alamo of sorts for these never-say-die Texans, who embraced this historical analogy.[51]

Significantly, this was not an abstract historical analogy because the very heart and soul of the Texas Brigade was inspired by the enduring spirit of the Alamo and the Texas Revolution. Consequently, these men were early consumed by the firm resolve "to maintain the reputation for desperate courage won for the 'Lone Star State' by the heroes of the Alamo," penned Corporal Joe Polley, 4th Texas, who proudly embraced the rich historical revolutionary heritage. After all, the Texans were now engaged in the second people's revolution, after their first revolution had been won barely twenty-five years before.[52]

This forgotten clash of no name between Union cavalry and only a handful of ragged Texas infantrymen was a representative example of an especially feisty fighting spirit. But perhaps Colonel John Bell Hood, a hard-fighting West Pointer who was not known for idle boasts, said it best. When reaping laurels as the regimental commander of the 4th Texas, Hood led from the front and "could double-quick the Fourth Texas to the gates of Hell and never break their line."[53] Despite a native Kentuckian but still possessing distinctive some southwestern qualities admired by the Texans, Hood "was as ambitious as he was brave and daring," making a perfect match for his brigade.[54]

First and foremost, Texas Brigade's members were largely middle-class yeomen of the southwestern frontier, mostly small farmers. They, ironically, had fulfilled the idealist visions of Virginia's second most famous Founding Father, after George Washington, but in the frontier lands west of the Mississippi. Indeed, Thomas Jefferson's cherished dream of a people's republic of self-reliant small farmers was his solution for the settlement of the West and the preservation of the most cherished republican virtues of America. Like most middle-class farmers who tilled the land of east of the Sabine River, they primarily raised corn and hogs, the basic western staples of the common people, including in the Mississippi Valley.

But many Texans had been ranchers of rancheros and raised cattle (first brought to the New World by the Spanish Conquistadors) on the wide prairies and plains, continuing the longtime traditions of the Tejano (Mexicans born in Texas) people. Even Nicholas A. Davis, the chaplain of the 4th Texas and a small slave-owner, wrote affectionately about "my ranch." However, contrary to existing stereotypes, these young men who hailed from the small farms of the Lone Star State seldom owned slaves, because they were members of a small property-owning class of the yeoman farmer. Knowing that he had much work ahead in regard to saving souls of brigade members who were well-known for trouble-making and unruly behavior, Chaplain Davis described these roughhewn Texans with admiration as "representative men from all portions of the State—young, impetuous, and fresh, full of energy, enterprise, and fire—men of action."[55]

Hailing mostly from the grassy prairies of central Texas, the pine and post oak belt woodlands, and cypress bayous of East Texas, these men represented virtually every occupation imaginable. Ending at the broad, gently-rolling grasslands of the central plains to the west, the piney woods of equally rolling hills—beyond (or west) the Sabine River's lower-lying plain) of East Texas, especially in the counties of Shelby, Sabine, Newton, Orange, and Jefferson, from north to south, along the Sabine and adjoining the Louisiana border—were an extension of the Deep South's sprawling pine belt. Beyond the piney woods region lay the fertile blackland prairie, to the north and just south of the east-west Red River that served as the Indian Territory's southern boundary, and the broad expanse of the post oak belt (to the south) of more hilly country than the pine country.

Hailing "from the hills and valleys of Texas," Chaplain Davis was astounded by the sight of men from "all trades and professions—attorneys, doctors, merchants, farmers, mechanics, editors, scholastics, [and] all animated and actuated by the self-same spirit of patriotism [and prepared] to place themselves on the altar of their country." Despite the occasional individual of means and education because many of Hood's men came from "some of the best families in Texas," the vast majority of Texas Brigade soldiers were closely connected to the land as farmers, hunters, and woodsmen. Some Texas Brigade soldiers had been "buffalo hunters," while others were cowboys from the wide plains and arid lands of West Texas.

Other Texas Brigade soldiers had been mustangers. They had made a profession of capturing wild horses (mustangs) in the low-lying, dry, and infertile region lying between the Nueces and Rio Grande Rivers. Drawing upon this cultural legacy with distinctive Spanish and Tejano antecedents, the men of Company "F," 4th Texas, were proud members of the Mustang Grays. These volunteers hailed from San Antonio de Bexar, Bexar County, which was located in the sprawling central plains. Early in the war, San Antonio was early secured by United States regular forces from the Headquarters of the Department of Texas, despite the anti-secessionist sentiments of many people of San Antonio that paralleled the views of Governor Sam Houston, who still cherished the Union.[56]

As published in the influential *Richmond Enquirer* in the nation's capital, the Texas Brigade soldiers bound for Virginia were described in glowing terms: "I have seen the men destined for the battlefields of Virginia and a finer set of men I never beheld. Of lithe and vigorous frames, they are the best fighters and marksmen in the state." This was the very description of the Texas western frontiersmen, who "had come altogether too far [expressly] in search of a fight" to allow any opportunity to pass by.[57]

Other Southerners viewed them as "the wild Texans," and expected "to see them with their hair down to their heels" and one of these men even looked "like an Indian!," in the words of one shocked Southern woman, who had already heard about these men from Texas.[58] Young Corporal Joe Polley, 4th Texas, emphasized with some understatement in regard to one of the secrets to the Texas Brigade's amazing success on the battlefield, including during the decisive showdown at Gettysburg, writing:

> Armed as most of the Texans were with Minie and Enfield rifles, and accustomed as they were to the use of fire arms from their earliest boyhood, their marksmanship proved

> so superior to that of the Federals that it was not long before their appearance on the firing line was hailed with delight by their comrade Confederates, and viewed with apprehension by the Federals.[59]

When Peach State soldiers of the 18th Georgia Infantry—which served in the Texas Brigade from the fall of 1861 to the autumn of 1862 and whose members were eventually to become nearly equals to the feisty Lone Star State soldiers but not quite—first saw the Texans, they were a bit intimidated by these fierce frontier warriors. Actually a veiled compliment but one with understatement, one 18th Georgia officer wrote with awe and apprehension in his journal how the Texas soldiers were "a right hard looking set of fellows."[60]

The most outward physical manifestations of the deep imprint left by the Texas frontier experience on these Lone Star State soldiers was their free-wheeling ways and their rough-hewn appearances that astounded even fellow Confederate soldiers. Despite being elite troops, on the field of strife, the homespun Texans looked the exact opposite. Partly out of inclination almost as if deliberately determined to present the striking contradiction between inferior appearances and superior battlefield performances—a symbiotic relationship in regard to the Texas Brigade—to fool their opponents, Hood's Texans almost defied description. This facade seemed to mock those finely dressed soldiers, especially the much-touted Virginians, who fought less well in crisis situations, like at Gettysburg, than themselves. Quite simply, Lee's Texans were without doubt the worst uniformed, shabbily attired, and seemingly most ill-disciplined soldiers in the army, or so it seemed. Revealing the extreme degree of their individuality, carefree spirits, unorthodoxy, and unbounded frontier-imbued sense of freedom, the Texas Rebels (from leading officers to the lowest private) acted exactly as they desired in camp and wore whatever they felt was the most comfortable, which had little to do with a proper uniform. Therefore, most of Lee's crack fighting men and the talk of the army looked like nothing more than farmers who were more focused on plowing straight rows in their cornfields.

Matching their carefree attitudes and excessive frontier individualism, the Texans' unorthodox dress was the most outward indication that these young Lone Star State soldiers were independent-thinking to an extreme degree. Most of all, they conformed to no military standard whatsoever, even if ordered so by General Lee himself. Clearly, these men were first and foremost Texians in the truest sense and still remained so on Virginia soil, despite the years that had passed since the bloody days of the Texas Revolution, while now serving in the army of the infant Southern republic.

Therefore, these resilient men remained strongly independent in mindset, attitude, and appearance, because they cared not for the army's rules and regulations or whatever headquarters or aristocratic and haughty generals expected of them. In true frontier fashion and in crossing the wide Potomac River like when George Washington's mostly Continental soldiers crossed the Delaware to attack a Hessian brigade (three regiments) at Trenton, New Jersey, on the snowy morning of December

26, 1776, bands of 1st Texas men, impatient to kill Yankees, advanced on their own to harass the Federals without Colonel Louis Trezevant Wigfall's consent or knowledge during the winter of 1861–1862.

Most of all, these young Texans were so individualistic that they spoke their minds boldly before high-ranking officers and remained very much citizen-soldiers to the end. These men were distinguished by a sense of unorthodoxy and defiant attitudes born of the character-molding western and frontier experiences. In an army known for the individuality of its troops, the Texas Brigade's soldiers stood out and wholly apart, because of an undisciplined style, unorthodox ways, and unconventional look all their own.

Additionally, the Texans also possessed a high-spirited attitude (both on and off the battlefield) that was all their own to also set them apart from Lee's other fighting men. They early gained a widespread reputation for the most outrageous breaches of discipline and protocol that were imaginable. To the utter despair of West Pointers and other well-educated military men, a decidedly unmilitary-like, casual informality existed between the Texas enlisted men and their own officers not seen in other command to such an excessive degree: another forgotten factor that paid dividends and was one secret behind the Texas Brigade's successes on the field of strife, including at Gettysburg.

In many ways, it was almost as if these clannish Texans were still back home and had to work in close harmony together, needing each other for survival on the southwest frontier. Officers and enlisted men were close and friends for the most part, which translated into good working relationships on the battlefield, because of extremely close bonds. Not only influenced by the frontier and western experiences, the combined natural impulse and intentional determination of the men not to wear proper uniforms or conform to strict military regulations and discipline off the battlefield like other troops were historical legacies left over from the western and frontier experience, including the Texas Revolution which had been won by equally unorthodox citizen-soldiers.

These ever-individualistic appearances and attitudes ranged from the highest ranking officer to the lowest private of the Texas Brigade to erase outward rank and class distinctions in the democratic tradition: in the sense, they were indeed a band of brothers and distinctively informal military force, even within the context of a strict military hierarchy. At the Battle of Gaines's Mill during the 1862 Peninsula Campaign, the captured colonel of the defeated 4th New Jersey Volunteer Infantry refused to surrender his sword upon demand to Tennessee-born Colonel John Cunningham Upton, who commanded the 5th Texas with his usual skill during this sparkling success. One of the Texas Brigade's finest regimental commanders, Upton was well known for his bravery on the battlefield, especially at Second Manassas. This curt refusal by the New Jersey colonel was forthcoming because this Texas colonel looked more like a ragged private than a regimental commander. However, under the circumstances, this indignant Federal officer could hardly be blamed for his logical deduction. At that time in late August 1862, Tennessee-born Colonel Upton, who had been a cattle rancher on the lush Texas prairies, wore "an old pair of pants, a dilapidated pair of cavalry boots, and an old cotton shirt, a slouch black hat, a huge sabre, with a pair of six-shooters—looking less like an officer than any of his men," wrote a highly-amused Private Robert Campbell.[61]

In the words of Corporal Polley, 4th Texas, Colonel Upton, who had migrated to Texas in 1859, was among the "adventurous, self-reliant and plain-mannered class of people to whom military uniform and a long unwieldy word were nuisances," wore "a woolen overshirt [that] constituted his uniform, and while his sword trailed at his side, he carried in his right hand, as was his habit, the long-handled frying pan in which he fried the bacon for himself and mess."[62]

During the Gettysburg campaign, civilian clothing-attired Arthur James Lyon Fremantle, the erudite English military observer for the British Army, could hardly believe his eyes upon getting his first close-up view of the Texas Brigade troops, whose lofty reputation had preceded them. Noting a host of unique qualities that separated them from Lee's other troops, the Briton wrote how "Hood's ragged Jacks [were] well known for its fighting qualities, certainly are a queer lot to look at. They carry less than any other troops, many of them have only got an old piece of carpet or rug as baggage, many have discarded their shoes in the mud, all are ragged and dirty but full of good humor and confidence in themselves and in their general [Hood]."[63]

As a sad fate would have it, Colonel Upton, in his mid-thirties and distinguished by high cheekbones and dark hair that might have reflected some degree of Native American blood in the family, was killed during the Texas Brigade's fierce assault at Second Manassas at the head of his troops of the "Bloody Fifth" Texas. Like many of his followers, the colonel fell during the winning of another impressive victory, after the smashing through the lengthy, blue battle-lines of two New York regiments.[64]

Lieutenant Philip Alexander Work's 1st Texas Infantry Regiment

However, no command in the Texas Brigade was more individualist or unorthodox in attitude, appearance, and performance than its crack regiment, the 1st Texas Confederate Infantry, which was destined to lead the assault on the Devil's Den and Houck's Ridge on July 2, 1863. As if to mask its lethality and elite qualities, the appearance, manner, and dress of the 1st Texas men were even more frontier-inspired and individualistic than any other regiment of Hood's brigade, including the "Bloody Fifth." The almost destitute, pauper-liked appearance of the men in the ranks earned the 1st Texas the much-deserved sobriquet of the "Ragged Damned First." Bestowing a stealthy compliment, Corporal Joseph Benjamin Polley, 4th Texas, wrote: "'The Ragged Damned First' was a peculiar regiment in many respects [because] Its personnel were as brave and daring as any, but they were never strong on dress, drill and discipline, as laid down in Hardee's tactics."[65]

By any measure, to say that the 1st Texas was a "peculiar" regiment was indeed a considerable understatement. But there was nothing at all peculiar or odd about the combat prowess (which was second to none, including when compared to the "Bloody Fifth") of the 1st Texas, especially in the attack. Corporal Joe Polley, 4th Texas Infantry, marveled at the unconventional nature and ever-orthodox appearance of the 1st Texas soldiers, who seemed to deliberately flaunt every army rule and regulation to the book and at every opportunity. He explained: "In the matter of dress ... the First Texans were neither dudes nor dandies [and] Their fondness for and frequent indulgence in games of cards, naturally had a disastrous effect upon the seats of their trousers." After what they demonstrated during the assault on the Devil's Den and Houck's Ridge, the 1st Texas soldiers, without seats in their pants and dirty rags for uniforms, were the elite troops of Hood's Texas Brigade, especially after they were unleashed upon the Yankees, who never knew what had hit them.[66]

In the fall of 1862, General Lee and the aristocratic Fremantle watched as the well-trained troops of Army of Northern Virginia marched past with discipline and with everyone in step that marked them as tried veterans. All except the Texans, who stood out because of their much different manner and distinctive look than the other Confederate troops. The cultured former member of His Majesty's Coldstream Guards and member of the English upper class was shocked by the sight of the Texans, who marched by with wide strides at their own deliberate pace and looked more like destitute beggars on London street corners, in Hyde Park, and on the slummy east side along the Thames River than Lee's crack soldiers of legendary renown. Like a proud and adorning father talking about his naughty children who had been spoiled, General Lee merely stated to the British observer and proper gentleman, who could hardly believe his eyes: "Never mind their raggedness, Colonel [as] the enemy never sees the backs of my Texans," who were his pride and joy.[67]

In fact, the Texans' dress became so appalling that Chaplain Nicholas A. Davis, the Presbyterian spiritual leader of the 4th Texas, wrote a desperate appeal to the citizens of Richmond. This heartfelt appeal was published in a Richmond newspaper in November 1862 not long after the army's return from the disastrous Maryland Campaign during the fall of 1862:

> ... our men are not all shod. On yesterday evening an order was read on dress parade to the effect that, being barefooted would not excuse any man from duty. Those who were without shoes, were ordered to make moccasins [in the frontier tradition] of raw hide, and stand in their places.... I ask the good people of Richmond and surrounding country, if they will stand by and see them go into the fight without shoes. We are too far from home to look to our [Texas] friends there for help.... We are from the far South, and the cold is severe to us [and] It will require at least one hundred pairs of shoes, and five hundred pairs of socks [for the Texas soldiers in the dead of winter].[68]

Not only in regard to their threadbare, makeshift uniforms, but also the Texans possessed the grizzled look of hardened veterans and robust physical appearance of tanned, muscular, and well-toned men from the western frontier. Such distinctive physical qualities, especially in regard to a generally taller height, also caused Hood's Texas soldiers to stand apart from Lee's other soldiers, especially easterners and city dwellers from Virginia Tidewater cities like Richmond, Williamsburg, and Fredericksburg.

Admiring the Texans' sheer physicality that paid dividends on the battlefield, Alabama-born Chaplain Davis, the promising son of an Alabama legislator, described "the tall forms of our boys" from Texas, remarking how they were more robust and generally taller than the average Confederate soldier. Such imposing physical qualities were partly a byproduct of the overall frontier experience, an active outdoor life, healthy climate with plenty of bright sunshine, ample food sources in a mild climate, long-growing season, working the land behind a plow, and the endless opportunities for outdoor activities, including hunting, swimming, and fishing.

The high percentage of tall, lanky forms distinguished the long-legged Texas Brigade soldiers from other Southern troops, especially from the Deep South. Overall, Southern soldiers, including those from Deep South regions that were more unhealthy and disease-ridden (especially yellow fever), such as Louisiana, were generally shorter, less healthy, and less robust than the western frontiersmen and yeoman farmers from Texas. One such imposing Texas Brigade soldier was Captain George T. Todd, who commanded Company "A" (the Marion Rifles from Marion County), 1st Texas. He stood 6 feet and 3 inches and was stoutly made. Likewise, "Big John" Farris, Company "C" (Leon Hunters), 5th Texas, was also physically imposing and a well-known Yankee killer.

Reflecting the popular style of the southwest frontier, the long hair worn by the Texas Brigade soldiers also gave them a distinctive frontier western look from easterners. Although especially prominent in the enlisted ranks, long hair was also common among the Texas Brigade's officers. First Lieutenant Benjamin A. Campbell of the Reagan Guards, Company "G" from Anderson County, 1st Texas, proudly wore "long curls that gracefully hung over his shoulders."[69] Lieutenant Campbell was destined to be killed in gallantly leading his men into the leaden storm on the second day at Gettysburg, where so many of Hood's attackers were cut down.[70]

Captain William Harrison Martin, who commanded the Henderson Guards of Company "K" (originally known as the Sandy Point Mounted Rifles), 1st Texas, likewise wore his hair long in the popular Texas style. Known to the boys as "Howdy," Martin was a natural leader with the gift of inspiring soldiers to follow him to hell and back, if necessary. But the Georgia-born "Howdy," who was age thirty-nine at the time of the Battle of Gettysburg and still a bachelor, was no country bumpkin as his colorful nickname seemed to suggest. The personable Martin was a savvy lawyer by profession in Henderson County, after moving to Athens, Texas, from Alabama in 1850. Then, as a popular politician who knew how to garner votes, he represented the people of Henderson, Limestone, and Freestone Counties in the Texas Senate from 1853–1858.

Despite gaining his unique nickname because of his penchant of shouting "Howdy" to high-ranking officers rather than a formal military salute, the unorthodox captain was destined to earn a major's rank for his leadership ability. In the heat of battle where he was known for his devil-may-care fighting style, the revered captain "would shake his long hair and look like he was mad enough to eat a Yankee raw." Both in terms of personal appearances, the Texas Rebels in fact looked much like the citizen-soldier Texians, who fought at the Alamo and San Jacinto more than twenty-five years before in 1835–1836, than the average Confederate soldier of the Army of Northern Virginia.[71]

Lethal Weapons from the Southwest Frontier

In what other fundamental ways did the overall frontier and western experiences in the untamed lands west of the Mississippi create the army's most durable and resilient fighting man, whose combat skills arose to fore in the struggle for possession of the Devil's Den and Houck's Ridge? First and most symbolically, the weapons that the Texas Brigade men first carried in battle were basically identical to the ones (essentially those used by Andy Jackson's volunteers—rather than his reliable United States regulars—at the Battle of New Orleans and in the War of 1812 and the Creek War) that first won the Texas frontier from hostile Native American tribes and Mexican soldiers, bands of wide-ranging guerrillas, and ruthless banditos of the borderlands.

Like the hard-riding Texas Rangers who had long fought like Comanches by relying upon stealthy hit-and-run raids and the deadly frontier art of ambush, the Texas Brigade soldiers also carried large Bowie Knives. These knives possessed symbolic meaning to these men largely because of the alleged heroic death of the Louisiana-born Jim Bowie, the Southwest's premier knife fighter and "a sort of gentlemanly desperado," on that awful early morning at the Alamo.

To enhance their lethality, the Texas officers and men also replied on the fast-firing Colt and Navy six-shooters that were the primary weapon of choice on the southwestern frontier. But thanks partly to the inspirational legacy of the Alamo's defense on March 6, 1836, the Southwest's most famous edged weapon (described in 1836 as "longer than a butcher knife, made to be carried under the coat, and called by the gentleman stabbers the 'Bowie Knife'") remained extremely popular among the Texans. Lieutenant M. C. Noble, Company "F" (Woodville Rifles), 1st Texas, carried a homemade 19-inch Spanish-style knife, with a wooden handle and brass guard, reflecting the Mexican (Tejano) influence and blending of two cultures on Texas soil, where people, food, and weapons had long mixed in a cultural fusion of the southwestern frontier.

In the war's beginning and responsible for arming themselves when they first formed volunteer companies that then entered Confederate service, almost every type of firearm had been carried by the Texas Rebels. These weapons included .54-caliber Mississippi rifles (United States Model 1841), fast-firing Colt revolvers (the .44- and

.47-caliber six-shooters—the famous Walker Colt—the weapon of choice of the Texas Rangers), repeating rifles, old shotguns (single and double-barrel), white-tailed deer rifles, Mexican-American War and Indian War weapons, etc. But by the time of the showdown at Gettysburg, the accurate, relatively light .577 Enfield rifle proved the favorite long-arm weapon of the Texans.

But revolvers remained a popular legacy from the southwest frontier. Long an especially lethal weapon of choice on the western frontier, Colt and Navy revolvers (the famed six-shooters) were most popular hand-held firearm among the Texan officers, because of their first-firing capabilities and the damage that could be inflicted in short order. One Texas Brigade company (Company "C," 4th Texas, in which five Talbot boys served, including a hard-fighting father-son team—J. B. Talbot, Jr., and Sr.—and four Wilson boys) was known as the Five Shooters. Texas Brigade officers often held popular shooting matches with six-shot revolvers to show-off their skill with their favorite weapon.[72] At this time and for ample good reason, the common conviction across the South was that a Texan "with his superior marksmanship could shoot down the Damn Bluebellies as fast as they would come in sight."[73]

Described across the South as the best shots in the Confederacy and for ample good reason, the frontier marksmanship of the Texas Brigade's common soldiers early became the talk of the Army of Northern Virginian. The Texas Brigade's unparalleled lethal qualities were perhaps most visibly demonstrated against the unfortunate soldiers of the 5th New York Zouaves at Second Manassas. Here, Hood's Division nearly destroyed General John Pope's Army of Virginia with a fierce flank attack that overpowered everything before it. Near the end of August 1862, the deadly Texas marksmanship demonstrated at Second Manassas appalled witnesses and created "Carnage Hill." The fast-firing Texas Rebels inflicted the highest number of fatalities (at least 120 5th New Yorkers of an exceptionally hard-hit regiment that was thoroughly decimated and routed by the charging Texans) suffered by any single regiment during a battle of the Civil War.

Such lethal marksmanship, which allowed the Texans to kill more Yankees than any other unit of the Army of Northern Virginia, was a key reason why the Texas troops were early and so often detailed by commanding generals for all-important rearguard duty to protect the withdrawing army's rear and to spearhead assaults, including at Gettysburg. An expert marksman, Sergeant Andrew W. Smith was elected captain of a specialized unit of "1st Texas Sharpshooters" in April 1862. Smith and his sharpshooters had been early assigned to the strategic sector at the Rohrbach Bridge (later dubbed Burnside's Bridge) sector at the southern end, or far right, of Lee's thin defensive line to assist General Robert Toombs's Georgia Brigade in holding firm against the odds. Early in the war, the Texas soldiers boasted: "... one Southerner with his superior marksmanship could shoot down the Damned Bluebellies as fast as they would come in sight"—a fact proven true at Gettysburg, where the Texas Brigade excelled beyond what was even imagined, especially at the Devil's Den and Houck's Ridge.[74]

Repeatedly, the high level of accurate marksmanship among Texas Brigade members astounded both friend and foe. Chaplain Davis described how in the heat of action, the Texas marksmen were successful in "picking off every one who showed his head" above good cover in the brigade's first battle. During the sweeping attack at Gaines's Mill that carried the day, one Texas soldier wrote: "One volley was poured into [the Yankee's] backs, and it seemed as if every ball found a victim, so great was the slaughter." Texas Revolutionary War veteran Colonel Jerome Bonaparte Robertson, a father figure to the teenagers in the ranks, never forgot how during the successful charge at Second Manassas that crewed up and spit out almost too many New Yorkers (hapless Zouaves who were cruelly decimated without mercy in a San Jacinto-like rout) to count: "Such was the impetuosity of the charge [not initiated by continued by the common soldiers in the ranks] and the unerring aim of my men, that very few, if any, of that regiment [5th New York Zouaves] reached the hill beyond" and safety.[75]

In his battle-report about the bloody contest that raged across the same ground where the Battle of First Manassas (or First Bull Run, the South's first major victory of the war just outside Washington, D.C., during July 1861) was fought, one officer marveled at the "well-practiced aim of the men of the entire brigade" that simply slaughtered the unfortunate New Yorkers.[76]

The renowned poet of Hood's Brigade bragged in true homespun terminology how the Texas boys "Can wallop ten to one, whether Yanks or Mexicans"; ironically, the same lofty equation about combat prowess that had been mistakenly embraced by the ill-trained citizen-soldiers of the Alamo garrison to play a key role in its destruction to the last man. No idle threat or mere braggadocio, this chauvinistic bravado that flourished among the Texas Rebels was in part a legacy of successful clashes against Native Americans and Latinos, including the regular army forces under General Antonio Lopez de Santa Anna during the final showdown on the Gulf of Mexico plain of San Jacinto and during the Mexican-American War of 1846–1848.

The heavily-armed Texas Brigade soldiers certainly looked like supreme Yankee killers, as if they had been specially molded by some Union-hating God. Like on the southwestern frontier while fighting for survival, they were armed to the teeth, and well beyond what was required in Confederate Army regulations. These Texans were lean, rugged-looking, conditioned by hardship, and sun-tanned from outdoor lives long before they entered Confederate service: the most formidable opponent that the brave men of the Army of the Potomac ever faced on the field of strife.[77]

The Distinctive "Texas Yell"

At the decisive moment of victory, a distinct yell of the victors erupted over the Devil's Den on the bloody afternoon of July 2, 1863, at Gettysburg. Indeed, another distinctive feature of the wild Texas frontier was the unique war-cry of the Texas Brigade soldiers that was entirely different and distinctive from that of any of Lee's other troops in the heat of battle. Indeed, the Texas war-cry was quite unlike the typical Rebel Yell. Higher-pitched, more piercing, and partly a byproduct of the often no-quarter combat long seen on the frontier and Indian warfare, the Texas yell was more of a Comanche war-cry straight from the windswept grasslands of the southern Great Plains than the high-pitched yelp-yelp commonly heard from Southern troops in battle.[78]

To other Army of Northern Virginia soldiers and the Texans themselves, this distinctive war-cry was commonly known as the "Texas Yell." The emotional and psychological effect of the "Texas Yell" helped to inspire Texas Brigade soldiers to do the impossible on one battlefield after another, including at Gettysburg, while instilling fear in their opponent. From Beaumont located just north of the gulf coast, where his family had moved from western Louisiana in 1859, the Louisiana-born Private William A. Fletcher, Company "F" (Company Invincibles whose members hailed from Jefferson, Liberty, and Washington Counties), 5th Texas, described: "When Hood's Brigade went into action, they raised the Texas yell, and ... its meaning was 'charge.'" Private Robert Campbell, 5th Texas, wrote how during the unstoppable attack at Gaines's Mill, "the boys gave a [Indian war] whoop, and with fixed bayonets, started at a run for them."[79]

As far back as their first fight of the Texas Brigade at the Eltham Plantation, located on the low-lying Virginia Peninsula, on May 7, 1862, the Texas Rebels unleashed a "whole-souled hearty yell" that had been heard so often in frontier conflicts from hard-riding Native American warriors bent on revenge for encroachment on their ancestral lands and Mexicans eager for vengeance for the loss of Texas, thanks to the surprising defeat of Santa Anna's forces at San Jacinto.

On Virginia's gory battlegrounds, the attacking Texans were all "yelling like mad men" of the Comanche nation. Because the piercing war-cry was entirely unique to the soldiers of Hood's Texas Brigade, this terrifying war-cry from the wildest and most untamed frontier in America, was long remembered, especially the Yankees, who heard it echoing over the fields and forests to early warn them that all hell was about to break loose.[80] Although the Texas war cry sounded like something from the dark depths of Hades, even Chaplain Davis marveled how "the full grown shout of success, which always tells what the Texans are doing, when they struggle for victory in the presence of mighty foes."[81]

Sterling qualities bestowed by the frontier and western experiences that made the Texans such fierce combat soldiers were an inordinately high degree of resiliency, individual initiative, and resourcefulness of the individual common soldiers. Consequently, these qualities of the men in the enlisted ranks, mostly humble privates, often rose to the fore on the field of strife in the absence of officers. Indeed, these distinctive frontier qualities that spelled the difference between victory and defeat on the battlefield, when many Confederate officers were killed or wounded.

During Lee's costly headlong attacks on Malvern Hill—the last high ground before the James River—on July 1, 1862 in the final clash of the Peninsula Campaign, Private Fletcher described how the common soldiers, acting and performing well like officers, instinctively filled the leadership void during the advance "our number gradually grew less and after our second advance we were, as far as I knew, without an officer [but] The remaining men continued doing as first directed and would advance" toward the row of blazing Union cannon.[82]

In such battlefield emergencies when so much was at stake and especially in regard to the showdown at Gettysburg, the Texas common soldiers always arose to the occasion primarily because they possessed the experience, flexibility, and resiliency to do so in crisis situations. Therefore, some Texas Brigade's successes resulted in part from the initiative of the privates rather than superior weaponry or leadership. With leading officers either absent or shot down, these Lone Star State men of the enlisted ranks continued to fight on their own in pivotal battlefield situations. Demonstrating that they were highly-adoptable veterans who adjusted quickly to the flurry of fast-paced tactical requirements, lowly and humble privates often led the way to victory. In the words of an astounded Chaplain Davis, who marveled at the resourcefulness of the hard-fighting common soldiers, who seemed to always rise to the occasion: "Our men do not need their chief officers to set them an example of bravery and daring. They only need to be told when and where to go" into battle.[83]

Such distinctive frontier qualities and western characteristics were not unlike the secret of Sam Houston's decisive victory at San Jacinto in April 1836. Unlike Santa Anna Lopez de Santa Anna's national army based on an inflexible Napoleonic model to the generalissimo's delight because he idolized the native Corsican, the Texians most often fought as frontier individualists without having received written or verbal orders from officers, remaining highly-tactical flexible and adaptive in fluid battlefield situations to exploit tactical opportunities. In fact, General Houston's men (from officers to privates) had literally forced their reluctant commander—a former United States officer who served under Andrew Jackson during the Creek War—to unleash a frontal assault on the vulnerable Mexican encampment on the hot afternoon of April 21. Before and after the assault, the Texians were well beyond the control of their frustrated officers, including General Houston, in destroying Santa Anna's advanced force in only twenty minutes. After the assault on the Mexican encampment became completely unmanageable, "Old Sam" admonished his men at the sight of the slaughter of hundreds of Mexican soldiers, including men who had attempted to surrender: "Gentlemen, I applaud your bravery, but damn your manners."[84]

Demonstrating tactical flexibility and adaptability on the field of strife, the Texas Rebels made their own tactical decisions in the heat of combat and on the fly, especially at Gettysburg. Almost always, this instinctive and natural decision-making of the common soldiers to continue the attack paid high dividends by exploiting available tactical opportunities, while most other Confederates troops hesitated, faltered, or halted when on the verge of victory.

These distinctive frontier qualities of the common soldiers gave the Texas Brigade an unmatched tactical flexibility and adaptability on the battlefield: a key advantage against Union soldiers, who fought more conventionally by the book and without comparable tactical flexibility. In the absence of orders from officers who were killed or wounded, especially during steam-rolling attacks, on the battlefield, this unique characteristic of greater initiative and tactical flexibility enhanced personal initiative and freedom of action for the common soldiers to immediately exploit battlefield gains and tactical opportunities that were most often fleeting. At a time when poor-quality Confederate leadership, especially because of ill-timed hesitation and the lack of aggressiveness, so often snatched defeat from the jaws of victory, privates, corporals, and sergeants of the Texas Brigade often deliberately acted on their own to exploit a tactical opportunity in full, before a clueless general located far to the rear at some remote headquarters issued an order to halt an attack on the brink of success or failed to ascertain the opportunity.

Such resourcefulness and flexibility of the Texas Brigade's common soldiers on the battlefield was no accident, as often believed by historians. Thanks to the molding process of the frontier experience and the rigors of western warfare, and as mentioned and noted, a large percentage of Texas Brigade members were already experienced soldiers and lethal frontier warriors before the war: invaluable experience that rose to the fore at Gettysburg on the afternoon of July 2. This higher level of experience was quite unlike that of raw citizen-soldiers in the East, including tens of thousands on both sides who had never fired a gun before at the war's beginning. Not seen elsewhere to such a degree, this unique situation of the Texas frontier and western experiences bestowed these weapons-savvy men with an invaluable early advantage, allowing them to repeatedly excel on the field of strife by a thorough utilization of well-honed skills and instincts.

Consequently, the first time that the Texas Brigade met the Yankees revealed a notable example of the clash of cultures and vastly divergent past experiences between the men in blue and gray and with predictable results. What developed was in essence a showdown that pitted frontier-influenced westerners against easterners in blue far removed from the frontier experience. Here, on the Virginia Peninsula, this distinctive western unit from the lands west of the Sabine first demonstrated a host of dominant cultural and combat qualities that made it so distinctive beyond other units, both North and South: a penchant for hard-hitting offensive thrusts, tenacity in refusing to relinquish ground; the resourcefulness of the hard-fighting common soldiers, who relied upon individual initiative to win victory on the battlefield; a heightened degree of tactical flexibility and adaptability, and the never-say-die determination of the men in the ranks to continue to exploit success without specific orders to do so.

Showdown at Eltham Plantation

During the baptismal fire on May 7, 1862, at Eltham Plantation in Kent County, Virginia, and directly east of Richmond, the Texas Brigade soldiers first established a fearsome reputation for combat prowess. This sharp clash on the Virginia Peninsula's tangled lowlands between the York and James Rivers occurred during the early stages of General George B. McClellan's push up the Virginia peninsula during his seemingly unstoppable attempt to capture Richmond, when General Joseph E. Johnston's Army retired west from Yorktown toward Richmond.

Here, on the south bank of the Pamunkey River at Eltham Landing, northwest of Yorktown and near the small town of West Point (hence, this fight was also known as the Battle of West Point), which had long served the Eltham Plantation for the transportation of goods, General McClellan made a determined bid to intercept the withdrawing Confederates heading closer to Richmond. He planned to strike Johnston's withdrawing forces on the flank with an amphibious landing of a large task force to catch the Rebels by surprise.

But General McClellan had not anticipated the sudden arrival of the Texas Brigade—and Wade Hampton's Legion—and young Colonel John Bell Hood, formerly the commander of the 4th Texas, who led the Texas Brigade. Johnston had correctly anticipated McClellan's attempt to flank his lengthy line of retreat by way of the York River. Here, at Eltham Plantation, Hood and his Texas Brigade first gained widespread recognition for meeting this serious Union threat with a hard-hitting style that was all its own.

To avoid any accidental firing between his troops who led the Confederate advance through the summer-like woodlands and toward the landing site so as not to alert the Federals, who had poured inland from transports, Hood prudently ordered his men forward early on the morning of May 7 with unloaded muskets so that no accidental discharge would alert the bluecoat interlopers. Leading the way before his Texas troops as usual despite wearing a resplendent colonel's uniform, the mounted Hood suddenly stumbled into a lengthy line of Yankee skirmishers hidden in a maze of tangled, heavy timber. Hood was about to be shot down at close range by a Union corporal standing only a few feet distant. Seemingly, "a military career of high promise seemed at its end."[85]

In the ranks of the 4th Texas, however, stood a self-reliant individualist named Private John Deal of Company "A" (Hardeman Rifles). Like so many other Texas Brigade members in the western frontier tradition, he thought for himself and on his own, regardless of directives from either West Point generals or headquarters. Consequently, the young private now wisely carried a loaded musket against orders. Acting instinctively, he quickly took a good firing position behind a stump and almost instantly shot down Corporal George J. Love, 16th New York. Private Deal, thereby, almost certainly saved Hood's life: a young rising star that was destined to become Lee's most aggressive and best division commander by the time of Gettysburg. In the Texas Brigade's initial encounter with the Yankees in the depths of the Virginia Tidewater, this episode was one of the first examples of the western frontier-induced flexibility and personal initiative of the ever-unorthodox Texas soldier rising to the fore.[86]

No Quarter Ways of the Southwestern Frontier

At Eltham Plantation on May 7, 1862, the Texas Rebels first demonstrated that they had brought the old ways of the Texas frontier—especially a well-honed, if not grisly, art of guerrilla and Indian warfare—with them to the more civilized world of old Virginia, where Southern hospitality and refined cavalier manners of the wealthy planter class were time-honored traditions. Chivalric and romantic notions of warfare (or what was considered to be Christian concepts—as opposed to so-called "savages"—from the Yankee or east coast perspective) were largely foreign concepts to the free-thinking frontiersmen in the Texas Brigade.

After all, they had known no-quarter warfare and the ugly realities of racial conflict with Native Americans and Mexicans for generations. With savagery on both sides in Indian warfare equally ruthless, such pervasive western frontier attitudes that rose to the fore ran contrary to longtime perceptions (extending back to ancient times, including the Greeks when they battled Trojans and Persians, or today's Iranians) of western society's romantic concept of "Good Death," which was romantically heroic in the popular Sir Walter Scott tradition of the day: popular and inspirational reading for the Civil War generation.

For these resourceful Texas frontiersmen in gray, therefore, the first meeting with the Federals naturally brought forth that same old kind of brutal warfare (as witnessed in both the Texas Revolution and Indian warfare), which had been long waged with deadly effectiveness on the western frontier. After pushing aside the first Union cavalrymen who protected the front before Eltham's Landing, the charging Texans then steam-rolled over two picket companies of the 16th New York Volunteer Infantry.

In one of these advanced New York companies, Private Francis Mummery, age twenty-one and an Irishman, was shot by the onrushing Texans. Private Mummery was cut down but he not out, however. After the Yankees, who had advanced too far inland to be adequately supported by gunboats, were hurled back to the Pamunkey River landing, and the Texans had secured their first sparkling success outside the capital of Richmond, the Irish fighting spirit of the injured Mummery had not diminished. Consequently, the bleeding Son of Erin gamely pulled out a pistol to get his revenge. He then shot down at least one Texas soldier, evidently in the back. The never-say-die New Yorker then continued to blaze away with his revolver until his ammunition was expended to seal his doom.

As if still fighting on the Texas frontier against a Mexican or Comanche, who certainly would have done the same to him if wounded in a typical war to the death on the western frontier, an enraged Texan cut the throat of the belligerent New York private, who refused to surrender, with a Bowie knife. As demonstrated on the gory field of San Jacinto on April 21, 1836, where the Texians' vengeful battle-cry was as much, if not more, to "Nock There Brains Out," as the more famous "Remember the Alamo," this was a "natural" act of no-quarter warfare. Indeed, because not wasting a single shot in a frontier style of fighting was a longtime priority in a harsh land where the simple rule of survival of the fittest dominated rather than the niceties and antiquated European-based ways of waging war, this "natural" act was committed without thinking by a Texan, who had only eliminated another pesky opponent who could not be allowed to exist because he had taken Texan lives.

The entire Alamo garrison had been killed to the last man on the morning of March 6, 1836, for a comparable reason, after refusing to surrender to Santa Anna's early demanded capitulation. Clearly, winning a decisive victory on a hard-fought field required what has been described as "a harder courage," and the Texans possessed this key, but harsh, frontier quality in disproportionate abundance, including in the war's beginning.

In the past, some Texas Brigade soldiers had very likely seen the throats of family members cut by Native Americans, or they themselves perhaps had once cut the throats of Mexicans and Indians in the vicious conflicts that had long raged across Texas. Rationalized in part by the belief that this was a "just" war in which God was on the Confederates' side during what was considered this holy war, the Texan's cruel act of dispatching a fallen opponent without mercy to eliminate an existing threat was in many ways only a natural frontier impulse and part of a survival instinct, which came as easily to these Texans as dispatching a Comanche warrior, who sought to wipe out his family stranded in a remote log cabin on the Texas prairie.

Clearly, this type of vicious no-quarter warfare was nothing new to many of Hood's Texan warriors, although the more pious men believed, in the words of one Texan soldier, that the ugly methods of killing without mercy on the battlefield was one of the "most blasphemous thing perhaps on earth." But of course, such ruthless acts that ensured survival had long ago become a widely-accepted practice out of necessity to exist on the Texas frontier, where the cruel Darwinian law of survival was paramount.

During the 1836 Campaign, Santa Anna's Mexican *soldados* had waged a savage brand of no-quarter warfare as learned from the Spanish, who had learned their lessons from the Islamic Moors of North Africa in Spain during a merciless religious, cultural, and racial conflict that spanned for more than six centuries on the Iberian Peninsula. Indeed, this no-quarter tradition was a dark legacy of not only southern European and Mediterranean religious, racial, and imperialist warfare learned from the Spanish and centuries of combat against the Moors (Africans), but also later from the cruel conquest of the Aztec civilization in central Mexico, and then in battling Native Americans in North America during wars of extermination.

This same Spanish-like way of waging war in all its brutality was demonstrated not only at the Alamo, but also at Goliad, Texas. This brutal brand of no-quarter brought from deep inside the Republic of Mexico resulted in two slaughters during the same month of March 1836. The Goliad massacre witnessed Santa Anna's premeditated and systematic slaughter of hundreds of mostly Anglo-Celtic prisoners, including their previously wounded commander Colonel James Walker Fannin. The unfortunate victims were mostly volunteers from the United States, and they were executed like sheep on the open prairies outside Goliad on Palm Sunday 1836: ironically, in a case of history coming full circle, the pitifully small band of surviving Texas Brigade men were destined to surrender on a Palm Sunday at Appomattox Country House, Virginia, in 1865 that they never forgot.

For the feisty citizen-soldiers of the Texas Revolution and the Texas Brigade, conflict against an opponent (red, brown, or white) was based upon two simple, but brutal, equations: "conquer or die" and "war to the knife and knife to the hilt," in the words of Texas Brigade soldiers, who waged war without remorse and in deadly business-like fashion, because it was a matter of simple survival.

A regular feature of irregular warfare on the western borderlands and as noted, this type of savage kind of fighting was learned the hard way by the Texans in an earlier people's revolution, where no-quarter became the accepted policy on both sides. In early 1836, General Santa Anna initiated his aggressive war of extermination, with the battle-cry of "Death to the Americans." On April 21, 1836, the Texans' awful retribution for past slaughters, especially at the Alamo and Goliad, was finally fulfilled with the massacre of hundreds of routed Mexicans, who were contemptuously called "Yellowbellies," at San Jacinto (some Mexicans were even scalped by these frontier fighters): a grim continuation of the harsh traditions of frontier and Indian warfare. Significantly, Texas Brigade soldiers of 1861–1865 still felt the need to adhere to the same business-like ruthlessness and terrible efficiency (necessary for acquiring decisive victory in this 1861–1865 war but more in regard to decimating enemy units rather than a deliberate no quarter policy of Union soldiers in the ranks) in regard to vanquishing an opponent, especially if they were from New York or New England.

Not understanding the cruel ways of frontier warfare or the no-quarter rules of survival of the fittest that had long governed harsh life on the Texas frontier, the 16th New York Infantry troops and the northern people were thoroughly shocked at the savage nature of Private Mummery's death at the Eltham Plantation. After all, the unfortunate private was found with his throat cut, which infuriated the boys in blue. But, of course, the northern people were not made aware that this brave Irish Yankee had continued to fight back with spirit, after he had been summoned by the Texans to surrender.

Also causing outrage was the fact that another New Yorker in blue suffered eight bayonet wounds: the high price paid for the folly of defiant men engaging the Texas warriors in hand-to-hand combat. Since the dangerous days of the Stephen Fuller Austin's settlement in the early 1820s, Texians, including women and children, had received uncommonly brutal treatment from Native Americans, and this type of brutal combat that was focused on exterminating an enemy was nothing unusual to the average frontiersman.

The outraged major of the 16th New York penned and then published an angry letter in a major newspaper denouncing "the most horrid barbarities perpetrated on the person, as that of [Private] Mummery whose throat was cut" by a Texan. According to the western frontier logic of one Texas soldier, who in a matter-of-fact manner provided a commonsense explanation that even the most upper-class easterners might understand, if unclouded by a sense of indignation: "... it was thought that a wounded man, whose line of battle had been driven from the field, and who thereafter continued to fight on his own account, deserved to be summarily dealt with so we cut his throat." In the Texans' initial battle at Eltham's Landing, this was the first incident that served notice to the Union Army and the northern people that a very different kind of soldier (the Texian who was in general more fanatical and ruthless in his quest to achieve a decisive victory than other members of the primary army defending Richmond) had made his appearance on the battlefields of the eastern theater.

Indeed, with the arrival of the Texas Brigade, a new and much harsher brand of warfare had come to the eastern theater at a time when the war was still looked upon a romantic adventure. This unsurpassed fighting man from the distant Texas frontier simply did not adhere to the established rules of warfare as taught at West Point or as deemed by the traditional chivalric values of eastern America. The kind of warfare brought by the Texans to Virginia was not understood by those refined young men and gentleman dandies from the fashionable parlors, upscale society, and fancy French restaurants of New York City, the tree-lined streets and manicured lawns of Philadelphia, or the social clubs of Boston's stylish upper class.

Quite simply, the average Texian frontiersman and yeoman farmer in gray and butternut, hailing from the most untamed frontier still left in America, which was still as dangerous as early Virginia had been during the colonial period. With a hard-hitting style, these Texas Rebels brought the ways of frontier warfare to the more genteel, cultured, and romantic-minded soldiers of the eastern theater to shock soldiers, politicians, and civilians.[87] Representing a killer instinct that equated to victory in this war when the fate of two nations was at stake, one Texas officer perhaps explained the simple rationale that equated to victory: "Oh this is fun ... to shoot them [the Yankees] down" in droves.[88]

Most importantly, such sterling qualities among the rugged fighting men resulted in a sparkling success at Eltham's Landing. Here, Hood's Texas Brigade, along with the rest of General William H. C. Whiting's Division which had been assigned by General Johnston to this key mission of the Union ambitious landing, hurled the bluecoat interlopers back to the landing and to their gunboats.[89]

This rough-and-ready Texan fighting man and his frontier means of waging war without traditional rules defied the conventional wisdom and the day's established military practices and warrior ethos, which especially shocked northerners and easterners, especially erudite New York City residents of the fashionable part of town. Widows and orphans across the North were early created by Texas Bowie knives and bayonets, and this kind of warfare stunned the more civilized Yankee world. In the Texas frontier tradition, the primary objective of Hood's men was all about utterly destroying and exterminating the enemy to the last man if necessary. A frontier product of western Louisiana and eastern Texas, Private William A. Fletcher of the 5th Texas, relished the spectacle of heaps of dead Yankees, which made his fondest dreams come true.

In time, such gory sights reaped by the harvest of Texas bullets and bayonets "elated him" and his hard-bitten Texas comrades, who fully realized that decisive victory in this war could only be achieved by killing as many Yankees as possible. For the Texians, this conflict was certainly no civilized brothers' war in the traditional sense, and sometimes to the consternation of the Texas Brigade's chaplains, such as Presbyterian Nicholas A. Davis, chaplain of the 4th Texas, and Chaplain J. R. Vick, a fiery Baptist minister of the 1st Texas. Chaplain Vick might have been related to Private William A. Vick, Company "M" (Sumter Light Infantry), 1st Texas, who died of disease in Virginia on August 3, 1862. The boys, especially the irreligious ones dominated by a youthful recklessness, in the ranks simply called them "Parson."

Most of all, Hood's Texans early understood the basic, but harsh, frontier equation that complete victory could only come not from precise battlefield maneuvers or civilized behavior to fulfill outdated chivalric traditions of far-away Europe, but by utterly wiping out the adversary in the tradition of Indian and guerrilla warfare on the western border. Engaged in a crusade that was a holy war against the Yankees and feeling a sense of exhilaration by the destruction of so many opponents, Private Fletcher delighted upon viewing the piles of Union dead on the battlefield, because it equated to a hastening of the war's end: "My thoughts on seeing the [clumps of Yankee] dead were without a pang of regret or sorrow."[90]

For Fletcher and many other Texas Brigade soldiers, the sight of large numbers of dead and dying Federals was emotionally and spiritually uplifting, succeeding in "Doing my soul good," in one Rebel's words upon viewing some of the most surreal carnage ever seen on an American battlefield.[91]

Born of an especially harsh, unforgiving environment, the Texans felt a special contempt for their ancestral enemies—first Native Americans and then Mexicans, although some Indians and Tejanos served in the Texas Brigade. In fact, the Tejanos in gray of Hood's Brigade continued the distinguished legacy of Captain Juan Nepomuceno Seguin's hard-riding Tejano company of Texas Revolutionary fame. This excellent Tejano unit, that won considerable Texas Revolutionary War recognition, consisted of patriotic Latino rancheros who rode like the wind. Seguin's citizen-soldiers possessed a well-deserved reputation as "the best horsemen in the world," making them more than a match even for the much-feared Comanche. Captain Seguin's patriotic Tejanos of the Texas Revolution hailed mostly from the cattle ranches in the San Antonio area, especially along the San Antonio River. Most significant, these Tejanos were among the first Texians to join the struggle for Texas independence against the encroaching centralized powers and the growing threat of Mexico. They fought with distinction at San Jacinto where the final success was achieved to shock the world by the winning of an improbable victory.

Besides their own performances, the past successes of Texians in arms from 1835–1836 only fueled the ever-growing sense of confidence and superiority of the Texas Rebels, causing them to sincerely believe that they could whip any number of Yankees in any battlefield situation. Such contempt for the enemy—Yankee, Indian, or Mexican—was expressed in a letter by Major Matt Dale, the 1st Texas Infantry's popular commander, who was killed in the war's bloodiest day at Antietam, of considerable ability. Born in Smith County, Tennessee, in 1830, Dale had crossed the Sabine and settled in Palestine, Texas, in 1852. With undisguised disgust, the major and former associate editor of the *Trinity Advocate* and state legislator (elected in 1859) wrote how at a moment of triumph during the fighting on the Virginia peninsula, the Yankees "ran like hounds as they are."[92]

Young Private Fletcher, another seasoned "product of a frontier environment," described the common sentiment among these hardened Texans, who in general were not so naïve as to be guilty of thinking too grandly or excessively romanticizing about the alleged majesty of war like the vast majority of young northern and southern soldiers, especially in the war's beginning. Most of all, the Texas Rebels, who generally and earlier embraced fewer romantic illusions, "understood war [was all about to] kill or capture [as many of the enemy as possible], and understood capture was not complete until the enemy was disarmed."[93]

For these highly-motivated soldiers of Hood's Texas Brigade, warfare most of all was a savage contest in which only the most ruthless, cunning, and resourceful combatants survived a life-and-death confrontation and prevailed in the end: a harsh reality that they fully understood from the war's beginning and in general more than other American soldiers, who only belatedly learned about the war's ugly side and surreal horrors.

Therefore, when the Texans met the Yankees head-on on the battlefield, as revealed at Second Manassas, they were early determined to destroy every soldier in blue until no one was left standing, knowing that this was a war of attrition as in the case of their infant republic that had been born out of the forge of an earlier revolution. To the Texas Brigade soldiers, this ruthless single-mindedness represented the true formula for victory in the tradition of the grisly nature of frontier and Indian warfare. Civilized rules of warfare as understood and faithfully practiced by easterners, North and South, in a more gentlemanly war were simply not part of the personal experiences or frontier culture of the Texas Brigade soldiers in their unforgiving world, which was defined by the lack of rules and niceties between opponents partly because of broad racial and cultural differences.

Elated instead of feeling repulsed by the bloody sights of slaughter, Private Fletcher wrote how the ghastly scene on one Virginia battlefield during the Seven Days fighting "was pleasing to the sight and pleasant for reflection [after ascertaining] a masterly piece of marksmanship—blue coats with bodies enclosed, lay in line for some distance, and so close that it put one in mind of a railroad grade with ties laid for ironing."[94]

In regard to the Confederate assaults on Malvern Hill in the last major clash of the Peninsula Campaign on bloody July 1, 1862 and as if writing about hunting white-tailed deer or turkeys along the Brazos River in the East Texas pine forests back home, Private Fletcher penned with an unconcealed glee of the sheer pleasure of shooting down Yankees and silencing a troublesome Union battery with deadly marksmanship:

"... what fine shooting it was, for we had a safe position, while they had as exposed a one as I ever saw men in—it looked like replacing the dead and wounded with live men to be slaughtered, with little hope of retaliation."[95]

Like his seasoned Texan comrades, Private Fletcher was especially lethal with his trusty rifled musket and steel bayonet. Even in a combat situation, he refused the coveted honor of carrying the 5th Texas' battle-flag simply because he might miss the fun of killing more Yankees, which he accomplished with a smooth efficiency without thinking or considering the widows and orphans that he created: "I have said I never would pick up a flag, going into battle, for I would not lay down my gun when I thought there was a chance to kill a Yankee." But this representative Texan attitude of the common soldiers was less pathological or psychotic—in regard to the wartime experience brutalizing individuals in a traumatic sense—as it would seem at first glance to modern readers, because such time-honored frontier concepts were revered and so deeply rooted in the searing Texas experience and frontier warfare against ancient foes.[96]

In terms of personal motivation, fighting spirit, and overall toughness, consequently, these rawboned Texans were more than a match for the men, especially city boys from the major northeastern cities, of the Army of the Potomac, when it came to frontier-style fighting of ambush, lightning-quick strikes, smashing heads with musket-butts, and hit-and-run strikes in the manner of guerrillas or Native Americans.

Quite simply in the eloquent, knowing words of the commander of a hard-fighting North Carolina brigade in the Army of Northern Virginia, General William Dorsey Pender (West Point Class of 1854 and fated to be mortally wounded at Gettysburg) explained in a letter why the Texas Brigade soldiers were superior fighting men: General John Bell Hood "has the best material on the [North American] continent without a doubt."[97]

But as mentioned, perhaps the most important factor that explained the Texas Brigade's success year after year was the overall experience, initiative, and quality of the common soldiers in the ranks, especially the privates and noncommissioned officers, such as Sergeant Shadrack "Shady" D. Roach. He was a tough Scotch-Irish fighter of Company "M," 1st Texas, who was killed at Antietam on September 17, 1862. By any measure, these were no ordinary fighting men, who had become in essence informal citizen-soldiers at an early age on the Texas frontier.

Here, they had early learned not only to fire weapons, but also to use the tomahawk. These frontier skills were additionally improved and well-honed as the war lengthened to become even more deadly, maturing to reach new heights of lethality across the eastern theater, especially at Gettysburg. Exactly where the bullets fly the thickest and in crisis situations, Hood's men often made their own tactical decisions on the fly in the heat of combat, knowing almost instinctively when to press the attack when the enemy showed signs of weakness or faltered.

On one Virginia battlefield when the Yankees finally broke and fled for their lives, Texas privates acted on their own, utilizing instincts and acquired tactical knowledge like a commanding officer. Knowing that now was exactly the right time to exploit the tactical advantage to the fullest to maximize success because greater opportunities were presented, one natural tactician from the enlisted ranks yelled, "Now's our time, boys!" What resulted was an unstoppable attack that gained more momentum and garnered additional success. Without the usual advantage of advice, detailed planning, or orders from high ranking officers, this was but one example of the common soldiers' rallying call that often won tactical successes on some of the hardest-fought battlefields of the war.

In the words of Corporal Joseph Benjamin Polley:

> The effect of the call seemed magical, for the words had scarce passed the speaker's lips when every member of the brigade sprang to his feet, gun in hand, and leaping over the breastworks, joined in a wild, reckless charge.... No order was given by an officer; none was needed. Each man wanted to do, just then, while the enemy were in confusion, what he felt sure he would be ordered to do, perhaps an hour later, when the Federals had recovered from their panic, and probably, received reinforcements. There was no alignment, no attempt at any [while] Company, regimental and brigade officers, following the lead of their men.[98]

During the bloody combat of the Seven Days Battle that raged in the forest-covered, low-lying Virginia Peninsula in the late spring and summer of 1862, Orlando Thacker Hanks, Company "K" (composed of St. Augustine County, Texas, soldiers who went to war with homemade bayonets created by a blacksmith from butcher knives), 1st Texas, caught the very essence of the Texans' fighting spirit that was destined to rise to the fore in the struggle for the Devil's Den. Hanks described how the high-spirited Texans, with fixed bayonets, seemed almost magically transformed when the word to attack rang down the line: "Then the order came 'Charge men.' You ought to have seen those Texans, every one to a man go forward [over rough ground and man-made obstacles] But that did not stop them; on they went, until they reached the enemy's breastworks [and the Yankees] are fleeing from them like rats from a burning ship.... We had nothing to do but shoot them as they went panic stricken" to the rear.[99]

Then, during the bitter struggle for possession of the Devil's Den and Little Round Top at Gettysburg on bloody afternoon of July 2, 1863, "every fellow [of the Texas Brigade] was his own general [and the] Private soldiers gave commands as loud as the officers—nobody paying any attention to either." On the all-important second day at Gettysburg and along with seasoned Alabama attackers of Brigadier General Evander McIver Law's Brigade advancing beside them to the right, or south, the 4th and 5th Texas came very close to capturing Little Round Top, and turning the tide at Gettysburg on the crucial day before "Pickett's Charge" was decisively repulsed to end lofty Confederate dreams.[100]

Ever-reliable Texas Scouts

In overall terms, the degree to which the frontier experience bestowed a host of specialized frontier attributes can be seen by the fact that Lee and his army of more conventional and traditional fighting men often relied heavily on the Texans as invaluable scouts. These former hunters and trappers had partly learned their skills from Native Americans and from the frontier experience in which hunting and self-defense were top priorities. Such reliable scouts, who gathered invaluable intelligence to illuminate tactical realities and opportunities for General Lee's headquarters, included trusty 1st Texas men like Privates George C. Sorell, Thomas W. C. Lake, Wilson J. Barbee, and Private John Burke. Of Scotch-Irish descent, Burke was a longtime "Confidential Scout" for General Lee. Indeed, the Texans "because of their familiarity with rough frontier conditions and their ability to shoot and to track were often employed as scouts by Confederate commanders" of the Army of Northern Virginia.[101]

One Company "E" (the Corsicana Invincibles of Navarro County), 1st Texas, soldier named Private John Burke, likewise of Scotch-Irish descent, also served as General Lee's "favorite spy." A private of the Marshall Guards (Company "E") from Harrison County, Burke was "an outstanding scout," while serving as another one of Lee's "Confidential Scouts." Burke was born in Philadelphia in 1830, and either lost his parents, ran away from home, or was abandoned, at age eleven. Burke, therefore, had grown up "on his own" on the mean streets of New York City, perhaps in the urban squalor of the Five Points, where many Irish immigrants and African-Americans lived in this crime-ridden section, in lower Manhattan. Here, he might well have lost an eye in a personal fight, gang altercation, or an accident.

The seductive lure of the West called to the ambitious young man, and Burke migrated to Marshall, Texas, becoming a shoemaker. Burke worked hard to get ahead, studying law at night to escape lower-class status. He joined the law practice of his brother-in-law, becoming "a prominent criminal defense attorney." Because of his intimate knowledge of New York City and Philadelphia and his street smarts, Burke was early utilized as a spy to gather intelligence in these major northern cities, and also in Washington, D.C. Private Burke was wounded barely a month before the first major clash of arms north of the Potomac during the struggle that swirled through the David R. Miller Cornfield at Antietam, ensuring that he missed the Texas Brigade's greatest challenge at Gettysburg.[102]

However, a good many Texas Rebels possessed woodsmen and scouting skills akin to Private John Burke. Having grown up with firearms and having used them either in hunting for sport and to put food on the table or fighting guerilla style against Indians and Mexicans, the average Texas soldier from the rural areas of Texas marveled how the opposing Yankees (probably city boys or rookies) were so unskilled and "poor in woodcraft or they would not have so exposed themselves."[103]

In addition, besides their high level of a vastly superior *esprit de corps* and *élan*, the Texas Rebels seldom turned to run in battle in part because in frontier warfare the turning of one's back to an enemy often meant death (besides, of course, a measure of shame) in the no-quarter tradition. There was no such comforting concept of surrender in the brutal warfare that had long raged on the Texas frontier.

General Hood's Texans never forgot how hundreds of Colonel James Walker Fannin's men had learned that terrible lesson the hard way during the Texas Revolution. On the bloodiest Palm Sunday, 1836, in the annals of Texas history, the mostly volunteers from the United States were brutally executed on the open prairie by Santa Anna's forces on the premise that all foreigners (they were heavily-armed United States citizens on Mexican soil and serving in organized military companies) captured under arms were to be exterminated as pirates (the United States was not at war with Mexico). Mexican lancers and bayonets then finished off the piles of wounded men after the initial volleys of Santa Anna's men had exploded at close range into the columns of defenseless prisoners. The grim death toll at Goliad reached around 400 volunteers, who never again saw their homes.

In general for the Texas Rebels and from the beginning, therefore, the mere thought of fleeing the battlefield was an entirely foreign, if not unimaginable, concept that was simply not an option to the Texans unlike so many other Civil War troops (North and South), especially in the war's early days. As Colonel John Cunningham Upton, commanding the 5th Texas, explained without exaggeration to a staff officer of General Richard Stoddert Ewell, who was destined to lose a leg, but still commanded the Second Corps at Gettysburg after having replaced "Stonewall" Jackson, on the bloody field of Gaines's Mill during the Peninsula Campaign: "... these are my men [of the 5th Texas], these are Texans, and they don't know how to run."[104]

Another key factor that made the Texas Brigade an elite command was the overall high quality of leadership at brigade, regimental, and company levels. Inspiring their men to do what was seemingly impossible on the battlefield, Texas leaders on all levels were not only experienced, but also consisted of a reliable and sturdy quality. Most of these were natural fighters, who were resourceful and tactically-talented, especially the battle-hardened sergeants. The colonel of the 5th Texas and Texas Brigade commander by the time of the climactic showdown at Gettysburg, Jerome Bonaparte Robertson, was a Texas Revolutionary War veteran. He utilized tactical lessons and skills at Gettysburg on the afternoon of July 2, 1863, which had been first learned in battling Mexican forces in 1836.[105]

The Irrepressible John Bell Hood

This overall high level of quality leadership, from brigade commanders down to non-commissioned officers, also played a large part in the transformation of the Texas Brigade into an elite unit that consistently out-performed Lee's other commands. The most positive leadership change in the Texas Brigade's early days was the replacement of its first commander, Colonel Louis Trezevant Wigfall, who had been promoted to a brigadier general's rank in October 1861. He was replaced by an aggressive, tactically astute, and natural fighter with almost limitless potential, John Bell Hood. Tall and physically imposing, Hood became the Texas Brigade's commander in March 1862, after relinquishing command of the 4th Texas upon earning a brigadier general's rank.

Formerly the 1st Texas' commander, the South Carolina-born Wigfall was a smooth-talking politician, who was more of a braggart and heavy drinker than gifted tactician and natural fighter like Hood. In one letter, one disgusted 1st Texas officer lamented how Wigfall "has one great fault. He loves whiskey too well." A man of the enlisted ranks of the 4th Texas laid full blame for Wigfall's unpredictable behavior and uncontrollable temper on the consumption of too much "apple jack and kindred refreshments which he was [always] so fond," which seriously affected his overall leadership ability.

In contrast, Hood was a highly-qualified, sober, and hard-hitting West Pointer with solid United States Army experience. Gaining a well-deserved reputation while leading the "Hell Roaring Fourth" with his usual aggressiveness, Hood had early turned his command into one of the army's finest regiments, especially when unleashed on the tactical offensive. Thanks in part to commanding such capable troops who seemingly were always impatient to launch the attack and wreak havoc among the enemy, General Hood evolved into one of Lee's best and most aggressive brigadiers.

Unlike the tactically-gifted Hood, Wigfall knew very little about the complexities about the complicated art of war. In a January 3, 1862, letter, Corporal Joseph Benjamin Polley lampooned his incompetent brigade commander for ample good reason:

> … if there is anything else that I have a right to complain of in common with every member of the brigade, it is of the vagaries and hallucinations of the brilliantly astute politician now in command of the brigade … whether it be due to constitutional nervousness, or to that produced by the Apple-jack, and kindred liquid refreshments of which he is [now] so fond, he has kept us for the last month … in a state of almost constant apprehension [for] he sees a Yankee in every shadow, hears one approaching in every breeze that rustles [and] orders the long roll sounded by the drummer…[106]

Not a harder hitting combat leader could have been chosen by President Davis to replace the alcohol-ridden Wigfall, when he became a Texas senator in the Confederate Senate in February 1862, than the young and dynamic Hood. Only age twenty-nine and the son of a respected physician, the Owingsville, Bath County, Kentucky-born General Hood possessed a heightened degree of natural aggressiveness and hard fighting instincts like the rawboned Texas soldiers, who he commanded with skill. Unlike the long-winded Wigfall, who boasted about himself as much as he drank the fine whiskey, and despite the promising son of a scholarly backwoods physician, Hood was a rangy frontiersmen from a border state divided by the war. Hood possessed his own distinctive western qualities, fulfilling the lofty expectations of his rawboned

Texans. Hood had received the nickname of "Sam" from his fellow cadets at West Point which indicated popularity, graduating from the prestigious military academy in 1853.

Best of all, he was an old Indian fighter from the regular army, which perfectly suited the prickly Texans, who respected no commander without battle scars, physical and mental, like Spartan warriors in an ancient time. Hood had even fought on Texas soil while serving in Colonel Robert E. Lee's Second United States Cavalry, before the insanity of the fratricidal conflict divided loyalties and destroyed countless lives. Hood resigned his officer's commission for the express purpose of fighting for the Confederacy. He considered himself an adopted Texan, especially with his native Kentucky having maintained its neutrality in the Civil War's early days. Therefore, this tough West Pointer, experienced in frontier duty and dangers in battling Native American warriors, had a good deal in common with the hard-fighting Texas Rebels, who knew a real fighting man when they saw one.

Consequently, a strong bond immediately developed between the gaunt, somber Kentuckian and his lively and high-spirited Texas Rebels, who loved nothing more than a good fight against the North's finest troops. The polished but acerbic Richmond diarist Mary Chesnut, a well-connected South Carolinian (married to a respected South Carolina's senator) in Richmond, wrote that General Hood possessed "the face of an old Crusader who believed in his cause, his cross and his crown, we were not prepared for such a man as a beaux ideal of the wild Texans." Consisting of so much excellent natural and experienced material that merged into unsurpassed lethal qualities, the Texas Brigade early benefitted from Hood's leadership. He knew how to best utilize his aggressive fighting men, especially kindred spirits from the western frontier.[107]

Before Hood's took brigade command in the spring of 1862, the Texans had already established a lofty reputation, which had preceded them to the eastern theater. In a July 30, 1861 letter to his parents, Lieutenant Robert Hugh Gaston, 1st Texas, wrote from the Confederacy's capital of Richmond: "The Texians have a great reputation here at fighters [and therefore] The people here look upon a Texian ranger (as they call all Texians) as a person who don't care for anything. They say that they had as soon fight devils at once as Texians [and] We will have enough to do [in the future] to sustain our reputation."[108]

As Hood had accomplished with his hard-hitting 4th Texas (one of the best Texas Brigade units after the unsurpassed 1st Texas), so he continued to fine-tune the Texas Brigade into a lethal fighting machine. General Hood's motto caught the essence of the Texas Brigade's fighting spirit: "let us stand or fall together" on the battlefield.[109]

In the insightful words of Colonel William Calvin Oates, who commanded the finest Alabama regiment in Hood's Division, the 15th Alabama, that proved its worth during the assault on Little Round Top at Gettysburg on July 2, 1863, Hood "drilled and disciplined [the Fourth Texas] until he made it one of the finest regiments in the army."[110] Indeed, this was one reason why Hood became the finest division commander in the Army of Northern Virginia by the time of the climactic clash of arms at Gettysburg.[111]

In addition, Hood also strengthened an already robust sense of *esprit de corps* in the Texas Brigade that paid high dividends on the battlefield, especially in regard to the second day at Gettysburg. Hood early "impress[ed] upon them that no regiment in that Army should ever be allowed to go forth upon the battle-field and return with more trophies of war than the Fourth Texas—that the number of colors and guns captured and prisoners taken, constituted the true test of the work done by any command in an engagement."[112]

In this clever way that fueled a healthy rivalry among the Texas regiments of his hard-fighting brigade, "Sam" Hood prepared his men for the most severe challenges of the war, including the struggle at the Devil's Den. He made them even more eager to undertake the most dangerous and risky assignment, either as rearguard defenders or in spearheading the attack. Thanks in part to his own western experiences as a young Second United States Cavalry lieutenant on the western frontier, Hood additionally improved elite soldiers, who were especially lethal on the battlefield.

As if to compensate for his emphasis on intense drilling hour after hour under the hot summer sun or in the snows of winter, Hood allowed his men to pretty much do as they pleased in camp and to go their own way. Because the tall Kentuckian, who intimately knew the typical psychology of these roughhewn westerners and their mysterious ways to the minds of shocked easterners, was dealing with fiercely independent and unorthodox soldiers. Indeed, with their trademark defiance, these men openly questioned authority and orders with seemingly endless repetition. Consequently, knowing their temperament and inclinations, Hood wisely ignored the strict requirements of endless regulations and strict protocol whenever his Lone Star State boys were off-duty and far from the enemy. But he only did so with the clear understanding of an unwritten mutual agreement that they, in turn, would always perform their best on the field of strife. It was an informal covenant of mutual consent and somewhat of a westerner's gentleman's agreement that paid impressive dividends on the battlefield, including in the struggle at the Devil's Den and Houck's Ridge.

This most unorthodox, frontier-like understanding between general and the enlisted men suited the ever-independent Texans perfectly well, because any type of traditional "group discipline, grated on the Texan frontier soul." This unspoken, but fully understood, informal pact between the common soldiers and their commander revealed that Hood was the ideal commander of a wild bunch of soldiers, who simply could not be disciplined in the traditional sense, or even according to the much looser Confederate Army standards. Almost certainly, the Texas soldiers could only have reached their full potential as elite fighting men second to none, including at Gettysburg, under the informal terms of this "less bridle the better," according to one Texan, who well understood the importance of this special arrangement and its corresponding high dividends paid on the battlefield.

As a westerner who fully understood the psychology of these contradictory Texas fighting men and willing to forget all about West Point's strict teachings when they were off the battlefield, Hood possessed the good sense to take these free-thinkers as he found them from the beginning, and treated them accordingly. In return, the Texans were supremely devoted to "our beloved General Hood," who they would follow to hell and back, if necessary. But most importantly and as part of the informal bargain between their brigade commander and the common soldiers, they always performed their best on the battlefield, accomplishing what other Confederate troops (even the most celebrated fighting men—Virginians, of course—who were long promoted in the influential Richmond press) were unable to achieve, especially against the odds and seemingly impossible situations. In this way, the incomparable Hood and the Texas Brigade repeatedly met the challenge on one battlefield after another. Hood inspired confidence by leading in front by bold example, such as during the Texas Brigade's successful attack on the Union defensive lines, bolstered by well-manned cannon, at Gaines's Mill, and on the afternoon of July 2, immediately before his troops overran the Devil's Den and Houck's Ridge.

In addition, the disproportionately high casualty rate suffered by the Texas Brigade gave enduring testimony that Lee's "Grenadier Guard" or "Old Guard" (a name that certainly would have caused Napoleon Bonaparte to smile, because of his own longtime reliance upon the elite Imperial Guard troops, who were distinguished by their physical height accentuated by tall bearskin shakos) was "time and again it was chosen for the most difficult, dangerous missions." One 4th Texas soldier, William R. Hamby, Company "B" (Tom Green Rifles) summarized how "when a regiment or brigade claims to have suffered heavily in battle, you ask for the list of killed and wounded [and] Judged by this standard, no brigade in the Confederacy has more bloody laurels or stands higher on the roll of honor than Hood's Texas Brigade."[113]

One modern historian emphasized without exaggeration how in analyzing the Texas Brigade's heavy losses and sacrifice on some of the hardest fought battlefields of this war: "... the known statistics of these [Texas] regiments are so remarkable [as it was] a record equaled by few, if any, organizations in the Civil War, or indeed, in modern warfare."[114]

The Texas Brigade's total casualties have been estimated at least 4,332 soldiers out of the estimated 5,300 men who served on behalf of the world's newest republic, as if they were defending the old "Lone Star Republic" against invaders and raiders from Mexico. But in fact, these statistics that spoke eloquently of the high price that had to be paid to establish an elite reputation in the Army of Northern Virginia was actually higher, because of poor record-keeping and incomplete and lost military records.

In consequence, one historian estimated that this frightful casualty figure of the Texas Brigade was actually even higher: around 4,700 Texas soldiers, including Texans who were not only killed, wounded, and taken prisoner, but also discharged because of wrecked health and lingering injuries, after arduous campaigning across Virginia, Maryland, and Pennsylvania.[115]

2

Distinguished Revolutionary Legacies

Other key factors seldom emphasized historians have played leading roles in fueling the Texas Brigade's superior combat performances. By the time of the Civil War, the spirit of the Texas Revolutionary generation was still alive and well across the Texas, and among the men in the ranks. This especially vibrant inspiration early convinced Texas Brigade members to march to the Virginia theater. Corporal Joseph Benjamin Polley, 4th Texas, perhaps said it best: the Texans "resolved to maintain the reputation for desperate courage won for the 'Lone Star State' by the heroes who at the Alamo fought and died that their comrades might at San Jacinto fight and win."[1]

Even among the Texas Brigade's many teenagers in the ranks, this historical, almost spiritual, legacy of the Alamo, and San Jacinto served as powerful motivating factors among Major John Bell Hood's common soldiers from beginning to end. These enduring revolutionary and historical legacies motivated them to perform exceptionally well and "second to none" on the battlefield. Unlike men from any other Southern state because of the difficult birth of the Republic of Texas, Hood's Texans closely embraced a dual revolutionary heritage and legacy: the inspirational traditions of the American Revolution and the Texas Revolution.[2]

Like other Americans of the Civil War generation, these young Texans, the descendants of men who fought in the American Revolution on the Mississippi's east side, were significantly shaped in overall psychological, spiritual, and emotional terms by the cherished revolutionary traditions, ideologies, and legacies of 1776. Consequently, large numbers of Texas Brigade soldiers, from high-ranking officers to enlisted men, were named after American Revolutionary heroes, especially Founding Fathers George Washington, Benjamin Franklin, and Thomas Jefferson, and even famed partisan South Carolina leader Francis Marion.

Handsome Benjamin Franklin Carter, the 4th Texas Infantry's commander, had been born in Maury County, Tennessee, in 1831, four years before the Texas Revolution's beginning. Making a fresh start in life in a new land, Carter had migrated to the banks of the Colorado River at Austin (which has been founded barely a decade before) in 1853. Here, he practiced law and became the mayor. Carter was idolized by the men in the ranks for not only his leadership skills, but also for the kindness that he demonstrated to the common soldiers. As a sad fate would have it, Carter was mortally wounded in the fierce assault on Little Round Top on July 2, 1863, after the capture of the Devil's Den.

In the ranks of the 1st Texas alone, the first and second name of the revered sage of Monticello, Thomas Jefferson who authored the Declaration of Independence and was known as the most intellectual Founding Father, preceded the last names of fighting men named Chambers, Kennedy, Rose, Reed, and Bowman. Naturally given the importance of a revered revolutionary experience that was not forgotten, the most common first and second Founding Father names among these Texas Brigade soldiers was that of George Washington. These were the first and middle names of no less than at least twenty members of the 1st Texas.

Of Scotch-Irish heritage, George Washington Armstrong, Company "A," 1st Texas, was one of these men. Armstrong was seriously wounded in the attack through the hellish Miller Cornfield at Antietam on September 17, 1862. Some 1st Texas men also might have known that their names followed in the tradition of an earlier generation of Texas revolutionaries, such as Lieutenant George Washington Main, born in Virginia in 1807. He was killed at the Alamo, when it was overwhelmed by thousands of attackers from the lands south of the Rio Grande River. In addition, a total of ten soldiers of the 1st Texas possessed the names of Ben Franklin, who was the brilliant Founding Father from Philadelphia.

Another four men who carried the names of Francis Marion, the famous guerrilla leader known as the Swamp Fox of South Carolina's Dee Pee River country, served in the 1st Texas' ranks, while keeping the revered memories of asymmetrical warfare and heroic resistance against the odds during the American Revolution alive. Of French Huguenot heritage and a Continental officer who survived the siege of Charleston, Marion kept the spirit of resistance against the British alive during the darkest days of the especially savage war (ironically, primarily between Americans because of the large Tory population that had sided with England) in the South Carolina. This bitter conflict was basically America's first civil war, and its atrocities revealed as much.

The young men and boys of the 1st Texas believed that they were the true inheritors of the American Revolution. When the Texans, the great-grandsons and grandsons of America's first revolutionaries, marched to the small, tobacco port of Yorktown, Virginia, during the opening stage of the Peninsula Campaign of 1862, this historical place still possessed special meaning in another people's revolution. Here, Lone Star State soldiers "grew quite enthusiastic over the fact that we were on historic ground, made sacred by [General George] Washington's great victory, and eloquently insisted that the scene should inspire us with extra courage and patriotism," wrote Corporal Joe Polley, 4th Texas, in a May 19, 1862 letter.[3]

When Texas Brigade soldiers viewed Thomas Jefferson's stately architectural masterpiece of Monticello, located just outside Charlottesville, Virginia, these young men and boys stood solemnly in respectful silence on this picturesque hilltop in Albemarle County. This generation of Texans viewed their people's struggle against the North's centralized government (as London had also represented an arbitrary centralized government to the colonists) as what was considered to be the Second American Revolution.

Even more, they firmly believed that the Confederacy, not the Union, represented the true core egalitarian and democratic values of the Founding Fathers and America's republic experiment, which needed to be saved by their people's revolution against the march of modernity. Therefore, the Texans strolled in silence and with reverence among "the sacred portals" of Jefferson's beloved architectural marvel of Monticello, while reflecting upon the distinguished legacy of "the famous statesman" and his "glorious memories" of a former revolution.[4]

Sacred Memories

Cherished revolutionary legacies were so vibrant that Hood's rawboned Texans were determined to live-up to the legendary revolutionary wartime accomplishments of their ancestors, who fought with distinction at the key turning point battles of Saratoga, New York, Kings Mountain, South Carolina, Cowpens, South Carolina, and Yorktown, Virginia. Equally symbolic, the American Revolution's inspirational influences had also similarly motivated the fighting men, both the Texians and United States volunteers, from 1835–1836 during the Texas Revolution. Chaplain Nicholas A. Davis, 4th Texas, summarized the almost spiritual power of this distinguished revolutionary heritage and analogy of 1775–1783 in simple, but eloquent terms:

> The patriots of the [American] Revolution were struggling for liberty, and so are we. They had been oppressed with burdensome taxation—so were we. They remonstrated—so did we. They submitted until submission ceased to be a virtue—and so have we.... Who would have believed that the Stars and Stripes, the emblem of liberty, would so soon become the ensign of oppression.[5]

Along with the significant influence of the frontier experience, however, no single factor more forcefully shaped the mentality and psychology of the average Texas Brigade soldier regardless of their age than the legacies of the Texas Revolution of 1835–1836. Indeed, even more than the revered memories of the American Revolution, the Texas Revolution was the most powerful single historical influence that most inspired and motivated Texas Brigade members to perform beyond expectations on one battlefield, including the capture of the Devil's Den on the afternoon of July 2. Unlike other fighting men of both North and South, this distinctive and unique revolutionary influence of a bloody revolutionary struggle on the southwestern frontier helped to fuel the Texans' combat prowess to unprecedented levels on battlefields, and especially at Gettysburg.

This powerful emotional and psychological, if not spiritual, legacy of the Texas Revolution was not a distant or abstract memory for Hood's men like in regard to the American Revolution, but an actual tangible and physical presence in the Texas Brigade's ranks. Indeed, Texas Revolution veterans served in the Texas Brigade's ranks, including Jerome Bonaparte Robertson, who faced his greatest challenge at Gettysburg. He had led Kentucky mounted volunteers and "join[ed] in the pursuit" of Mexican forces after General Houston's one-sided victory at San Jacinto on the gulf coastal plain. Most symbolic for leading the Texans into the midst of the largest battle on the North American Continent and the bloody showdown at Houck's Ridge, the Devil's Den, and Little Round Top, Robertson commanded the Texas Brigade on a true day of destiny, July 2, 1863.

As in regard to America's first revolution, some younger Texas Brigade soldiers were named to honor Texas Revolutionary heroes. These 1st Texas soldiers included Sergeant Crockett English and Private Crockett Dunlap. Of course, these men had been named in honor of Davy Crockett, the famous Congressman from Tennessee and recent migrant to Texas in a classic and tragic case of bad timing. After all, Crockett's death in battling to the bitter end at the Alamo was never forgotten by the Texas Brigade's soldiers, who were extremely proud about what happened in the name of battling for liberty on the morning of March 6, 1836.

Catching the mood at the time, one Tennessee newspaper reporter lamented how "there is something in the untimely end of the poor Tennessean, that almost wrings a tear from us [especially since he was] butchered by such a wretch as Santa Anna." Most symbolic, Company "I," 1st Texas, was known as the Crockett Southrons, and these young men from Houston County, Texas, fought the bluecoats in the same spirited manner as David Crockett during his short career as a Texas Army private, who enjoyed the confidence of the diminutive garrison, when under siege.

When the ever-optimistic Texas Rebels first marched off to war in the heady spring and summer of 1861, Texas Revolutionary War veterans (political leaders, former Texas Rangers, and windy orators of Texas) had long filled these young men with martial tales of the glories of the Texas Revolution, especially in the great victory at San Jacinto. Thus, these highly respected individuals reinforced the already strong link between the 1835–1836 revolutionary experiences and the Confederacy's own revolutionary tradition that came dramatically to life in 1861. In the tradition of the American Revolution in regard to General George Washington's and the French Allies' decisive victory at Yorktown by forcing the surrender of General Charles Cornwallis' Army in October 1781, the Texians had won the independence of their frontier republic on the gory field of San Jacinto. But even stunning defeats in the Texas Revolution before Sam Houston's miraculous victory at San Jacinto infused among the Texas soldiers "many painful, and pleasing, and glorious reminiscences connected to the Alamo [which invigorated] every Texan spirit," while bestowing Hood's Texas Brigade with a distinguished revolutionary legacy that was never forgotten.

A fiery Texas Rebel and former Texas Ranger leader, Colonel John Salmon "Old Rip" Ford, emphasized the importance to the inspirational analogies between the

American and Texas Revolutions by writing how the Texians' struggle against Mexico: "involve[d] all the principles for which our forefathers fought in the revolution of 1776." To Colonel Ford, who served in the western theater during the war years, and the Texas Confederates, the fight for Texas independence had been the sacred "cause of constitutional government, for the rights of man, for liberty" in the tradition of the American Revolution.[6]

Therefore, even before Houston's sparkling victory on the gulf plain of San Jacinto along the brown waters of wide Buffalo Bayou on a decisive spring afternoon near the head of Trinity Bay, he was already known across the United States as "the Washington of Texas."[7] Emphasizing the importance of American Revolutionary War ideology that had been born of the Age of the Enlightenment as a motivating factor, General Houston had inspired his Texians and United States volunteers in the fight against Mexico with the war cry: "Our cause is the cause of all mankind—tis the cause of human Liberty!!!"[8]

Most symbolic, Houston's own eldest son, Sam Houston, Jr., born at Washington-on-the-Brazos, where the Texas Declaration of Independence had been hastily signed by delegates on March 2, 1836 to create a new republic and gain greater support—especially military—in the United States, in late May 1843 and who proudly wore the gray, was told by his proud warrior father (since the days of the Creek War when he served as a United States regular at the Battle of Horseshoe Bend, Alabama) in a May 22, 1861 letter: "... go to war if you wish to do so. It is [a man's] duty to defend his Country; and I wish my offspring to do so..."[9]

Ironically, by the time that this letter was written, Houston had been forced out of the governor's mansion at Austin in mid-March 1861 by the rising secessionist tide and for failing to take the required oath of loyalty to the Confederate States of America, after Texas departed the Union with much fanfare. After joining the 2nd Texas Confederate Infantry that served with distinction in the western theater, Sam Houston, Jr., nearly lost his life during the brutal slugfest along the Tennessee River at Shiloh (or Pittsburg Landing that was owned by Pitts Tucker). During a charge through the springtime Tennessee woodlands of early April 1862, Houston's pocket Bible, carried in his breast pocket, stopped the Federal bullet that had been aimed at his heart to save his life on this bloody battlefield in Hardin County, Tennessee.[10]

Even more ironic, by the time that they marched off to Virginia, the Texas Brigade's soldiers no longer saw the Unionist Houston as an idol and the revered hero like their fathers to reveal not only a considerable generational split, but also changing times. As a fearful Private John Camden West, 4th Texas, reasoned in April 1863 when he was concerned about the homeland's safety because Houston was running for governor since "His election will be an invitation to Yankee invasion."[11]

The legacy of invoking the memory of Revolutionary War heroics from 1775–1783 to inspire the fighting men of Texas were nothing new. During the Texas Revolution from 1835–1836, a Methodist preacher and veteran of the Battle of New Orleans, January 8, 1815, reminded the Texians of his congregation that "the same blood that animated the hearts of our ancestors in '76 still flows in our veins." Therefore, the Texians who fought in the Texas Revolution were widely praised across America as "the brave sons of Washington and freedom." Symbolically, when the newspaper of the Texas Brigade was published during the winter of 1861–1862 at Dumfries (which had been settled by Scottish immigrants from the Celtic town of the same name on the Atlantic's other side), Virginia, the publication was named *The Spirit of '61*, which echoed the Spirit of '76 in overall idealistic terms.

For the younger Texas Brigade soldiers, the dual legacies of the American Revolution and the Texas Revolution were something that was precious, playing a key role in the creation a never-say-die soldiery, despite the odds or seemingly no-win situation. Stirring memories of the American Revolution heroics, from General Washington's late December 1776 Delaware crossing in harsh weather to win a dramatic victory at Trenton and to the final showdown at Yorktown, motivated the citizen-soldiers of the Texas Revolution, just like the Texas Revolution inspired Hood's men at Gettysburg. The heroics that stemmed from these dual revolutionary legacies challenged the Texas Brigade's soldiers to not only equal, but also to surpass the distinguished military feats of their revolutionary forefathers, whose battlefield achievements had become the stuff of lore.[12]

Most symbolic, zealous volunteers for the South united as one in Austin to form a volunteer company that was appropriately named the Travis Rifles. This infantry command became officially known as the Travis Guards, Company "G," 6th Texas, which originally was to have joined the Texas Brigade in Virginia. However, the Confederate regiment was kept in the West by self-serving Confederate leaders. Consequently, this company of Texas Rebels, who never reached Virginia, had been named in honor of the Alamo's martyred commander, Lieutenant Colonel William Barret Travis.

Indeed, young Travis, a former Alabama lawyer who had been born in South Carolina, served as an inspirational role model to these young men in gray and butternut throughout the war years. After all, Travis's last words to rally a defense of the weak north wall on the fateful, early morning darkness of March 6, 1836, had been "Come on Boys, the Mexicans are upon us, and we'll give them Hell." Symbolically, this fine volunteer company of young Texas Rebels was commanded by Captain Rhoads Fisher. His father, Richmond, Virginia-born John, who was proud of his brother (William S. Fisher) for having led a volunteer company to victory at San Jacinto, had signed the Texas Declaration of Independence on March 2, 1836, at Washington-on-the-Brazos to create the world's newest experiment in democracy, the Republic of Texas.[13]

Texas Brigade soldiers were inspired by Travis's famous words (in essence the unofficial Texas declaration of independence) as written in his February 24, 1836, letter during the siege of the Alamo, "I shall never surrender or retreat" and "Victory or Death!" The native South Carolinian's eloquent words of courage and a desperate defiance in the face of impossible odds and an inevitable cruel fate were addressed "To the People of Texas and all Americans in the world." By the time of the Civil War, even some infants of Texas Brigade members were named in honor of the martyred heroes of the Texas Revolution. Such inspirational examples revealed the powerful influence, emotional appeal, and spiritual legacy of the Texas Revolution to the average Texas Brigade soldier, who fought and died during the bitter struggle for possession of the Devil's Den.[14]

As if attempting to validate the legitimacy the South's own audacious experiment in nationhood, the revolutionary heritage of the Texas War for Independence was warmly embraced not only by the Lone Star State soldiers, but also by the people of the Confederacy, including its austere president from Mississippi, Jefferson Davis. In the war's beginning, Private T. D. Williams, Company "E" (the Lone Star Guards which had been organized in McLennan County), 4th Texas, wrote:

> President [Jefferson] Davis anxiously awaits our arrival [to Virginia], having great confidence in the world renowned courage and prowess of Texans, so you see we have a great responsibility resting on us in order to sustain the well merited renown of our revolutionary sires of San Jacinto and '36 [and] I believe our boys can and will do it.[15]

When President Davis, a patrician member of the planter aristocracy and Mexican-American War hero of the February 23, 1847 Battle of Buena Vista, which had raged fiercely in the rugged terrain of the arid mountains of northern Mexico, addressed the newly-arrived Texans in Richmond, he proclaimed: "Texans! The troops of other states have their reputations to gain; the sons of the defenders of the Alamo have theirs to maintain!" Essentially a sacred trust between their nation's leader and the common soldiers from the Lone Star State, the president's words were a direct challenge that the Texas Brigade's soldiers took most seriously, and they demonstrated this fact in deadly earnest during some of the hardest-fought fields of the Civil War, especially at Gettysburg.[16]

Such priorities of the Texas soldiers motivated them to repeatedly rise of lofty standards of the revered Texas Revolutionary heroes, who they hoped not only to emulate but also to out-perform, if possible, on the battlefield: a forgotten factor that partly explained the tenacity of the struggle for possession of the Devil's Den. Like the Texas Revolutionaries had been motivated to repeat the heroics of their American Revolutionary ancestors, so the Texas Rebels were determined to not only duplicate the feats of their American and Texas Revolutionary ancestors, but also to create their own distinctive chapter in the history of the South's struggle for independence.

In the words of Chaplain Nicholas A. Davis, 4th Texas, who emphasized the closeness of the connection (a true symbiotic relationship) between the past and present in regard to the sacredness of the revolutionary tradition that was resurrected in full force during the spring of 1861: "To-day, we make history for the world to read." While the average Civil War soldier on both sides was initially concerned about demonstrating sufficient bravery ("The Red Badge of Courage" syndrome that became a popular cultural concept of the Civil War generation) to manfully stand-up to the first fire (the so-called "seeing the Elephant"—something novel and unique—to the boys in the ranks on both sides) during the war's early days, the average Texas Rebel was already supremely motivated and inspired, if not heavily burdened, by the weight of revolutionary and historical legacies by exceptionally high expectations.

Consequently, Texas Brigade soldiers fully expected that they could achieve another San Jacinto-like victory at places like Gettysburg to ensure a new nation's independence. Even the chaplain of the 4th Texas, Chaplain Davis, wrote with pride how the Texas Rebels were determined "to represent the ancient valor of Texas on a distant theatre" of war in a distinguished manner. But instead of an overpowering burden that often impaired abilities on the battlefield because of the weight of excessively high expectations, this lofty challenge only enhanced the combat prowess and determination of these men to win a decisive success at all costs, while fueling the fighting resolve of Texas Brigade soldiers in hellish places like the Devil's Den.[17] As early as October 29, 1861, therefore, Private Jack Burke, Company "A," 5th Texas, already hinted of the lofty expectations because of an early acquired reputation for excellence in a letter: "We are armed with Enfield Rifle[s] and said to be one of the finest regiments in the service."[18]

Perhaps a seventeen-year-old soldier from Houston, Texas, named Private Robert Campbell, Company "A" (Bayou City Guards), 5th Texas, best described the powerful symbolic, emotional, and psychological meaning of the Texas Revolution to the common fighting man, especially in regard to the Battle of Gaines's Mill, Virginia. Here, General Hood led the furious attack of the Texas Brigade against a lengthy row of roaring Union artillery pieces and lines of bluecoat infantry. With "comrades falling on all sides," Private Campbell wrote how the steam-rolling Texas attackers took heart upon the sight of "the Lone Star flag, which had been upon the field of 'San Jacinto' [and the banner now] cheered us on" to victory at Gaines's Mill.[19]

Unlike other Americans (North and South) and demonstrating pride in their distinctive heritage shared by no other state, Hood's Texas soldiers closely embraced three distinguished revolutionary legacies, experiences, and traditions unseen elsewhere in unison. They were strongly influenced by each righteous struggle for self-determination to fulfill lofty republican aspirations based on Age of Enlightenment ideology: the American Revolution, the Texas Revolution, and what this new generation of Texas fighting men viewed as the true Second American Revolution (not the War of 1812) that began in the exciting spring of 1861.

Most of all, for these highly-motivated Lone Star State soldiers, the Texas Revolution had been an epic struggle for liberty that has been described by one modern Texas historian as the "Texian *Iliad*." For the Texas Brigade soldiers, the Texas Revolution provided the most immediate and enduring lesson of a successful revolution against a powerful central government in Mexico City that led to the fulfillment of the great dream of independence. Rebelling against the centralized authority of Mexico and dictator Santa Anna, Texas won its independence more than a quarter century before the Civil War, but that legacy remained as vibrant, as if won only a few days before. Joseph Benjamin Polley, a member of Company "F" (Mustang Greys), 4th Texas, and whose father's home housed the first Texas Congress of a new republic in 1836, described: "Not a Texan there, whether by birth or adoption ... resolved to maintain the reputation for desperate courage won for the 'Lone Star State' by the heroes who at the Alamo fought and died that their compatriots might at San Jacinto fight and win."[20]

Imbued by the historical legacies of the Texas Revolution and the defiant words of Lieutenant Colonel Travis who had promised "never to retreat," the Texans remained highly motivated from beginning to end, because of this ensuring historical and cultural legacy that shined brightly in hearts and minds. Translating into a superior *élan* in the most severe battlefield crisis situations like at the Devil's Den, Texas Brigade members performed heroics with monotonous regularity, because it was expected of them and almost a birthright. In the words of one member, the Texas Brigade's soldiers continued the revolutionary tradition of defying a far-away tyrannical central authority by "emulating the bravery and heroism of [South Carolina's James Butler] Bonham, [whose young brother—Milledge Luke Bonham—served as a brigadier general for the Confederacy] Travis, Crockett and their compatriots in the Alamo," which had become legendary across America by 1861.[21]

During the struggle to gain possession of the Devil's Den, consequently, younger Texas Brigade soldiers sought extremely hard to duplicate the heroics of their fathers and grandfathers in the Texas Revolution, while older men sought to reclaim the martial glories that they themselves had won at San Jacinto with courage and audacity. Not surprisingly, therefore, the Texas Brigade soldiers possessed the very "aura of the Alamo about them" when they marched on the field of Gettysburg. Representing a unique Texas Revolutionary heritage, Company "I," 1st Texas, was known as the Crockett Southrons, and these Houston County men backed-up that name by hard fighting, regardless of the battlefield situation.

A reliable volunteer company was appropriately known as the Milam County Greys, which reflected a distinctive revolutionary heritage. Destined to become Company "G," 5th Texas, this volunteer unit, consisting of men from Milam and Cameron Counties, was named in honor of diehard republican Benjamin Rush Milam, a freedom fighter during the bloody struggle for Mexican independence against the Spanish. He was killed when shot in the head while leading the attack, including on the Mexican-held Alamo, which resulted in the capture of San Antonio in mid-December 1835. The Kentucky-born Milam became one of the first heroes of the Texas Revolution, and his heroic death inspired other revolutionaries to faithfully serve the cause of Texas.[22]

During the bitter struggle to win Texas independence, the "Mexicans have been taught a lesson which they will not soon forget, that Americans know their rights, and asset and protect them."[23] The Texas Brigade's soldiers were determined to teach the central government in Washington, D.C., and its minions a comparable lesson that they would never forget, including on the field of Gettysburg. Supremely motivated by the inspiring historical legacies of these three distinct revolutionary traditions of the American Revolution, the Texas Revolution and the so-called Second American Revolution (the last two raged within only twenty-five years), Hood's Texas Brigade possessed a much more lengthy and more intimate (and hence overall meaningful) revolutionary experience and intimate revolutionary tradition than any other Americans by 1861: the inspirational and ideological influences that played a key role in greatly enhancing the combat prowess of the Texas Brigade.

Of these three revered revolutionary traditions, the first two were successful, while the third was doomed to failure. Some younger Texas Brigade soldiers even believed that they could win this third revolutionary experience practically on their own at Gettysburg, when everything was at stake: an over-confidence fortified by the frontier experience and the winning of Texas independence.

The Texas Rebels were also imbued with a sense of mission that was a legacy of the spirit of Manifest Destiny (a distinct corollary and byproduct of the frontier experience and the relentless push of the American people toward the setting sun from the beginning) that led to the 1845 annexation by the United States of Texas and then the Mexican-American War's outbreak that had been sparked by the self-sharing annexation. General Hood's Texans believed that a special destiny and responsibility had been placed firmly in their hands in part because the Confederacy possessed its own distinctive sense of Manifest Destiny, which was not unlike that of the once-proud Republic of Texas. All in all, therefore, no other Army of Northern Virginia's soldiers possessed a greater sense of destiny for themselves and their southwestern homeland than the Texans, who envisioned the Southern nation expanding west and to the tropical islands of the Caribbean.

This heady sense of a special destiny motivated the Texas Brigade soldiers to achieve feats in battle that no other unit in the Army of Northern Virginia so often or so consistently accomplished on the battlefield. Such uniqueness and distinctiveness were additionally reinforced by the fact that the Texas Brigade was the only Lone Star State unit to serve in the Army of Northern Virginia during the four years of war. Therefore, Hood's Texas Rebels believed that their battlefield performance at Gettysburg represented Texas and every Texan, while garnering ever-lasting distinction under the microscope of Lee's eyes and the Richmond press.

Consequently, the Texas Brigade soldiers felt that it was their sacred duty to demonstrate the same heroic qualities of the Texians of romantic and enduring legend, from early settlers who battled the ruthless Comanche to homespun Texas revolutionaries who had vanquished Santa Anna's forces at San Jacinto, for the new Confederate nation to appreciate in full. After the repulse of the Army of the Potomac's first attempt to capture Richmond in the summer of 1862, Chaplain Davis described how the Texas Brigade troops, at no small cost, successfully "Sustained the pride of the Lone Star State [and now] They were looked upon by thousands as the flower of the Southern Army."[24]

In his Second Manassas battle report on the bloodletting that resulted in one of Lee's most spectacular victories on Virginia soil, Colonel Jerome Bonaparte Robertson, the savvy Texas Revolutionary War veteran who had ridden west across the Sabine River with a Kentucky volunteer company and then pursued the Mexicans south to the Rio Grande after the one-sided victory at San Jacinto, wrote with pride how "All, both officers and men, sustained well the reputation of the Lone Star State flag, under which they fought through the battle."[25]

Other respected Texas Brigade leaders, besides future Texas Brigade commander Robertson, were veterans of the Texas Revolutionary War and later conflicts with Mexico. Tennessee-born Captain William Harvey Sellers was a 5th Texas lieutenant, the assistant adjutant general of the Texas Brigade, and an esteemed member of Hood's staff. He had migrated to Texas in 1835, and fought in the Texas Revolution as a newly-arrived volunteer. Sellers then later served in the ill-fated Texian expedition launched to capture the Mexican town of Mier on the Rio Grande, northwest of Brownsville. Along with the rest of the members of the overly-ambitious 1842 Texian expedition, Sellers was captured and imprisoned in Mexico City.[26]

Stephen Heard Darden was another Texas Brigade officer with Texas Revolutionary War experience. Born in Fayette County, Mississippi, on November 19, 1816, he migrated to Texas in 1836 for the express purpose of joining the revolutionary struggle against Mexico. Darden represented Gonzales County (named in honor of the first battle—the "Lexington" of the Texas Revolution—that resulted in a first 1835 victory at Gonzales), Texas, in the House of Representatives. Ironically, he had initially opposed the drive of Texas politicians to secede from the Union like Houston, but eventually joined the popular consensus that demanded breaking away. After leaving his Gonzales County farm behind, this reluctant secessionist first served as a lieutenant of Company "A," 4th Texas, before his election to captain in late May 1862.[27]

In the true revolutionary tradition, even the favorite songs sung (although often sung out of tune and with too much vigor) with such unbridled enthusiasm by the Texas Brigade soldiers reflected the unique legacies of the Texas Revolution. This was another means of transferring the struggle's spiritual essence to a new generation of young revolutionaries—young innocents who became cannon fodder at Gettysburg because they believed that their respected leaders had served them capably—who thought in idealistic terms. The most popular of these frontier tunes was a jaunty song of Irish antecedents known as the "the Yellow Rose of Texas."

According to popular legend, General Santa Anna, a crass opportunist when it came to exploiting Mexican and Tejano ladies, had been surprised by the Texian attack on the afternoon of April 21 at San Jacinto, because of a sexual escapade. He was supposedly dallying in his silk headquarters tent, while under the influence of liberal doses of opium and sex, with an attractive mulatto slave woman named Emily Morgan (actually, the woman now in Santa Anna's camp was Emily D. West, a free black woman from New England, who had been working at New Washington, Texas), the alleged "Yellow Rose of Texas."[28]

Throughout the war, Texas women—mothers, daughters, sisters, wives, and lovers—also played their patriotic roles in motivating the young men and boys of the

Texas Brigade. In the words of one 4th Texas soldier, who was the only married man of Company "E" to his astonishment when in his late twenties, wrote:

> By their smiles they inspired and encouraged the soldiers in the field. By their frowns and scorn they drove the laggards to the front. By their tears, their sympathy and their prayers they upheld and stimulated the weak, the weary and the wounded [and this was] the glorious heroism of the noble women [of Texas].[29]

For such reasons, Private Jack Burke, Company "A," 5th Texas, penned to a Texas friend in an October 1861 letter: "Give my love to all the girls in your section.... By the way, have you seen my 'Bayou Belle' lately?... Remember me to your mother and sisters and all at home."[30]

However, not every Texas mother sent her young son off to war with unbridled enthusiasm. A vexed Joseph Benjamin Polley penned to his sister Hattie on September 20, 1861:

> That Mother should give me so little credit for strength of mind as to suppose I could be persuaded by any one to a course which I believed wrong and that she should harbor ill feelings towards this one, who has ever proved himself a true friend ... is a source of real grief to me—David Houston did urge me to go [to war] but my mind was made up before he conversed with me [and] I think mother is wrong in making David suffer for an uncommitted act [because] I am the one to be blamed if any ... that she should regret any connection with the army is natural [and] I am now enlisted in the Confederate Service for the war.[31]

Marching off to war because he was "not resolved not to remain quietly at home another moment while a foe is on our soil" in part because feisty Texas women who hardly allowed it because they had their own reputations in the community at stake, Private John Camden West, 4th Texas, exemplified the diehard commitment among Texas Brigade members, writing in his diary, "I am perfectly willing to give all [including his life] I have if the sacrifice will aid my country in achieving its liberty."[32]

Forgotten Scotch-Irish Roots

A well-educated, transplanted South Carolinian who regretted the absence of the more cultured Deep South planter class world that he had left behind for a new life on the unruly Texas frontier, West was emboldened by the great personal "satisfaction of striking a blow in the holiest cause that ever fired the breast of man [while reminding him of] reading the stories of [Scottish patriot William] Wallace" and other Celtic nationalists and revolutionaries, especially generations of rebels of Ireland, who struggled for their people's freedom and country's liberty.[33]

In fact, with the Texas Brigade's soldiers consisting largely of Anglo-Celtic fighting men, it came as no surprise that some of Hood's followers even looked almost like Celtic rebels of old. One Texas Brigade soldier wrote to a friend in late October 1861 and informed him: "I have changed much in appearance since you [last] saw me. I've got a fierce mustache, my whiskers have grown long enough for me to twist around and put into my mouth to chaw on [and] I imagine myself a 'huge' soldier."[34]

All of these diverse factors (environment, experience, leadership, *esprit de corps*, historical and dual revolutionary legacies, southwestern frontier culture, psychology, and time-honored Texian traditions) explained why the incomparable fighting men of the Texas Brigade compiled the finest combat record of any troops in Lee's Army of Northern Virginia and were "second to none" in regard to elite troops.[35]

Therefore, one Confederate general and division commander early complimented the performance of the Texas scouts with the most appropriate historical analogy in his official February 1862 report, because their "conduct deserves praise and invites emulation, and is worthy of the success of men who, many years ago, gallantly defended their cause at the Alamo and San Jacinto."[36]

3

Sturdy Foundations for a Superior Performance at Gettysburg

No regiment of the Texas Brigade was harder fighting or more resilient than the crack 1st Texas, and this was demonstrated in full in the struggle for possession of the Devil's Den and Houck's Ridge. Even among other regiments of the Texas Brigade, the combat prowess of the 1st Texas was universally admired throughout the arm.

By the time of the dramatic showdown at Gettysburg, the 1st Texas had already emerged as the most effective regiment of this crack brigade either in spearheading the attack or protecting a withdrawal. Hailing from Tyler, Anderson, Harrison, St. Augustine, Trinity, Nacodogches, Galveston, Polk, Sabine, Livingston, Marion, Cass, Newton, Cherokee, and Harris Counties, the men of the twelve companies of the 1st Texas (the only Lone Star State regiment of Lee's Army with a dozen companies) often covered the rear of Lee's Army during its most risky withdrawals, including after the miserable defeat at Gettysburg. In addition, the 1st Texas soldiers, who hailed mostly from the piney woods and post oak belt of East Texas, nestled between the Indian Territory to the north and Louisiana—and to a lesser degree Arkansas—on the east, were among the deadliest marksmen in the Army of Northern Virginia.

In contrast to its spotless combat record and in a striking paradox, no regiment in the entire Army of Northern Virginia was known for greater indiscipline or more widespread raggedness in overall appearance than the 1st Texas. Inspection reports recorded the total apathy of the 1st Texas boys for the strict requirements and exacting details of army regulations. Fighting Yankees and reaping decisive victories were the only priorities, if not obsessions, of the 1st Texas soldiers, who fairly lusted for every opportunity to meet the boys in blue, even as the war grew bloodier and more horrific.

This tough frontier regiment was bestowed with the nicknames of the "Ragged Old First" and the "the Ragged First" Texas. These 1st Texas soldiers, nevertheless, consisted of "the cream of Texas manpower," as demonstrated at Gettysburg. From the beginning, the fiercely independent 1st Texas soldiers were literally in charge of this regiment (not unlike the men of Houston's Army who played the largest role in orchestrating the showdown at San Jacinto by leading the reluctant general to decisive victory), because of their excessive individualism and their own concepts of democracy that superseded matters of rank.

The regiment's first commander, Colonel Louis Trezevant Wigfall, the blustering politician who drank excessively even by lofty frontier Texas standards, which was no small feat, learned as much the hard way. He had first migrated to Texas in 1848 long after the Texas Revolution. From the beginning, Colonel Wigfall was no match for the rebellious antics of the high-spirited 1st Texas soldiers. In the words of Joseph Benjamin Polley, 5th Texas: "The First Texas had run him half-crazy with its unwillingness to submit to the rigorous discipline he would have enforced."[1]

Indeed, when Wigfall found one carefree Texas guard relaxing on the ground and with his musket leaning against a tree, the incredulous colonel snapped, "Do you know who I am, sir?" The Texan remained composed and perfectly calm in the face of the direct challenge of the regimental commander, replying with an East Texan drawl that reflected Deep South antecedents, "Wal, now 'pears like I know your face, but I can't jes' call your name—who is you?" When informed that Wigfall was the regimental commander, this still unimpressed soldier, without rising or observing high rank in anyway, merely extended his hand, and said, "I'm pleased to meet you. My name's Jones."[2]

Wigfall restrained his strong desire to harshly discipline his soldiers, which had initially bolstered his popularity. But on March 14, 1862, Joseph Benjamin Polley penned in a letter:

> Col. Hood has obtained his commission as Brigadier General and has been assigned to the command of the Texas Brigade in place of Genl Wigfall [who] resigned. The loss of him as colonel is very severe on us—all the men had great faith in him and none whatever in ... our present Colonel. The latter does well enough to manage a [news]paper and do the mere work of political machinery, but has no military talent whatever [and] Great dissatisfaction exists in the regiment [4th Texas] against him. I hope he will have sense enough to resign ere we are called into battle.[3]

But a more telling incident than in regard to the nonconforming Private Jones developed when one 1st Texas soldier named Ebin Andrews displayed extreme laxness (which was so epidemic throughout the 1st Texas that it became a trademark) on guard duty one night during an *ad hoc* inspection. He was given a tongue lashing by a respected Confederate general from Louisiana, after the Texas private nonchalantly shouted, "Oh Hell! I thought it was the relief" upon the approach of the group of stern-faced senior officers. The general then abruptly grabbed Andrews's weapon out of his hands and mocked, "you are a fine soldier to give your gun to a man [and now] What are you going to do?" In response, Andrews drew a pistol from his belt and shoved it into the general's face with the serious threat, "Give me my gun or I will blow Hell out of you."[4]

In the most unorthodox manner possible, the ragged 1st Texas private had made his point to the stunned general, who was left speechless and much chagrined at having been humbled by the defiance of a proud common soldier in the ranks. But this was the kind of raw material that rose splendidly to the fore during the challenge of overrunning the Devil's Den.

Consisting of hardy yeoman stock and with largely Scotch-Irish antecedents, the 1st Texas soldiers hailed from the pine forests, bayou country, and small farms of east and southeast Texas. A total of nineteen Texas counties were represented in the regiment's ranks. However, Anderson County, with its county seat at Palestine, Texas, dominated with two companies ("H" and "G"), consisting of men from this single county located in the Trinity River, which flowed southeast into the Gulf of Mexico. Even in the 1860s, east Texas was yet mostly wilderness area and still a rough-and-tumble frontier region, despite its close proximity to the bayous and swamps of western Louisiana.[5]

Here, along the coastal plain lowlands of east Texas where brownish-hued Buffalo Bayou and the San Jacinto River met, Sam Houston's feisty citizen-soldiers had thoroughly vanquished Santa Anna's forces at San Jacinto: a stirring memory not forgotten by the 1st Texas soldiers, even while they launched their assault on the Devil's Den and charged over the open fields with fixed bayonets. From 1861–1865, the Texas Rebels repeatedly sought to win their own San Jacinto and a glorious victory, especially in the showdown at Gettysburg, where they went for broke like on no other battlefield of this war. However, year after year and as a tragic fate would have it, the endless search for winning another San Jacinto was nothing more than a one-way ticket to a shallow grave for a good many young men and boys of the 1st Texas.

These men fought to preserve what they and their families had gained in having settled to make self-sufficient lives for themselves. Mississippi-born Sergeant David H. Hamilton, Company "M" (Sumter Light Infantry whose members hailed from Sumter County), 1st Texas, described the rich land that his family had settled after moving west from Mississippi to east Texas in 1846. Here, they farmed on a small section of fertile prairie known as Hamilton Prairie: "... with the exception of the several prairies, the county [Trinity] was covered with a splendid and dense forest of large trees of hardwood and pine.... It was a hunter's and fisherman's paradise, and the best cattle range in the world."[6]

The Texas Invincibles (a name that was not as much of an exaggeration compared to non-Texas units, and later officially became Company "K," 1st Texas) was commanded by Captain Benjamin Franklin Benton. Like many other 1st Texas soldiers, the captain was named for the wise Philadelphia diplomat, who had played the key role in securing the French Alliance of 1778, Benjamin Franklin. The young soldiers of Company "K" hailed from the Texas counties of San Augustine, Newton, Sabine, Harrison, and Nacogdoches.[7]

Native Americans in Gray

Still another unique factor distinguished the 1st Texas from its sister regiments of the Texas Brigade, and it has been mostly forgotten and overlooked by generations of historians. Private Fletcher, who always "had made the practice of wearing my cartridge box to the front when battling" for the faster loading of his Enfield rifle, wrote how the "1st Texas Regiment had a company with quite a number of Indians enlisted" to serve Texas and the Confederacy. Most of these Native Americans, such as a warrior named Battise, hailed from the grassy prairies—the southern extension of the Great Plains—of Texas. Also known as Isaac, he served in Company "B," Livingston Guards, which consisted of men from Polk and Livingston Counties. Some Indians who served in the Texas Brigade hailed from the Alabama–Coushatta Reservation. When shelled by Union artillery while serving on Virginia soil during the Peninsula Campaign, these Native Americans "protested against such warfare, as the fellow who shot those big guns were out of reach of their rifles, and they were not having an equal show."[8]

Native Americans serving beside American revolutionaries was nothing new in the annals of American military history. During the French and Indian War, three entire companies of the most famed ranger command in American history, Major Robert Rogers's Rangers, consisted of Native American warriors. Like in regard to the Texas Brigade, Indians of the Mohawk, Stockbridge, and Mohegan tribes were allowed to serve in the ranks. These stealthy and knowledgeable warriors had proved invaluable in bestowing not only guerrilla-like tactics upon the Rogers's Rangers, but also Indian dress suitable to their advantage to meet the stern demands of wilderness warfare.[9]

In addition, sizeable numbers of warriors from the Stockbridge, Oneida, and Tuscarora tribes provided invaluable assistance to the Americans during the 1777 Saratoga Campaign in upper New York State during a key turning point of the American Revolution. Terrifying the interlopers, they played a role in helping to force the surrender of the British, Hessian, and Loyalist army of General "Gentleman Johnny" Burgoyne at Saratoga to win the victory that convinced the French to sign the 1778 Alliance.[10]

Volunteers of these initial Texas companies of the future 1st Texas had first marched to war with a wide variety of uniforms and equipment. The young soldiers of Captain Benton's company wore a gray-uniform with collars and cuffs trimmed in light blue. They also carried their own colorful company battle-flag like other Texas volunteer infantry units, such as Company "F," the Marshall Guards, whose members hailed from Harrison County in the piney woods country along the Sabine River. This silk banner of the Texas Invincibles of Company "K" was a source of pride to the men, especially those who fought and died to save it on the battlefield.

When the soldiers of the Texas Invincibles departed for Virginia in the late summer of 1861 to the jaunty Irish tune of "The Girl I Left Behind Me," they were armed with large butcher, or Bowie, knives. Physical legacies and reminders of the martial traditions of the Texas Revolution and as noted, these Bowie knives, the southwest frontier region's side weapon of choice, were named for Kentucky-born Jim Bowie. A former slave trader, the popular Louisianan had served as second in command of the diminutive Alamo garrison, until sickness reduced him to a bed in a dank room along the south wall, where he was killed in the final assault while still confined inside an adobe room near the Alamo's main gate.

Calculated to terrorize the Yankees, these fearsome weapons were skillfully fashioned from sawmill blades by local blacksmiths, including African-Americans (slave and free) who were well-known for their artisan skills. These fierce-looking weapons, some more than a foot in length, were attached to muskets to create homemade bayonets that were most imposing to an opponent on the battlefield: an innovative, but inferior, match to the steel bayonets of Union soldiers, which had been produced by modern northern factories of the nascent Industrial Age.[11]

Some African-Americans went to war with the Texans as officer's servants, and they often paid a high price for their service. A proud member of Company "C," 4th Texas, William Henry Foster lamented in a January 17, 1862 letter how "Lem's negro died at the hospital."[12]

From San Augustine County, which had been named after Saint Augustine of Hippo (part of ancient Rome's north African empire in today's Algeria), Private Orlando Thacker Hanks of Captain Benjamin Franklin Benton's Texas Invincibles (Company "K," 1st Texas) described: "Our bayonets were butcher knives made by our blacksmiths out of old files [and] Some were about twelve inches long [while] Others were 16 or 18 inches long…"[13]

So eager were Virginia-born Captain Frederick Samuel Bass and his volunteers of the Marshall Guards (Company "E," 1st Texas) to reach the seat of war in Virginia that they departed Harrison County (in east Texas and located near the Louisiana border) and headed for New Orleans without wasting the time that it would take for local tailors or women to sew uniforms. Therefore, these over-anxious volunteers arrived in the Crescent City without uniforms, but soon had them made by local tailors.[14]

Hailing mostly from the community of Palestine, Anderson County, the soldiers of John R. Woodward's Reagan Guards, also known as the Anderson County Guards (future Company "G," 1st Texas), wore dark uniforms with bright red stripes. This was the most unusual uniform of not only any 1st Texas company, but also of any other Texas Brigade company. These colorful uniforms were soon worn out and promptly replaced by more durable garments. But this unconventional uniform was actually appropriate garb for the unorthodox soldiers of the Anderson County Invincibles, who seemingly always defied convention and the rules, but never lofty expectations on the battlefield, including at the Devil's Den.

These Texans (of eventually Company "G," 1st Texas) also clothed themselves in captured parts of Union uniforms and civilian garb in the days ahead. For instance, Major Matt Dale, 1st Texas, described in a June 1862 letter to this brother how during the Peninsula campaign of 1862, "our men … provided themselves with a large number of [Union] blanket[s,] knapsacks & haversacks [and] oil cloth overcoats, &c &c from the Yankee camp…" This homespun, make-shift uniform of the 1st Texas soldiers beguiled the fact that these rough-hewn frontiersmen and farm boys were not only the elite soldiers of the Texas Brigade, but also of Lee's Army of Northern Virginia.[15]

In striking contrast, the finest uniforms of the 1st Texas were worn by the men of the Star Rifles or the Marion Rifles, Company "D," 1st Texas. Most symbolic for a new generation of revolutionaries, Marion County had been named after the famed "Swamp Fox" Francis Marion of the Santee River country of South Carolina. A diminutive South Carolinian whose unimposing size masked a host of sterling leadership qualities and strength of character, Marion's feats during the darkest days of the revolutionary struggle in the South, after Charleston's capture that was a monumental disaster for the patriot cause, were legendary and vibrant in popular memory, including in Texas.

These Lone Star State soldiers from Marion County (located in east Texas and among the gently rolling hills drained by the waters of the Red River basin and whose eastern border touched Louisiana) wore tight-fitting uniforms. These tailor-made uniforms were distinguished by half a dozen rows of blue piping that spanned horizontally across their upper torsos. Wide blue collars and rows of brass buttons also highlighted the distinctive look of the Company "D" soldiers, who were true fighting men as they demonstrated in full during the attack on Houck's Ridge and the Devil's Den.

However, the most distinctive aspect of the uniform worn by the men of the Star Rifles was their large black felt Hardee Hats. Along with their large Bowie knives that they wore in thick leather belts to present a fearsome warlike appearance, which well-suited the high spirits of these Marion County men in the ranks, these high felt hats were turned up on one side in stylish fashion. Large silver stars, which symbolized the Lone Star State that possessed almost sacred meaning to the Civil War generation of Texans, held up one side of the black felt hats. Ironically, these hats were the same as those worn by the crack fighting men of one of the most famous combat units of the Civil War, the hard-fighting Iron Brigade, Army of the Potomac. As fate would have it, the Texas Brigade met these tough westerners, including crack fighters of the 24th Michigan Volunteer Infantry, in blue in the killing fields of Antietam north of Sharpsburg during the first phase of the battle.

In this so-called brothers' war—a concept that was mocked by the surreal blood-letting at Gettysburg—regiments on both sides were organized in local communities across Texas before journeying east to protect the new nation's capital. But the 1st Texas was a notable exception to the rule. These volunteers of the future 1st Texas were so eager to kill Yankees that they refused to wait for orders and the regiment's official formation. Instead and on their own, companies of zealous volunteers left independently for the front—hundreds of miles to the Virginia theater—with the officers who they had chosen by democratic vote (in the western frontier tradition) to lead them in the manner of the Texas Revolution's citizen-soldiers, who won glory at San Jacinto on a hot afternoon on the gulf coastal plain.

Eager for the opportunity to meet the Yankees, the first eight companies of the future 1st Texas journeyed eastward for the Virginia Theater on their own like volunteers from the United States had poured into Texas from the opposite direction in 1835–1836 to join the Texians' struggle for liberty. Heading east, the Texas Confederates first traveled to New Orleans and then on to Richmond during the summer of 1861. So eager were the young men of some companies to depart that they traveled to

Virginia without orders or directives of any kind: setting a familiar pattern for future independent-minded performances, when the Texans so often openly defied authority, army regulations, or even orders, including even the failure to halt steamrolling Federal charges which simply could not be stopped by officers' orders. A distinction of which they were immensely proud, the volunteers of the future 1st Texas Infantry were the first Texans to reach the main theater of operations in Virginia.

As could be expected, the long-anticipated arrival of these men all the way from the southwestern frontier had early drawn a great interest from the locals and the eastern newspapers. At the new nation's capital of Richmond (after having been moved from Montgomery, Alabama), where the infant Confederacy's three leading newspapers were published, these eight companies first were organized into the 1st Texas Infantry Battalion. Colonel Wigfall, the ex-United States senator from Texas, then took command of the unruly volunteers. The four remaining companies of the unit that became the 1st Texas also traveled eastward individually, reaching Virginia in the summer and autumn of 1861.

Bringing up the rear, the last unit (the Sumter Light Infantry) was led by a young lawyer named Howard Ballinger, Company "M." These young rebels from Trinity County, named after the Trinity River that flowed along its southeastern border, arrived in Virginia during the spring of 1862. Also known as the Silver Greys, Company "M" was organized at Sumpter, Trinity County. The company consisted of "about 125 men and boys, about half boys, from 17 to 19 years of age," wrote Sergeant David H. Hamilton. Uniquely, the 1st Texas was composed of a total of twelve companies instead of the standard ten companies of a typical Confederate regiment. By the time of the 1862 Maryland campaign, no other regiment of Army of Northern Virginia was composed of twelve companies.

Service in the Confederacy was looked upon by these Texans as almost a religious-like experience and sacred duty. Indeed, for the Texans, this conflict against the President Abraham Lincoln Administration and the centralized government located in Washington, D.C., was a righteous crusade and a holy war, just like in battling against Native Americans and the Mexicans for the possession of the land that they loved. From the beginning, the Texas Rebels, wrote one chaplain, were eager for this "pilgrimage to the great Mecca of their hopes, the 'Old Dominion,'" where many of their ancestors had hailed. The Trinity County boys of Company "M" (known as the Silver Greys because of their uniforms' distinctive color) were especially anxious to reach Virginia, being "afraid they would not get there in time to help take Washington": a common misconception that revealed excessive innocence and a telltale sign that the war would almost certainly last much longer and be far bloodier than anyone on either side originally imagined.[16]

All of the volunteer companies that merged together to create the 1st Texas were organized independently, and had been raised by men who commanded these units prior to their arrival in Virginia. Consequently, the 1st Texas Confederate Infantry was not officially organized until the fall of 1861 at Dumfries, Virginia, located about halfway between Richmond and Washington, D.C. Here, near the Potomac River just to the east, the Texas Brigade was officially created from the newly arrived Texas regiments that were the only Lone Star State troops in the Army of Northern Virginia: the Texas Brigade's birth, this Trans-Mississippi command consisted of the 1st, 4th, and 5th Texas.

The 18th Georgia only became part of the Texas Brigade because they were encamped near the Texans among the heavily-forested rolling hills of the Dumfries area situated just west of the Potomac and south of George Washington's Mount Vernon, which was located on a commanding bluff that overlooked the wide river that separated Maryland and Virginia. This fine Georgia regiment was dubbed by the Texans the "3rd Texas," after this reliable Peach State command proved its fighting qualities and reliability on the battlefield. Indeed, the Georgians were worthy fighters, earning the rare respect of the Texas boys. What was formed at a relatively obscure place in Virginia shortly became "a great fighting machine, one of the best produced in America."[17]

An Elite Regiment's Composition

The 1st Texas, which attacked the Devil's Den and Houck's Ridge, consisted of companies from across the prairies, bayou country, and pine forests of east and southeast Texas: Company "A" of the Marion Rifles from Marion and Cass Counties; the Livingston Guards of Company "B" from Polk County and mostly from the town of Livingston and Livingston County; Company "C," which was known as the Palmer Guards from Harris County, primarily the city of Houston, and also including volunteers recruited in New Orleans and Pensacola, Florida; Company "D" was the Marion Rifles, or the Star Rifles, from Marion County; Company "E" (the Marshall Guards, or Bass Grays) from Harrison County; Company "F" (Woodville Rifles) from Tyler County and primarily the town of Woodville; Company "G" (Reagan Guards or the Anderson County Invincibles) from Anderson County and mostly from the community of Palestine; the Texas Guards of Company "H" from Anderson County (also known as the Anderson County Guards) principally from Palestine; Company "I" (Crockett Southrons) from the port of Galveston on the gulf coast and Houston, Cherokee and Sabine Counties; the Texas Invincibles of Company "K" from San Augustine, Newton, Sabine, and Nacogdoches, Counties; the Star Rifles (also known as the Lone Star Rifles) of Company "L" from Galveston; and the Sumter Light Infantry of Company "M" (Silver Greys) from Trinity County. Texas Revolutionary War legacies were seen in the name of the Crockett Southrons of Company "I," and the words spoken and stories told by the common soldiers in the ranks.[18]

These volunteer companies included friends, neighbors, and relatives not only from the same county and rural areas, but also often from the same community. Companies also often consisted of kinship groups and even family-like units. For instance, seven Oliver brothers (only four survived the war) served in the Marion County Rifles, or Star Rifles, of Company "D," 1st Texas.[19]

Young, handsome, and dark-featured, the Oliver boys, Absalom, Henry (who died of pneumonia in 1862), Thomas, William (mortally wounded at Chickamauga), and John, marched off to war with unbridled confidence, while wearing fancy gray uniforms and high Hardee-style hats. As their photographs have revealed, these men wore their tall, dark hats with one-side turned up in a jaunty manner. As mentioned, this side of the hat was kept upright by an iron or Silver Star that, of course, represented Texas.[20]

A total of seven brothers (including twins) from Kickapoo, Texas, located northeast of Palestine, and named after the Kickapoo tribe, fought for the Confederacy. From the small town nestled beside the trickling waters of Kickapoo Creek, five soldiers of the Knight clan served in the Texas Guards, Company "H," 1st Texas. Long a guiding spiritual light and moral force, their austere Knight family patriarch was a Methodist preacher of east Texas. Two of these soldiers of the Texas Guards (also known as the Anderson County Guards), brothers Privates William Henry Knight and James Polk Knight, were destined to fall wounded at Antietam that claimed so many 1st Texas lives during the nightmarish combat.[21]

In Company G's ranks (the Reagan Guards), 1st Texas, at least three Watts boys, Andrew Jackson Watts, Benjamin Franklin Watts, and F. J. Watts—known as Willis, Julius, and Sandy—hailed from the town of Palestine. While charging beside his fellow Anderson County Invincibles (the Reagan Guards), Julius had his "arm off at Sharpsburg," or the Battle of Antietam, as called by Southerners. In the same company, three other Wren boys served in the ranks, including Sergeant William C. Wren, Richard F. "Little Dick" Wren, and Private Richard H. "Big Dick" Wren.[22]

Rich Ethnic Diversity

Interestingly, to contradict the popular stereotype of the typical Texas Rebel or Southern cracker of a homogeneous combat unit, a good many Germans and Irish, mostly immigrants who had migrated to southeast and east Texas in the 1840s and 1850s, served in the 1st Texas and the Texas Brigade. In the 1st Texas, Private Patrick Murphy, Company "A," and Private Lawrence "Larry" J. Byrnes, Company "B," were among soldiers born in Ireland. The 1st Texas men born in Germany included such Teutonic warriors as Private Joseph Rints, Company "A," and Private Henry P. Schultz of Company "K."

This Celtic-Gaelic and Teutonic flavoring that made the Texas Brigade's ranks more colorful and diverse was a most symbolic one. After all, Germans and Irish served in large numbers in the Texians' ranks during the Texas Revolution. For instance, at least fifteen defenders who died at the Alamo were Ireland natives. These were the Alamo's most forgotten defenders. One Texian described the Texas Revolutionaries as both "the sons of [George] Washington and St. Patrick," revealing how this was very much of a Celtic-oriented uprising against Mexico in the tradition of the many people's rebellions against England on the Emerald Isle. Symbolically, a young German fifer had played the spirited tune, "Come to the Bower," that helped to inspire Houston's daring afternoon attack of the Texians, including a good many Sons of Erin, onward through the open meadow of tall Buffalo grass that lay before Santa Anna's tented encampment at San Jacinto.

Despite the fact that most Texas Brigade's soldiers descended from the Scotch-Irish of Ulster Province, north Ireland, this did not mean that anti-Irish sentiment (especially in regard to Irish Catholics) did not exist in the ranks, however. Sergeant David H. Hamilton, Company "M," lampooned the size of the lice that afflicted the men, writing how "occasionally you would find one with 'R.I.B.' (Royal Irish Brigade) in gilt letters on his back," before was dispatched by fingernails. For many provincial backwoods boys, the Irish were detested only slightly less than America's ancient enemy of two wars, the hated British. In overall terms, this colorful ethnic diversity that existed in the Texas Brigade (in contrast to the popular White Anglo-Saxon Protestant—WASP—stereotype of the Confederate soldier) represented the unique, but often-forgotten characteristics and dynamics of western settlement that allowed for wide-ranging ethnic and cultural diversity in early Texas.

However, mirroring prewar migration patterns and demographic realities, the vast majority of Germans fought for the North, and proved to be fiercely patriotic to their adopted nation. In addition, soldiers of Latino descent also served in the 1st Texas and Texas Brigade. Private Willoughby Tullos of Company "M" was one such individual. His name reflected the fact that his mother was Anglo and father was Hispanic (Latino). The Tejano contribution continued the distinguished Texas Revolutionary War tradition of hard-fighting Tejanos, who fought against their native countrymen from 1835–1836.[23]

The significant influence of a vibrant Tejano culture was alive and well in the Texas Brigade's ranks throughout the war years. Spanish words were sprinkled in the everyday vocabulary of the Texas Brigade's soldiers. For instance, in a December 5, 1861 letter to his sister, Hattie, Joe B. Polley described how for added warmth against the harsh winds and snows of winter, "We intend putting up a regular Mexican jacal."[24] In the same letter, Polley wrote: "Jack [Sutherland] is playing the fiddle out in the open sun. So you may be sure he is not very bad off and Remember me to the boys [including] Pancho [a Tejano friend or ranch hand] and others."[25]

Sons of Solomon, Forgotten Hebrew Warriors

Even more, the other forgotten men of the Confederacy, Jewish Rebels also served in the ranks beside the Galveston County boys of Company "L," the Lone Star Rifles, 1st Texas Infantry. Devoted to the ancient religious teachings of the Torah that emphasized the sacred law of God as bestowed to the Hebrew people by the ancient prophet Moses, Jewish soldiers, such as Privates Jacob Frank and H. Cohen, hailed from the busy port of Galveston, where Gulf of Mexico commerce had long thrived. Private Frank met an untimely death in the bloodletting in the Miller Cornfield at Antietam, while Private Cohen also fell wounded in the same western Maryland tempest on September 17, 1862.[26]

Also from this Galveston company—known as the Lone Star Rifles (or the Star Rifles)—were two Schadt brothers, Privates William and Charles Schadt. A victim of a tragic fate, Charles lost his life at Eltham Plantation, Virginia. The Schadt boys had been born in Germany, migrating to Texas in 1846 when the Mexican-American War erupted. Fulfilling the White House's sound strategic plans (the so-called Anaconda Plan) of the South's subjugation that had been early embraced by General Winfield Scott, who had become America's greatest military hero in capturing Mexico City, the powerful United States Navy gained control of Galveston Harbor on Christmas Day 1862 to tighten the Union blockage not long after the 1st Texas fought against the odds and a cruel fate at Antietam. Such Federal naval threats to Galveston, the largest port city in Texas, and its population (where the families of many Texas Brigade members resided) only fueled the motivation of the Galveston soldiers of Company "L," 1st Texas, to greater exertions to reap a decisive success, especially in Pennsylvania during the summer of 1863.[27]

Other Texas Brigade regiments besides the 1st Texas were also distinguished by a high degree of diversity, which shattered the popular stereotype of the average WASP soldier in gray and butternut. With some surprise, if not a measure of disgust, Tennessee-born Valerius "Val" Cincinnatus Giles, a member of Company "B," 4th Texas, wrote: "There was a mess in my company of foreigners, who were immigrant Irish and Emerald Islanders who often used the phrase, 'Holy Saint Patrick.'"[28] The boyish-looking "Val" also described the combat prowess of one resourceful "Mexican Confederate" (a Tejano in gray), who served in the Texas Brigade, and evidently a 4th Texas soldier.[29]

A more typical volunteer of the 1st Texas was sixteen-year-old Private James Henry Hendrick from San Augustine County. His father was a Kentuckian who had taken his family to Texas in 1824 to begin life anew in east Texas. Then, the fighting Kentuckian served in the Texas Revolution. Private Hendrick marched off as "a mere striping of a lad," but when he returned to Texas to recuperate from a nasty Antietam wound, he had been transformed into a "matured man." The feisty Private Hendrick of Company "E" (Marshall Guards) then rejoined his Harrison Country comrades, dying in the Battle of the Wilderness, Virginia, in May 1864. Like many other Texas Brigade members, the body of Private Hendrick lies today in a lonely grave only known to God. Ironically, an optimistic Private Hendrick was convinced that decisive victory would be quickly won by the newest generation of revolutionaries on American soil. In his naïveté and innocence, he had believed that "I would not be surprised if we were all home in December" for Christmas 1861.[30]

Like other Texas Brigade members, Chaplain Davis, 4th Texas, greatly admired not only the fighting qualities but also, ironically, even the devil-may-care attitude of the rambunctious 1st Texas boys. Like General Hood, this man of God fully understood the correlation between the two seemingly incompatible qualities. He wrote: "The First Texas, of which regiment, we cannot speak too highly—These are the men who came from their distant homes, at their own expense, before the President [Jefferson Davis] had called upon Texas for troops, to assist in this great struggle [and] They are a lively, merry set."[31]

After Colonel Wigfall gained a brigadier general's commission and took command of the Texas Brigade during the autumn of 1861, a new commander of the 1st Texas was named. Promoted to colonel, he was a large-sized leader of Scotch-Irish and Celtic descent like most Texas Rebels, Hugh McLeod. Born on August 1, 1814, in New York City, where so many Irish had migrated before the Civil War, McLeod was a West Pointer (Class of 1835). From the beginning, he was determined to mold his men into the best-drilled and hardest-fighting soldiers of the Army of Northern Virginia.

This diehard Celtic-Gaelic warrior had formerly led the Galveston men of Company "L," the Lone Star Rifles (or Star Rifles). Then, McLeon served under Colonel Wigfall as the lieutenant colonel of the 1st Texas. McLeod early gained an opportunity to demonstrate his worth as the 1st Texas' commander. McLeod's background made him an excellent leader, despite having graduated last (like George Armstrong Custer in his West Point Class of 1861) in his class of fifty-six cadets, after entering the famed military academy on the Hudson River in September 1831.

Newly-minted Second Lieutenant McLeod had been assigned to Fort Jesup, Louisiana, near the Texas border along the Sabine River. Not able to resist the opportunity, he left his men in regulation blue uniforms—regular United States troops—behind to join the Texas Revolution, resigning his commission in late June 1836. McLeod then remained in the Texas military, serving as an officer in the Army of the Republic of Texas and also during the Mexican-American War. Continuing to wage war against the Mexicans, who were determined to conquer Texas, after losing their promised land after the Texas Revolution, McLeod had led Texas troops during the disastrous Santa Fe Expedition in an attempt to capture the economically-vital city in New Mexico in 1841.

A Renaissance man of the Texas frontier, this dynamic Celtic soldier also served in the legislature of the Republic of Texas in the 1840s. For all of these reasons, McLeod was popular with the roughhewn boys of the 1st Texas, especially because of his service in the Texas Revolution. Captain Todd of Company "A" (the Marion Rifles consisted of good fighting men from Marion County where the county seat was the town of Jefferson—named after Thomas Jefferson—on the Big Cypress River) described McLeod as "the gallant old hero." Fate was not kind to Colonel McLeod, however. The warm-hearted "jovial" Scot-Irishman died of pneumonia (like Henry Oliver of Company "D," 1st Texas) in the tented encampment near Dumfries, Virginia, during the freezing weather on January 2, 1862. Unlike the fate of almost all Texas Brigade's dead who remained where they fell on the battlefield and in camp, McLeod's body was shipped back to Texas by the family for burial, while generations of the McLeod clan lay in final resting places in the Scottish Highlands.[32]

Year after year and on one battlefield after another, especially in the furious attack on the Devil's Den and Houck's Ridge during the second day at Gettysburg, the 1st Texas demonstrated an exceptionally high quality. The striking paradox and seemingly contradiction that these 1st Texas soldiers were the worst looking and acting soldiers—in terms of dress, indiscipline, and overall appearance off the battlefield—in the Army of Northern Virginia only heightened their reputation for outstanding combat achievements against the odds. Indeed, 1st Texas inspection reports revealed that the unit was perhaps the most deplorable regiment, in terms of meeting inspection requirements, expectations, and standards off the battlefield, of all the regiments of Lee's Army: a fact that served as a contradictory, if not perverse, source of pride for these most unconventional 1st Texas soldiers.

Clearly, regimental members possessed their own unique personal value systems and unorthodox evaluations upon which they based their self-worth not taught at West Point or Southern military academies, but in the life-or-death school of hard knocks on the Texas frontier, which translated into superior battlefield performances. However and as mentioned, Chaplain Davis, 4th Texas, understood how this shoddy-looking facade hid the elite qualities of the 1st Texas when unleashed on the battlefield. Therefore, he wrote: "… though often hungry and 'ragged,' [the 1st Texas troops] have shown in numberless instances, that they can march as far, and fight as hard, as any troops in the service." All energies and efforts of the 1st Texas soldiers were directed at only one purpose: reaping decisive victory, and this was especially the case at the Devil's Den and Houck's Ridge. In consequence, they proudly sported a widespread reputation as unsurpassed "fighters and frontiersmen" of an army dominated by Virginians, especially among the highly-touted leadership corps.[33]

Throughout the conflict, the unruly 1st Texas troops were inspired by the Texas Revolution's heroic legacies by the sight of their regiment's beautiful "Lone Star" State flag: the revered national banner of the Texas Republic. These history-conscious Texas soldiers never forgot when "Mrs. Wigfall presented our battalion with a beautiful flag. It has the Texas star on it. Colonel Wigfall says that the star is a piece of his wife's wedding dress," wrote Private James Henry Hendrick of Company "E" (Marshall Guards), 1st Texas, in a letter.[34]

In the words of one soldier, who marveled at the flag's powerful emotional and psychological effect on the common soldiers in the ranks: "The 1st Regiment was so proud of this flag that they carried it in a silk oilcloth case, and never unfurled it except on reviews, dress parades, or in battle [and] The entire brigade was proud of it; and when we saw it waving in the Virginia breeze, it was a sweet reminder of home, a thousand miles away."

Over-sized by design compared to the typical Confederate battle-flag for emotional effect among the average fighting man not unlike the "Star Spangled Banner" of Fort McHenry that flew with defiance during the mid-September 1814 British bombardment that had inspired the defenders, this colorful banner was highly "prized" by the 1st Texas soldiers. No one bothered to mention or acknowledge that the Lone Star State flag was in fact "a modified American flag," dominated by red, white, and blue colors. The 5 by 8-foot battle-flag was made of silk, and it had been stitched by Mrs. Louis T. Wigfall and daughter Lula in the spring of 1861.

No one ever forgot how during the summer of 1861, the regimental colors were formally presented to the 1st Texas during a respectful ceremony in the regiment's tented encampment located outside Richmond by the general's daughter, Lula. "When presented to the regiment by a noble Texas girl on the banks of the Potomac, it was bright and glorious, and, like the character of the fair donor, was 'pure as the beautiful snow' [and] Twelve hundred Texans cheered it to the echo when it was kissed for the first time by the breeze of classic old Virginia," wrote one soldier of the impressive ceremony.

The prized silk flag of the 1st Texas was distinctive in overall appearance as well as in design and color composition. This was the distinctive "Lone Star" flag of the independent Lone Star Republic. Two horizontal sections of white and red made-up two-thirds of this beautiful silk flag, with white on top and the red on the bottom. A vertical blue section (the remaining one-third of the flag) bordered the wooden staff.

Additionally, in the middle of the flag's vertical section was the large white star, made of expensive wedding dress silk, displayed on a navy blue background. By the time of the Maryland campaign during the late summer of 1862, this blue backdrop of the silken banner was distinguished by the painted names of the hard-fought Virginia Peninsula battles like "Seven Pines." Below the large white star that symbolized the still revered Republic of Texas and the Texas Revolutionary heritage had been painted the name of the Battle of "Gaines Farm [Mill]" in large white letters.

On the field of white on the top half of the 1st Texas flag was the name of the Texans' first battle, "Eltham's Landing": the first Southern victory reaped on the Peninsula during the Union drive on Richmond. On the corresponding bottom half of the flag, on a red background, was the name "Malvern Hill": the last engagement of the bloody Seven Days fighting before Richmond, when repeated Southern assaults had been hurled against the high ground line bolstered by a large amount of Union artillery and cut to pieces. The magnificent flag of bright colors was the pride of the 1st Texas soldiers, who fought with their hearts.

Possessing far more symbolic meaning than the typical standard red battle-flag with the St. Andrews Cross that the flag-bearer of the 1st Texas also carried, this distinctive "Lone Star" banner was a sacred emblem to the 1st Texas soldiers. Consequently, these young men and boys repeatedly sacrificed their lives to protect and save the precious banner to keep it out of Yankee hands. The capture of the regiment's flag was seen as the ultimate disgrace and humiliation.[35]

The sacredness of the regimental flag was seen in soldiers' solemn words. In a March 14, 1862 letter to his father, Joseph B. Polley, 4th Texas, described: "... we formed on the color line where Col. Hood gave us a short talk and presented us with a flag from Miss [Lula] Wigfall whom he aptly christened the 'Daughter of the Regiment.' She was to have presented it through her Father, but the weather was unfavorable."[36]

Destined to suffer a severe wound during the raging combat that swirled through the Miller Cornfield at Antietam, Corporal William David Henderson Pritchard of Company "I," the Crockett Southrons of Houston County, wrote in a letter:

> ... we were shown the distinguished honor of having a most magnificent Lone Star Flag presented to us by President Davis as the gift of Mrs. Davis and Mrs. Wigfall. It is said to have been made out of their wedding dresses. The flag was usually large and beautiful.

> That part next to the staff and about one fourth of its length was white, with a large blue star in the center. The upper half of the remainder was a bright blue, and the lower half was a rich purple and the whole bordered with a heavy golden fringe, and it was fastened by a heavy cord and tassel. The material was of very fine satin and was of such weight that [color bearers] had to wear a belt and socket to carry it.

In presenting the flag to the 1st Texas at Richmond with an eloquent speech, President Davis emphasized: "That the soldiers of other states had a reputation to gain, while the soldiers of Texas had a reputation to maintain."[37]

In moral, symbolic, and psychological terms, the importance of the "Lone Star" flag to the 1st Texas soldiers was almost beyond measure. To these young men, this colorful banner not only represented home, family, and state, but also much more. Indeed, this "Lone Star State" flag represented the distinctive and storied history of Texas, a spirit of nationalism from the days of the young republic, and a special identification with the hundreds of martyred volunteers of the Texas Revolution. Consequently, the Texas Rebels who fought and died on Virginia soil still possessed the memories and legacies of an entirely separate sense of national destiny of an independent country nearly a decade before Texas entered the Union. Noah Smith, a volunteer soldier of the Texas Revolution, wrote how "to my knowledge the first Lone Star flag used in the revolution was gotten up at Gonzales for [Stephen Fuller] Austin's army" at the revolution's beginning.[38]

The psychological importance of the Lone Star State flag can hardly be overestimated in terms of its overall effect on the common soldiers, when they were engaged on the battlefield, especially at Gettysburg on July 2, 1863. Commanding the 5th Texas and the future commander of the Texas Brigade, dark-haired, bearded Colonel Jerome Bonaparte Robertson, emphasized how during the Texans' sweeping charge at Second Manassas to reap victory: "All, both officers and men, sustained well the reputation of the Lone Star flag, under which they fought through the battle." As in late August 1862, the 1st Texas and Texas Brigade repeatedly sustained the "well the reputation" of the Lone Star State and its heroic past of Texas history.[39]

Also on the bloody field of Second Manassas, Captain "King" Bryan, who was destined to gain a lieutenant colonel's rank in leading the 5th Texas, never forgot the sheer majesty of the sight of the "Lone Star" flag in battle. This magnificent sight inspired the Texas soldiers to new heights when they viewed it waving through the acid, sulfurous palls of smoke: a stirring and emotional image that motivated the Texas soldiers to greater exertions, which resulted in larger clumps of Yankee dead and the sweet taste of victory. Throughout the swirling combat, this cherished banner, which proudly proclaimed a distinctive heritage and heroic past of the Lone Star State, was "bore high above all others which were then floating over the field, as a beacon for our men..."[40]

Capable and experienced leadership also explained why the 1st Texas became the premier combat unit of the Texas Brigade. Captain Frederick S. Bass, destined to command the 1st Texas and the Texas Brigade during the final surrender at

Appomattox Court House, Virginia, on Palm Sunday 1865, possessed solid military experience. He trained his soldiers of the Marshall Guards (Company "E" and also known as the Bass Grays) in the grassy meadows of Harrison County for months before finally departing for Virginia. Ironically, Bass had been born in Brunswick County of the Tidewater in southern Virginia along the North Carolina border in June 1829. He had attended the Virginia Military Academy at Lexington, Virginia, graduating second in his class in 1853.

Now leading Company "E," 1st Texas, Captain Bass was the former president of Marshall University at Marshall, the county seat of Henderson County, which was nestled in Texas' northeast corner. But more importantly, in military terms, he had served as the school's instructor of military tactics beginning in 1857. Therefore, members of the Marshall Guards were considered by many officers to have been one of the Texas Brigade's best-drilled companies. Quite simply, "there was no finer drilled organization in the South."[41]

All in all, the elite quality of the 1st Texas and the Texas Brigade in general was in part attributed to the invaluable influences and experiences of leaders, who had graduated at West Point and VMI. These two educational institutions were the leading military academies in America, North and South, respectively. [42]

Another highly-respected leading citizen of his community, Dr. Albert Gallatin Clopton, organized and then led a 1st Texas company from Marion County. He commanded the Marion Rifles of Company "D" (the Star Rifles), 1st Texas. These Marion County soldiers were led by a man of considerable intellect and ability. By the time of the bitter fighting of the Seven Days, Captain Clopton had risen through the ranks, serving as the 1st Texas' major.[43]

Lieutenant Colonel Philip Alexander Work

Perhaps the most promising young leader of the 1st Texas was the dark-haired, bearded captain of the Woodville Rifles of Company "F," Philip Alexander Work from Tyler County in east Texas. He was a signer of the Texas Ordinance of Secession in Austin on February 1, 1861. But Work ended his promising political career because of his desire to lead Texas troops in battle.

He continued to excel at the challenges of leadership until becoming the commander of the 1st Texas by the time of the Battle of Gettysburg. In the war's beginning, he raised the Woodville volunteers (the Woodville Rifles), who hailed from Tyler County. Then, Work led one of the first eight Texas companies—Company "F" (Woodville Rifles)—that arrived heavily-armed and eager for action in the Virginia Theater. A highly-respected, popular leader of ability as demonstrated when he had been elected by the people to the Texas state secession convention in 1861, the Kentucky-born Captain Work became the lieutenant colonel and commander of the 1st Texas by the time of the 1862 Maryland campaign. Despite his age, born in February 1832 and barely out of his twenties, Work was the ideal regimental commander. He proved to be a resourceful and experienced commander, who was supremely devoted to his rawboned soldiers from the southwest.[44]

The winter of 1861–1862 was spent by the 1st Texas and the Texas Brigade in the Dumfries, Virginia, area. Dumfries was located north of Fredericksburg and about 40 miles south of the great goal of Confederate ambitions that lay inviting amid the lowlands of the Potomac, Washington, D.C. Here, "we became well drilled and disciplined [*sic.*], seasoned soldiers, inured to camp life, and the rigors of a severe winter," wrote Captain George A. Todd of Company "A." In addition, the reliable 1st Texas soldiers were often engaged as scouts, skirmishers, and rearguard protectors during this first winter of the war. No troops in the army at an early date were better at these demanding tasks of critical importance than the men of the 1st Texas, especially reconnaissance and intelligence-gathering missions.[45]

A faithful spiritual voice of the Texas Brigade, Chaplain Davis wrote about the 1st Texas when first viewing this crack regiment of rugged frontiersmen, woodsmen, and yeoman farmers from west of the Sabine River: "We here with the 1st Texas Regiment, commanded by Col. [Hugh] McLeod.... The 1st Texas was composed of companies that had hurried to Virginia on the first breaking out of hostilities; they had come on without any regimental organization, and were at first formed into a Regiment and placed under the command of Col. Wigfall [and then] When the brigade was formed..."[46]

Here, in the cold rains and snows that fell during the winter of 1861–1862, the 1st Texas soldiers prepared to come to grips with the Federals, wherever they were found. Chaplain Davis wrote: "A cheerful spirit pervades all the camp. And all [the Texas Rebels] are looking for the northern mercenaries & anxious for them to come." As always and since first reaching the major bone of contention in the eastern theater, Virginia, the Texans were all "spoiling for a fight."[47]

The Potomac defensive line and the Texas Brigade's position at Dumfries were evacuated during the second week of March 1862. Then, the troops of the Texas Brigade earned the key assignment of serving as the dependable rear guard, when the Confederates marched south to align along a new defensive position based upon the high ground around Fredericksburg to protect Richmond. Deliberately employing an Alamo-like analogy that appealed to the emotions of the common soldiers, Hood addressed his lengthy formations of the 4th Texas, consisting of soldiers from Travis, Gonzales, Robertson, Guadalupe, Bexar (San Antonio de Bexar, which was the home of the Alamo), McLennan, Grimes, Walker, Navarro, and Henderson Counties, proclaiming: "Ours is the last Brigade to leave the lines of the Potomac [and] when the struggle does come ... let us stand or fall together."[48]

Then, with a greater Union threat brewing, the Texas Brigade shifted farther south below Richmond while General George B. McClellan, who commanded the Army of the Potomac, launched an amphibious landing from the Chesapeake Bay to gain a position southeast of, or below, Richmond. From beginning to end during the struggle for possession of the Southern nation's capital, the Texans were utilized as trustworthy rear guardian protectors of the army that was literally fighting for its life. The reliability, sharpshooting skills, and fighting spirit of the Texas Rebels were already becoming legendary even at this early date. In regard to highly-specialized skills that made the Texas Brigade especially lethal, the 1st Texas soldiers were early considered among the best fighting men of the Confederacy.

Without fully understanding how thoroughly the Texans could be relied upon in any emergency situation, Chaplain Davis mused over a haunting question that oddly perplexed him, although the answer was obvious: "Why our men were so often used as the rear guard, not only to the army corps, to which they belong, but detailed for other portions, as in the case of [Wade] Hampton's Legion [of South Carolina] in evacuating the Potomac, I never could imagine unless it was for their superiority in woodcraft and skirmishing."[49]

With General Hood commanding the Texas Brigade since March 1862, the Texans served under their best commander just in time for their first challenge, when McClellan's Army of the Potomac marched upon Richmond with the determination to win the war in one stroke. By this time, the 1st Texas possessed a new commander to replace the popular Colonel McLeod, Colonel Alexis T. Rainey, who was cut down in the nightmarish combat at Gaines's Mill, from Palestine, Texas. He was originally the captain of Company "H," the Texas Guards, or the Anderson County Guards. The former lawyer was not only a good commander, but also a popular leader of the 1st Texas.

Meanwhile, the capable Captain Philip Alexander Work was promoted to lieutenant colonel, when Rainey took command of the 1st Texas. Chaplain Davis wrote in glowing terms of the leadership skills of young Work:

> At the expiration of twelve months he was elected Lieutenant-Colonel of the 1st Texas Regiment, of which, he has been in command since the battle of Gaines' Farm; and from his gallantry in the field and constancy with his command, he well deserves to have rank as he has command; for although Colonel Rainey is a gallant officer, he has been unable since his wound at Gaines' Farm to be on the field. [Lieutenant] Colonel Work has been present in every battle, and with his men in every march of the campaign.[50]

Meanwhile, to face the new threat below Richmond, the Texas Brigade soldiers took position in the earthen defenses of Yorktown, Virginia, to confront the massive Army of the Potomac. By this time during the early spring of 1862, the Texans, in one captain's words, were "in fine spirits [and most] anxious for a fight" with the hated Yankees.[51] General Joseph E. Johnston confronted McClellan and his mighty war machine on the Virginia Peninsula in the showdown to determine Richmond's fate during the greatest crisis yet faced by the Confederacy. When the Southerners evacuated the Yorktown defenses, including those from the 1781 siege, and withdrew northwest toward Richmond with Yankees close behind, the 1st Texas and the Texas Brigade's remainder served as the rearguard.

Soon to protect the withdrawing army in this vital role, the 1st Texas first led the advance of a Confederate division toward the Eltham Plantation, located directly east of Richmond, on the south bank of the Pamunkey River to confront an amphibious landing by Brigadier General William B. Franklin's Division to gain the flank of the withdrawing Southern Army. However, after landing, Franklin delayed in advancing his forces inland because of unfamiliarity about the area and fear of a Rebel ambush, allowing the opportunity for the Confederates time to deliver a counterblow. Here, the fight at the Eltham Plantation erupted on May 7, 1862, and the Texas Brigade, especially the 1st Texas, received its first opportunity to inflict a punishing blow.[52]

The hot fight that raged across the low, underbrush-tangled ground of the Virginia Peninsula opened when Colonel Rainey ordered the 1st Texas color bearer "to unfurl the Lone Star flag and 'give them hell,' [and to] aim low and, damned it, shoot them'!" Here, the Texas Brigade men early proved its combat prowess at Eltham Plantation in New Kent Count, Virginia. But this sharp clash was primarily a showcase performance for the 1st Texas, which demonstrated its worth like South Carolina's Hampton Legion.

After having taken good cover in an underbrush-clogged ditch upon ascertaining Union forces advancing from the muddy landing, the 1st Texas soldiers unleashed their first volley, which "seemed to mow down the whole front rank" of the Federals, according to Chaplain Davis, who early learned about the ugly ways of war. Federal survivors of the close-range volley immediately withdrew, after having been caught by surprise. Then, to exploit the tactical advantage and maintain the initiative, Colonel Rainey "ordered us to charge them which we did promptly & they fled in the greatest confusion," penned a 1st Texas officer in a letter.

From beginning to end, Rainey's 1st Texas bore the brunt of the Battle of Eltham Plantation. This initial confrontation set the trend for the prominent role of the 1st Texas in future engagements in future years, including at the Devil's Den and Houck's Ridge on July 2, 1863. A native of Indiana, Lieutenant Colonel Harvey H. Black, the former captain of the Marion Rifles of Company "A," was killed, and more than a half dozen 1st Texas soldiers fell wounded, including Captain H. E. Decatur of Marshall, Texas, who was mortally wounded.

With loads of "buck and ball" unleashed at close range from a row of smooth-bore muskets, the 1st Texas Rebels played a larger role in driving the Federals back and containing the threatening landing of General William B. Franklin's troops than any other unit. Not surprisingly, therefore, the 1st Texas suffered the highest losses of the Texas Brigade, establishing a future trend that continued to hold true on the afternoon of July 2, 1863.

Clearly, besides a harbinger of events to come, including at Gettysburg, this was an auspicious first encounter with the Yankees for the young men and boys of the 1st Texas, which began to establish a reputation as the Texas Brigade's best unit. Most importantly, the Texans' hard-hitting offensive effort at Eltham Plantation on May 7, 1862 prevented Franklin's corps from striking either the flank or rear of the Confederate Army. In the words of a thankful President Davis, the Texans "saved the rear of the army" at the Battle of Eltham Plantation, which nevertheless has remained one of the forgotten engagements of the Civil War. Captain Todd described: "… we were much enthused over our success in our first fight."[53]

Besides the 1st Texas, the 4th Texas and 5th Texas also made names for themselves during their baptismal fire in the fight just outside this obscure landing in New Kent County. In the words of a Salem, North Carolina-born soldier of the 4th Texas, we "went to fighting in true earnst [*sic.*] … and soon set them to running."[54]

But in his revealing letter, this 4th Texas soldier saved his most glowing words for "The First Texas Regt. [which] met them and after firing three vollies [*sic.*] charged them at the point of the bayonet and completely routed them, driving them back to their gunboats…. Yankee reports of the engagement say it was the hottest fight on the Peninsula."[55] General Gustavus W. Smith penned in a letter how when they were unleashed at Eltham Plantation, "the Texans won immortal honor for themselves, their State, and for their commander [and] With forty thousand such men, I would not hesitate to invade the North, and would before winter, make them sue for peace upon our terms, or destroy their whole country." Most importantly, the repulse at Eltham Plantation made General McClellan even more cautious, slowing his advance up the Peninsula and toward his target of Richmond. General Johnston and the Confederacy gained valuable time, which was much-needed for the overall defensive effort. No troops played a larger role in securing the South's first victory on the Virginia Peninsula than the 1st Texas, whose members basked in the newly-won laurels.[56]

Referring to the clash at Eltham Plantation, General Samuel W. Melton described: "… here we first had a fair sample of your Texans, under Hood. They are, incomparably, the best fighters in the confederacy; men upon whom one could depend under all circumstances—who seem to fight for the very love of it."[57]

Even though the contest at Eltham Plantation was a relatively minor affair when compared to the upcoming battles around Richmond, it placed General Hood and his high-spirited Texan warriors, and especially the 1st Texas, at center stage in the national spotlight. In part to lift morale in the beleaguered city, Richmond newspapers praised the Texans' aggressiveness, while Union newspapers described the ferocity of the Lone Star State soldiers in combat. Even at this early date, the Texans were possessed with a "superlative morale among men who ere long [became] the most renowned Brigade of the entire Army."[58]

Part of the high morale stemmed from the fact than instead of the Yankee stereotype of Texas savages who were little different from Native American warriors, these men represented a moral soldiery, who believed in the righteous of their cause and that God was on their side. Therefore, what was created was a diehard determination that bordered on the fanatical, because they felt that they were engaged in a holy war and moral crusade. In a May 22, 1862, letter written just outside Richmond, Joe B. Polley wrote that "though McClellan's grand army is with ten miles of Richmond [we will] see the town burned down level with the ground before [we] surrender it. Here we are bound to fight" to the bitter end.[59]

The moral side of the average Texan in the ranks also was revealed by one 4th Texas soldier in a letter to his family. Revealing the soft and seldom-seen side of a holy warrior who shot Yankees in the head and plunged bayonets into an enemy's midsection, he described the fight at Eltham Plantation, where he demonstrated a combat tenacity that paradoxically combined with a measure of human kindness: "Our Company behaved gallantly, we killed about 30 and took 22 prisoners. I, my self, killed 1 dead, broke another's leg and took 2 prisoners. I felt sorry for the poor fellow whose leg I broke, so much so, that I tied it up for him, gave him a drink of water and put him in as comfortable a position as I conveniently could."[60]

But the stiff challenges for the hard fighting 1st Texas men were only beginning during this all-important campaign at the gates of Richmond. During Johnston's gradual withdrawal toward the capital on the James River, the Texans were again utilized as dependable rear guard protectors with their newly-earned fame as the victors of Eltham Plantation: the position of honor given to the most reliable troops, when so much was at stake.[61]

Throughout the campaign to determine the fate of Richmond and as noted, the Texas Rebels were repeatedly employed repeatedly as scouts, intelligence-gatherers, and sharpshooters to harass the advancing Union troops and probe for weaknesses. Especially from the advantage of natural cover of trees, ravines, and high split-rail fences that lined the Virginia farmers' fields of the peninsula's lowlands, these 1st Texas marksmen and frontiersmen became an absolute "terror" to the Yankees. Consequently, the Texans early gained a reputation for ferocity that spread consternation throughout the Army of the Potomac.[62]

The greatest challenge for the Texas Brigade and the hardest fighting to date was about to erupt at Gaines's Mill during the savage battles of the Seven Days. Out of desperation and after he took charge of the army after Johnston fell wounded at Seven Pines in early June, Lee took the offensive to hurl McClellan's forces from Richmond's vicinity and back down the Virginia Peninsula from where the Army of the Potomac had advanced with so much confidence. The fight at Gaines's Mill was described by some soldiers as the "most bitter of the war" to date.

Private Robert Campbell, Texas Brigade, certainly believed as much. He wrote how "at no point did the Yanks seem so defiant and immoveable [*sic.*] as at Gaines Mills" on September 27, 1862. Poised along commanding high ground known as Turkey Hill located north of the Chickahominy River and before a watery morass called Boatman's Swamp, this Union strong-point held by the Fifth Corps was the key to the battlefield. Here, General Fitz John Porter's left was well-entrenched in an excellent defensive position that was considered virtually impregnable. Earlier Southern attacks had failed to break through this strong defensive line, before the men of the Texas Brigade were unleashed with fixed bayonets. By this time, this Union position was widely viewed as a "death trap" for any attackers, who dared to strike.[63]

But this formidable defensive position would not become a "death trap" for the Texas Rebels, who were not daunted by the imposing challenge. After fixing bayonets on the run, the tide of howling Texans descended upon the Federal lines with the swiftness of Comanche raiders. After charging across a wide stretch of open ground and through the underbrush-choked swamp and tangles of abatis, they smashed through multiple lines of the Fifth Corps. After cutting down bluecoat gunners in a flurry of stabbing bayonets and clubbing musket-butts, the Texas attackers, which included the tough Peach State men of the 18th Georgia, captured fourteen pieces of artillery and Union battle-flags. While leading his 1st Texas forward, Colonel Rainey was cut down, ending his military career because of the severity of the wound. Although still only a captain and despite his relative youth, Work took command of the 1st Texas after Colonel Rainey's fall.[64]

Then, the Texas marksmen regrouped in timely fashion to repulse a desperate attempt by the charging troopers of the 5th United States Cavalry to recapture the lost artillery. Unleashing a blistering volley, the Texans blasted away and shot Yankee cavalrymen out of saddles with ease, as if shooting turkey gobblers off treetop roasts in the tall cypress towering above the clear waters of the Trinity and Colorado Rivers in east Texas.

All in all, the hard-charging Texans achieved significant gains at Gaines's Mill, after spearheading the dramatic breakthrough of the blue lines on the Federal left. In fact, the Texas Brigade's "charge saved the day for Lee" (his first success since taking command of the army after General Johnston's wounding) at Gaines's Mill. But the victory was not a cheap one for the Texas Brigade. Nearly 600 Texas boys were either killed wounded or captured in the bitter fighting at Gaines' Mill, where the reputation of the Texas Brigade reached new heights across the South.[65]

With the wounded Colonel Rainey recuperating from his wound, Captain Work of the Woodville Rifles, Company "F," from the Sabine River country of Tyler County, retained command of the 1st Texas in the days ahead. As the senior captain of this most unconventional, but elite, regiment of unorthodox fighting men, he was now on his way to retaining permanent regimental command.[66]

Fortunately, the Texas Brigade was not heavily engaged for the remainder of the Peninsula Campaign in the contest over the possession of Richmond, but losses steadily mounted nevertheless. On June 30 at Frayser's Farm, "nearly all of Company 'M' of the First Texas was killed or wounded" by an exploding shell after a direct hit in the ranks. Also known as the Silver Greys, this Trinity County company that had been so cruelly victimized by Union artillery was the Sumter Light Infantry. As could be expected, this company of rambunctious young men had been named in honor of the first Southern success at Fort Sumter. Of course, the masonry fort in Charleston harbor had been named after the famed South Carolina partisan leader of the American Revolution, who arose to the fore after the 1780 fall of Charleston in the embattled low country of South Carolina, Thomas Sumter.[67]

After the slaughter of the Seven Days, the 1st Texas soldiers and the Texas Brigade "were now looked upon by thousands as the flower of the Southern Army" and incomparable fighting men of unique distinction. Even more, the Texas Brigade was viewed far and wide as "the pride and glory of the Army of Northern Virginia," which was dominated by Old Dominion leaders, including Lee and his top lieutenants, especially the West Pointers. Richmond society, newspapers, and politicians buzzed about the stirring battlefield exploits and fighting skills of the Texas Brigade soldiers.[68]

With much pride, Private James Henry Hendrick of the Marshall Guards (Company "E") from Harrison County penned in a July 13, 1862 letter: "... our brigade distinguishes itself in the fight [but] We lost a great many men [and] The Yankees fight well [as] They will stand and shoot all day with us. The only way we can whip them is to charge them. They will not stand the bayonet."[69]

But this "glory" won by the Texas Rebels only came at a frightfully high price. During the charge at Gaines's Mill, the 1st Texas lost fourteen killed and sixty-four wounded, including Colonel Rainey. Rising to the challenge, Kentucky-born Lieutenant Colonel Philip Alexander Work, aggressive and highly-capable, was now the ideal commander of the 1st Texas soldiers. He was officially promoted to that rank on June 27: a well-deserved advancement, without a hint of the ever-pervasive army politics or back-door dealings that so often elevated unqualified men beyond their means in other Southern commands.

At age thirty, Lieutenant Colonel Work demonstrated that his rise was not the product of campaigning for votes or politics, but by tactical skill and leadership abilities. Because of a bureaucratic technicality with Colonel Rainey remaining on the muster rolls as the 1st Texas's colonel although his fighting days were over, Work only held a lieutenant colonel's rank instead of that of a full colonel. Even though, wrote Captain Todd who led the Marion and Cass County soldiers of Company "A", he was "a very small man" and more of an intellectual and scholarly type than a stereotypical frontiersman, Work was highly respected by his men.

Ambitious and hard-working, Work had been admitted to the bar of Texas at only age twenty-one. Work also possessed military experience prior to the Civil War. He had served as the orderly sergeant of a mounted company of hard-riding Texans on the western frontier. Like so many other Texas Brigade officers, Work intimately knew the ways of Indian and guerrilla warfare. Work's invaluable frontier tactical lessons, insights, and skills made the 1st Texas more formidable, especially in regard to the upcoming challenge at the Devil's Den and Houck's Ridge.

A man of many talents and varied interests, the newly-promoted lieutenant colonel also had been a leading politician of the Palestine, Texas, region. Work had represented the good people of Tyler County when he had signed the Texas Ordnance of Secession. However, Work had missed the secession convention that voted to depart the Union, because he already had left civilian life to fight for his country conceived in violent revolution. He returned home to raise his volunteer company ("F") of Tyler County Rebels and then rushed his volunteers to Montgomery, Alabama, the Confederacy's first capital, to enter the conflict as soon as possible. Most of all, "from his gallantry in the field and constancy with his command, he well deserves to have rank as he has command [of the 1st Texas and he] has been present in every battle, and with his men in every march of the campaign" from the beginning.[70]

After Gaines' Mill, additional fame came for General Hood and his hard-fighting Texans at Second Manassas, when Lee launched the offensive with his usual vigor, after skillful maneuvering undetected by the Yankees, including dividing his army, to catch the Federals by surprise. Most of all, General Lee sought to destroy General John Pope's Army of Virginia, sensing a golden tactical opportunity that he was determined to exploit to the fullest. Troops of Hood's Division embarked upon a reconnaissance in force on the night before the Battle of Second Manassas to ascertain weak points in the Union position. However, the Texans soon ran headlong into a force of Yankees advancing in the darkness.

Before he could draw his revolver from its holster, however, Lieutenant Colonel Work, now leading the 1st Texas' advance and reconnoitering on his own before his regiment to ascertain the exact location of Federal positions, suddenly ran into the enemy. A shadowy figure appeared before the 1st Texas' commander, and then said to Work, "Yes, cease firing; we are Rebs!" With that, Lieutenant Colonel Work screamed, "You are a damn Yank! Give 'en hell, boys!" At that moment, the colonel was clubbed down with a Union musket-butt. Hand-to-hand combat then erupted in the night, with bayonets, musket-butts, and even fists used by both sides. But despite his diminutive size in contrast to his large-sized opponent, the lieutenant colonel prevailed in the end, overpowering the Yankee. In the words of an incredulous Captain Todd: "[Lt.] Col. P. A. Work, our commander, a very small man physically, got into a rough and tumble fight with a big Yank, and marched him to the rear" as a prisoner.[71]

But Work proved his greatest value as the 1st Texas' commander during the bloody showdown at Second Manassas, where the Lee won still another masterful victory. On the hot afternoon of August 30, with General James Longstreet, the commander of the First Corps and Lee's top lieutenant, planned to assault General Pope's vulnerable left on the old First Manassas battlefield, at Henry Hill, with around 25,000 troops, Hood's Texas Brigade once again played a key role. A fitting compliment to the unit's combat prowess, Longstreet wisely chose Hood's Texas Brigade "to lead the assault" and gain the imposing Henry Hill plateau. The bloody Battle of Second Manassas resulted in one of the finest days for the Texas Brigade, adding to an already lofty reputation for not only combat prowess, but also for combat ferocity.

With the 1st Texas initially advancing in front as "the regiment of direction" for Hood's Brigade that emerged from a belt of woodlands around 4 p.m., the Texans spearheaded the final assault of Longstreet's Corps on left of Pope's Army. Lieutenant Colonel Work, who refused to leave his regiment despite his painful head injury suffered the night before, continued to lead his crack 1st Texas forward. As usual, the colonel's example inspired the 1st Texas soldiers onward in the assault. Surging across open ground, the Texans moved with discipline in what one Company "B" (Tom Green Rifles), 4th Texas soldier, Granville Henderson Crozier, who was wounded in the assaults at Gaines's Mill and Second Manassas, described as "a magnificent sight" to one and all.

A veteran regiment of highly-touted New Yorkers, who were fresh after having been spared the bloodletting of the previous day, August 29, stood in the path of the

Texas Brigade's onslaught. The New York boys, known as (Abram) Duryee's Zouaves, possessed a fine combat record. They also were proud of a widespread reputation as one of the army's best-drilled units. However, these facts had created a good deal of hubris among the New York officers and men, fueling overconfidence before meeting Lee's best fighting men from far-away Texas. Wearing the brightly-colored Zouave uniform inspired by the French Zouaves, who had long fought against the Islamic warriors of Bedouin tribes in North Africa, these New Yorkers were the army's most splendidly-uniformed soldiers by this time: the very antithesis of the ragged Texas Brigade soldiers, especially the 1st Texas boys.

The Texas assault was about to be unleashed upon the more than 500 "red breeches Zouaves" of General Daniel Edgar Sickles's Excelsior Brigade. These were not New York rookies, but veterans of the bitter fighting of the Seven Days. By this time, Colonel Duryee's Zouaves of the 5th New York possessed a widespread reputation for parade ground precision and distinguished membership with more than half a dozen future generals in its ranks. Their lofty reputation—like the Texas Rebels but for different reasons—had preceded them to the field of Second Manassas.

But, wrote Chaplain Davis in mocking fashion, "our men were not frightened at their red breeches, nor the appearance of their red skull-caps, with cow-tail looking tassels, but they seemed to be fired afresh for the combat." Making General Hood extremely proud, the tide of yelling Texas Rebels surged through the steamy, Virginia woodlands of late August on the run with clattering gear and high spirits. With fixed bayonets, they descended upon the hapless New Yorkers like wolves upon sheep in a great killing field.

Attacking south toward Pope's vulnerable left, the Texans moved so swiftly over the open ground that they caught the Yankees by surprise and before they were ready to receive the assault moving at such a brisk pace. The startled bluecoat skirmishers from New York hardly had time to fire a few hasty, ill-aimed shots before they turned and fled the fast-approaching Texans. After smashing through the thin skirmish line of the 10th New York, the Texans then poured without a halt toward the main line of the 5th New York with a speed that even amazed Texas officers. Even more, the onrushing Texas Rebels advanced closely on the heels of the retiring New York skirmishers to exploit the tactical advantage to the fullest.

When the Texans struck, the unready New Yorkers, who were positioned just before an expanse of dense woodlands, hardly knew what had hit them. The initial Texans' volley, which suddenly poured out of the thick timber of summer, at close range destroyed half of the 5th New York, which was entirely exposed on open ground. More than 300 Empire State men went down in the explosion of gun-fire, falling victim to the vicious fire at close range.

Then, sensing the kill by the sight of so many falling bluecoats who littered the ground in sickening clumps, the Texas Rebels let loose a cheer, and then charged with steel bayonet sparkling in the sunlight. Packing a mighty punch, the Texans tore into the thinned line of New Yorkers and the remaining survivors, who were left standing half-stunned by the terrible punishment, after having taken a devastating fire. Six-shooters,

.577 Enfield rifles, and bayonets and musket-butts were handled with deadly efficiency by the unleashed westerners. Piles of red-stained New York City men were laid low by the fury of the ruthless Texans, as if they were attempting to outdo the more than 500 Mexicans left dead on the bloody field of San Jacinto on another tragic day of revenge.

In horror, one Yankee described the surreal slaughter in which "not only were men wounded and killed but they were riddled" by Texas bullets. With the Texans screaming like banshees and swiftly curling around both of the New Yorkers' flanks, now hanging in mid-air, the 5th New York, exposed in an open field, was simply crushed under with weight of the onrushing Texas Rebels. Himself amazed at the extent of destructiveness delivered by his brigade, Corporal Polley, 4th Texas, wrote with supreme satisfaction in a letter: "Not fifty of the Zouaves escaped whole" during the thorough decimation.

Unable to stand-up to the Texans' accurate fire and jabbing steel bayonets, what little remained of the New York regiment fell apart and disintegrated under the onslaught. Almost to a man, the surviving New Yorkers fled "like dogs," running for their lives. With the bluecoats on the run, the Texans instinctively continued onward without being told and followed close behind with victory cheers. Intoxicated by their success, they pursued their defeated opponent with abandon that could not be controlled, as if on a festive fox or coon hunt in the pine forests of east Texas.

Captain Todd, Company "A," 1st Texas, described how "our regiment, literally ran over a regiment of N.Y. Zouaves, with red caps and jackets, who surrendered to us." Aligning along a slight ridge to catch their breath in the day's intense heat and to deliver more punishment upon the New Yorkers from the high ground, the panting Texas Rebels, as if in a turkey shoot, fired down the slope to kill additional numbers of Duryee's Zouaves, who fell in droves. Then, the slaughter of the unfortunate New Yorkers continued unabated downhill for two hundred yards through the woodlands to a brushy low spot along Young's Branch, a tributary of Bull Run that trickled through the dense forest that had become a grim killing ground.

The contest turned into another San Jacinto-like annihilation of a reeling opponent similar to the tragic fate of Santa Anna's routed Mexicans at the scene of the greatest slaughter at Peggy's Lake, after their thin defensive line was broken by Houston's afternoon attack that had caught them by surprise. Now additional doses of death and destruction were inflicted by the fast-firing Texans upon the New York Zouaves in the wooded ravine of Young's Branch. Corporal Joe Polley described: "… not waiting to reload, the Texans rushed after the fugitives, and, clubbing their muskets, continued the work of destruction until every enemy in sight was left prone on the ground." Clearly, by this time, the Texans were a lethal killing machine even without loaded muskets, leaving behind them a gory scene of carnage.[72]

Indeed, of the more than 500 New Yorkers in action at Second Manassas, only around sixty men escaped the Texans to reach safety with many horror stories to tell. Incredibly, the Texans had shot down, bayoneted, or clubbed more almost 300 Fifth New York soldiers in only ten minutes of perhaps the most concentrated and swiftest slaughter of the entire Civil War. Here, the Texas Rebels "met [Dan] Sickle's 'Excelsior Brigade.' and almost annihilated it [because] the ground was piled with the slain" New York soldiers, who had the misfortune of tangling with Lee's finest combat troops. Ironically, the Texans were destined to face Dan Sickles' men at the Devil's Den and Houck's Ridge in the following summer at Gettysburg.

Out of some 500 Empire State soldiers, a staggering total of 120 New Yorkers were killed on the field, and even more men later died of their wounds. This was "the largest loss of life in any battle of the entire Civil War" for a single regiment, North or South. Even more, this rare complete success was a gory tribute to lethal fighting qualities that were second to none in the Army of Northern Virginia at this time. What the Texans had accomplished was nothing less than the slaughter of "the flower of those two (New York) regiments," wrote one Confederate, who basked in the success.

Echoing General Sam Houston's April 1836 grim rationale in regard to the slaughter at San Jacinto, General Hood merely concluded that his uncontrollable Texas frontiersmen had "slipped the bridle and went wild." Not even the 5th New York's utter destruction caused the breathless Texans to halt their charge, and the "Lone Star State" soldiers, with their fighting blood up, continued to steam-roll onward to achieve more success, including the capture of battle flags. With the Texans out of control in reaping additional gains in continuing the attack, Rebel support troops on either side were unable to keep up with the sweeping Texan charge fueled by a momentum all its own. In total, the Texas Brigade attacked nearly three-quarters of a mile and all the way to the high ground of Chinn Ridge, smashing one Union brigade, overrunning another, and capturing a battery.

The full extent of the carnage, where the Texas Brigade mauled the 5th New York that now barely existed as a regiment, was surreal. Corporal Polley was shocked by "the ghastly, horrifying spectacle that met our eyes[because] nearly an acre [was filled with] killed and wounded Zouaves, the variegated colors of whose gaudy uniforms gave the scene ... the appearance of a Texas hill-side carpeted in the spring by wild flowers of many hues and tints." Ironically, at this time, not a greater contrast could have been found between the appearances (also in terms of combat prowess) of opposing troops: the urban Zouaves from New York City, wearing perhaps the Union Army's finest uniforms, *versus* the unwashed, ragged frontiersmen and yeomen farmers from the Lone Star State. But once unleashed on the battlefield, it was the Texans' unsurpassed frontier skills and superior fighting abilities that shined the brightest on the gory field of Second Manassas.[73]

Therefore, in summary, one Texas Brigade soldier, Bennet Wood, crowed with a mixture of pride and contempt that burned deep inside his Lone Star State soul, wrote how the "Zouaves who were pitted against the Texas Brigade, I guess, were all killed, for the earth was strewn with them and I never heard of one after that day. If any escaped they changed their big legged pants for another uniform."[74]

The sparkling victory at Second Manassas was complete for Lee, opening the door for the invasion of the Promised Land of Maryland in September 1862. Once again, the

Texas Brigade achieved gains far beyond expectations and its numbers. Against the odds, the Texas Rebels captured five artillery pieces and eleven Yankee banners, but losses were heavy. One-half of the Texas Brigade (628 men) was cut down in the bitter fighting and lengthy charge to win the day: the highest Texas Brigade numerical loss during the war. The 5th Texas lost more men (225) than any regiment of the Army of Northern Virginia. Many of the best and brightest members of the Texas Brigade were eliminated in one of the most hard-hitting charges of the war. In a relatively short time, half of the Texas Brigade was cut down immediately before the arduous Maryland Campaign.[75]

Chaplain Davis wrote a lasting testimonial to the Texans' superior marksmanship, which was especially evident on the Second Manassas battlefield where they had charged for hundreds of yards to sweep everything before them: "... the line of their flight was marked by the carcasses, which fell from their ranks.... Hundreds of them [now] were hilled up like a potato-patch on the field."[76] After the battle, General Hood marveled at the amount of awful destruction that had been inflicted by his Texans: "Men who fight in this way, can never be whipped." In fact, "no troops in General Lee's army bore a more conspicuous part in this great battle or contributed in a greater degree to achieve the victory than Hood's Texas Brigade."[77]

But despite its success and heavy losses at Second Manassas, the 1st Texas' finest day to date was still to come—the epic clash of arms at Gettysburg. All previous battles were destined to pale by comparison to what lay ahead in the great showdown between the Army of Northern Virginia and the Army of the Potomac in the great killing fields of Adams County, Pennsylvania.

To successfully meet the challenges of the showdown at Antietam, Work was fortunate to have a most dependable and capable top lieutenant as his right-hand man in Major Matt Dale. In May 1862, he had been promoted from lieutenant of the Reagan Guards of Company "G" (a fine unit from Anderson County that he had helped to raise among his Palestine friends and neighbors) to major, after nearly a unanimous vote by the 1st Texas soldiers. The Tennessee-born Dale had been an enterprising Nashville printer before migrating to Texas in search of new opportunities that he found as editor of the *Trinity Advocate* located in Palestine, Texas. Most importantly, he was cool in action and aggressive on the battlefield.

As explained an admiring Chaplain Davis: "He was no office seeker, but his gallant conduct and general affability won him a host of friends, who forced positions upon him." In 1857, Dale had been elected to represent the people of Palestine, Anderson County, Texas, in the state legislature. He had been one of the first men in Anderson County to volunteer to serve in the Reagan Guards of Company "G," winning election to lieutenant. Despite suffering from a serious bout with disease throughout the summer of 1862 and since stationed at Yorktown, on the Virginia Peninsula, that "has reduced me somehow," he continued to serve faithfully in the ranks as best he could in order to continue to lead his boys.

Dale was promoted to the well-deserved rank of major in May 1862. In a letter to his brother, Major Dale wrote with pride of "my promotion [from captain] to Major." Major

Dale made-up one-half of an excellent leadership team, along with Lieutenant Colonel Work. Both men were the same age (thirty) and in the prime of life. The two dynamic officers possessed an abundance of vitality, tactical flexibility, and aggressive instincts that made these two men highly-effective combat leaders. By the time of the Maryland Campaign, Major Dale was the second highest-ranking officer of the 1st Texas. These top two officers of the 1st Texas held much future promise, including when they returned to Texas after the war, if they could survive the ever-increasing level of bloodletting. All in all, the 1st Texas could not have hoped for more capable leaders than Work-Dale leadership team.[78]

Ambitious and highly-motivated, Major Dale was proud of his rise to major, because he had earned it the hard way at a time when so many officers, including generals, had relied on friends in high places to secure high promotions. He, therefore, took his added responsibility most seriously, leading the 1st Texas by bold example and from the front. But this young man with a talent for writing and expressing lofty ideals with eloquence was haunted by a dark premonition of death by the late spring of 1862. For the prophetic Dale, the ugly realities of an increasingly brutal war had become a personal nightmare that seemed about to consume and destroy him like so many others.

The stoic young major wrote to his brother, Williamson Dale, on June 7, 1862:

> [In this savage war] many of us will be laid low [and] If this should be my lot, I want you to manage my little affairs, pay the last cent I owe with lawful interest, divide what is or may be left equally between Mother, brother Isaac's little boy Matt, and your own children. Educate the children and teach them to hate the Yankees, and I will rest easy beneath the sod.[79]

At this time, Dale did not know that he indeed would shortly be lying "easy beneath the sod" in a final resting place of Washington County in western Maryland in less than three months, after Lee's Army crossed the Potomac River. With his gloomy premonition of impending doom but never thinking about turning back on his role or responsibility, Major Dale had just scribbled out his last will and testament. As if anticipating the war's bloodiest day at Antietam, he fully expected that the worst lay in store for him after having witnessed so much slaughter and barely surviving some of the war's most brutal fighting. Indeed, Major Matt Dale would not live to again see his beloved Anderson County, nestled between the Trinity and Neches Rivers around 150 miles north of Houston, home or family. Like so many other young men and boys of the 1st Texas, he was destined to fall in the lush cornfield of farmer David R. Miller at Antietam during "the Thermopylae of the Texas Brigade," wrote Joe Polley, 4th Texas.[80]

In a letter, Colonel Edward Bragg, commanding the 6th Wisconsin, Iron Brigade (one of the best combat units in the Army of the Potomac), described the 1st Texas Rebels and the sad fate of their revered leader, Major Dale:

> ... the Rebels fought like demons [and] They are the dirtyist, lousyist, filthiest, piratical looking cutthroats a white man ever saw.... Officers & men alike—in filthy rags [and

> one dead major had fallen] with fiery courage, worthy of a State having an Alamo for its nursery cradle [in the 6th Wisconsin's line and] he was wearing a lady's watch presumably a talisman given him by a wife or finance.[81]

What Colonel Bragg had described were the hardiest fighters of the Army of Northern Virginia in part because they were much closer to the frontier experience than any of Lee's other troops, while embracing the dual legacies of the Texas Revolution and the Republic of Texas. In consequence, the Texans held a seemingly limitless measure of contempt for the "the swells and dandies of the Army," especially easterners, including Virginians in gray, who, in turn, looked with disgust upon these elite fighting men as little more than a "gang of Texas Coyotes," although they were the army's finest troops.[82]

One 4th Texas soldier from the plains of west Texas perhaps best summarized the wide gulf of cultural and societal differences that existed between the frontier Texians and cavalier Virginians—from opposite sides of the Confederacy—by describing the popular Texan sport of "Comanche hunting." In describing what were in essence two different cultures and worlds, he drew upon an unique distinction by emphasizing to some Virginians how during "the spring of the year, we make up what we call 'Comanche Parties,' like you F.F.V.'s [First Families of Virginia] make up fox-hunting parties here in Virginia, just for the fun of it ... we charge them with a yell ... and chase 'em and shoot 'em on the wing, just like partridges."[83]

But now a cruel fate had reversed that former role, because the Texas soldiers had become pawns and cannon fodder in this most cruel war in American history. They were now as fated for destruction (ironically, like the Native Americans of Texas, including the Comanche) in part because they were repeatedly employed in crucial combat situations that demanded a frightfully high sacrifice. Nothing in the world now could save the young Texas soldiers from the escalating rate of attrition that so cruelly culled the ranks without mercy. Tragically for them, the greatest slaughter of the war still lay ahead: a rendezvous with a cruel destiny in rural south central Pennsylvania, where unknown and obscure places, like the Devil's Den and Little Round Top, in Adams County, Pennsylvania, were about to become famous.

The typical fighting spirit of Texas Brigade members was perhaps best represented in the stoic words of John Camden West, Company "E," 4th Texas. West wrote to his wife, whose prized tintype, along with his well-worn pocket Bible, he carried close to his heart, including on the fatal field of Gettysburg: "I started from Texas to find a fight, and I have made a success of it."[84]

As fate would have it, the greatest battle for the Texas Brigade was now on the horizon at a remote community first established by James Gettys in Adams County, Pennsylvania: a small market and crossroads town of barely 2,000 people named Gettysburg. The Texans were about to be hurled into the vortex of what they believed was the climactic showdown between "the combined forces of good and evil," in Private West's words, to determine the future destiny of America.[85]

4

The Formidable Challenge of Capturing the Devil's Den and Houck's Ridge, the Army of the Potomac's Left Flank

Caught in a brutal war of attrition that the Confederacy could never win despite all of the heroics of his fighting men who continued to bravely sacrifice themselves in unparalleled numbers because they believed victory was on the horizon, therefore, General Robert E. Lee led his Army of Northern Virginia north in his ambitious second invasion of the North. Lee's overall goal was to deliver a decisive knock-out blow to the Army of the Potomac. Like an increasing number of men in the veteran ranks of his hard-hitting army, he realized that it was now or never for the Confederacy.

Quite simply, if a decisive victory was not won on northern soil by the Army of Northern Virginia during the summer of 1863, then the Confederacy was doomed. The barren strategic results of Lee's most recent victory (still another pyrrhic one) at Chancellorsville, Virginia, in early May 1863 only demonstrated the truth of this grim, undeniable reality for Southern fortunes—still another pyrrhic victory. If the Army of the Potomac, the North's primary eastern army assigned to protecting Washington, D.C., was not vanquished in the days ahead, then it would be only a matter of time before the South's experiment in nationhood succumbed to an early death.

Clearly, by the summer of 1863, when the fatal arithmetic became even more obvious and ominous after 13,000 Southerners had been cut down in the savage fighting at Chancellorsville, including Thomas Jonathan "Stonewall" Jackson who was his top lieutenant, Lee was desperate. Of course, the battle-hardened men of the Texas Brigade felt much the same way. Clearly, the stakes could not have been higher for either the Confederacy or the Army of Northern Virginia by this time. Therefore, the invasion of the Keystone State beckoned as never before.[1]

For the South's soldiers, invading northern soil for the second time, especially with a more powerful army than during the Maryland Campaign of the late summer of 1862, was an exhilarating experience. This was an opportunity to accomplish what had not been achieved during the failed Maryland Campaign that had sputtered to a dismal end in the killing fields of Antietam: the reaping of a decisive success over the Army of the Potomac, which would be the delivering of a masterstroke. For such reasons, an epic clash of arms—the largest and most decisive battle fought on the North American continent—was inevitable north of the Potomac and only a matter of time: the three-day Battle of Gettysburg, southeastern Pennsylvania.

While encamped at Chambersburg, Pennsylvania, just northwest of Gettysburg in the south central part of the Keystone State, an upbeat Private John Marquis "Mark" Smither, 5th Texas, Brigadier General Jerome Bonaparte Robertson's Texas Brigade, Major General John Bell Hood's Division, General James Longstreet's First Corps, wrote with pride to his mother in a June 28, 1863: "... we have carried the war into the enemy's country [when] We crossed the Potomac at Williamsport, Md., [on June 26] and marched into this state the same day [and] we now have seventy five or eighty thousand as good troops as ever shouldered a musket, confidant [*sic.*] of victory."[2]

What the ragged Texas soldiers now saw in this area (not touched by the war) north of the Potomac's shallow and cold waters was a bountiful land of plenty that delighted the eye, especially among the farm boys in gray and butternut, as far as one could see. In a letter, Private John Camden West, of the same regiment, described the natural beauty of Maryland and Pennsylvania with a sense of wonder:

> ... we passed [through the] most thoroughly improved [lands] I ever saw. There was not a foot of surplus or waste territory [and] Wheat, corn, clover, half a dozen varieties of grass, rye, barley—all in full growth and approaching maturity—met the eye at every turn [and] The barns were, however, the most striking feature of the landscape [because they were better than] three-fourths of the dwellings in Texas.[3]

Likewise, in a letter to his mother, James E. Hendricks, of Company "E" (Marshall Guards), 1st Texas, was astounded by what he saw around him. He looked at this lush and picturesque land of plenty in absolute wonder, writing how this "is the finest country I have seen."[4]

In high spirits and with soaring confidence during the bright skies of late June, Lee's men were eager to meet the Yankees on their home soil to give them the thorough trashing, because God was on their side, or so they sincerely believed. In the ranks of Company "B" (Tom Green Rifles), 4th Texas, young Van C. Giles later mused: "It is fortunate that we were gay on the way to the battle, for all gaiety was [soon] replaced by grim realities and bitter fighting on the field."[5]

But not everyone in the ranks was buoyed by soaring spirits because thousands of soldiers in lengthy columns were treading across northern soil for the second time in the army's history. From the small community of Corsicana, Texas, Private James M. Polk, Company "I" (Navarro Rifles), 4th Texas, thought back upon those early and much more innocent days when the war seemed like a grand adventure and the opportunities for reaping glory had seemed endless. Now reflecting upon the loss of so many comrades who were no more and now mostly buried in the soil of Virginia, young Polk "could not help but think how different [this increasingly brutal war of attrition now] was from the way it was pictured out to us in war speeches at the commencement" of the conflict.[6]

All the while, the marching Confederates continued onward with confidence, while their colorful war banners waved in the warm breeze. But these young men and boys who had won dramatic victory across Virginia seemed to be pulled farther east toward the rising sun and along the dusty roads of Pennsylvania by a strange destiny toward the little town of Gettysburg. Numerous cold, clear waters of a good many springs along their trek had recently improved health and lifted spirits among the dust-covered men in the army's ranks. Private John Camden West described in a glowing letter how "I think I have seen more than fifty springs equal to those of Barton, San Antonio, San Marcos and Salado," Texas.[7]

Trudging through the rising clouds of dust with rifled-muskets on shoulders, the Confederates were impressed by the sheer beauty of the fertile lands, mostly covered in nearly ripe fields of wheat that revealed Pennsylvania's bounty. But the local citizens, who were mostly Germans and Unionist to the core with their boys fighting at the front, including in the Army of the Potomac, left something to be desired to the invaders' way of thinking. In his letter, Private John Mark Smither described the scene that greeted the Texas Brigade soldiers when marching east through the picturesque town of Chambersburg on June 27:

> Chambersburg is about as large as Houston [Texas] and is the prettiest place I ever saw, laid out with regular Dutch [German] precision, the girls (and they were beauties) in town, were Union to the back bone and had capital sport at our shabby and military appearances but as a general thing our boys took it good humoredly and marched by in silence [and] I wish I could described [*sic.*] to you [mother] my feelings on entering Chambersburg ... it was a feeling of exultation."[8]

But this sense of "exultation" turned into astonishment and a resurgence of Texas pride among the Lone Star State men, who learned that their lofty reputations for combat prowess had preceded them. These men already knew that the Texas Brigade's reputation for superior combat prowess could not have been higher than across the South at this time, but no one expected in the ranks that the command's fame was alive and well even in the North.

In his letter that revealed how the Texas Brigade's reputation had already spread far north among the civilian population, Private John Mark Smither explained:

> [When marching through Chambersburg] we passed a crowd of people who enquired of me what troops were passing and on receiving the answer of "Texas Brigade" one turned around to the rest and remarked "they are the ones that have killed so many of our soldiers!" [and indeed] we have come in collision with Pennsylvanians on every one of our battlefields and I expect [that the Texans] have actually killed more of them than the rest of our soldiers in this army and they are pretty good soldiers too, have enough of the

> Dutch [German] in them to make good Hessians. We are all in splendid health and spirits in fact I never saw this army in better...[9]

Indeed, the soaring morale of Lee's troops could not have been higher, while they marched with impunity across Pennsylvania soil with a confident step and flags flying. These heady days of endless optimism disguised a host of grim and harsh realities for the young men and boys of the Army of Northern Virginia. Taking the war to the enemy was the fondest of dreams of Lee's soldiers, and now that intoxicating vision had become a happy reality.[10] Thinking more like a savvy politician than a Virginia general, Lee hoped to revive the northern peace party, the so-called "peace Democrats"—with a dramatic success north of the Potomac, leading to recognition for the Confederacy and an established peace.[11]

In pushing east toward its initial target of Harrisburg, the capital of Pennsylvania, and also the more lucrative target of Philadelphia (the North's second largest city) farther to the east if the capital was captured, the soldiers of the fast-moving ranks of the Army of the Northern Virginia were unknowingly now headed toward the largest and most climactic battle ever fought over heart and soul of America. One Texas officer lusted at the mere thought that once Harrisburg was captured by Lee's interlopers who believed that anything was possible, then "the way will be clear to Baltimore[,] Philadelphia[,] [and] Washington and so on."[12]

As revealed in a letter, a confident private of the 4th Texas was likewise dreaming of glory that was seemingly about to be reaped on northern soil. Sensing a golden opportunity, he wrote how "Baltimore would have been ours," if all went well in Lee's great invasion by an army that seemed invincible at this time, after what had been repeatedly demonstrated by the South's primary eastern army on Virginia soil.[13]

Lieutenant Colonel Arthur James Lyon Fremantle, the astute English observer with Lee's command, doubted that the troops of the Army of Northern Virginia could achieve such lofty goals based upon mere appearances of the men in the ranks. However, the aristocratic Briton, of the Coldstream Guards, was guilty of a gross underestimation in regard to the fighting prowess of Lee's men. For instance, he could hardly believe the disturbing sight of the men of Hood's Division, because what he saw was the antithesis of troops of the British Army. He penned these veterans "are certainly a queer set to look at ... all are ragged and dirty, but full of good-humour and confidence in themselves and in their General, Hood."[14]

After an accidental clash of vanguard of both armies—the Union cavalry advance under Brigadier General John Buford, who commanded the First Cavalry Division, Major General Alfred A. Pleasonton's Cavalry Corps, Army of the Potomac, and Lieutenant General Ambrose Powell Hill's Third Corps troops—that erupted just northwest of Gettysburg, where ten dusty roads met to make this community now strategic, on the morning of July 1, Lee hurriedly concentrated his scattered forces, while inflicting damage on the advance elements of the Army of the Potomac, which was scattered and not united like his army. All the while, the battle grew and swirled out control, drawing units of both armies like a magnet.

Meanwhile, the vast majority of the more than 90,000-man Union Army, under newly-appointed Major General George Gordon Meade was still pushing north from western Maryland. These veteran Federals were determined to reach the field of strife, which was situated amid the lush farmlands of Adams County, Pennsylvania. After taking a severe beating when hit in front from the west and also from the north by Lieutenant General Richard Stoddert Ewell's Second Corps that had reversed course from the Harrisburg area, the battered Federal units, the first on the field, were defeated and hurled rearward, losing Gettysburg to a relentless tide of howling Confederates. On the heights beyond and south of the town, the Federals made their defensive stand on high ground of Cemetery Ridge, with the army's main position also aligned along Cemetery Ridge that expanded south of the town.

On fateful July 1 after an accidental clash of arms at a place and time not of his own choosing, General Lee found himself making some of the most important decisions of the war because of situational circumstances, as opposed to orchestrating tactical developments as throughout the past. His decisions had to be made in regard to an all-important battle that had spiraled out of control. Nevertheless, with nearly 70,000 troops eventually available to him, Lee had remained offensive-minded because of the tactical opportunities that had been presented to him.

Most of all, he knew that the reeling Confederacy desperately needed a decisive success to ensure a long life, exploiting the tactical advantage to the fullest until the Federals formed on the high ground beyond Gettysburg by the night of July 1. Most of all, he was determined to make the most of what he hoped was an opportunity to destroy the Army of the Potomac, which had still to unite at Gettysburg with the Fifth and Sixth Corps still pushing north from the farmlands of western Maryland.

Therefore, on the morning of July 2, 1863, Lee decided to exploit the significant gains achieved by his army on a scorching Wednesday July 1. The sweet taste of success had only made Lee more aggressive at Gettysburg, because he knew that everything was now at stake for his army and nation. He possessed ample good reason to be supremely confident at this time.

In fact, he believed that what now lay before him was the long-awaited opportunity to win it all. As mentioned, the largest battle ever fought in North America had begun when a light skirmish had escalated into a major clash. But everything had suddenly changed for Lee because of the arrival of his Second Corps, called back just in the nick of time from near Harrisburg: fortune smiled on the Army of Northern Virginia under these fortunate circumstances that had seemingly been ordained by a kind fate. Lee believed in the miracles of Providence, and such now seemed to be the case: the simplistic mentally that dominated his thinking on July 2 and July 3, and, unfortunately, for the common soldiers in the ranks.

He had seen God's handiwork, or so he believed, when thousands of battle-hardened veterans of General Ewell's Second Corps had charged south to smash into the exposed right flank of newly-arrived Union infantry brigades of the First and Eleventh Corps, from left to right, while they had initially faced Third Corps troops, led by an ailing West Pointer General Ambrose Powell Hill, attacking through the broad fields from the northwest: a tactical recipe that had resulted in the hurling of the Yankees through the town of Gettysburg.

Of course and thinking like Napoleon Bonaparte whose aggressiveness had always reaped dramatic victories across Europe until he sought to do the same in ill-fated Russia in 1812, General Lee saw the situation as a golden opportunity to vanquish the Army of the Potomac, before it was united in its entirety along the high ground of Cemetery Ridge. However, he ignored the fact that the Federals fought more tenaciously than ever before, because they now possessed the psychological advantage of defending northern soil: like the key advantage held by his troops in defending Virginia.

Therefore, and even though much of the Army of the Potomac now held the high ground of Cemetery Ridge and Cemetery Hill and Culp's Hill (just south of town, the two key elevations—the northern end and flank of Meade's sprawling defensive line—that General Ewell had failed to capture with his Second Corps late on July 1, after hurling the Federals through Gettysburg) and under the command of highly-competent Meade, Confederate confidence was extremely high for the inevitable showdown on July 2. Lee could almost taste the winning of a decisive success at long last.

After all, this talented Mexican-American War veteran, the hero of the South and its most successful commander, was a master in the art of delivering a masterful decisive blow that had often sent the Union Armies reeling, becoming the most successful battlefield commander in American history. With his fighting blood up and tasting victory on July 1, he believed that the showdown at Gettysburg on July 2 would be no different, feeling that it was now or never for inflicting a mortal blow on his nemesis, the Army of the Potomac.

Almost a classic case of hubris by this time, confidence for ultimate Confederate success was sky-high, because the Army of Northern Virginia had never known defeat, especially in offensive operations. Lee planned to repeat the astounding success of Longstreet's assault, which had been spearheaded by Hood's Texas Brigade to smash through the vulnerable Union left flank to nearly destroy General John Pope's Army of Virginia at Second Manassas, or even "Stonewall" Jackson's lengthy flank march to ease into an advantageous position to tear into Union Army's right flank at Chancellorsville.

Thanks in part to a faulty intelligence report from a low-ranking officer (captain) that led him to believe that the Union left was entirely exposed and vulnerable, Lee was determined to repeat that tactical magic by rolling-up the left flank of Meade's Army poised on Cemetery Ridge. If this winning tactical formula of smashing into the enemy's flank and rolling it up could be repeated as at Chancellorsville, but this time on Adams County, Pennsylvania soil, then the war's most decisive victory would be reaped.[15]

Therefore, Lee was obsessed with delivering a decisive blow, and for ample good reason. Before the recent success at Chancellorsville, General Hood's Texas Brigade had led Longstreet's assault of 25,000 troops to victory on August 30, 1862, which was one of the finest days of the Army of Northern Virginia. Now, on an equally scorching July 2 in southeastern Pennsylvania, Hood's Texas Brigade was likewise about to play another leading role in the tactical offensive.

At this time and as mentioned, Hood was Lee's finest division commanders because of his superior tactical skill, leadership qualities, and aggressiveness. The Texas Brigade, which now possessed "a reputation that was nonparalleled in the army," was the best combat unit in Longstreet's First Corps, which was the finest corps of the hard-hitting Army of Northern Virginia. Destiny itself now seemed to be calling for Hood's Division and the Texas Brigade to outdo its previous tactical performances that had resulted in impressive victories.

At this time, the men of the Texas Brigade were ready for action. After a long march east, that had consumed the entire night, since the early afternoon of July 1 and toward where they heard the battle raging fiercely on the first day, the troops of Hood's Division finally reached the heavily-timbered Seminary Ridge in mid-morning of July 2. Because Lee believed that the Federal left hung in mid-air, Longstreet's Corps was to advance south to stealthy slip into an advantageous tactical position to turn and roll-up that vulnerable southern flank. As in the past, Lee placed his faith in his right-arm and trusty "old war horse," General Longstreet, to deliver the flank attack with his crack First Corps.

But because of a Union signal station situated atop the open, rocky crest of Little Round beyond where Cemetery Ridge flattened out in extending south, Longstreet's flank march had to backtrack to avoid being seen from the high ground. The movement caused confusion, frustration, and the loss of much precious time on a hot afternoon—nothing went right for ambitious Confederate plans and delicate timetables, which were shattered.

But instead of finding a vulnerable left flank and relatively few Yankees as so optimistically expected, Major General Lafayette McLaws, Longstreet's division commander of the First Corps that led the march, shortly discovered that the Federals were ready and waiting in large numbers. From the crest of Warfield Ridge, a southern extension of Seminary Ridge, and the shelter of the George Adam Biesecker's Woods, McLaws could hardly believe his eyes, because he had been informed by Longstreet that he would find no Union troops, especially in large numbers, in his front.

Lee's vision of striking a weak position had vanished, because General Dan Sickles' Third Corps had advanced west around two-thirds of a mile and without Meade's orders from Cemetery Ridge to gain the higher ground and more defensible position along the Emmitsburg Road Ridge. In an embittered letter to his wife Emily, a frustrated McLaws blamed Longstreet for not having properly reconnoitered the ground, before deploying his divisions, as if the Third Corps was still on Cemetery Ridge, where it should have been as General Meade had ordered. With McLaws' Division in Biesecker's Woods and now facing northeast toward Sickles' Third Corps aligned across high ground, Longstreet ordered Hood to push farther southeastward through the open corn, wheat, and oat fields of the Biesecker Farm and then down Warfield Ridge and then to lead the attack on the far right, or south, in order to strike

Meade's true left flank. Therefore, the Texas Brigade, along with the division's other three brigades, was directed to take position on the far right, or the southern end of Lee's battle-line in preparation for delivering another Second Manassas-like blow.

After passing before the silent ranks of the frustrated men of McLaws' Division, now positioned below, or opposite, the high ground of the Joseph Sherfy Peach Orchard, which dominated the high ground (between Seminary and Cemetery Ridges) on the Emmitsburg Road and along the Emmitsburg Road Ridge, now occupied by Sickles' Third Corps, the troops of Hood's Division pushed southeast on the double through the fields of summer and the blistering heat of early summer. Sickles' defensive line was based on the high ground of the Peach Orchard salient, and McLaws' soldiers were aligned just southwest of this strong point—the Peach Orchard salient—and faced thousands of Federals and numerous batteries of artillery.

General Hood's around 14,500 infantrymen of four seasoned brigades (and three veteran batteries) pushed steadily south down Warfield Ridge until finally halting in the refreshing shade and relative cool of the southern end of Biesecker's Woods, southwest of the Peach Orchard, on the reverse, or west, slope of the heavily-wooded Warfield Ridge. As mentioned, Warfield Ridge was located at the southern end of Seminary Ridge, and was a continuation, or southern extension, of that ridge that generally ran north–south and parallel to Cemetery Ridge.

Here, in the eastern part of the Biesecker farm and Biesecker's Woods, the Texas veterans stood in a lengthy column amid the virgin timber that covered the western slope of Warfield Ridge like a green carpet. The lines of McLaws' Division were aligned to the north to the Texas Brigade's left. All the while, a heightened state of anxiety dominated the heat-filled woodlands, and not a breeze stirred to disturb the heavy foliage of the most important summer in the Confederacy's history. Hearing the orders that they knew meant hard and bloody work up ahead, the Texans were ordered to load and cap their .577-caliber Enfield rifles, as so often in the past before successful battles. Then, with the tension high and anxiety on the rise like the day's heat, the grim-faced Texans waited patiently for the inevitable orders to move out to once again meet the boys in blue. All the while, they basked in the much-needed respite on such a scorching hot day, especially after the lengthy flank march south.

These soldiers from the rolling prairies of central Texas and the pine and oak forests of east Texas had no idea that they had just marched across property owned by a free black farmer and blacksmith named James Warfield, for which the ridge, whose reverse slope was timbered, but open on the crest, was named. Meanwhile, Longstreet's troops remained under the good cover of Biesecker's Woods. Most importantly, the quiet woodlands of farmer Biesecker, who was another hard-working and industrious German farmer in an area heavily populated by Teutonic agriculturalists, who had made this land so productive, concealed the build-up of Longstreet's First Corps from prying Yankee eyes, especially the bluecoat signalmen atop Little Round Top.[16]

Poised on the high ground of Warfield Ridge, which veered in a slightly southeasterly direction as the southern extension of Seminary Ridge, after having moving south down the ridge and nestled in the quiet woodlands in full summer foliage and tense soldiers in gray and butternut, Private John Camden West described his innermost thoughts in a letter to his family far-away: "We kept in this line so long, and I was so tired, I went to sleep and dreamed about you [his 'Precious Wife' as he addressed his letters] and mamma and little sister, and I asked God to take care of you if I am taken away from you," while battling for God and country.[17]

In the ranks of Company "C," 4th Texas and contradicting the stereotype of the uneducated frontier warrior from Texas, Private William Henry Foster, who had been wounded in the attack at Gaines's Mill along with his brother, Private Robert V. Foster, was without any popular literature to have recently occupied his mind in part, because "I tried to buy a volume of Shakespeare in Richmond, but they were too heavy to carry in my knap sack [and] If I had one now, I would not take twice the value for it."[18]

Although long delayed after the wasting of so many precious hours, the stage was finally set for the opening of the second day's battle on the far south of Lee's sprawling battle-line. In a letter, Private John Mark Smither, 5th Texas, described the overall tactical situation on July 2 in basic terms: "... the next morning [*sic.*] it was discovered that the Enemy had taken position on an extensive range of mountains [Cemetery Ridge and then Little Round Top later in the afternoon] about 1 ½ miles from Gettysburg. Our [First] Corps, by this time having all come up, Genl Lee, knowing the Enemy, could not be routed unless they were driven from this place gave the order for the heights to be stormed."[19]

Unfortunately for the Army of Northern Virginia, Meade now had almost all of his sizeable army on the field and in good defensive positions by noon of July 2. He had negated Lee's ambitions of early striking hard to catch his opponent by surprise and inflicting a mortal blow before all of the Army of the Potomac arrived from western Maryland.[20] One wary Union captain, Samuel Fiske, predicted prophetically in a letter that Lee was almost certainly about unleash a hard-hitting strike in the "old Jackson style" and "launch the heaviest kind of an attack, which will give all of us as much battle as we can wish for" at Gettysburg.[21]

But unfortunately for Confederate fortunes at Gettysburg, the revered "Stonewall" Jackson was no more (unlike his great dream of invading the North that had been now fulfilled by the Army of Northern Virginia), having been accidentally mortally wounded by nervous North Carolina soldiers in a so-called "friendly" fire incident with grave repercussions. Fearing a sudden attack from Union cavalry known to have been in the area, the veteran North Carolina men had fired a volley that cut down Jackson on the night of May 2 in the haunted, darkened forests of Chancellorsville.[22]

Formulated earlier at headquarters, General Lee's ambitious plan called for unleashing the attack of Longstreet's First Corps to roll-up the Army of the Potomac's left, which he believed did not extend significantly all the way down Cemetery Ridge, and hung in mid-air amid the open fields: an ideal target. Therefore, he had planned to launch an attack in echelon northeast up the Emmitsburg Road to eventually gain the southern end of Cemetery Hill, which was located at the northern end of Cemetery

Ridge. The assault was calculated to swarm into the rear of the Federals defending Culp's Hill and East Cemetery Hill, where the bluecoat defenders had earlier thwarted General Ewell's Second Corps. Lee envisioned a simultaneous assault across a broad front: Ewell's Second Corps striking from the north, while Longstreet's First Corps hit from the south to deliver a simultaneous one-two punch that was calculated to deliver a devastating blow to achieve a decisive victory.

However, the Confederates, including the Texans, were now destined to pay a high price for a series of errors that had long delayed the assault and the wasting of so much precious time. The average common soldier in the Texas Brigade's ranks was not aware of all of the complex factors on multiple levels that had caused the extensive delay in launching the attack on July 2.

First, convinced by Longstreet's tactical reasoning and special request, Lee himself had early given Longstreet permission to wait for the arrival of Brigadier General Evander McIver Law's Alabama Brigade (five veteran regiments), Hood's Division, which had been far to the rear in guarding Lee's flank at New Guilford, Pennsylvania. For nearly an hour, this ill-fated decision delayed the flank march, which had finally began just after the noon hour, to gain Meade's left flank, because Law's Brigade, consisting of the 4th, 15th, 44th, 47th, and 48th Alabama regiments, was the last unit of Longstreet's Corps to reach the field. As Longstreet appreciated, young General Law was every inch of a fighter.

But other reasons existed to explain why not only had the entire morning of July 2 passed by without a Confederate attack to the far south, but also most of the afternoon, which had been wasted by Longstreet's tortured march south to get into a proper position to fulfill Lee's tactical ambition of rolling-up the Union Army's left flank. First and foremost, Longstreet's planned flank march of 5 miles—which was to have taken only around two hours—south had been doomed from the beginning. Faulty intelligence from Captain Samuel R. Johnston's early morning reconnaissance and the unknown nature of the ground to the south, including an elevated point near Black Horse Tavern, a two-story, stone structure located on March Creek and 2½ miles southwest of Gettysburg that would have revealed the trek (that of course needed to be unseen for Longstreet to retain the element of surprise) to vigilant Union signalmen perched atop Little Round Top, resulted in the time-consuming countermarch.

After these extensive delays of a hot day that also slowed down the march, Longstreet's Corps of two divisions, one under Hood and the other commanded by General McLaws, situated north of Hood, were in position and ready to attack by the late afternoon. From the edge of the darkened woodlands, Longstreet and his top officers, especially McLaws who faced the Peach Orchard salient, now realized that they faced a serious dilemma of the first magnitude: instead of the open ground leading to the southern end of Cemetery Hill and a wide open Emmitsburg Road that led northeast toward Gettysburg, the entire Third Corps of Sickles' Corps, bolstered by rows of Federal artillery whose iron and brass barrels glistened in the sun, blocked the way to the northeast toward Cemetery Hill.

Fate itself had seemingly conspired to sabotage Lee's battle-plan. Against Meade's wishes and to his utter astonishment, General Sickles, an independent-minded former New York City socialite and self-serving politician who was largely at odds with top leadership, especially General Meade, had earlier advanced his entire Third Corps of more than 10,000 troops from his assigned place (the south or left flank) on the Cemetery Ridge Line to the Peach Orchard on the Emmitsburg Road. He had decided to move forward to the higher ground along the Emmitsburg Road Ridge, because he was considered that his left would be vulnerable because Cemetery Ridge, which he was ordered to hold at the southern end of the line, decreased dramatically in height on the south and just north of Little Round Top.

In truth, this commanding ridge, especially the hill of the Peach Orchard salient, along the Emmitsburg Road offered an overall better (or so it seemed to the free-thinking Dan Sickles, who was not impressed by West Point-trained officers because of his arrogance and ego of considerable size) defensive position that was higher in elevation than the lower end of Cemetery Ridge before Little Round Top's northern end, because this sector (that Meade wanted him to occupy to anchor his left flank) consisted of low ground, which was vulnerable in consequence. However, the advance of the entire Third Corps so far west without orders compromised Meade's entire Cemetery Ridge defensive line, especially his southern flank that was now advanced far before his main defensive position.

The early morning intelligence by Captain Johnston, who almost certainly never advanced as far as Little Round Top, hastily gathered that morning, about visible Federal dispositions upon which Lee's plan had been based was now entirely obsolete by the late afternoon, because of Sickles' advance so far before the main Cemetery Ridge defensive line. Therefore, no one had realized that Longstreet's much-anticipated open road to deliver a powerful blow to Meade's unprotected left flank was now blocked by thousands of veteran soldiers of the Third Corps, until it was too late.

But like Longstreet and now the highly-respected leader chosen to begin the day's assault from the extreme south, Hood did not like what he saw—thousands of good fighting men in the lengthy, blue ranks of the Third Corps ready for battle just northeast up the Emmitsburg Road. Because Sickles had formed a lengthy defensive line whose northern arm (that ran northeast along the Emmitsburg Road) and the southern arm (that ran along the Wheatfield Road that extended southeast toward Little Round Top) faced any Confederate advance northeastward up the Emmitsburg Road and toward Gettysburg, this new tactical situation now required a frontal instead of a flank assault, which Lee had originally envisioned to turn Meade's left flank.

Indeed, Sickles' move around two-thirds of a mile west to the high ground had drastically changed the entire tactical situation to completely sabotage—although unintentionally—Lee's master plan. However, the Third Corps' advance so far west to gain the high ground of the Emmitsburg Road Ridge and the Peach Orchard and subsequent deployments resulted in Sickles' troops having to cover a far wider front.

This *ad hoc* tactical situation left the Third Corps's defensive lines weak because the independent-minded New Yorkers had too few troops to protect the sprawling length of his new advanced position so far before Meade's main defensive line. Most importantly, this inherent weakness was especially the case on the Sickles' far left flank, which was weak and vulnerable, because of his line's over-extension that now left the southernmost flank dangling in mid-air: a golden tactical opportunity for Lee's attackers to turn and roll-up Meade's entire left flank.

Consequently and as General Meade, a precise former civilian engineer who had rightly become infuriated by Sickles' unauthorized advance before the main line, and his top generals fully realized, Sickles' push west and all the way to the Emmitsburg Road Ridge had created a greater tactical opportunity for the success of Longstreet's upcoming assault. Indeed, with the limited number of available Union troops unable to cover such a wide front, the Third Corps was spread so thin that Sickles was unable to anchor its left on Little Round Top, or its right on the Second Corps's left that remained in line on Cemetery Ridge, as Meade had ordered. A strict West Pointer (Class of 1853) and Mexican-American War veteran who was well known for a short fuse and hot temper that earned him recognition as "the Old Snapping Turtle," General Meade's disdain for political generals reached a new high on July 2, and for ample good reason.

Hood's Veteran Texas Scouts Advance

Before reaching the Emmitsburg Road, which the Warfield Ridge intersected, because haphazard, inadequate Confederate intelligence had already failed miserably on July 2, Hood had dispatched his best Texas scouts to gather reliable information—he rightly trusted these experienced men—and the most recent intelligence about the unfamiliar ground that lay before him. The native Kentuckian knew that the little information that had been gathered by Captain Johnston's earlier reconnaissance ordered by Lee to the south to ascertain the location and strength of the Union left flank was badly out-dated by this time.

Therefore, General Hood's orders to the six-man team of scouts mostly from his old 4th Texas, but also Wilson J. Barbee, 1st Texas, to go forth to ascertain the true situation was important. These were dependable men with ample western frontier experience and skills in intelligence gathering, including behind enemy lines. Hood's decision to order this party of trusty scouts to embark on a vital intelligence-gathering mission to acquire the latest information about Federal dispositions, especially the exact location of the Union left flank, was extremely wise under uncertain circumstances.

For ample good reason, Hood was no longer relying on General Lee's or Longstreet's headquarters because they were operating on and had made tactical decisions based on outdated intelligence that was now absolutely worthless, after General Sickles' advance west with his entire Third Corps. From "my picked Texas scouts [who were sent forward] to ascertain the position of the enemy's extreme left flank," in Hood's words, the opportunistic general so beloved by his Texas soldiers shortly correctly learned "that I could march through the open woodland pasture around Round Top, and assault the enemy in flank and rear; that their wagon trains were parked in rear of their line, and were badly exposed to our attack in that direction."[23]

Most importantly and incredibly, General Hood learned from his just-returned scouts around 3:30 p.m. that Big Round Top, situated just to Little Round Top's south, was free of Union troops, along with the area to the rear immediately east of Big Round Top: vital information not ascertained by Captain Johnston. Even more, Sickles' left flank was weak and vulnerable, hanging in mid-air. Colonel Charles H. Weygant, 12th New York Volunteer Infantry, lamented the weakness of Sickles' left for a long list of very good reasons: "When the battle opened there was nothing to our left but a section of [Captain James E.] Smith's battery [4th Independent New York Battery positioned atop the narrow crest of Houck's Ridge], the remaining guns of which were in position a short distance to our rear."[24]

However, as Longstreet discovered in regard to Lee's ambitious tactics that he had attempted to alter for permission to conduct a wider flank movement farther south around the Round Tops, Hood's prior orders for the assault were unbending and without flexibility because Lee's mind had been made-up: "The instructions I received were to place my division across the Emmitsburg road, form a line of battle, and attack" up the Emmitsburg Road.[25]

But the ever-aggressive and flexible General Hood would not be denied. He was only too aware that top Confederate leadership, including Lee, had already failed to live-up to lofty expectations, because of fast-paced recent developments and that they were unaware of the true tactical situation on the far south. After all, Lee was headquartered in the Widow Thompson house, which was located just northwest of Gettysburg, and far from Longstreet's sector far to the southeast.

Therefore, Hood's well-honed veteran instincts rose to the fore (not unlike Sickles in moving west from the vulnerable, lower end of Cemetery Ridge, where the high ground ended to leave Third Corps defenders on low ground just north of Little Round Top and at a tactical disadvantage) because he sensed that his division, which was to open the assault northeastward in echelon from the southwest, would be cut to pieces by a strict adherence to Lee's original orders. Based on faulty intelligence and as noted, Lee's earlier orders had not taken into account the westward advance of Sickles' entire Third Corps of two divisions to the Peach Orchard to secure the all-important high ground (the Emmitsburg Road Ridge) along the dusty Emmitsburg Road. Of course, Lee's orders had been written in part to avoid natural obstacles and rough terrain, like the Devil's Den, in regard to the upcoming assault.

Dan Sickles' Vulnerable Far Left Flank

General Hood knew that if he obeyed Lee's orders to the letter in regard to attacking northeast up the east side of the Emmitsburg Road, then the troops, especially his precious Texas troops, would be raked by a blistering flank fire from a row of New York artillery pieces of a fine 135-man battery positioned atop Houck's Ridge and a good many bluecoat infantrymen of the Third Corps, whose lengthy battle-line extended as far south as the Devil's Den, at the ridge's southern end. Here, Sickles' left was held by a brigade (the Army of the Potomac's largest) of more than 2,000 men of half a dozen regiments, along with two sharpshooter companies and a six-gun New York battery, under Brigadier General John Henry Hobat Ward, of Major General David Bell Birney's First Division, Third Corps. Born in New York City in 1823 and educated at Trinity College, Harford, Connecticut, Ward was a capable and experienced commander, who had served with distinction in the Mexican-American War like Lee and Longstreet.

After performing an invaluable reconnaissance in the Emmitsburg Road sector that revealed Longstreet had been extending his line farther south, members of Hiram Berdan's Sharpshooters had earlier alerted General Ward of the growing threat. This vital intelligence had led to the all-important securing of the strategic high ground of Houck's Ridge, which was the first high ground situated just west of Plum Run and before Little Round Top, to protect the weak left flank of the Army of the Potomac. Quite simply and despite its strength, Ward's command was too small to defend the far left flank of Meade's Army.

Consequently, Houck's Ridge and the Devil's Den, located at the ridge's southern end, was now the true left flank of the Union Army, before the later establishment of the defense of Little Round Top (destined to become Meade's second left flank) by the four regiments of Colonel Strong Vincent's Third Brigade, First Division, Fifth Corps. Along with Houck's Ridge, the Devil's Den, of little importance to local farmers because nothing could grow there because of the expanse of massive boulders and ledges, had suddenly become the most important spot on the Gettysburg battlefield on the afternoon of July 2.

Therefore, General Ward's key mission of holding this crucial high ground—Houck's Ridge and the Devil's Den—before the heights of Little Round Top, farther east on the other side of Plum Run and its boulder-strewn valley, could not have been more important by this time. Ironically, General Meade, back on Cemetery Ridge at his headquarters in the Lydia Leister House on the Taneytown Road to the northeast, never saw or knew anything about the Devil's Den at this time.

Because of the excellent defensive position of these veteran Union troops on the dominant high ground of Houck's Ridge, this elevated fire from the east would rake and enfilade the right of Hood's advancing troops to ensure not only high losses, but also perhaps even the early breaking-up of the assault, while his attack northeast up the Emmitsburg Road would then run headlong into the considerable artillery might of the formidable Third Corps at the Peach Orchard salient.

All in all, therefore, Hood envisioned the horrific prospect of his crack division—the army's best fighting men—getting hit hard by a frontal, right flank, and rear fire, if he advanced northeast up the Emmitsburg Road as ordered by Lee. Ironically, to Hood's astute tactical way-of-thinking that revealed his high experience level and tactical insights, Lee's once-bright idea of unleashing a devastating flank attack now resulted in a potential flank disaster. This would indeed be the case if Lee's orders were now followed to the letter and as earlier planned back at his Widow Thompson House headquarters located on the Seminary Ridge's crest (General Meade's headquarters was situated on parallel Cemetery Ridge) and immediately on the north side of the main road, the Chambersburg Pike, leading into Gettysburg from the west. Here, just northwest of Gettysburg, Lee had long fumed about Stuart's absence, which reduced his intelligence-gathering capabilities.

Therefore, like Longstreet, the gifted West Pointer, age forty-two, who had appealed in vain for Lee to alter his offensive plans, Hood attempted to obtain permission from Longstreet for a wide flank movement with his division (like Longstreet had desired to accomplish with his entire corps) around the Round Tops and based on the most recent intelligence gained from his reliable Texas scouts. These Lone Star State men had ascertained that an extensive wagon train lay ripe for the taking in the Round Top's rear along the north–south running Taneytown Road, where Meade's headquarters was situated to the north in the Lydia Leister (she was a widow like Mary Thompson) House.

Most of all, Hood, consequently, wanted to outflank the Union left by sending a brigade south to circle around the Round Tops and strike into Meade's left flank from the south and into his rear from the east. Hood hoped that the scout's timely intelligence would convince Longstreet to alter the battle-plan once Lee gained the latest intelligence to understand the wisdom of such a maneuver.

However, to their shock, both Generals Longstreet and Hood were rebuffed (four times in Hood's case during this ill-fated afternoon when time was precious and rapidly fading away), but the stubborn Lee who would not bend or give an inch, because the overall tactics of turning Meade's left flank remained exactly the same and he felt that he possessed the best plan. In this sense, Lee's tactical inflexibility reflected his outsized ego and a shocking degree of hubris born of so many prior successes across Virginia. Quite simply, he had won too many victories to start doubting his own tactics and decision-making processes, or having second doubts at the last minute.

But to be fair to Lee and his decision-making at this time, he also realized that no additional time could be wasted on a day which so much valuable time had already slipped away. Having already made up his mind and almost as if not believing the most recent intelligence reports in an overly-ambitious campaign distinguished by the lack of good intelligence—Stuart and his three cavalry brigades were still absent from the army—that had left him groping in the dark, Lee was most of all determined to remain true to his original plan of continuing the assault in a bid to destroy the Army of the Potomac with one overpowering blow. Most of all to Lee, this meant rolling up Meade's left by an assault northeastward and parallel to the Emmitsburg Road, according to the originally-designed plan. Longstreet, therefore, had no choice but to put aside all of his objections and those of Hood, despite the value of the recent intelligence.

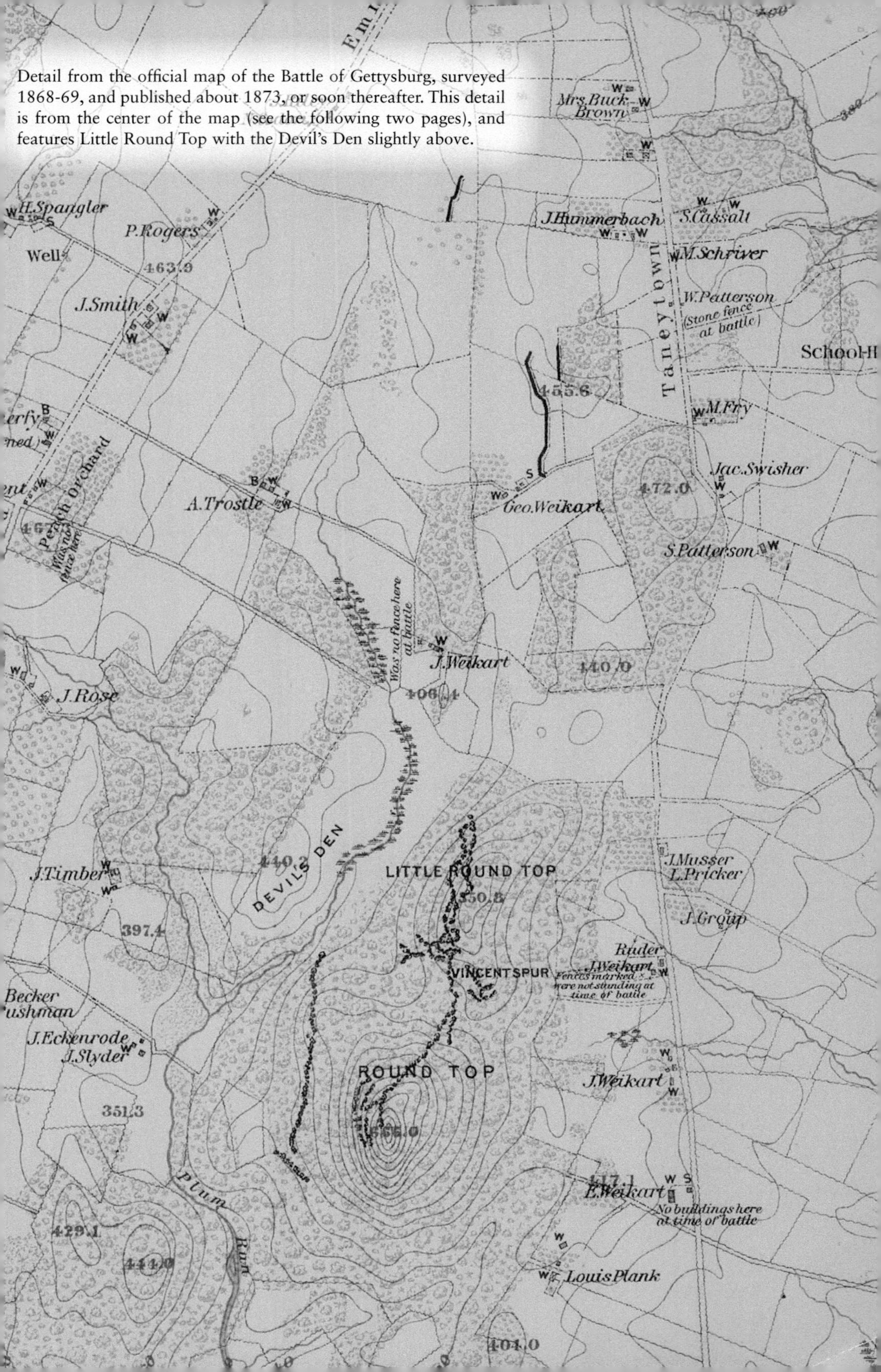

Detail from the official map of the Battle of Gettysburg, surveyed 1868-69, and published about 1873, or soon thereafter. This detail is from the center of the map (see the following two pages), and features Little Round Top with the Devil's Den slightly above.

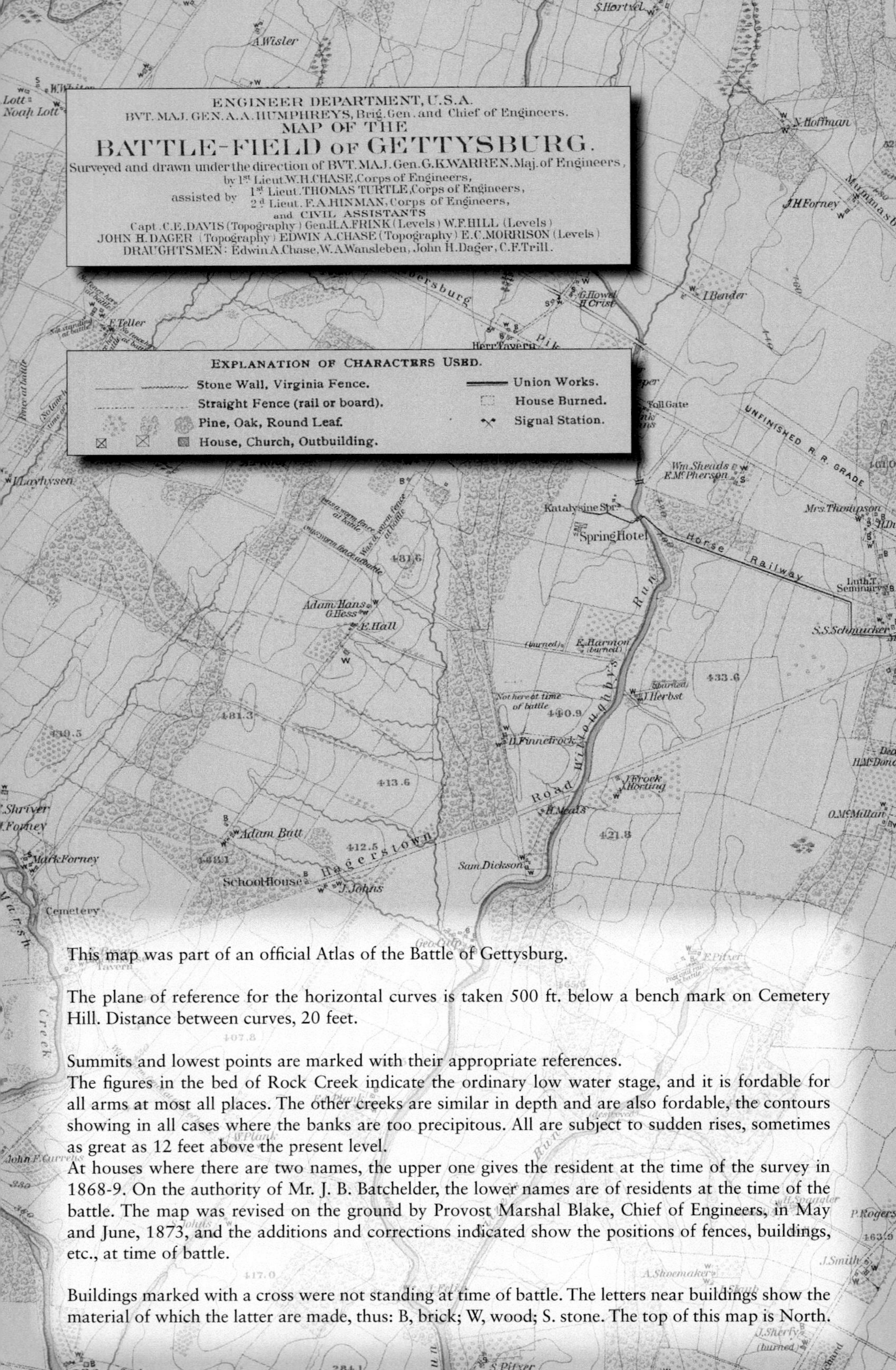

This map was part of an official Atlas of the Battle of Gettysburg.

The plane of reference for the horizontal curves is taken 500 ft. below a bench mark on Cemetery Hill. Distance between curves, 20 feet.

Summits and lowest points are marked with their appropriate references.
The figures in the bed of Rock Creek indicate the ordinary low water stage, and it is fordable for all arms at most all places. The other creeks are similar in depth and are also fordable, the contours showing in all cases where the banks are too precipitous. All are subject to sudden rises, sometimes as great as 12 feet above the present level.
At houses where there are two names, the upper one gives the resident at the time of the survey in 1868-9. On the authority of Mr. J. B. Batchelder, the lower names are of residents at the time of the battle. The map was revised on the ground by Provost Marshal Blake, Chief of Engineers, in May and June, 1873, and the additions and corrections indicated show the positions of fences, buildings, etc., at time of battle.

Buildings marked with a cross were not standing at time of battle. The letters near buildings show the material of which the latter are made, thus: B, brick; W, wood; S. stone. The top of this map is North.

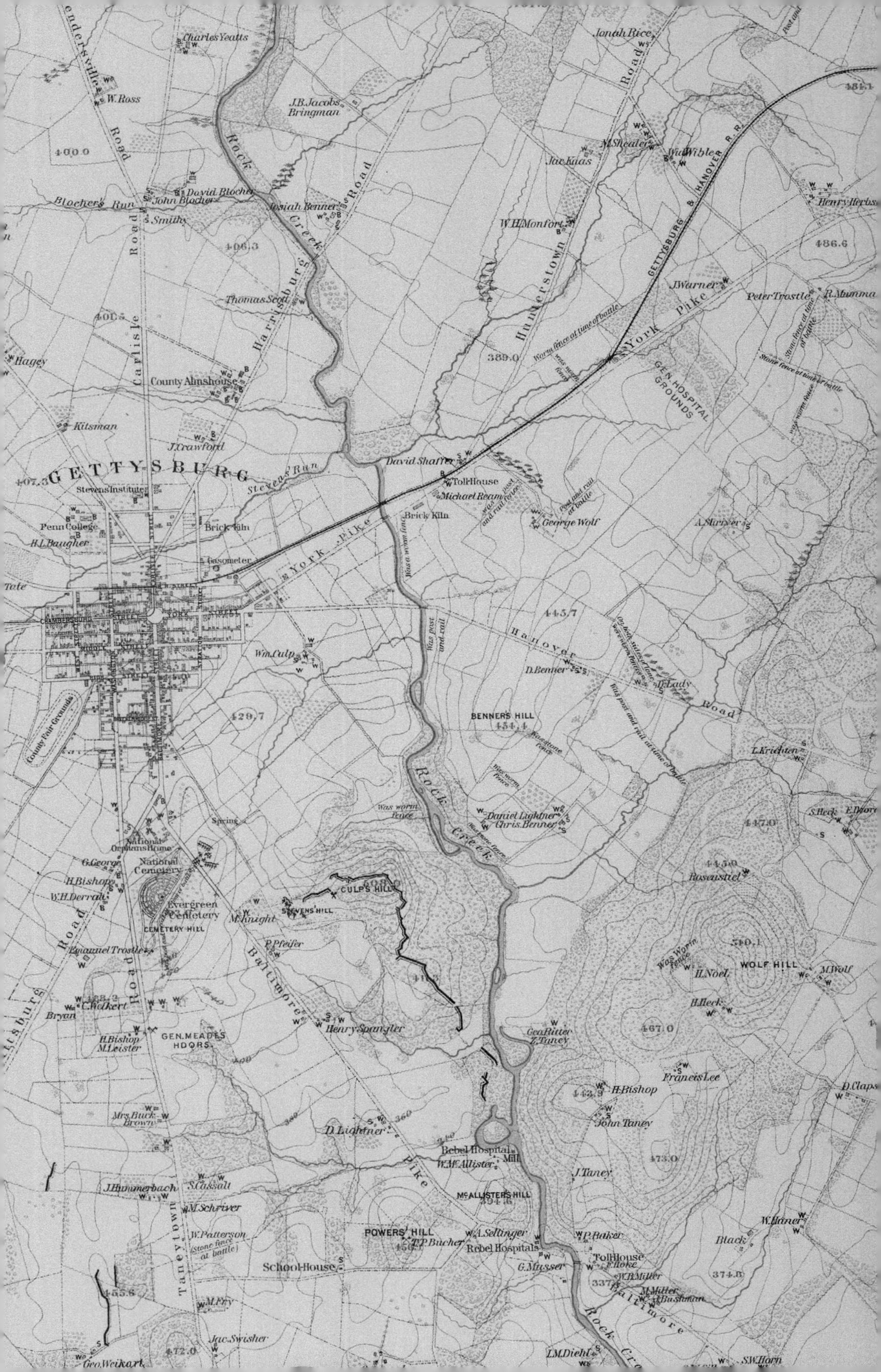
GETTYSBURG
Rock Creek
Harrisburg Road
Carlisle Road
Hunterstown Road
York Pike
Hanover Road
Baltimore Pike
Taneytown Road
GETTYSBURG & HANOVER R.R.
GEN. HOSPITAL GROUNDS
BENNERS HILL
CULPS HILL
STEVENS HILL
CEMETERY HILL
WOLF HILL
POWERS HILL
McALLISTERS HILL
GEN. MEADES HDQRS.
National Cemetery
Evergreen Cemetery
County Almshouse
Stevens Institute
Penn College
County Fair Grounds
Rebel Hospital
Rebel Hospitals
School-House
Toll House
Brick Kiln
Gasometer
Blochers Run
Stevens Run
Charles Yeatts
W. Ross
J.B. Jacobs
Bringman
David Blocher
John Blocher
Smith
Josiah Benner
Thomas Scott
Hagey
Kitsman
J. Crawford
H.L. Baugher
Jonah Rice
M. Shealer
Jac. Kaas
Wid. Wible
W.H. Monfort
J. Warner
Peter Trostle
Henry Herbst
David Shaffer
Michael Ream
George Wolf
A. Shriver
Wm. Culp
D. Benner
L. Krichten
Daniel Lightner
Chris. Benner
Rosenstiel
H. Noel
H. Heck
M. Wolf
Geo. Ritter
Z. Taney
H. Bishop
Francis Lee
John Taney
J. Taney
D. Claps
M. Knight
P. Pfeifer
Henry Spangler
G. George
W.H. Derrah
Emanuel Trostle
C. Weikert
Bryan
M. Leister
Mrs. Buck
Brown
D. Lightner
W. McAllister
J. Hummerbach
S. Cassatt
M. Schriver
W. Patterson
(Stone fence at battle)
A. Sellinger
T.P. Bucher
G. Musser
P. Baker
W.R. Miller
M. Miller
M. Bushman
W. Haner
Black
M. Fry
Jac. Swisher
Geo. Weikart
I.M. Diehl
S.W. Horn
400.0
406.3
400.5
407.3
389.0
486.6
445.7
454.4
429.7
447.0
445.0
467.0
473.0
394.6
455.6
472.0
374.8

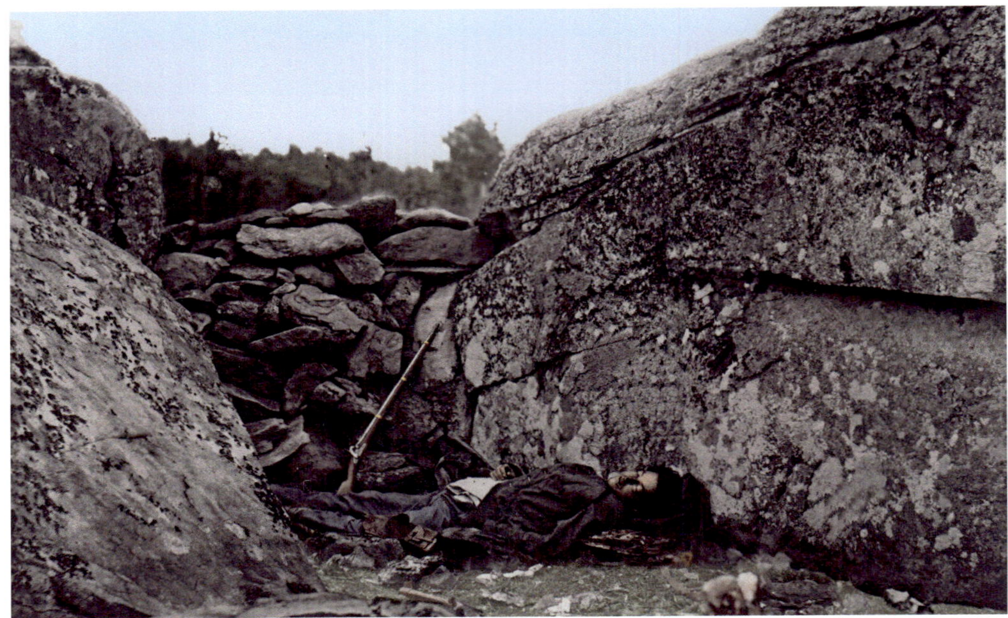

This is a colorized version of one of the most iconic photographs of the Civil War—the dead Southern "sharpshooter" of the Devil's Den. This famous photo was taken on July 6, 1863, which was four days after the young soldier was killed during the attack on the Devil's Den. Erected on the night of July 2, 1863, the rock wall situated between the two boulders protected Southern marksmen, when they targeted the defenders of Little Round Top (in the background) just east on the other side of Plum Run.

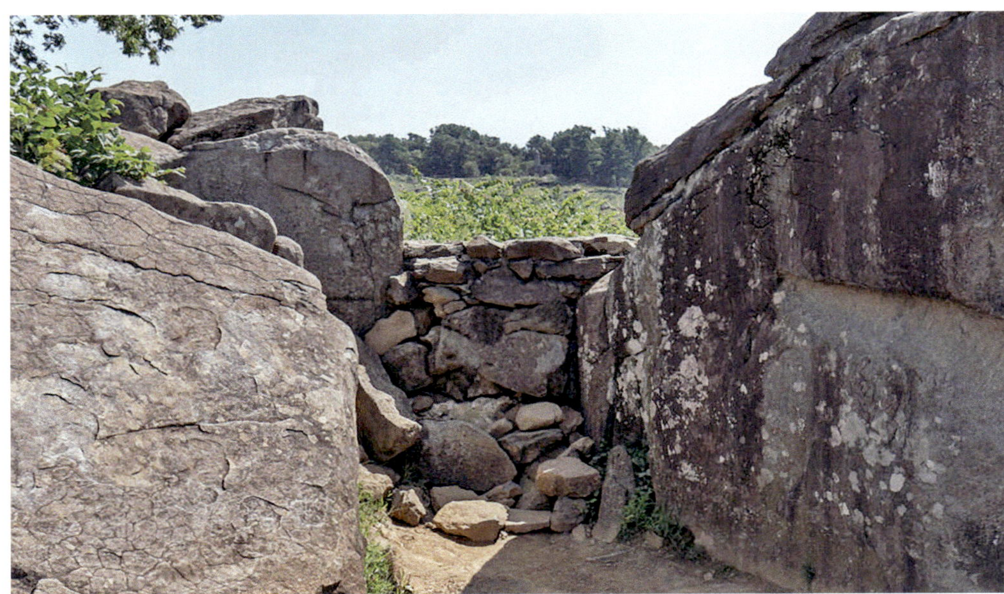

A modern view of the same location. The imposing stone monument to the brave men of the 44th New York Volunteer Infantry, Colonel Strong Vincent's Brigade, can be seen atop Little Round Top.

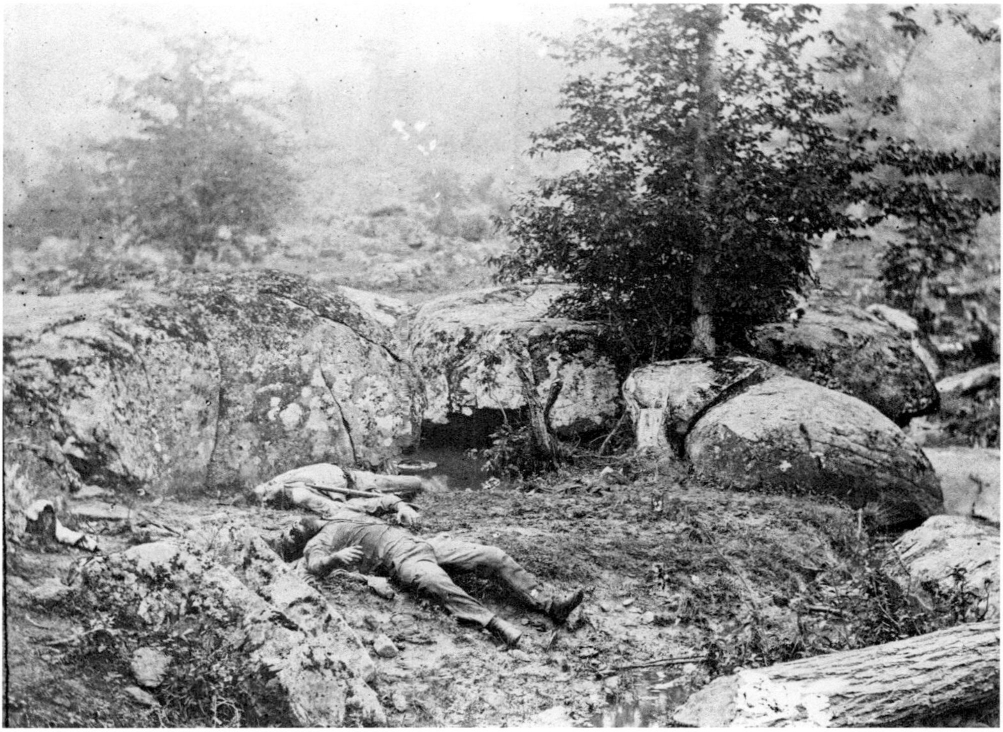

Two dead Southern soldiers in the "Slaughter Pen", which was located between the Devil's Den and the Round Tops. This famous photograph was taken on July 6, 1863, which was four days after the two young men were killed.

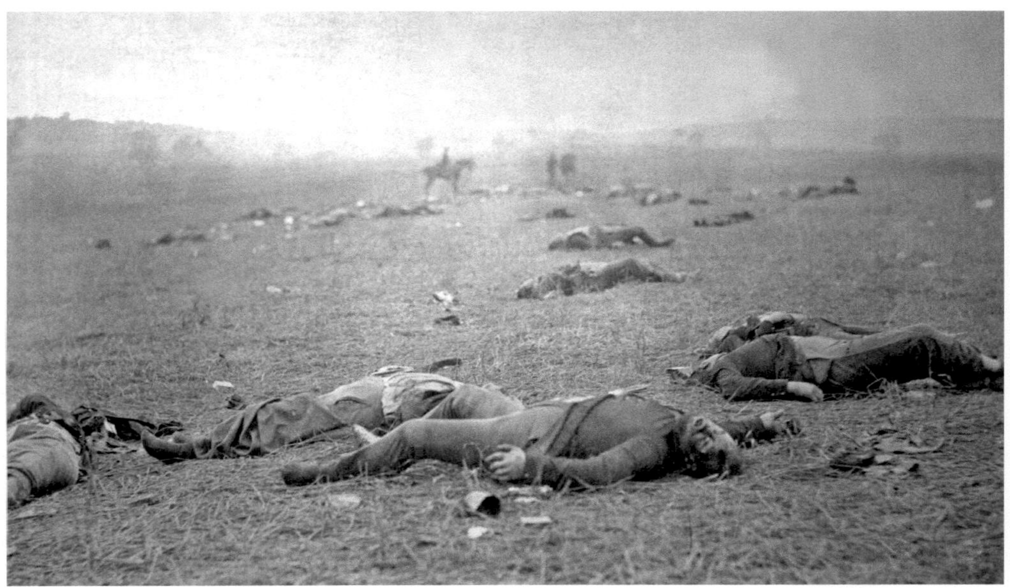

The grim harvest of the second day at Gettysburg. This photo of Union dead was taken on July 5. These were fallen soldiers of the Third Corps, which defended the Devil's Den.

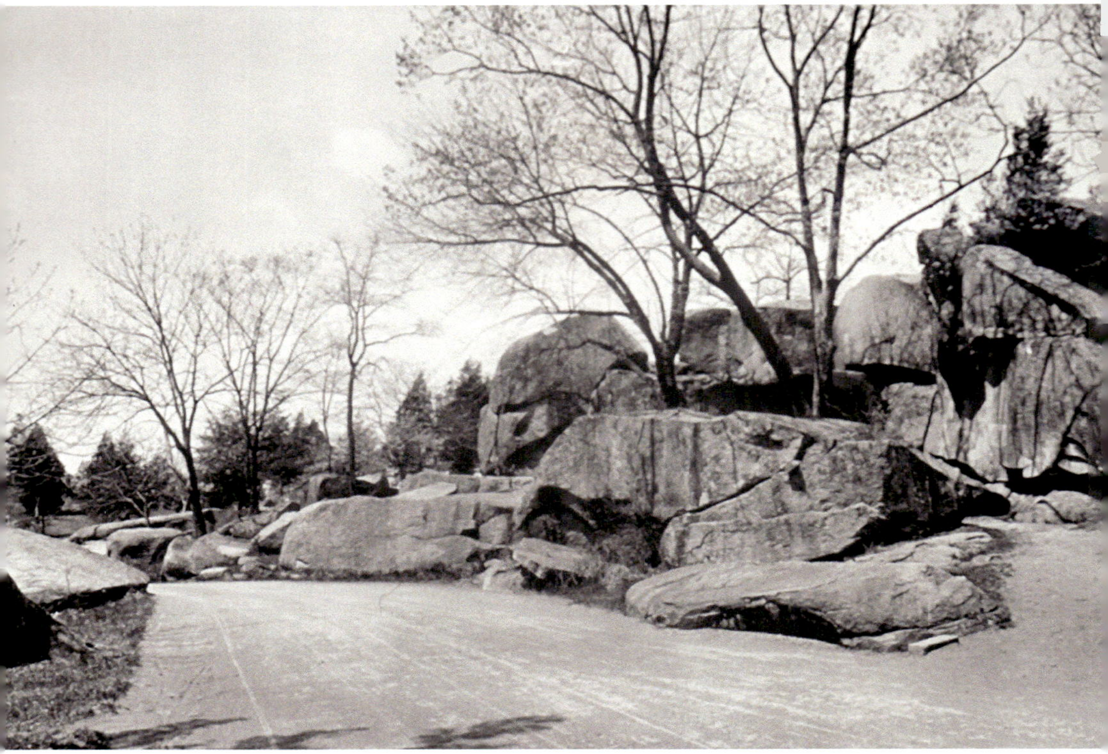

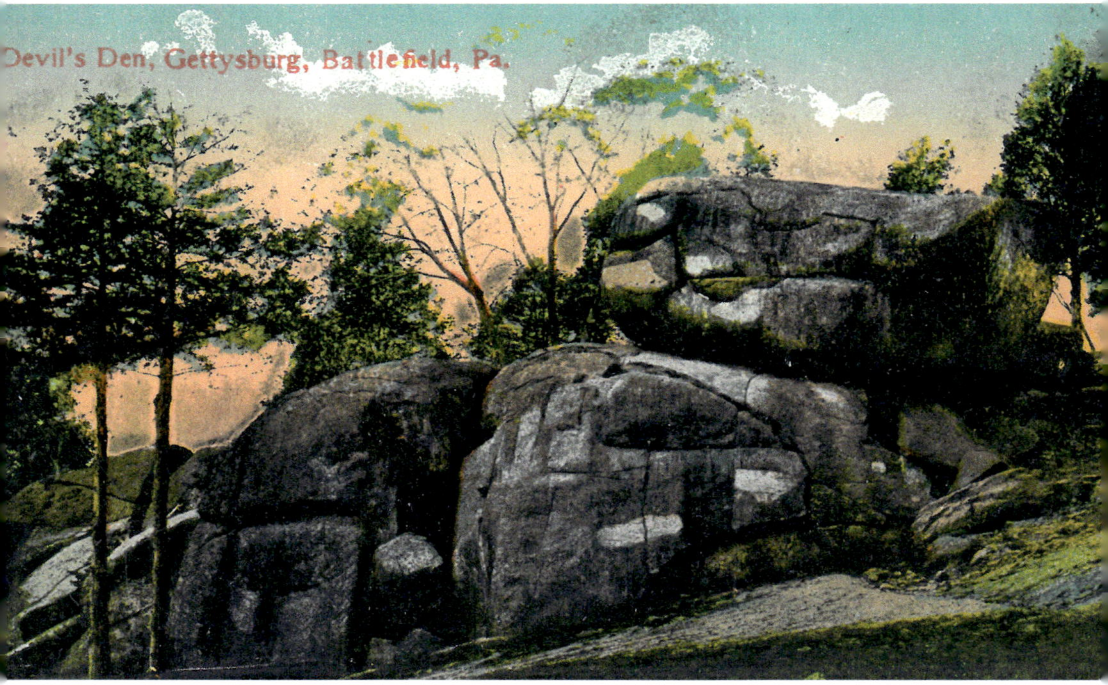

A *c.* 1910 colorized postcard photograph of the eastern face of the Devil's Den, which has been the most popular view of this hard-fought sector on the bloody second day.

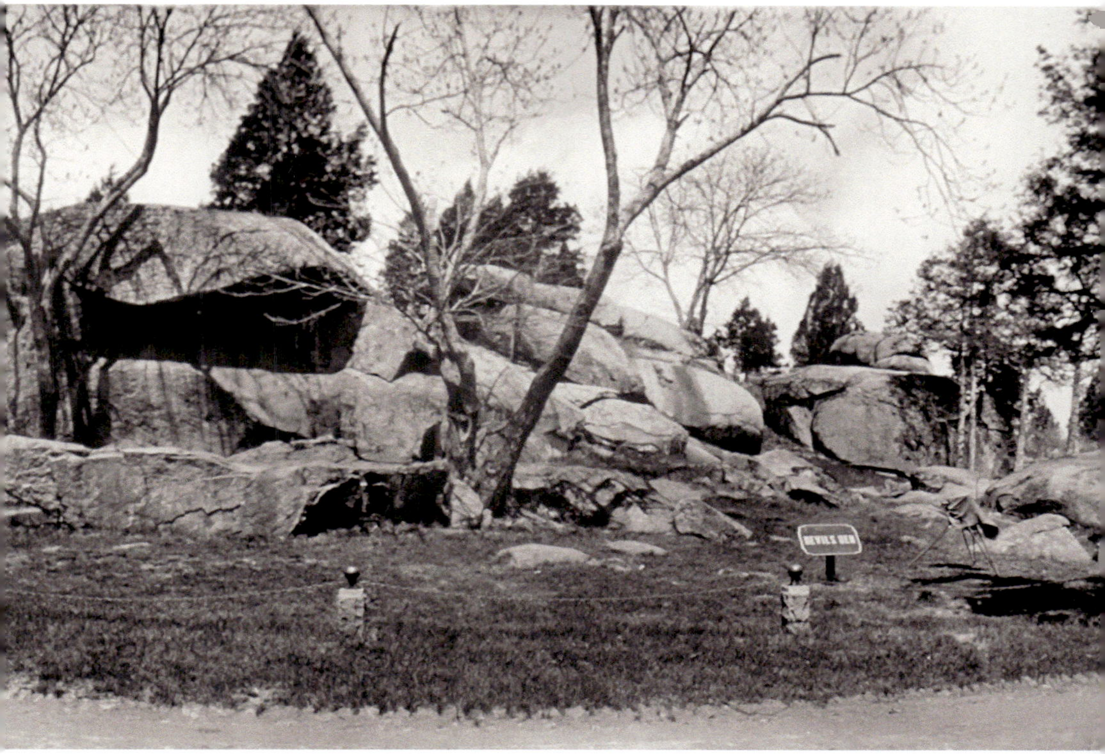

Panoramic view of the huge boulders of the Devil's Den that became Gettysburg's Most Hellish Battleground on the decisive afternoon of July 2, 1863.

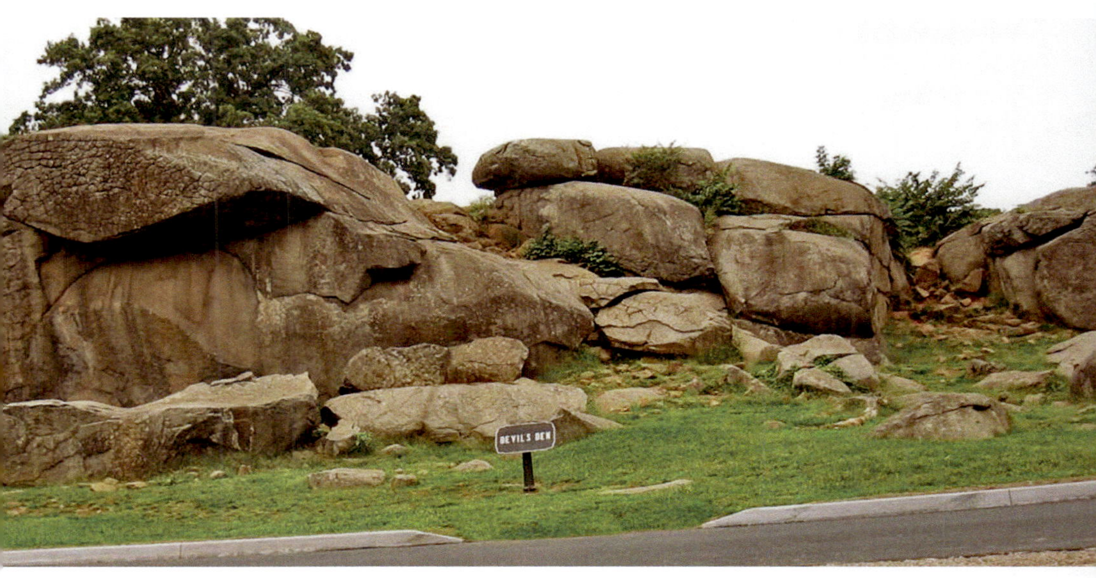

A modern view of one of today's most heavily-visited sectors on the entire Gettysburg Battlefield—the unearthly-looking landscape of the Devil's Den.

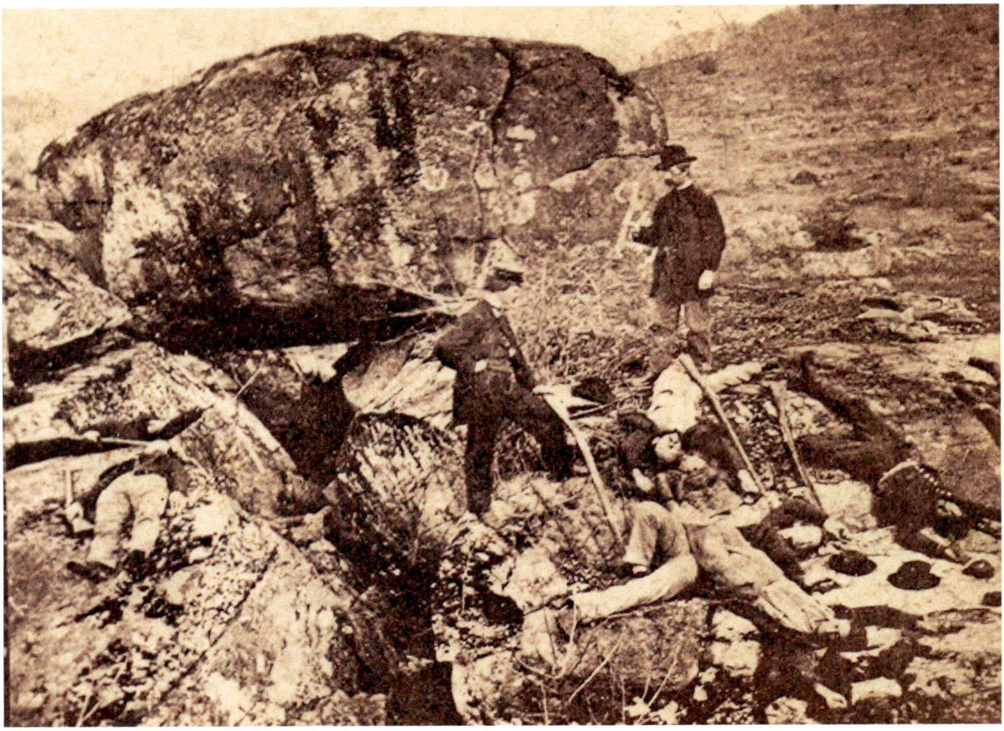

A photograph of Union soldiers posing as dead bodies atop a boulder of the Devil's Den. These "fake" photos were taken at some point during the fall of 1863.

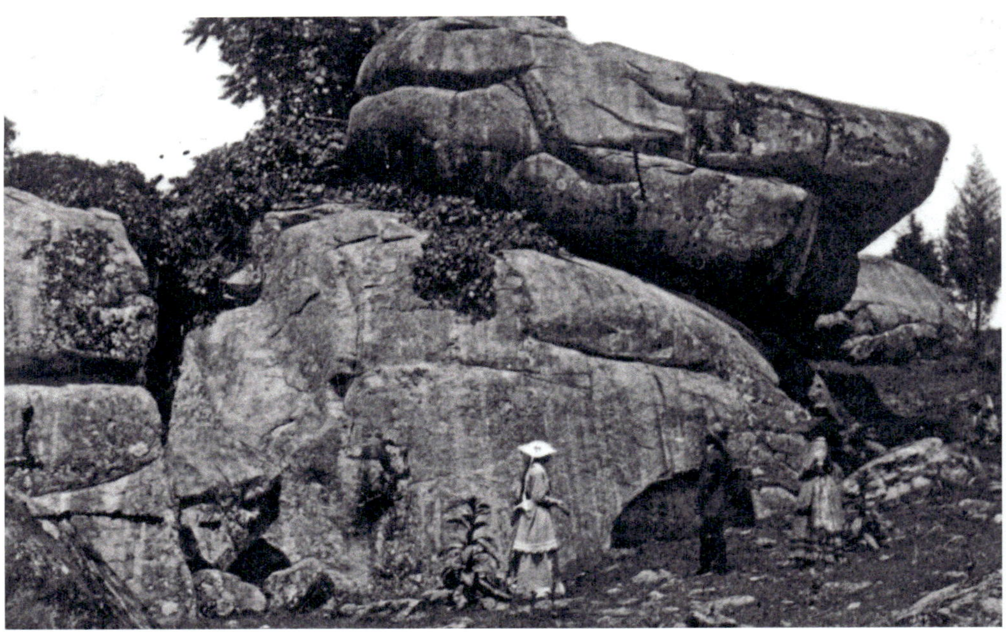

The giant boulders of the eastern face of the Devil's Den have been long popular with tourists since the battle and to this today.

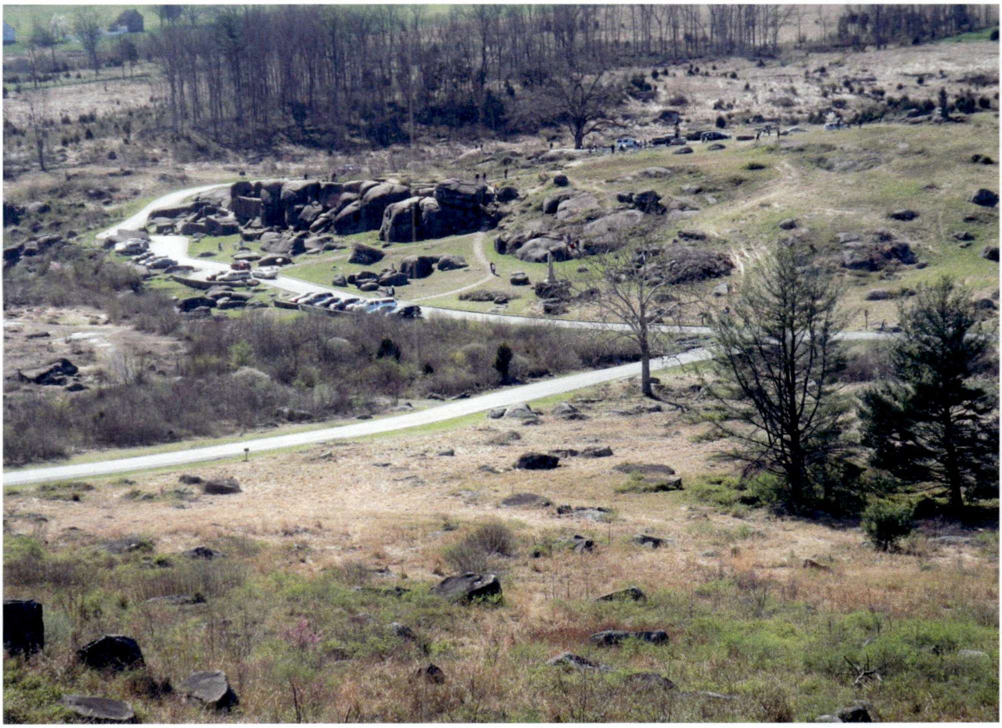

Devils Den from Little Round Top. *Courtesy: Wilson44691, 2 April 2016, Wikimedia Commons*

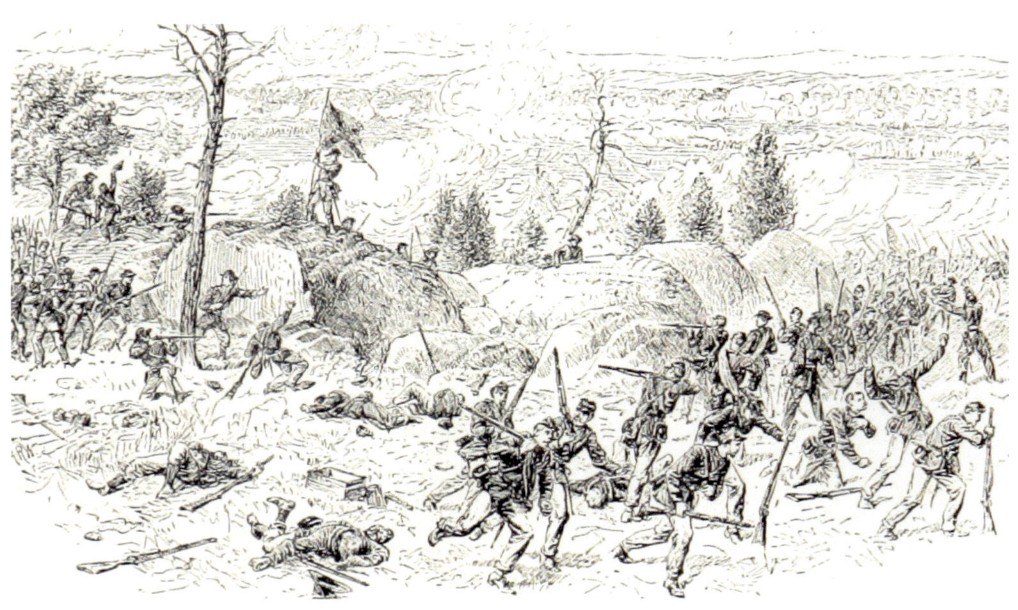

The struggle for Devil's Den, from a wartime sketch reproduced in the 1887 book *Battles and Leaders of the Civil War*, being for the most part contributions by Union and Confederate officers, based upon "the Century War Series", volume 3.

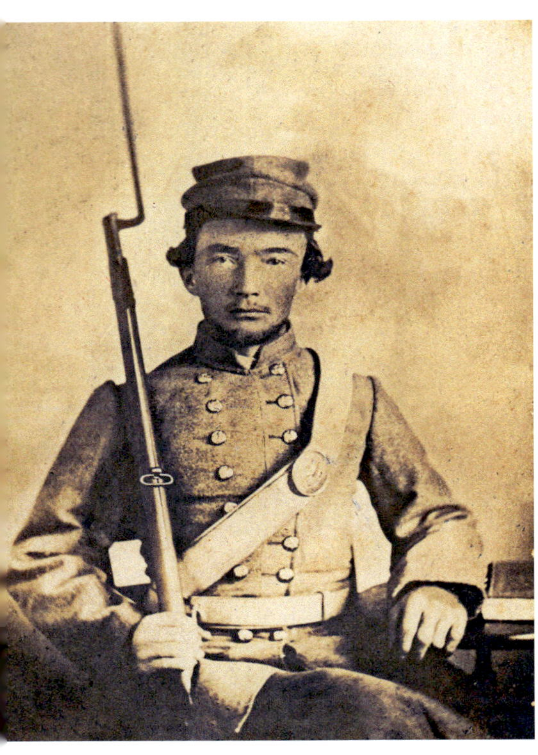

Rare 1861 photograph of a proud volunteer of a Georgia Infantry Regiment, Army of Northern Virginia. *Author's Collection*

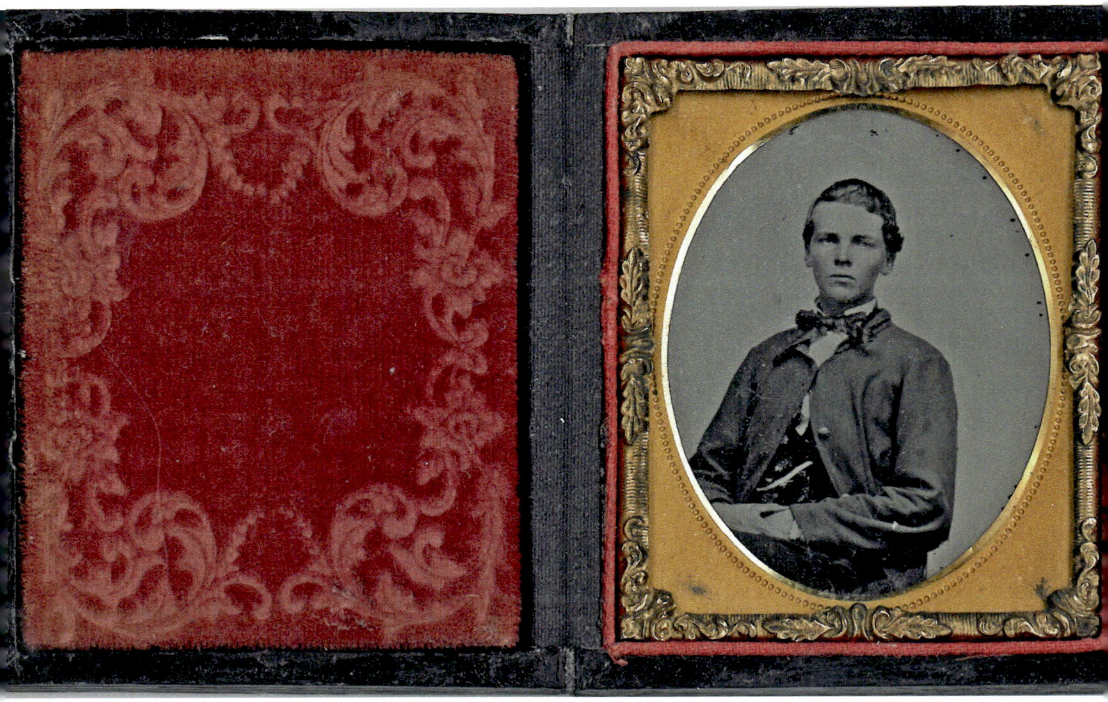

Tintype of a young Union volunteer wearing a civilian vest and expensive gold chain and watch under his blue uniform coat. *Author's Collection*

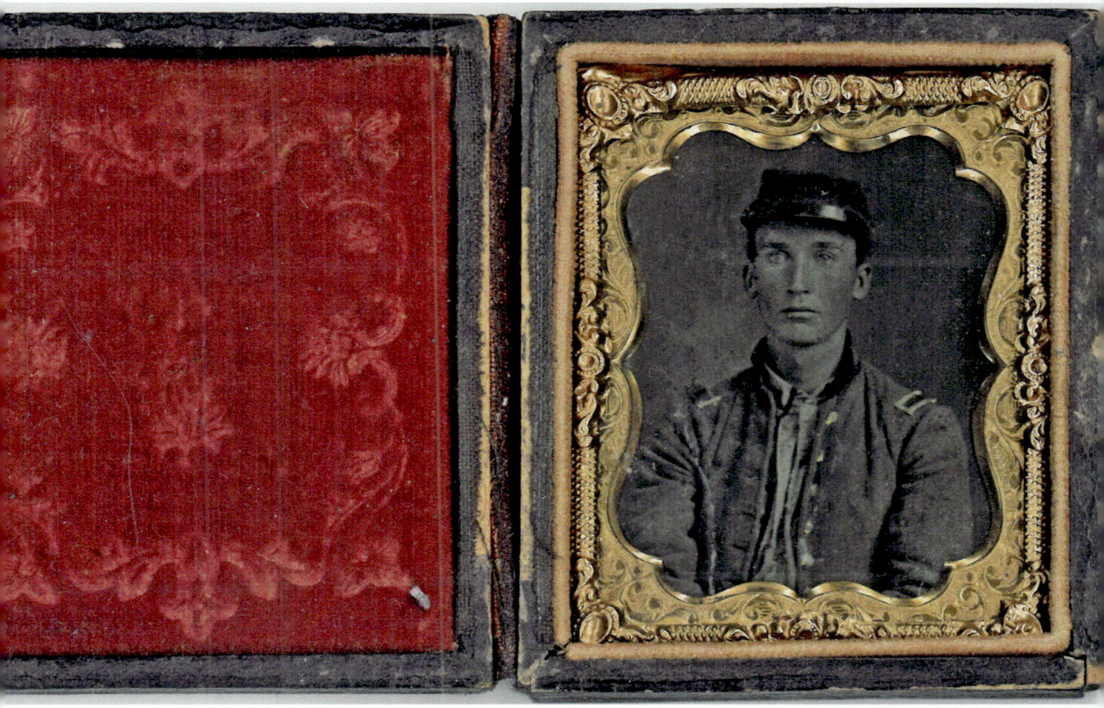

Above: Tintype of a Union lieutenant of an infantry regiment. He might have commanded his company on the battlefield, if the captain was killed or wounded in action, which was often the case. *Author's Collection*

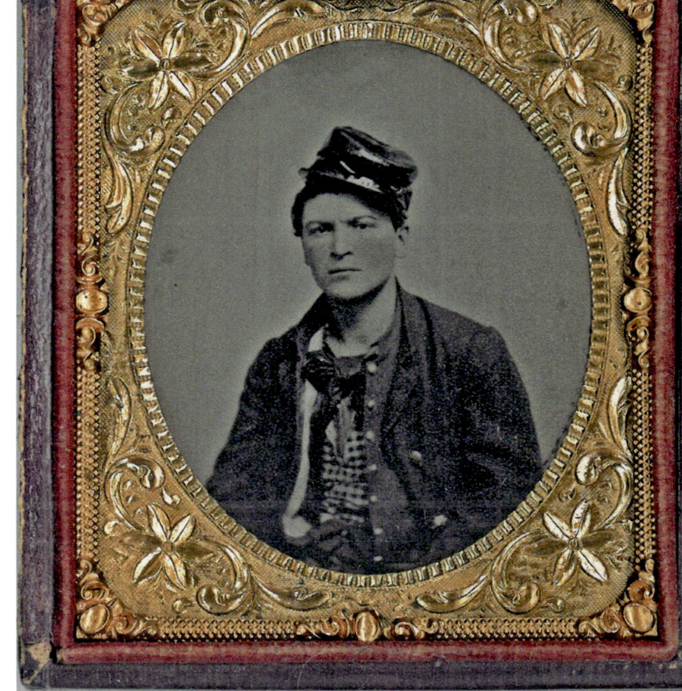

Left: A fresh-faced Union volunteer wearing his new kepi at a jaunty angle. He also wears a checkered shirt under his uniform coat. This photo was taken not long—perhaps on the same day—after his enlistment in an infantry regiment. *Author's Collection*

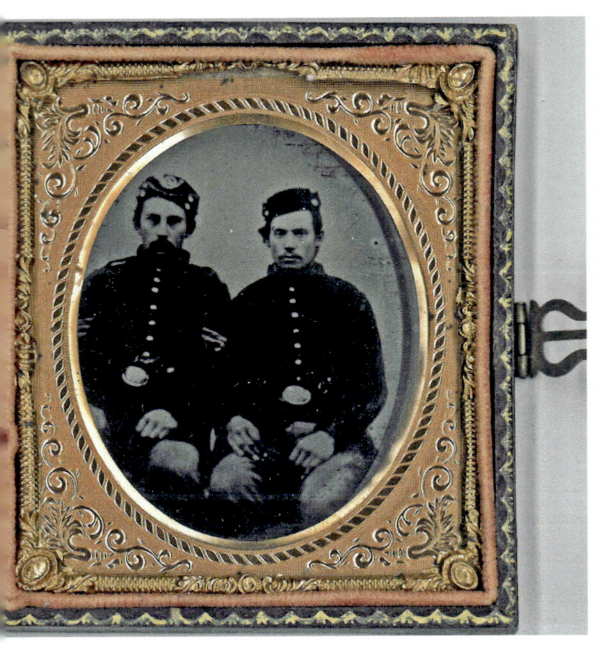

Two Union soldiers, probably members of the same company of their infantry regiment, posing for the photographer. *Author's Collection*

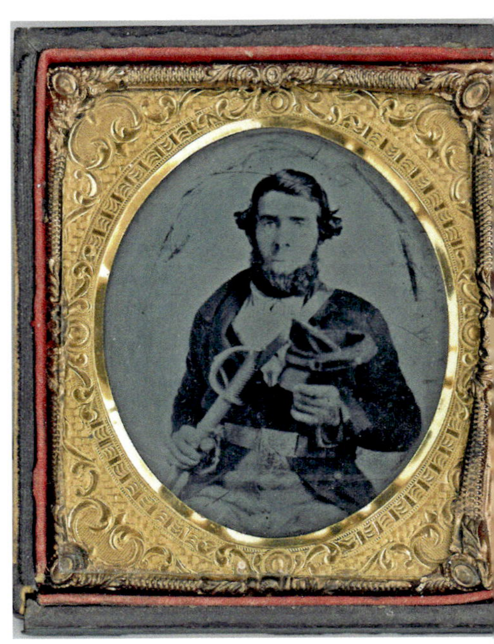

Bearded Southern cavalryman proudly posing with his prized sword in one hand and his kepi in the other. *Author's Collection*

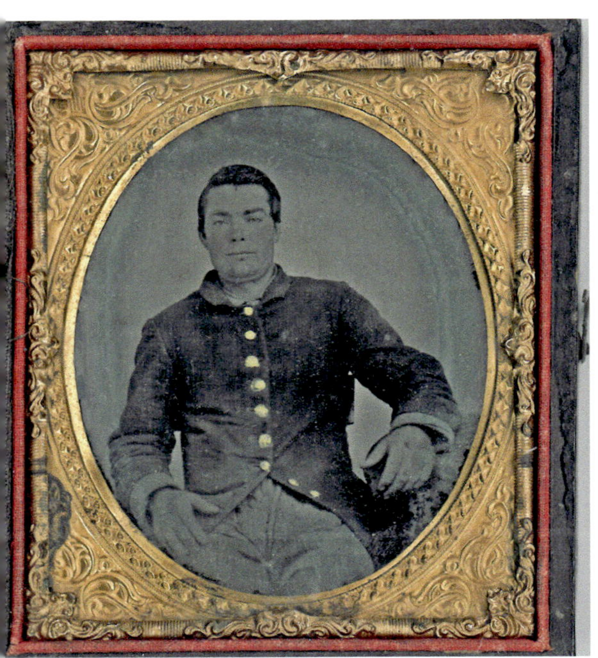

A typical Federal volunteer who risked his life on the battlefield in the war to save the Union.

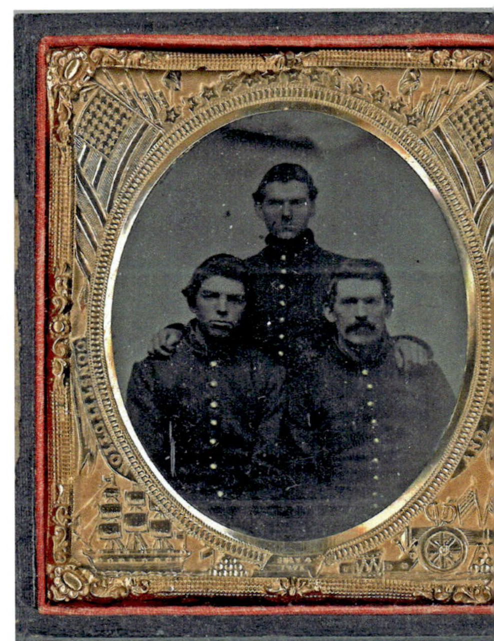

Tintype of three friends who fought for the Union, perhaps at the Battle of Gettysburg. The patriotism of these infantrymen has been appropriately represented on the brass mat of the photograph by the words of "Constitution and the Union." *Author's Collection*

Left: Tintype of a very young Southerner who is wearing a common soldier's kepi. It is not known but he might have served as a drummer boy, who were mostly teenagers or preteens. *Author's Collection*

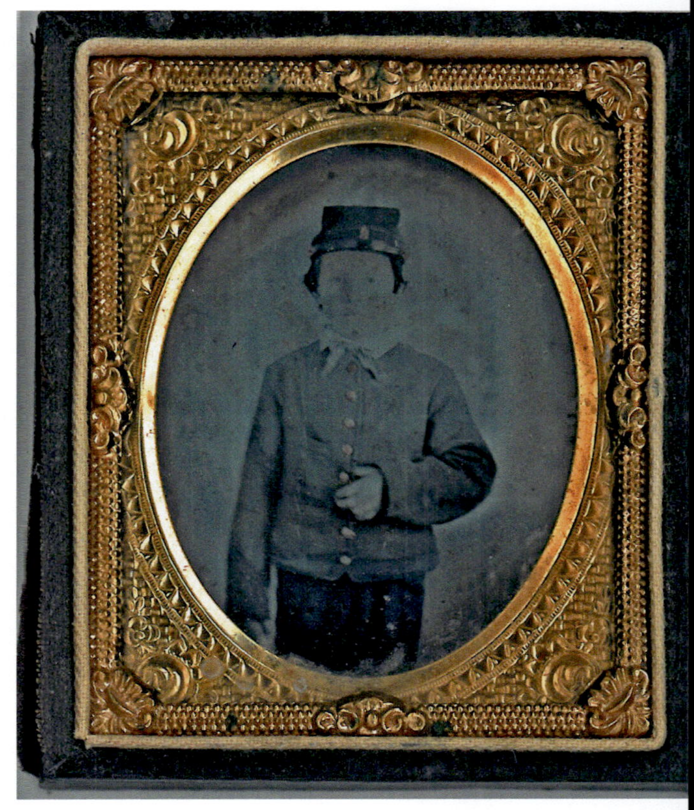

Below: Unique artistic pose of a soldier who looks like he might have been of Italian descent. If so, then he might have served in a regiment from New York City, which contained a large Italian population in 1860.He has a Bowie knife by his side, while his arm rests on the tip of his saber. *Author's Collection*

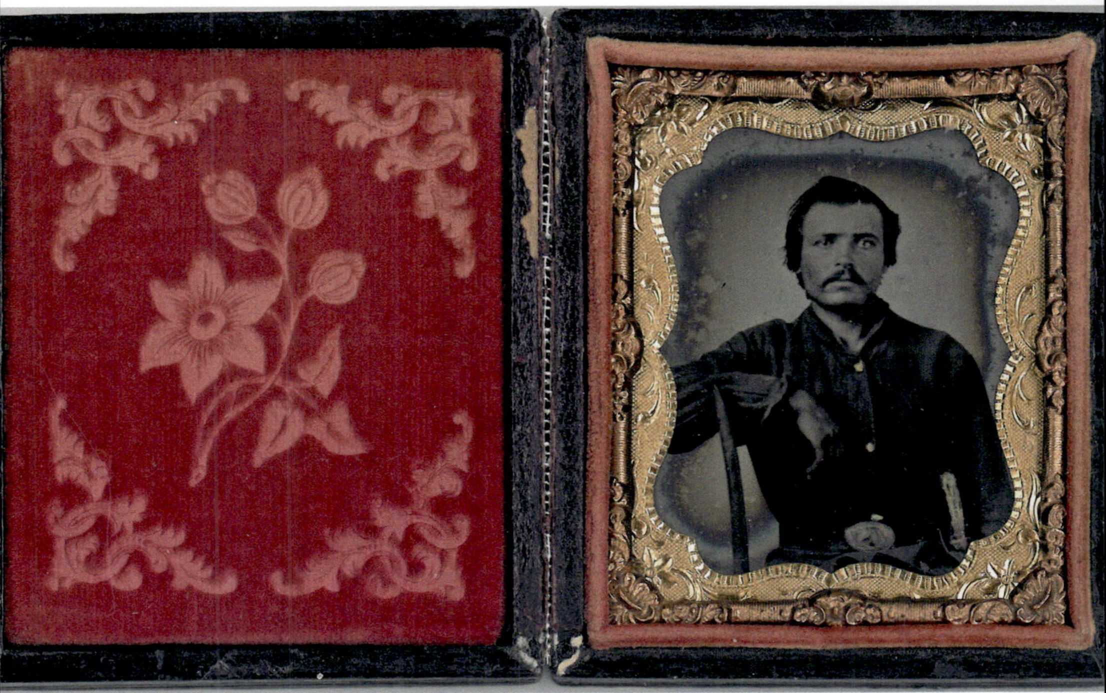

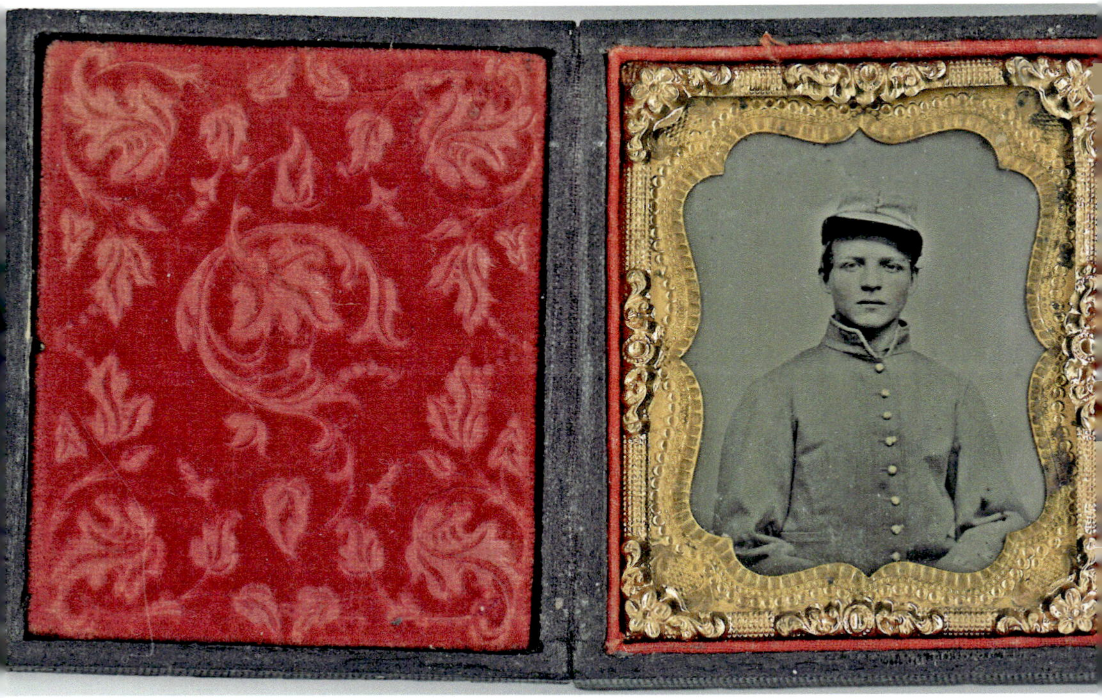

Tintype of a proud infantryman who served in a Massachusetts Regiment. *Author's Collection*

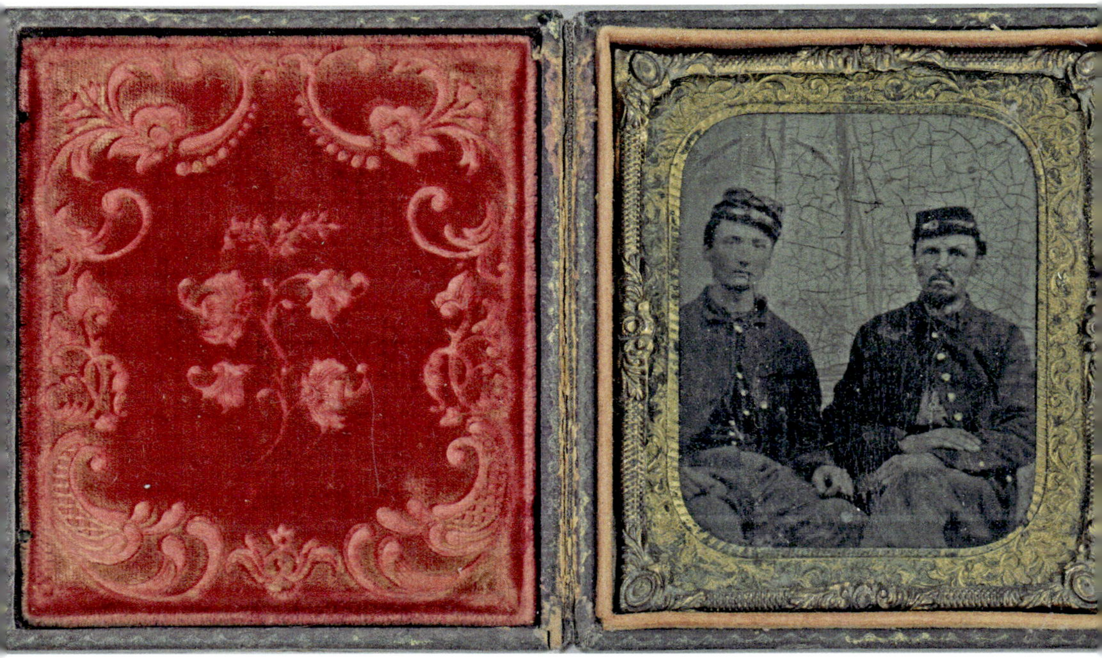

Two Union soldiers pose for the cameraman. *Author's Collection*

Left: Wearing a black Hardee Hat with a high crown, this young western Union soldier met a cruel fate in October 1862. He was severely wounded in battle and died after his leg was amputated by a Union surgeon. The young man is wearing a cotton homespun shirt, which was probably made by his mother before he marched off to war. *Author's Collection*

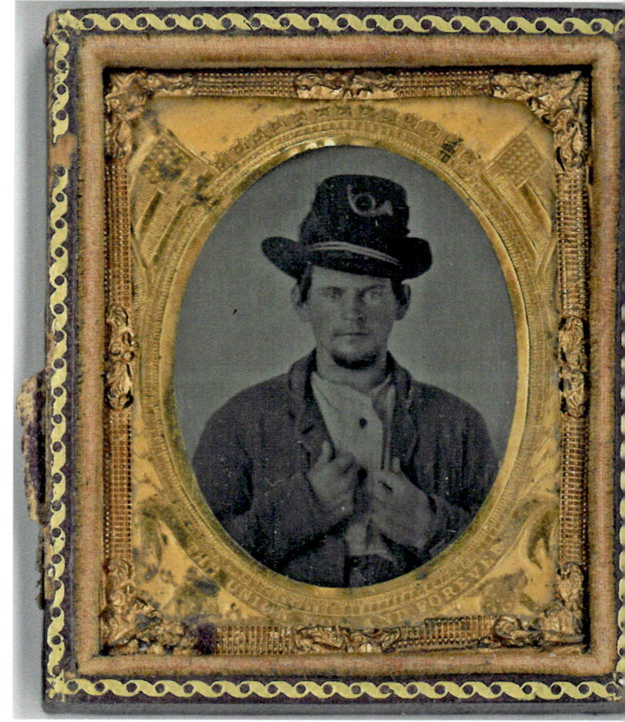

Below: Tintype of a Union corporal in a very common pose before the lens of the cameraman in his studio. *Author's Collection*

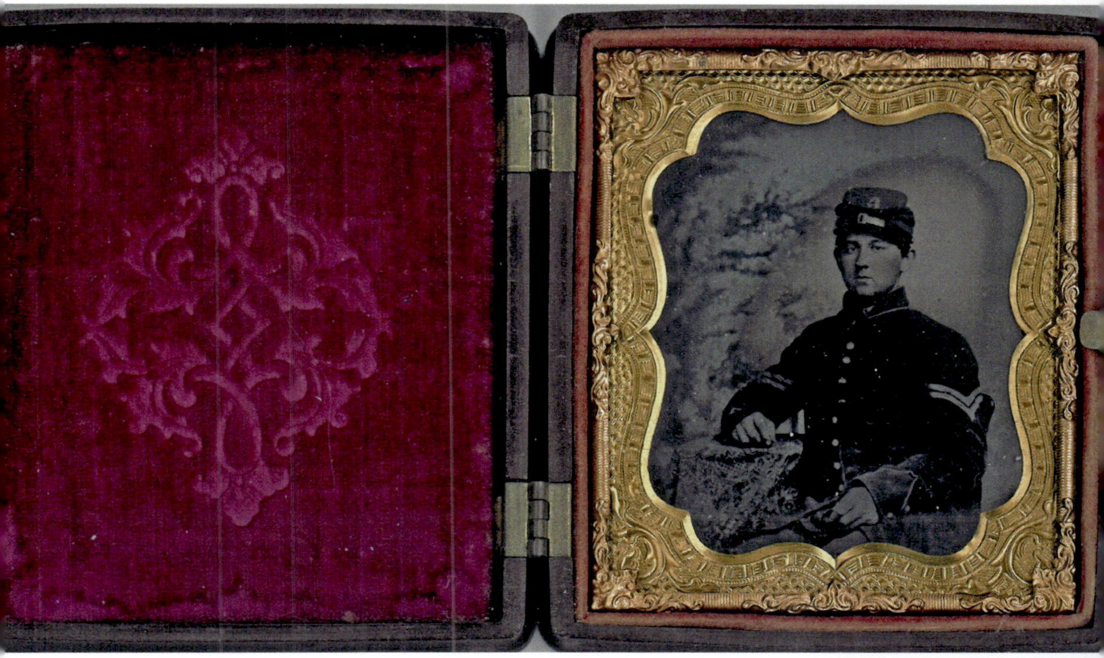

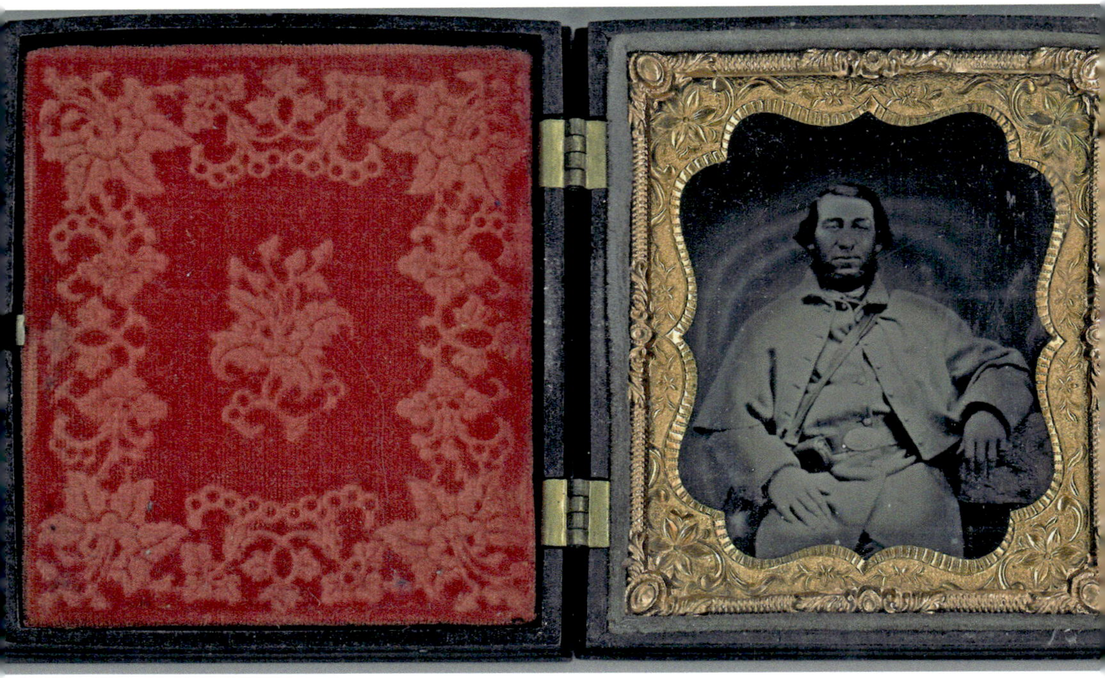

Tintype of a Federal infantryman wearing a winter uniform, including heavy army overcoat. Quite likely, a roving photographer had established a makeshift photographic studio in a town near the army's winter encampment. *Author's Collection*

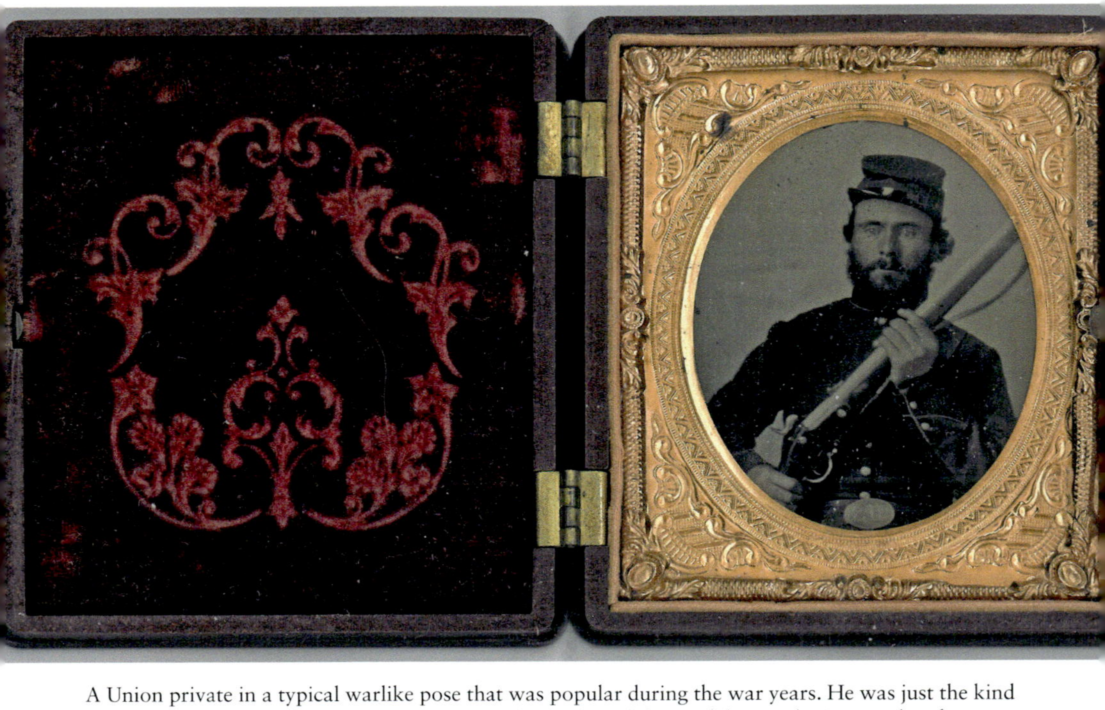

A Union private in a typical warlike pose that was popular during the war years. He was just the kind of determined common soldier who fought to the death in defense of the Devil's Den on the afternoon of July 2, 1863. *Author's Collection*

Near 4 p.m. on this humid afternoon when the day's intense heat had not diminished like the army's overall chances for success, "Old Pete" Longstreet now prepared to unleash his First Corps, with McLaws' Division surging northeast up the Emmitsburg Road to hit the Cemetery Ridge defenders on the left flank. Originally, Hood had been ordered to advance in echelon in conjunction, but belatedly according to the echelon concept, with McLaws, but he now planned on his own to attack straight ahead (or eastward) toward the high ground to the east instead of northeast up the Emmitsburg Road. After his protests against attacking northeast up the Emmitsburg Road to avoid the flank fire on the high ground (Houck's Ridge and later Little Round Top) to the east had been rejected by both Lee and Longstreet, Hood was determined to still overcome the odds under the circumstances and as best he could.

Therefore, Hood now planned to attempt to achieve the greatest possible tactical results, and this requirement meant not attacking up the Emmitsburg Road as originally directed by Lee, after his innovative plan for an outflanking movement to the south around the Round Tops had been firmly denied. He had ascertained that the true left flank of the Army of the Potomac lay on Houck's Ridge, which represented the southern end of Dan Sickles' line. First and foremost, the imposing threat of Union infantry of Sickles' Third Corps on Houck's Ridge and in the Devil's Den to a lesser degree not only had to be reduced, especially the artillery, but eliminated, because Hood was correctly convinced that this concentration of force represented the true Union left flank, if not located at the base of Big Round Top, which was targeted by the right of Law's Alabama Brigade of five veteran regiments.

Hood, therefore, planned to attack straight eastward to not only directly strike, but also to turn Meade's left flank with the Texas Brigade and Law's Brigade, while his two other seasoned brigades—basically reserves—then followed in support of his two front-line brigades leading the way. Most significantly, for the crucial mission of attacking the Union left flank head-on, Hood had chosen his hardest-fighting brigade (the Texas Brigade was also in much better physical shape than Law's weary and late-arriving brigade) for the job of delivering the key blow.

Indeed, because he could see the strength of Third Corps artillery and infantry on the high ground of Houck's Ridge that was not wooded, Hood's well-honed instincts told him that this was the true left flank of the Army of the Potomac. In this regard, Hood was correct. In consequence and in accordance with Lee's plan of turning the Union Army's left flank, this key high ground position and especially the New York guns positioned atop Houck's Ridge had to be overwhelmed first and as fast as possible in order to unhinge the entire Union defensive line not only of the Third Corps centered on the high ground of the Peach Orchard, but also Meade's main line situated along Cemetery Ridge north of Little Round Top. Most importantly, General Sickles had left Little Round Top—and Big Round Top just to the south—undefended and ripe for the taking, after having moved his corps so far west over the open fields to the Peach Orchard on the Emmitsburg Road Ridge, which was located northwest of Little Round Top.

Houck's Ridge and the Devil's Den, which protected the Houck's Ridge defenders on the south like a Stone Age bastion, was now the Union Army's extreme left flank, and it was General Ward's crucial mission to hold it at any cost with his regiments of the Third Corps. No longer about to lead his division in an assault in echelon northeast and up and parallel to, and just east of, the Emmitsburg Road, Hood planned to hit the true left flank lay to the east at the Devil's Den and Houck's Ridge. As noted, the Devil's Den, the pile of jumbled boulders and ledges, was the southern end of Houck's Ridge: an ideal defensive bastion.

Not farmed because it was so rocky and used only as a grazing area for cattle because only grass could grow on the crest of thin topsoil, this narrow ridge, which was distinguished by an open and barren crest, was named after the seventy-six-year-old farmer John Houck. As fate would have it, this odd-looking and surreal place later known as the Devil's Den had suddenly become important to both armies. Although his troops faced east toward the Devil's Den and were fated to be the first division to begin Lee's ambitions assault in echelon, Hood still envisioned a broad flank movement to the south that was to turn Meade's left by extending his battlefront farther south in an attack east instead of northeast and parallel to the Emmitsburg Road.[26]

Nevertheless, attacking eastward meant a headlong assault against a strong high ground position, and much hard fighting lay ahead, before the blazing sun of July 2 sank over the Cumberland Mountains to the west. Veterans in the Texas Brigade's did not like the prospect to assaulting high ground, because of the inevitable high losses and the possibility of suffering a sharp setback for the first time.

With some disgust, a frustrated Private John Mark Smither, 5th Texas, wrote in a July 29, 1863 letter to his mother: "Genl. Hood on being ordered to take the place, protested, saying he could take the place very easily by flanking around the mountain, but no, Bullhead Longstreet [who was only obeying Lee's orders] ordered him to go straight forward" in the assault.[27] Other veteran common soldiers, such as Private John Camden West, 4th Texas, were also convinced that the proper tactics on this crucial afternoon—the most important of the war—were those advocated by young General Hood.[28]

Golden Tactical Opportunity

Based upon the timely information that he had gained from his Texas scouts at around 3:30 p.m., Hood knew that the Round Tops were now vulnerable and ripe for the taking by his southernmost troops (Brigadier General Evander McIver Law's Alabamians), but only if he did not attack northeastward: a tactical situation that would not last long, however. Because no Federal reinforcements had been hurried south to bolster the Union Army's left flank and Sickles' unauthorized advance west to the Peach Orchard sector and the Emmitsburg Road Ridge to cover such a wide front of nearly 3,000 yards in length, this situation meant that Little Round Top and

Big Round Top still remained undefended at this critical moment when Hood planned to strike.[29]

Indeed, this tempting tactical situation that presented an opportunity to Hood was only temporary, however. To compensate for Sickles' decision to advance so far beyond the main Cemetery Ridge line to infuriate Meade who now gained still another good reason to detest non-professional and disobedient political generals, the commander-in-chief made the prudent, wise decision to advance the newly-arrived 11,000-man Fifth Corps (which served as the army's reserve until the Sixth Corps' arrival on the field—the last army corps to reach the battlefield—and Meade's old command) and have it in positioned about a mile northeast of Little Round Top and just below the Baltimore Pike to reinforce the Third Corps (still on its own and exposed in the open fields and farmlands) isolated around two-thirds of a mile before the Cemetery Ridge Line, if necessary.[30]

Clearly, in regard to Lee's orders—reconfirmed by Longstreet—to attack northeast up and parallel to the Emmitsburg Road, Hood believed that Lee had bypassed and missed the greatest opportunity to win the battle by moving south to ease around the twin elevations of the Round Tops to gain Meade's vulnerable rear. He now prepared for action, but only "under urgent protest." Therefore, Hood planned to attack straight east with the Texas Brigade to overwhelm Houck's Ridge, where the four cannon of Captain James E. Smith's 4th New York Independent Battery (Meade's true left flank at this time before the occupation of Little Round Top) stood on the ridge's barren crest that dominated a wide area of open ground to the west. Here, the four 10-pounder Parrott rifles, manned by veteran Empire State gunners, were in a dominant and "excellent position," in Smiths' words, after much effort by the enterprising bluecoat gunners in getting the artillery pieces up the steep, boulder-strewn eastern slope of Houck's Ridge.

Atop the barren crest, the New York guns commanded this advanced (westward) spur that angled off of Cemetery Ridge on the other side of Plum Run just to the east. This north–south running crest of Houck's Ridge was so narrow and boulder-strewn that it reduced overall defensive capabilities. Therefore, the unit's other two 10-pounder Parrott rifles could not be aligned by the gunners atop the commanding ridge, where they were badly-needed to protect the army's left flank during the most decisive afternoon of the war.

Instead, these two guns, situated on lower ground to the rear, were positioned to guard the gorge below the Devil's Den, if the Rebels attempted to surge through this natural avenue, despite the boulders and rugged terrain. But because of the relatively few numbers of bluecoats that were available in this key sector, the highly-capable Captain Smith, born in 1832 in New City, Rockland County, New York, was unable to protect these two cannon with infantry support.

Positioned at the southern end of Houck's Ridge and supported by the 4th Maine Volunteer Infantry to its rear, Smith's four New York guns now anchored the left of the Army of the Potomac to present a formidable objective to Hood's men. Significantly, these guns literally stood atop (although on the ridge proper farther north) the mass jumble of boulders known as the Devil's Den, where the left of the Maine regiment was anchored. Because of its elevation and the open, barren crest that served as an ideal firing platform for artillery unlike the crest of either Little Round Top or Big Round Top on the other side of Plum Run, Houck's Ridge was a strong defensive position and solid anchor for the left flank of the Army of the Potomac. The cannon of Captain Smith's expert New York gunners overlooked the open ground of the so-called "Triangular Field" to the west, promising to inflict severe damage on any Rebel attackers caught in the open.

Meanwhile, the ever-aggressive General Hood prepared to assault Houck's Ridge and the Devil's Den with primarily the 1st Texas, on the left or north and with assistance from the 3rd Arkansas on its left, to turn the left flank of the Army of the Potomac. Then, with the 4th and 5th Texas on the right, or south, he also planned to completely outflank the Federal left by a wider southward advance on Little Round Top as part of his "digression" once "we get under fire," in Hood's promise to Lieutenant Colonel Philip Alexander Work, who commanded the 1st Texas. Hood planned to use his own tactical flexibility and "latitude" in his orders to turn the Union left in the best way that he could, because so much was at stake this afternoon.[31]

As Lee's best division commander and finest major general, Hood's level of tactical ability was considerable because he was "the most highly regarded fighting general in the Army of Northern Virginia" at this crucial moment, when decisive victory (if he could turn Meade's left as envisioned) seemed to be in his tactical grasp.[32]

Upon the refusal of Hood's fourth request to be allowed to outflank the Union left by dispatching a brigade south of the Round Tops to gain the Army of the Potomac's rear, Longstreet informed the native Kentuckian, who he trusted immensely, with stoic resignation that "We must do the best we can."[33]

Now Hood, a decade younger in age than General Longstreet, was determined to do just that on this day of destiny in Adams County, Pennsylvania, so far from Texas and loved ones at home.[34] In a letter, Private John Camden West penned of the greatest disagreement that arose to frustrate and divide the highest levels of Confederate leadership on this seemingly ill-fated second day, which was the most crucial of the three days at Gettysburg, when complete unity of tactical thought and purpose was necessary for success: "Generals Longstreet and Hood were opposed to attacking the enemy in a position of their own choosing."[35]

Actually and although not fully realized at the time by top Confederate leadership (except for Hood who was the youngest division commander and now felt considerable frustration toward his seniors and superiors), especially at the Widow Thompson House on Seminary Ridge, Hood's Division was now presented with an excellent opportunity to turn the left flank of the Army of the Potomac. As mentioned, the decision of General Sickles to anchor the left flank of his Third Corps at Houck's Ridge and the Devil's Den with Ward's brigade of veteran troops had dramatically changed the tactical situation from Lee's original intention of attacking northeast up and parallel to the Emmitsburg Road.

Now, the high ground of Houck's Ridge and the Devil's Den had suddenly become the most important on the Gettysburg battlefield, representing the true left flank of the Army of the Potomac. In a bid to win it all, Lee's offensive plan (originally McLaws' mission as the foremost division, if everything had gone according to plan) was to turn the Union left flank, and now Hood's troops, now south of McLaws' Division, were presented with the tactical opportunity to do just that if they successfully overran the high ground that loomed before them: not one, but two parallel high ground positions, Houck's Ridge and then Big Round Top and Little Round Top, which this lesser elevation was not yet occupied by Colonel Strong Vincent's brigade, of the Fifth Corps. Unfortunately for the Texans, nature had seemingly favored the Union in having created dual elevations before Hood's Division: a natural and ideal defense in depth that was extremely formidable, if held by sufficient numbers to veteran troops and well-served artillery.[36]

Shortly, under the late afternoon light when the heat of this second day in July was as blistering as at the noon hour, the Texas soldiers, with newly loaded Enfield rifled-muskets, remained concealed on the reverse, or western, slope of the southern end of Seminary Ridge. Here, the shade of the dense woodlands now offered a refreshing respite from the scorching heat to the sweat-stained common soldiers. While under cover of the hardwood timber of Warfield Ridge at the southern end of the Biesecker's Woods to ensure that no hint of Confederate concentrations were seen, never were Texas Brigade members more exhausted and worn-down by this time, after marching for most of July 2 to reach the battlefield in time. In uniforms covered with dust, Hood's men now looked like tramps, but held their lethal Enfield rifles, clean and shiny, with pride.

All the while, the lateness of the day, nearing 4 p.m. on this decisive afternoon in Adams County, told these veterans that something had gone terribly wrong in the highest levels of planning at headquarters among the army's top commanders. After all, Lee's assaults were usually unleashed at dawn to catch the Yankees by surprise, but this was not the case on the most important day at Gettysburg! Hoping for the best despite the ominous warnings that things were not going right on July 2, the Texas Brigade's soldiers could only hope that their leading officers, especially their young, but capable, division commander, would be able to develop winning tactics, because an overly-ambitious and ill-conceived battle-plan that had already gone awry.

Most of all, these veterans of hard-fought battles across Virginia and in Maryland (Antietam) hoped that a good many lives would be saved by Hood's well-known concern for the welfare of his boys. As fate would have it to fulfill Lee's ambitious offensive plan, the Texas Brigade was aligned in a north–south direction at the southern end of the Confederate battle-line along the crest of Warfield Ridge, from where Longstreet's assault would begin in echelon. Lee viewed in echelon attacks as the best possible opportunity-creating tactics, because this echelon concept of staggered assaults was based on the premise that the first strikes would cause a hasty realignment of defenders, who would be weakened and less prepared to resist the next attack—to the north on the afternoon of July 2—in consequence.

As ordered, Hood deployed his crack division of four brigades in two assault lines—two brigades in the front line and two brigades in the second line—from north–south and across the Emmitsburg Road at an angle that paralleled the north–south running road. On the high ground of the northern end of Warfield Ridge and north of its highest ground farther south down the lengthy ridge that paralleled the Round Tops to the east on the other side of Plum Run, General Jerome Bonaparte Robertson formed his Texas and Arkansas troops (four regiments, three Texas and one Arkansas) in the first line of battle.

Here, he positioned his hard-hitting Trans-Mississippi troops to the left, or north, of Law's Alabama Brigade on the open, high ground on the right of Lafayette McLaws' Division and the 3rd Arkansas, just west of the Emmitsburg Road and immediately south of the modest J. Timber house. The small house was located across from the tall timber of Biesecker's Woods and situated on a commanding knoll just east of the road. The 3rd Arkansas, which had joined the Texas Brigade to replace the South Carolina infantry of Hampton's Legion in the fall of 1862 after the Maryland Campaign and thereby earned the distinction of having been the last regiment to join the Texas Brigade, held on the brigade's left flank.

Fortunately for the Texas Brigade on this day of destiny, the 3rd Arkansas was a veteran combat unit, having served in the Virginia Theater since the summer of 1861. A former lawyer from Hamburg in southeast Arkansas, the North Carolina-born Colonel Van Hartrog Manning commanded the 3rd Arkansas, which had been organized during the spring of 1861. This excellent regiment included such hard-fighting companies like "The Arkansas Travelers" (Company "A"), "The Hot Springs Hornets" (Company "F"), and "The Three Creek Rifles" (Company "G").

To the right of the 3rd Arkansas while positioned along the crest of Warfield Ridge, meanwhile, the men of the 1st Texas prepared to surge eastward just north of the stone Michael Bushman House. This house lay in the shallow valley (mostly covered in open fields) through which the north–south flowing Plum Run, which was bordered by thin belts of timber on both sides, ran along the base of Little Round Top. Open fields flowed east toward Houck's Ridge, the Devil's Den, and Little Round Top before the Texas Brigade's right and the ground gently descended to the east all the way to trickling waters of Rose Run, a tributary of Plum Run before the 1st Texas, which entered Plum Run at a point before the 4th and 5th Texas on the brigade's right.

Looking most imposing on the other side of the two parallel creeks (the smaller Rose Run and the larger Plum Run that flowed in the valley on the east side of Houck's Ridge), the Texans saw the entire north-south length of the open, bare, and rocky slope of the western face of Little Round Top under the bright July sunshine and only slightly obscured by a thin, heat-haze of early summer. Ironically, Houck's Ridge before Little Round Top's higher ground was less immediately perceptible to the view of the Texans, because it was a lower elevation and also due to the fact that the tall timber, bright green in full summer foliage, which ran along the course of Rose Run and also the southward-flowing Plum Run.

Meanwhile, to the south of the 1st Texas, the 5th Texas was about to move forward and directly over the open ground and farmers' fields toward the John Slyder house, which lay in the picturesque valley just west of Rose Run, and 80-acre farm situated directly west of heavily-timbered Big Round Top. Looming high like a natural citadel on the skyline to the southeast, Big Round Top dominated Little Round Top to its north. All in all, the upcoming advance of the Texans was sure to be swift and relatively easy because of the open fields and gently descending ground on the west side of Rose Run. The immediate environs of Rose Run offered the first initial natural barriers that would slow the attack east and toward the formidable high ground that towered above the small creek of clear, cold water that the Texas boys could now only dream about drinking on this sweltering afternoon. Therefore, the securing of this refreshing liquid remained only a fantasy for the thirsty Texans. Meanwhile, the heat of day continued to rise on this afternoon, just before the approach of new weather front of cooler air, which would shortly bring rain, which many of these Texas soldiers would never see.

A Feisty Irish Battery Commander

Before the lengthy lines of Texas soldiers, two 12-pounder Napoleon pieces and two 10-pounder Parrott rifles of Captain James Reilly's Tar Heel State battery were positioned in the open field along the crest of Warfield Ridge and beside the Emmitsburg Road. As so often in the past, this fine North Carolina battery supported the Texas Brigade, and was positioned "a little in the rear" of the 1st Texas, after the guns had been unlimbered by strong-armed artillerymen to align on the brigade's left-center. Of all the cannon of the Divisional Artillery Battalion of Longstreet's First Corps, Reilly's battery was destined to be located farther south than any guns in Lee's Army at the time of the assault. Officially designated as the Rowan North Carolina Artillery, but more commonly known simply as Reilly's battery for its colorful Celtic-Gaelic leader who tolerated no nonsense from any of his young gunners, this battery had been first attached to the Texas Brigade in the autumn of 1862.

With a well-deserved reputation as "Old Tarantula" (like General Meade's "Old Snapping Turtle" nickname because he was also crusty and hot-tempered) for his toughness and still speaking with a thick Irish brogue, the stout Reilly hailed from Ballydonagh. The small town was located near Athlone, County Westmeath, in the rich farmlands of central Ireland. As a teenager overcome with wanderlust, the Irish lad had run away from home and joined the British Army, but was retrieved by his angry mother. His mother proved as hard-headed and strong-willed as her son.

Like so many of his fellow countrymen, he fought with a typical Celtic-Gaelic tenacity and high spirit in honor of "St. Patrick [patron saint of Ireland and the] hoully saints," in his own words. A highly-capable battery commander, the blue-eyed and dark-haired Captain Reilly, of short stature but fierce fighting spirit, was a defiant Irish Catholic.

Most importantly, he possessed abundant artillery experience, and his qualities were sorely needed on the decisive afternoon of July 2. This hard-fighting Irishman was a Mexican-American War and United States Army veteran of the triumphant march of General Scott's Army on Mexico City and the so-called "Halls of Montezuma."

Ironically, Reilly, who had enlisted in August 1845, had served in the United States battery under Lieutenant Henry J. Hunt, who now commanded Meade's powerful artillery arm with great skill, taking advantage of high ground opportunities on Cemetery Hill and Cemetery Ridge. He was still the life partner of another Irish immigrant, Ann Quinn, who he had married at St. Paul's Roman Catholic Cathedral in Brooklyn, New York, not long after the Mexican-American War's conclusion.

Always providing timely support and an accurate fire in dependable fashion, he had previously supported the Texas soldiers on past battlefields by his well-honed skills in orchestrating the fire of his six 12-pounders. All in all, Captain Reilly, who spoke with a thick Irish brogue, had made the North Carolina's Rowan Artillery an elite "long arm" command by this time.

Also part of Major Mathias Winston Henry's Battalion, the other battery of Hood's Division was Captain Alexander C. Lanham's North Carolina Branch Artillery, which was positioned to the right of Reilly's guns. Here, the three Napoleon 12-pounders and one 12-pounder Howitzer of the North Carolina Battery promised to offer excellent support for the upcoming infantry assault upon the high ground that loomed before them to the east. After extending the lengthy line south toward the Emmitsburg Road, the troops of Work's 1st Texas was positioned along the open ridge-top in the rear of Captain Reilly's battery on the right of the 3rd Arkansas, and the Lone Star State regiment's right was anchored on the Emmitsburg Road and along the ridge-top upon which the road ran.

The 1st Texas's battle-line continued to extend south along the high ground of Warfield Ridge, crossing the narrow, dusty road until Work's right was situated on the east side of the Emmitsburg Road, where it adjoined the left of the 4th Texas. Aligned along Warfield Ridge, the 5th Texas was positioned entirely east of the road and held the right of the Texas Brigade, which was adjoined by young Brigadier General Evander McIver Law's front-line Alabama troops, with the 4th Alabama (the brigade's left flank) on the right of the 5th Texas, to the south.

Positioned farther down the ridge to the south along higher ground than where the Texas Brigade was aligned to the north and hence the ground dropped more sharply here than before Robertson's Texas Brigade, the five Alabama regiments of Law's Brigade were also aligned in a north–south direction like the Texas Brigade's regiments. Because of its position located on the far south on the right flank of Hood's Division, Law's Brigade was chosen as the "brigade of direction" for the upcoming assault, because of Lee's plan to attack in echelon. Unlike the Texans who stood before the barren western slope of Little Round Top directly, the Alabama soldiers could only see the southwestern face of Little Round Top and looked east more directly toward Big Round Top, while Robertson's men now viewed the entire western slope, bare and rocky to present an ominous appearance, of the ugly hill with some foreboding.[37]

A member of Company "F" (Company Invincibles), 5th Texas, William A. Fletcher looked with sadness upon the Texas Brigade's reduced ranks now positioned in a lengthy line along Warfield Ridge and immediately before its greatest challenge. He now saw how "our brigade ranks were well depleted [and] we did not make a very long battle line."[38]

Therefore, the Texas Brigade soldiers hoped that the fire of the roaring field pieces of the irrepressible Captain Reilly, "that gruff old Irishman," in the words of Private Val C. Giles, Company "B," 4th Texas, would make up for numbers and knock out opposition, especially the artillery, protecting the Union's Army left flank. However, expressing a commonplace view about the Irish that was more based on popular racial stereotypes than facts, this young Texas private possessed no deep love for the Irish, who he viewed with some provincial distaste as "foreigners," which was a common view at the time.[39]

Private John Camden West, 4th Texas, was likewise influenced by pervasive anti-Irish stereotypes that were so popular throughout America, but even more in the northeastern part of the United States, especially in the major cities like New York, Boston, and Philadelphia than in the South. Only recently, he had been obsessively concerned and "afraid that the Irishman [in gray] will get drunk and lose this" letter to his wife.[40] And as revealed in a letter that at least indirectly complimented the well-known work ethic of the Irish who usually engaged in menial labor in both the North and South before the war, Joseph Benjamin Polley described to his mother in a June 10, 1862 letter how he had "learned to work like an Irishman."[41]

Like so many other Texas Brigade soldiers who already had been saved by the accurate and timely fire of Reilly's North Carolina guns on previous battlefields, Private Giles felt admiration for the hard-fighting Son of Erin. He described how the hot-tempered, but highly capable, Captain Reilly "had been an artillery sergeant in the old Army [and] an old Irishman, rough, gruff, grizzly, and brave. He loved his profession and knew his business."[42]

Final Preparations

With Robertson's and Law's brigades side by side as the division's front-line troops and positioned along the lengthy expanse of Warfield Ridge, General Hood felt increased confidence in the fact that Law's Alabamians, consisting of around 1,600 men, was now the brigade of direction for the assault farther south. Therefore, on the far right and the southernmost of Lee's troops, Law's brigade would begin the assault in echelon, according to Lee's directives: a tactical situation that meant that Robertson's Texas and Arkansas would lurch forward not long after the Alabama troops to the south stepped off their commanding perch of Warfield Ridge, and then descended east along a gentle slope into the shallow valley of Plum Run.

Most importantly, Law's Alabama Brigade, on the far south of the lengthy battle-line, was assigned the crucial mission of turning the Union left, which Hood believed might be located either at the base of Big Round Top or Little Round Top. Clearly, the sight of Union signalmen at Little Round Top caused Hood worry, but Little Round Top was still unoccupied by any unit of the Army of the Potomac. But at this time and directly before Lieutenant Colonel Work and his 1st Texas, Houck's Ridge was the true left flank of the Union Army (or the Third Corps in this case) before Little Round Top was occupied by arriving Fifth Corps troops.[43]

The stiff challenge of overpowering Meade's left flank situated on Houck's Ridge and the Devil's Den, at the ridge's southernmost end, only reconfirmed, in one soldier's words, that "There was a kind of intuition, an apparent settled fact, among the soldiers of Longstreet's corps [that] when the hard, stubborn, decisive blow was to be struck, the troops of the first corps were called upon to strike it."[44]

For such reasons, and with the barren, rocky western slope of Little Round Top looming before him, and after the Texas Brigade had taken devastating losses in past battles for so long in the past, one veteran private from Company "A," 5th Texas, was overcome by the extent of the formidable challenge that lay ahead. While Captain Reilly's guns were aligned on Warfield Ridge, he suddenly stepped out of the tattered ranks of gray and butternut without permission from any officer, but with a pressing personal mission of a spiritual nature in mind.

Knowing that the unleashing of still another frontal assault against a high ground position was only a matter of time, this common soldier, who was as ill-clothed as he was undernourished, from the bustling Gulf of Mexico port of Galveston, "started to offer prayer, something that I had never heard of in our part of the line under like conditions."[45] Clearly, under these trying circumstances, these words of hope and faith were timely, because these hardened Texas veterans felt correctly that they were about to embark upon still another deadly odyssey, and one from which a good many men would never return.

Eighteen-year-old Private Albert Cuthbert Sims, Company "F," 1st Texas, now faced Houck's Ridge and the Devil's Den in part because his twin brother had recently given his life for the Confederacy and also because still another brother wore the gray. In his own words: "I was so crazed with grief for him [when he died] who had been my constant associate form [*sic.*] infancy that I resolved to go to that then seeming[ly] far off land Virginia to fight the battle[s] of my country."[46]

Now freed of the dense woodlands that filled the reverse slope of the lower end of Seminary Ridge (actually Warfield Ridge) like a green blanket, the Texas soldiers could see the glimmers of late afternoon sunlight—which thankfully did not shine into their eyes as if they looked west—reflecting off the four New York artillery pieces atop Houck's Ridge, with the larger Little Round Top looming to its rear. What these Lone Star State veterans saw before them was ominous, and enough to cause a heightened sense of anxiety. Most of all from the commanding ground of Warfield Ridge, the Texans saw that Houck's Ridge (at this time, they did not know the name of either elevation, either Houck's Ridge or Little Round Top) served as an ideally elevated artillery platform that dominated a wide area, especially the broad, open fields to the west that extended all the way to Warfield Ridge's crest.

The Texas Rebels could also see the glistening of the bayonets and accouterments of hundreds of Union soldiers of a powerful brigade (Brigadier General John Henry Hobart Ward's command, First Division, Second Brigade, Third Corps) more than a mile away to the east. But most daunting of all to the 1st Texas soldiers was the sight of the broad expanse of open ground, which descended all the way down the open slope leading to Rose Run that ran about halfway across the wide expanse of open fields to the ridge, before the ground ascended up to farmer John Houck's Ridge and its row of four artillery pieces.

The barrels of Captain Smith's New York cannon sparkled in the bright, early July sunshine from the commanding ridge-top devoid of timber unlike almost all other hills and ridges in Adams County. With an open, rocky western slope not unlike Little Round Top to its rear, Houck's Ridge looked sufficiently menacing to guarantee a high cost of lives of a good many Texas boys in the upcoming assault. But most ominous of all was what the Texans saw behind the first ridge was the far higher ground that was even more dominant and threatening, the barren western slope of Little Round Top that rose up from the valley of Plum Run.

All in all, Little Round Top was eerie-looking, especially when nestled amid a picturesque pastoral landscape of green and gold—seemingly anything but the stereotypical grim killing ground at first glance—that advertised the fertility and abundance of an agriculture paradise. The entire western face of the mountain loomed up ominously like the Rock of Gibraltar to seemingly mock Lee's lofty ambitions of turning Meade's left flank in one powerful blow.

Presenting an usual appearance at this time, timber was noticeably absent along Little Round Top's rock-strewn western slope, whose strange-looking sterility and barrenness beguiled the green richness of all around it, including the heavily-timbered north, east, and south sides of Little Round Top. Instead of giant trees, which had been earlier logged for sale to the townsfolk in Gettysburg because this steep, boulder-strewn ground could not be farmed, the slope was studded with large boulders. Rising up above most of the open slope, a large cluster of boulders (almost in essence a smaller Devil's Den that consisted of around 10 acres) dominated Little Round Top's northwestern face.

Never before facing such a formidable high ground challenge that initially took his breath away because he immediately understood the high price that would have to be paid for taking the heights, Lieutenant Colonel Work described Little Round Top as "a mountain knob (the name of which I learned long afterwards was 'Round Top')..."[47] Likewise, William A. Fletcher, Company "F," 5th Texas, only learned many years later of the name of the mean-looking, rocky hill for which so Texas soldiers were to ultimately die in repeatedly crashing against it with mad abandon and fixed bayonets, because of the lofty nature of Lee's ambitions that stemmed from his Chambersburg Pike headquarters at the Widow Thompson House and his firm conviction that his most unconventional, but best, fighting men were invincible: "I learned some time afterward that the peak was called 'Roundtop' or 'Heights.' Have never learned whether it was named before or after the battle."[48] In a letter, Rufus King Felder, 5th Texas, described Little Round Top more realistically and as a much more challenging, "a high mountain" distinguished by "an almost perpendicular peak."[49]

But the most descriptive words came from one 4th Texas soldier, who emphasized that Little Round Top as "a mountain where it was very steep and [contained] rock[s as] large as a meeting house."[50] In a letter to his mother, Private John Mark Smither, 5th Texas, penned how the high ground loomed up like an ancient castle and quite unlike anything seen in Texas, because it was "a very high and steep mountain about 2 miles high," which was of course an exaggeration.[51] One Southern officer described heavily-timbered Big Round Top, that dominated Little Round Top, its twin, just to the north and the surrounding countryside, as "a volcano."[52] This was no exaggeration in regard to its overall menacing and formidable appearance of the high ground, especially upon looking up from the hill's base situated deep in the valley of Plum Run, which promised a fiery explosion of musketry, if gained and defended by large numbers of Yankees before the Texans' arrival.

But at this point in the battle's opening phase on the far south, Little Round Top was not now important or Lee's principal target, because it was not so written in any orders or since it was still not occupied by Union troops. Indeed, at this time and as mentioned, the Union left was firmly located firmly on Houck's Ridge and the Devil's Den, and not Little Round Top. Little Round Top only became important much later in the conflict and after the struggle for possession of Houck's Ridge and the Devil's Den had erupted in full fury.

But for now, everything—the fulfillment of Lee's primary objective of turning the Union left and then rolling up Meade's battle-line from south to north and deciding the war's outcome as envisioned from his headquarters—now depended very much upon what the Texas troops could accomplish in overrunning the high ground before them on this scorching afternoon. Most importantly at this time, General Lee and the Army of Northern Virginia were most fortunate that the army's finest combat troops had been positioned in exactly the right place immediately before the most vital tactical objective and given the most vital mission: the striking and then turning of Meade's left flank to secure a long-elusive decisive victory. Indeed, the 1st Texas directly faced Houck's Ridge and the Devil's Den, which was certainly one of its greatest challenges of the entire four years of war.

Not long after the battle-hardened troops of the Texas Brigade were aligned astride the Emmitsburg Road, Captain Reilly's battery, located in rear of the 1st Texas, had finally opened fire on the four brass artillery pieces of Captain Smith's New York Battery atop Houck's Ridge, along with Latham's North Carolina Battery on the right. In the words of teenage Private Albert Cuthbert Sims, 1st Texas, "No sooner were we in position than did our canon [*sic.*] open fire through a skirt of timber which lay in our front, which was eastward; to which the enemy replied promptly, knocking out a man here and there. To avoid much danger as possible, we were ordered to lie down until all were in readiness."[53]

In a heartfelt letter to his young son, "My Dear Little Man," who he feared he might never see again, Private John Camden West, Company "E," 4th Texas, described the horror: "We were standing in an open field [on exposed Warfield Ridge], under the shot and shell of these batteries, for half an hour, before we moved forward, and a good many soldiers were killed all around me. One poor fellow had his head knocked off in a few feet of me, and I felt all the time as if I would never see you and little sister again."[54]

To the right of the 1st Texas, a shell exploded in the midst of the line of the 4th Texas, knocking fifteen men out of the ranks. A member of the Five Shooters of Company "C," 4th Texas which was known as the "Hell Roaring Fourth," Captain Delimus et Ultimus Barziza had migrated to Texas in 1857, possessed an University of Baylor law degree and practiced law in Robertson County. Proud of his Italian heritage as indicated by his dark hair and thick moustache and beard, he described how the troops lay "flat on the ground, keeping their places in ranks" in a display discipline under the steady pounding from the angry New York guns.[55]

The well-educated Barziza was a realist and fatalist, believing that when the Army of Northern Virginia crossed the cold waters of the Potomac, this had been "the Rubicon of our hopes."[56] Under the shellfire of the New York guns atop Houck's Ridge, he never forgot how the 4th Texas men now "generally try to sink themselves into the earth. Nearly every face is overspread with a serious, thoughtful air."[57]

On the brigade's right flank and as previously mentioned, the religious-minded east Texas soldier of Company "A" (Bayou City Guards), 5th Texas, who had stepped before the ranks of his solemn-faced comrades to deliver an impromptu prayer service, had his holy work suddenly interrupted when an irritated officer, no doubt thinking that the *ad hoc* religious service was not good for morale before an assault, ordered him back into line. Clearly, the officer knew that his men needed to hear encouraging words and not something that sounded like a funeral service.

With chaplains not immediately available at the front because they almost always served in rearward positions at the field hospitals, common soldiers took the initiative, filling in for chaplains, such as Private John Stevens, Company "K" (Polk County Flying Artillery), 5th Texas. This "prayer service" by a soldier of the Bayou City Guards was just in time, because no sooner had this religious-minded man resumed his place in the ranks of Company "A", when a shell exploded above the company, knocking three of his comrades out of line.[58]

The extent of the stern challenge that stood before the Texas Brigade's ranks was most convincingly made while the four Union artillery pieces of Captain Smith's New York Battery, aligned atop Houck's Ridge from north to south, continued their hot fire on the lengthy formations of the troops of Hood's Division aligned along the Emmitsburg Road, which was located just before the tree-line of the reverse slope of Warfield Ridge and just behind the dusty road.

Because the Emmitsburg Road ran atop Warfield Ridge in the tradition of country roads lining atop ridges to follow ancient Native American and old game trails, the southern extension of Seminary Ridge and tall, virgin timber in full summer foliage stood behind them, Hood's troops made good targets for the veteran artillerymen of the four 10-pounder Parrott rifles that were especially accurate at long-range, because they were rifled artillery pieces served by seasoned gunners. On high, open ground, the Texans were easily visible to the veteran New York artillerymen from their commanding perch atop Houck's Ridge.

Displaying a deadly accuracy, Captain Smith's cannoneers had been earlier inflicting considerable damage on Southern batteries located on Seminary Ridge north of Warfield Ridge, enfilading Rebel artillery units before turning their wrath of Hood's newly-arrived troops. Even before the attack was ordered by Hood, therefore, casualties among the Texas Brigade began to escalate because of the New Yorkers' skill in sighting targets and hitting them at long-range. And this ugly toll reaped from the gray and butternut ranks continued to grow every minute under the intense artillery punishment.[59]

Despite this artillery hell endured by the troops aligned along Warfield Ridge, the determination to succeed this afternoon in Adams County could not have been higher among the Texas Brigade men. In the 4th Texas' ranks, one officer from Robertson County emphasized how, "Everybody was confident and in the highest spirit of enthusiasm."[60] Earlier in the war, one young Texas Brigade soldier named Thomas "Tom" Bates, who risked his life on Virginia soil with so many of his friends and neighbors never returned to tell the tale, wrote to his grandmother, Elizabeth Bates, of the strategic possibilities if decisive victory was secured by the boys in gray: "… if we whip the Yankees this time we will be sure to take Washington," D.C.[61]

But now that exact high stakes situation legitimately applied to the decisive showdown at Gettysburg on the afternoon of July 2, when the war might well be decided at long last. If Hood's troops could turn the left flank of the ill-positioned Army of the Potomac, then Meade's Army would be vanquished and the war virtually won for the beleaguered Confederacy. Clearly, the stakes could not have been higher for Hood's men now aligned in lengthy formations.

As usual and despite the extent of the formidable obstacles that lay before them and the increasing feeling—almost a second sense—that today was the war's most decisive day that had made even these veterans much quieter and more reflective than usual even before an attack, the battle-hardened soldiers, with .577-caliber Enfield rifles loaded, aligned in prone positions along and parallel to the Emmitsburg Road were ready for action. Veterans like Val C. Giles, Company "B" (Tom Green Rifles), 4th Texas, cherished "my old Enfield." as much as a wife or lover. Indeed, very good, almost loving, care toward a soldier's Enfield rifle often spelled the difference between life and death, especially in close combat situations. The seriousness of the deadly work that lay ahead meant that the usual banter and jokes were no longer forthcoming from the ranks as in the past.

Despite their ragamuffin appearances that were at least better than their 3rd Texas comrades (now serving in the Department of Texas), who wore even fewer articles of standard Confederate gear compared to the 1st Texas men, Work's veterans were ready for the challenge. Some 3rd Texas soldiers, mostly from central Texas, including Travis County(that included the capital of Austin), which had been named after the Alamo's South Carolina-born commander, William Barret Travis, even wore Mexican sombreros to reflect a distinctive cultural mixture on the southwestern frontier.[62]

In addition when encamped around Richmond just before the ill-fated invasion of Pennsylvania, some 1st Texas soldiers wore new civilian hats, especially the popular stovepipe hates, that had been knocked off the heads of curious train passengers, who peered out windows to ascertain a deliberately-provoked 1st Texas disturbance to spark their curiosity, only to have their headgear knocked off by men with long pine boughs.[63]

After the cruel decimation in the Miller Cornfield at Antietam on September 17, 1862, the Texas Brigade's ranks had been bolstered by recruits from Texas. Never having seen combat and about to be hurled into the midst of Gettysburg's raging storm and the war's largest and most important battle, thirty-one-year-old Private Joseph E. Love, now holding an Enfield rifle and carrying a canteen marked "5 Tex" was one of these nervous rookies, who hoped he would not fall crippled or maimed for life in his first action. A proud member of Company "A" (the Bayou Guards), 5th Texas, Love had enlisted on April 1, 1863, barely three months before the holocaust at Gettysburg. Like other rookies, this was Private Love's last battle. He was destined to shortly be cut down, falling mortally wounded in his first battle.[64]

Private Albert Cuthbert Sims, Company "F," 1st Texas, was another new recruit, who had much to prove (to himself and others) this afternoon. He had enlisted in April and joined the Texas Brigade's ranks on May 8, 1863, after the lengthy journey from Texas.[65] Such new men, not yet traumatized by the war's horrors, had infused the Texas Brigade with a much-needed resurgence of strength and vitality just in time for the command's greatest challenge. However, on the fatal field of Gettysburg, these young soldiers who had been so recently back home in Texas had little idea of the harsh reality that awaited them at places like the Devil's Den, as now fully realized by the Texas Brigade's veterans.

As wrote one 4th Texas soldier, who had grown cynical, but entirely realistic: "If Fortune favors the brave, Death does not."[66] About to engage in his first battle and wondering "if it [will] be the last?," Private John Camden West, 4th Texas, at least felt some consolation before the assault, because "I have requested my friends to save my Bible and the little tin cup … in case of my fall" in battle.[67] At this time, perhaps a mounted Texas officer still rode before the ranks with his leather boots in Texas-made iron stirrups that were smaller and more decorative than usually worn by Confederate officers, reflecting distinctive Mexican cultural and ranching influences of the Tejano people.[68]

Here, on Warfield Ridge, the Texans were waiting for the arrival of 4 p.m. orders to begin the assault, because of what the officers had told them. In the words of James Henry Hendrick, Company "E," 1st Texas, from a letter: "It was understood by all that we were going to make the attack at four o'clock."[69] Therefore, all extra gear had already been piled-up by the 1st Texas men in small clumps to the rear to not weigh down the attackers and impede the advance across such a lengthy stretch of the open ground. This wise lighting of heavy personal loads of excess equipment of removing haversacks, blanket-rolls and knapsacks, including those of United States Army issued that had been captured from the Federals—dead, wounded, and prisoners—on past battlefields, had come as a welcomed relief to the average soldier in the ranks.

At this time, the 1st Texas soldiers still wore a wide variety of uniforms, or what was left of uniforms by this time, and even some civilian apparel. Since each company that formed the 1st Texas had been organized and uniformed independently before journeying to Richmond on its own, these companies still retained their unique qualities and characteristics. Most of all, therefore, the 1st Texas was still distinguished by its tattered and ragged appearance that often brought a great deal of laughter from the enemy when regimental members had been captured.

In the 1st Texas ranks and as during 1862, some soldiers wore brass regimental numbers and company letters on the crowns of cadet-pattern forage kepis. A top officer of the Marshall Guards (Company "E") from the piney woods of Marshall County in east Texas, Lieutenant Eli N. Baxter wore a kepi with the brass letters of "M G" for Marshall Guards at the high point of his hat's crown, and a brass number "1" (for 1st Texas) sandwiched between the brass letters "M G" and the brass letters of "Texas." The men of Company "D" (the Star Rifles), 1st Texas, wore tall Hardee-style hats as opposed to the standard forage caps, providing a distinctive look which was closer to that of the elite fighting men and hardy westerners of the Iron Brigade than other Confederate troops of Lee's Army.

At this time, some Texas hats now might have been decorated with deer tails from the cocky bluecoats of the famed Pennsylvania Bucktails, 13th Pennsylvania Reserve Regiment. These hard-fighting Pennsylvania boys had been vanquished by the Texans in the tangled lowlands of the Virginia Peninsula. In the past, these had been worn as trophies to a victory that was still looked upon fondly by these men on the afternoon of July 2.

But the majority of these 1st Texas soldiers wore slouch or planter's hats, as if still living in peace at home on the ranch or small farm, before the war's insanity had changed their lives forever. Cotton haversacks, knapsacks, and rolled-up blankets—filthy and lice-ridden—had been removed to leave a light and lean soldiery for faster movement in the upcoming assault. While the Confederates first marched through Pennsylvania towns, northern citizens had marveled how lightly the ragged invaders traveled on this grueling campaign north the Potomac.

But now just before the attack on Meade's left flank positioned on Houck's Ridge and the Devil's Den, consequently, the fighting men of Lee's elite brigade were now more mobile and agile because of their lighter loads. A handful of soldiers might have carried high-quality tin canteens made in Prussia and marked "TEXAS" in the center, while other soldiers wore heavier canteens, including some of superior quality imported from England, made of cedar or cherry wood. These canteens were no longer filled with the much savored "apple-jack brandy" that they had once carried to help them to endure their odyssey, when far-away from such grim killing fields as Gettysburg. Now these mostly wooden canteens were low on their contents, and contained only warm water.

Some of Hood's Texas officers, perhaps wearing .36-caliber Colt Navy revolvers manufactured by the Dance Brothers in Galveston, wore frock coats. Other officers also wore rectangular brass belt plates with the Texas star design, and two-piece sword-belt plates for sabers most likely made in the manufacturing center of New Orleans, with a Texas star (the Lone Star—the official state seal and the former symbol of the Republic of Texas) within a decorative wreath. Officers and enlisted men also wore brass buttons distinguished by the trademark Texas Lone Star and the five letters of Texas at each point of the star. In addition, other Texas soldiers wore brass star insignias, with company and regimental designations, on breast pockets. With pride, some men wore "the 'Lone Star' on his cap," to represent the home state so far away. Meanwhile, soldiers of Company "E," 4th Texas, were noted for wearing distinctive brass buttons with the letters "LSG," the Lone Star Guards.[70]

An unknown number of Texas Brigade weapons, rifles, and revolvers of the men in the ranks were almost certainly produced at the arsenals at Austin and San Antonio. Some trusty Enfield rifle muskets (which were accurate up to a range of 1,000 yards) of the Texas soldiers might well have been made from where a good many soldiers in the ranks hailed, the town of Tyler in northeast Texas. Here, the private firm of Yarbrough, Biscoe, and Short provided small arms, including the prized Enfield rifle. But this locally-made rifle was of an overall poorer quality compared to those finely-crafted rifles manufactured on production lines of experienced workers in industrialized England—the 9-pound Enfield rifles (the standard weapon of the British Army) imported from England and run through the gauntlet of the Union blockade. The western Confederacy relied upon these imports, after the large Enfield rifle plant at New Orleans became unavailable and inoperable, when the South's largest city fell to the Union Navy in the spring of 1862.

Most of the 3,000 Tyler-made Enfield rifles, marked "Texas Rifle," "Tyler," and "Cal. 57," respectively on the brass front plate, were carried by soldiers in campaigns west of the Mississippi, but almost certainly some of these weapons were brought east by recruits who filled the Texas Brigade's ranks, including in April 1863. Indeed, "many rifles produced at the Tyler, Texas, Armory ended up in the hands of Texans."[71] In a letter, Private John Camden West, 4th Texas, best summarized what an Enfield rifle meant to the average fighting man in the ranks, and it was a great deal: "I love my musket next to my wife and my country."[72]

But contrary to Private West's conviction, the love among comrades (one fundamental reason why they fought so hard and died together at Gettysburg) exceeded even the bonds between the trusty .577 Enfield rifle and the young men and boys in the ranks. Of course, these bonds were strongest among relatives, especially father-son fighting teams and groups of brothers, who served in the same companies: highly effective, if not fanatical, familial bands of fighters. The four Perry brothers of the Marshall Guards (Company "E" and representing the town of Marshall, Harrison County, in northeast Texas), 1st Texas, were one such family group of determined fighting men.

Forged by deep family ties and the war's demands, the bonds that existed between Eugene, Clinton, Howard, and Sidney Perry were strong and tight, until the slaughter at Antietam took all four brothers from the ranks. Lieutenant Clinton E. Perry and Private Howard Earle Perry were killed on the field and Private Eugene Osceola Perry and Private Sidney Franklin Perry were wounded. But now, just before the Texas Brigade's sweeping assault on the Devil's Den and Houck's Ridge, only Privates Eugene Osceola Perry and Sidney Franklin "Bose" Perry were left standing in the ranks of Company "E" to do their duty for God and country. "Bose" was about to be cut down in the forthcoming attack on the Devil's Den and Houck's Ridge, falling to achieve the decisive victory that was destined to never come. But Private Eugene Osceola Perry would not survive the battle of the Wilderness in Virginia in May 1864.[73]

Most importantly on the blistering afternoon of July 2, the Texans were in high spirits, and not deterred by the sight of the high ground before them. Almost incredibly, they were not discouraged about either the loss of life from the severe bombardment of Captain Smith's New York guns on Houck's Ridge and other Third Corps guns, or the prospect of charging headfirst into "the next slaughter pen," in Private Fletcher's words, hoping to win the long-awaited decisive victory on northern soil to reverse the war's course. If successful in the upcoming assault, then the Texas soldiers could almost envision themselves marching down the broad expanse of Pennsylvania Avenue in a much dreamed-about victory parade, after capturing Washington, D.C., and delivering a death-blow to the Union and the hated Lincoln Administration.

In fact, a good many Texas soldiers had long desired for nothing more than the opportunity to even up scores with "Old Abe" and reap a long-awaited measure of revenge for his forceful coercing the Southern states back into the Union. During the defense of Richmond during the Peninsula Campaign of 1862, a confident Lieutenant Robert Hugh Gaston, Company "H," 1st Texas, wrote in a letter to "Dear Pa & Ma," how President "Lincoln has said that he would dine at Richmond before long. We would all be glad to see him & would give him a very warm reception."[74] Now after perhaps winning a decisive victory at Gettysburg as fondly envisioned, optimistic Texas Brigade soldiers could almost picture themselves marching as proud conquerors into the streets of Philadelphia, Baltimore, and Washington, D.C., because, in the spring 1863 words of Private John Camden West, "no army on earth can whip these men" of the Texas Brigade.[75]

Of course, the Texas Brigade's soldiers now served in the ranks because of the massive political backlash from Lincoln's 1860 election and the common perception—fueled by John Brown's October 1858 raid on the United States Arsenal at Harpers Ferry, Virginia, to capture weapons to arm blacks to spark slave revolts—that the

Kentucky-born president was a fanatical abolitionist, who would support slave insurrections across the South, including in Texas. With Lincoln's election, therefore, editors of the *Texas State Gazette*, Austin, Texas, had informed readers that Texas families were now under threat from "the torch and the poison of the fanatic, the murderer, and the robber." With the memory of the tragic fate of the hapless French colonists of the Caribbean island of Saint-Domingue (today's Haiti) after the most successful slave revolt in the history of the western hemisphere in the early 1790s, the horrifying fear of slave revolts, sparked by abolitionists who were seen as part of a larger northern conspiracy as commonly believed across the South, played a disproportionate in leading to the secession of Texas.

Therefore, to protect the home front, in the midst of a large slave population thanks to a dominant cotton culture of east Texas, from the most nightmarish possibility of all (slave insurrection), the people of Texas had left the Union and its citizens took up arms.[76] With a successful assault that might win decisive victory at Gettysburg, consequently, the Texas boys could then settle old scores with President Lincoln, and eliminate forever what they perceived as a major threat (slave revolt) to families back home.

Under the searing sun of the humid afternoon of July 2 and about to embark upon their greatest challenge in the war's most important battle, the high *esprit de corps*, morale, and *élan* of the Texas Brigade soldiers, with their trusty Enfield rifles in hand and bayonets by their sides, was quite remarkable under the circumstances. After all, during the last invasion of northern soil during the previous last summer, the 1st Texas had lost at least 82.3 percent (actually higher) of its strength (the highest percentage regimental loss of any Confederate regiment during the war), while the 4th Texas lost nearly 54 percent of its strength in the same battle on the bloodiest single day of the war, Antietam.[77]

The 5th Texas, containing soldiers from Polk, Trinity, Liberty, Washington, Harris, Jefferson, Montgomery, Milam, Walker, Leon, and Colorado Counties, was likewise hard-hit on the bloody morning of September 17, 1862. The 5th Texas lost such good soldiers like a Jewish Rebel named A. F. Woolfe, who served as a private in Company "A" (Bayou City Guards). Woolfe hailed from Houston, which was less anti-Semitic than the North because the port possessed multi-cultural and cosmopolitan qualities. A member of Company "F" (Mustang Grays), 4th Texas, Private Simon Woolfe was another Hebrew warrior who served in the ranks. He was known not only for reading the Torah, but also for his quick reflexes and accurate fire that saved the lives of comrades in close combat situations. Woolfe was mortally wounded at Antietam, falling to rise no more.[78] The name of Woolfe had been long connected with the annals of Texas history, including during the course of the Texas Revolution. Symbolically, three Hebrew males, Abraham (Anthony) and his two young sons (Michael and Benjamin), of the Woolf family died at the Alamo during the surprise Mexican attack on the early morning of March 6, 1836.[79]

Standing in the 1st Texas' thinned ranks, Private George Anthony Walker, Company "B," who was fated to be killed outside Richmond in late August 1864, represented the most direct link to the heroic story of the Alamo. Here, George's father, Jacob Walker, died. The Tennessee-born Walker was the brother of mountain man Joseph R. Walker, who had trapped and explored the Far West. Jacob Walker, who had served as a proud member of Captain William Ridgeway Carey's artillery company whose citizen-soldier members manned the light artillery pieces on the elevated wooden firing platform in the Alamo church's rear, was killed by *soldados* in a flurry of jabbing Mexican bayonets, when cornered inside the smoke-filled church on that bloody morning.

The young private's mother, who never saw him again, was finely-educated Sarah Ann Vauchere Walker. She was born in 1811 and hailed from an aristocratic old French family from Mississippi. She had married Walker in Nacogdoches, Texas, in 1827. Sarah received the news of not only her husband's death at the Alamo in the late winter of 1836 but also that of her Texas Brigade son, who was described by a comrade as "a good and brave soldier." As a staunch Texas patriot during the turbulent course of the Texas Revolution that included a legendary 300-mile ride by her to warn Sam Houston and his forces at Gonzales of an anticipated Indian attack, the blue-eyed, blonde-haired Sarah, who spoke French and Latin with ease, was as feisty as her husband and son, who gave their lives for God and country.[80]

But the tragedies that destroyed the harmony and lives of the Walker family were representative of the sad fate suffered by hundreds of widows and orphans of Texas Brigade soldiers across the state, as the war lengthened and fatalities steadily-increased to frightful levels. The misery and sadness of relatives were destined to reach new heights by what was about to play out in full fury at the Devil's Den, Houck's Ridge, and Little Round Top on bloody July 2, 1863. After the decimation of Hood's troops, literally the best and brightest of Texas, in the nightmare of the killing fields of Antietam, General Lee had asked in astonishment, "Great God, General Hood, where is the splendid division you had this morning [September 17, 1862]?" Stunned by his heavy losses and the extent of the slaughter in the Miller Cornfield situated north of the town of Sharpsburg, Washington County, Maryland, Hood replied with an anguish that hid a deep sorrow that tore at this heart and soul: "They are lying on the field where you sent them, sir.... My division has been almost wiped out."[81]

Paradoxically, the men of the regiment (1st Texas) that had suffered the most of any regiment on either side in the hellish cornfield of farmer Miller were now perhaps the most determined men to achieve a decisive victory at any cost to ensure that frightful loss was not in vain. Consisting of soldiers from Tyler, Cass, Anderson, Houston, Trinity, Cherokee, Galveston, Marion, Harrison, Polk, Nacogdoches, Newton, Sabine, and San Augustine Counties, Lieutenant Colonel Philip Alexander Work's 1st Texas soldiers took inspiration from the fact that their skilled handiwork with the Enfield rifled-musket was lethal and that their color bearer, George A. Branard, now carried the Lone Star State flag in the front rank.

Meanwhile, the vast majority of Lee's regiments, except Virginia commands (represented by blue state flag with the famous Latin motto of "*Sic Semper Tyrannis*"—

"thus always to tyrants") and North Carolina units, flew no state flags. One 1st Texas officer described his regiment's "Lone Star State" flag as "a beautiful banner [that was] made by Mrs. Wigfall [and] It is the finest one I have ever seen." In the upcoming contest for possession of the Devil's Den and Houck's Ridge, the common soldiers were highly-motivated to live-up to their lofty reputation as exceptionally "strong on drill and discipline": qualities that revealed an elite soldiery.[82]

Here, at Gettysburg, the beloved "Lone Star" flag meant something very special to the Texas men, representing not only homes and families, but also a turbulent decade of Texas as an independent republic: a heady, but extremely difficult, nationalistic experience shared by no other state in either the Confederacy or the Union. In the words of one Texan, John Salmon Ford, a Texas Ranger and veteran of the Texas Revolution, this was "the glorious banner of our fathers ... the national flag they adored and almost worshipped [*sic*.]" in consequence.[83]

In addition on July 2, 1863, the band of 1st Texas survivors sought to perpetuate the legacy of their beloved first lieutenant colonel and "jovial" West Pointer who had been immensely popular, Hugh McLeod, and his own personal connection to the Texas Revolution. At least one soldier called Bailey's Prairie home, and he greatly admired McLeod. Bailey's Prairie had been first settled by James Britton Bailey, a War of 1812 veteran, in 1818, which was even before the settling of the Austin Colony. Bailey's Prairie was located in southwest Brazoria County and located just east of the Brazos River. From the picturesque grasslands of Bailey's Prairie, Corporal Joe Polley described how "McLeod was a valiant soldier in the Texas Revolution," and his vivid memory and sad death (January 2, 1862) from disease at Dumfries, Virginia, was still remembered by the 1st Texas soldiers at Gettysburg. Therefore, on this afternoon, his men, who still loved him as a brother and friend, wanted to strike a righteous blow in the name of the popular Scotch-Irishman to continue McLeod's distinguished legacy.[84]

At this time, the Texas soldiers were also motivated to add new laurels to their legendary combat record. They had not been unleashed in the attack since charging through the Miller Cornfield at Antietam on September 17, 1862. Although General Lee fully appreciated the combat prowess of the Texas Brigade, less truly distinguished commands, including the famed Stonewall Brigade of Virginia soldiers, had received more recognition, because of the biased Virginia press centered in Richmond. Here, four major newspapers, the Confederacy's most influential publications, steadily churned out stories, including fanciful ones, which endlessly promoted the heroics of Virginia troops at the Texans' expense.

General McLaws, a heavily-bearded Georgian who clashed with General Longstreet on July 2, said it best in a letter to General Richard S. Ewell, who now commanded the Second Corps after having taken "Stonewall" Jackson's place: "... there is a strong feeling growing among the Southern troops [including Texans] against Virginia, caused by the jealousy of her own people for those from every other state" in the Confederacy, because "no matter who it is may perform a glorious act, Virginia papers give but a grudging praise unless the actor is a Virginian. No matter how trifling the deed may be which a Virginian performs it is heralded at once as the most glorious of modern times."[85]

Now on July 2, the Texans' sterling reputation now called for even a higher level of valor and sacrifice, with battlefield accomplishments coming full circle to fuel the command's fighting spirit and revolve. After all, it was the crucial assignment of the Texas Brigade to turn the left flank of the Army of the Potomac, which, if successful, would drive a nail into the coffin of the North's primary eastern army and change the course of the most murderous war in American history.

Meanwhile, the 1st Texas men never forgot the summer of 1861 words of President Davis. One 1st Texas officer penned in a letter:

> [On the last day of July, President Davis (a revered Mexican-American War veteran who had gained a national reputation for his heroics in leading his Mississippi Regiment with skill in a key situation at the battle of Buena Vista in northern Mexico on February 23, 1847)] told the Texians that they already had a reputation for bravery and patriotism which it would be very difficult to maintain. He closed [his address] by saying that he would expect to see that banner [the "Lone Star State" flag] on the battlefield, where musket balls fell thickest, where the blood of heroes flowed freest and death's brief pang was quickest.[86]

Guaranteeing still another superior combat performance against the odds, they had to reap a decisive victory not only for the Confederacy to win its independence, but also to relieve the suffering of families and friends back in Texas that was extremely vulnerable to Union invasion. At this time, wives, mothers, sisters, and even half-grown children now attempted to operate their middle class-sized farms and ranches on their own as best they could, which was not enough, without their men laboring by their side.

By this time, the overall situation in Texas could hardly have been worse, and the Texas Brigade's soldiers learned as much through the sad letters received in a steady flow from home. After the capture and occupation of New Orleans, which then served as a refuge for pro-Union Texians in exile, on May 1, 1862, the Trans-Mississippi Department, despite the Confederacy's largest theater of operations, had become little more than the Confederacy's abandoned orphan child to a largely apathetic Richmond. Viewed of relatively little importance by Richmond politicians, including President Davis and especially the ever-Virginia-first Lee, the Trans-Mississippi Theater, where the Confederacy's first internal disintegration began to steadily erode the fabric of a fragile Southern nationalism, had been little more than a cast-off theater for the inferior service of a long line of incompetent, mediocre Confederate leaders, including those men exiled by Lee from the Army of Northern Virginia, unable to live up to the Virginian's high expectations.

Without adequate manpower reserves (ironically, thanks in part to so many Texas soldiers fighting and dying on fatal fields like Gettysburg), resources of every variety, capable leadership, economic stability (because of inflation that made a pound of coffee in San Antonio cost $7 when a Texas Brigade private made $11 per month), overall unity without deep class divisions (a classic case of a rich man's war and a poor man's fight), and faltering willpower of the home front because of such negative developments, the overall resistance effort and morale west of the Mississippi, including Texas, was simply not up to the formidable challenge under such disadvantageous circumstances.

Therefore, Southern nationalism and the overall resistance effort weakened and lagged behind across the vast expanse of the Trans-Mississippi, leading to an early demoralization of the home front, which suffered from severe shortages of food, money, and clothing. This disastrous situation, especially the loss of Vicksburg, Mississippi, on July 4, 1863, weakened the will to support the Confederacy that seemingly only brought greater hardships and suffering to the common people of Texas, while their boys fought and died in the eastern theater.[87]

But paradoxically, instead of returning to Texas by deserting and although torn between their moral duty to families and their military commitment to the new Southern republic, the Texas Brigade's soldiers remained steadfast. While thousands of other Southerners, especially westerners, deserted to return home, the Texans faithfully remained in the ranks in part because they knew how badly they were needed by Lee and his army that had long consistently relied upon their combat prowess to win victory, especially at Gettysburg.

The Lone Star State soldiers were convinced correctly that the only way to win this war and the best way to protect Texas was by their own upcoming battlefield performance on the afternoon of July 2, if they were able to turn the Army of the Potomac's left flank. Rather than returning to Texas to forsake the struggle, consequently, the men in the ranks thought more in terms of securing larger numbers of roughhewn farm boys, hunters, and yeomen farmers from their home state to bolster their ranks and make-up for devastating losses. Therefore, ever-mindful that this brutal conflict was a lengthy war of attrition which was gradually dooming the Confederacy to a premature death and the ash heap of history, an increasingly anxious Lieutenant William Henry Gaston, 1st Texas, wrote back to his family: "If there are any boys in Smith County who are anxious to get into the war, you can tell them to come on."[88]

He also penned another letter home to his Smith County, Texas, parents in regard to his two younger brothers, who he viewed as future soldiers who were bound to join the struggle: "Tell John & Mc if they are still going to school, that I want to find them considerably advanced [and] to be practicing with the rifle, for they may have to meet the Yankees sometime."[89]

Clearly, to the Texans, this increasingly bitter struggle was a holy war that had to be fought to the bitter end. As one 1st Texas soldier explained the essence of this crusade that was in part fought for righteous Christian values in their minds, informing the regimental chaplain, or "Parson," which revealed one secret (religious zeal) that explained the superior combat prowess of the 1st Texas, "I believe I am an instrument in the hands to punish those damn Yankees and you bet I am going to give them hell."[90] These words captured the spunky fighting spirit of the Texas Brigade soldiers, while partly explaining the ferocity of the upcoming assault and superior combat performance at the Devil's Den, Houck's Ridge, and Little Round Top.

Because the Texas Brigade soldiers fought more than 1,000 miles away from their Trans-Mississippi homeland, the only way that these elite fighting men could relieve their people's suffering was by winning a sparkling victory at Gettysburg. Unlike the vast majority of Lee's other soldiers mostly from east of the Mississippi, especially Virginia, the Texans clearly possessed more pressing home front-related reasons to vanquish the Yankees this afternoon in Adams County, Pennsylvania, before it was too late for not only the Army of Northern Virginia and Confederacy, but also for Texas.

Indeed, these seasoned Texas had been early convinced that "if we conquer the Yankees in one or two more pitched battles, the war will soon end," but such had not been the case during the first two years of bloody war. Only stalemate and more slaughter at an unprecedented rate had occurred to a degree unimaginable by these young men from Texas at the war's beginning.[91] Indeed, one survivor long remembered how the trek to Warfield Ridge and to a rendezvous with destiny at the Devil's Den and Houck's Ridge had been "the last march for many of the poor fellows" of the Texas Brigade.[92]

Therefore, the upcoming assault on the high ground and desperate bid to turn Meade's left flank offered Hood's men the golden opportunity to not only deliver a death blow to its principal opponent, but also to reap a decisive success second to none. After all, throughout the past, even the hard-earned success in former battles had been illusionary, which had proved fleeting. Even Lee's greatest victories at Second Manassas, Fredericksburg, and Chancellorsville had been nothing more than pyrrhic successes gained at a fearful price: the loss of some the best and brightest, especially among the riddled officer corps, of the Army of Northern Virginia.

But now what was presented to the Texas Brigade was a rare opportunity to achieve a truly meaningful success that would neither be just another case of wasted valor or a pyrrhic victory that cost too many precious lives for no gain. In a letter written just before the Battle of Gettysburg, perhaps no Texas Brigade soldier caught the overall mood better than Private John Mark Smither, 5th Texas. Burdened with a creeping sense of guilt so common with combat veterans, who somehow survived in living through one nightmarish slaughter after another, he was stoically resigned to a tragic fate, if decisive victory could be secured at the southern end of Lee's battle-line:

> I feel so utterly unworthy after being carried safe through the perils of so many battles when friend after friend was shot down at my side, it may be that I am destined to be killed in the next fight but if my life is a drop in the bucket towards restoring liberty & peace to our Confederacy I could not devote it to a better cause.[93]

Like many of the younger men in the ranks, Private John Mark Smither was especially close to his mother. Ironically, this July had special meaning for this soldier of limitless faith in his cause, people, and command. Reflecting on the course of his life, Private Smither thought about his far-away Texas home, when his mother "gave me your blessing and told me to go and serve my country!"[94]

In the veteran ranks of Company "B" (Tom Green Rifles), 4th Texas, Val C. Giles recalled the lofty egalitarian aspirations and republican visions of the Founding Fathers and the revolutionary generation, who fought and died for the great dream of "American independence, the very thing that we were then struggling for" on the blood-stained field of Gettysburg.[95]

As General Hood fully understood at this time, one of the keys to his planned successful offensive effort against the formidable high ground positions on Sickles' left flank in his front—Houck's Ridge, Devil's Den, and Little Round Top, if seized and occupied by Union troops—was the realization that he needed not only an ample amount of artillery, but also close artillery support for his attackers: the traditional "flying artillery" advancing with the infantry to provide close range-fire to knock-out opposing Union batteries and smash lines of supporting infantry. Therefore, with keen foresight, Hood directed that two of his four batteries were to remain limbered, with horses and gunners ready to advance to support the infantry on his order "at a moment's notice."[96]

But unfortunately for the Texas Brigade's fate, Hood and Lee never had enough artillery at Gettysburg to their entirely correct way-of-thinking, especially on the battle-line's southern end, where accurate long-range guns were needed to match the superiority of the 10-pounder Parrotts of Captain Smith's New York Battery. Symbolically, this same deficiency in artillery was now mirrored in Texas in regard to the inadequacy of the homeland's defense. Desperate officials of the Texas military board even conducted an extensive search for Sam Houston's famed cannon, the "Twin Sisters" that had helped to secure his miracle victory at San Jacinto along Buffalo Bayou on the bloody afternoon of April 21, 1836.

Ironically, in the war's beginning, some Texas Brigade soldiers had trained in a camp of instruction, established by the governor, along the sluggish waters of Buffalo Bayou, where Houston's Army had emerged like a ghostly apparition to unleash the afternoon assault that caught Santa Anna by surprise at San Jacinto, much like before pushing on to Virginia. Houston's only two guns at San Jacinto had been donated to the Texian war effort by the patriotic citizens of Cincinnati, Ohio, after having been cast at the Greenwood and Webb foundry in the "Queen City" on the Ohio.

After a thorough search, the famed "Twin Sisters," small iron 6-pounders that had played an outsized role at San Jacinto, were eventually found in Louisiana. On April 20, 1861, the two guns were then returned to Texas to defend the state's vulnerable borders, arriving on the twenty-fifth anniversary of their first firing at Santa Anna's *soldados* on the day before the Battle of San Jacinto.[97] Ironically, the "Twin Sisters" had gamely defended the people and city of Galveston, Texas, including the Battle of Galveston, on January 1, 1863, reviving the special memory of San Jacinto.[98]

Revealing the extent of the worry among Texas Brigade members about the plight of the vulnerable home front, a concerned Lieutenant Robert Hugh Gaston, who hailed from Mount Sylvan, Smith County, Texas, penned in a mid-June 1862 letter: "We have heard of the demand to surrender Galveston. You must meet them as best you can," almost as if apologizing for the fact that he was serving in Virginia and unable to aid in the homeland's defense. The brother of the "Boy Captain of the Texas Brigade," William Henry Gaston, Alabama-born Robert or "Billy," Company "H" (the Texas Guards), 1st Texas, had been killed at age twenty-one during the savage combat of Antietam barely three months after he penned this letter to his parents, who had migrated from the Deep South to Texas in 1849. The blood-stained body of "Billy" had been found in the slaughtered 1st Texas' ranks among the clumps of dead. He had fallen "farther within the Union lines than any other" in the nightmarish combat that raged through the tall, green stalks of the Miller Cornfield.[99]

But most ironic of all, the Texas Rebels could have now used the "Twin Sisters" for Hood's upcoming attack against the Devil's Den and Houck's Ridge, when adequate close-range artillery support (essentially as "flying artillery") was sorely lacking on this all-important afternoon. Seemingly almost instinctively realized by Texas Brigade members by this time, Gettysburg was destined to be the showdown at San Jacinto, where winner and loser were determined by a decisive clash of arms. Although San Jacinto had brought decisive victory and because of the Confederacy's agonizingly slow death by way of gradual attrition and declining will of the Southern people with each new defeat and higher losses, Gettysburg's results lingered until permanently finalized with Lee's surrender at Appomattox Court House, Virginia.

A Dream Deferred

Most of all at this time and fully realized by the men in the ranks, Lee and his Army of Northern Virginia now needed additional hard-fighting Lone Star State units to enhance the overall chances for battlefield success. What few Texas infantry regiments—only three depleted units—that Lee now possessed at Gettysburg was certainly not enough to achieve a decisive victory on the southern end of the army's battle-line.

General Lee's past requests for additional Texas regiments for the creation of a full Lone Star State division had been ignored by the governor and other Texas politicians. The combat prowess and lofty reputation of the Texas Brigade had led to its thorough decimation on one battlefield after another to significantly reduce its overall combat capabilities, especially because of the officer corps' decimation, by this time. These shining characteristics were now needed more than ever before for the climactic showdown at Gettysburg.[100]

Almost prophetically, General Lee had eagerly requested far more Texas fighting men from cantankerous Texas Senator Wigfall. He was "the most reckless of the Texas rabble-rousers," who drank had hard as he fought, but he was unreliable.[101]

Only four days after the Battle of Antietam, an impatient Lee, in perhaps his most solicitous letter to date, wrote to Wigfall about what he needed the most in order to enhance his army's overall combat prowess for future battles like Gettysburg:

> I have not heard from you in regard to the new Texas regiments which you promised to raise for the army. I need them very much. I rely upon those we have in all our tight places, and fear that I have to call upon them too often. They have fought grandly and nobly, and we must have more of them. Please make every possible exertion to get them on for me. You must help us in this matter. With a few more regiments such as Hood now has, as an example of daring and bravery, I could feel more confident of the campaign.[102]

During the Peninsula Campaign after the Texans had demonstrated their superior combat prowess to one and all, John H. Reagan, the respected Postmaster General of the Confederacy, wrote: "General Lee urged me to aid him in getting a division of Texans for his command, remarking that with such a force he would engage to break any line of battle on earth in an open field."[103]

However, good infantry regiments like the 3rd Texas remained far away in the Department of Texas along with the 6th Texas. In regard to the 6th Texas, fate had intervened at the last minute to ensure that this fine regiment never fought at Gettysburg. The 6th Texas was to have joined Hood's Brigade in Virginia, but the Confederate commander of southwest Texas, General Hamilton P. Bee, who won recognition at First Manassas, placed the regiment under his command. Then, in October 1862, when the regiment was finally dispatched to Arkansas "the military situation there soon dictated that the Texans not go any further east," wrote a frustrated William J. Oliphant, a 6th Texas soldier of Scottish, French, and English descent, whose family had migrated to the bustling frontier town of Austin in early 1853.[104]

Therefore, Lee's ambitious dream of an all-Texas Division (which almost certainly would have been the best divisional fighting machine in the Army of Northern Virginia) was never realized, remaining nothing more than a fantasy of the commander-in-chief. Unfortunately for the overall offensive effort at Gettysburg that was a desperate bid to win it all on the afternoon of July 2, General Lee, and the Confederacy, the long-awaited reinforcements that would have resulted in the creation of an entire division of Texas Rebels never became a reality.[105]

Still another missing ingredient in regard to overall chances for Confederate victory this afternoon was the fact that Lee's most reliable top lieutenant, Thomas Jonathan "Stonewall" Jackson, was no more. Many Confederates had prophetically anticipated the worst for Southern fortunate thereafter, especially in regard to the second invasion of the North. In a prophetic May 12, 1863 letter to his father, Corporal Joe Polley, 4th Texas, quite correctly wrote with sorrow how General Joseph "Hooker's grand army [of the Potomac which was now Meade's Army after Lincoln had sacked the bombastic 'Fighting Joe' Hooker, who boasted more than he fought] was badly beaten by our own hero Lee [at Chancellorsville] But our victory cost us a man whose equal we may never find—'Stonewall' Jackson [and] The moral effect which this will have on both armies will be great and very hard to counteract."[106]

Especially in regard to the Battle of Gettysburg, Corporal Polley had made a classic understatement. In a letter that revealed his spiritual faith, Private John Camden West, 4th Texas, lamented the strange twist of fate that had resulted in Jackson's death by the fire of nervous Confederate veterans from North Carolina, which "is a sad calamity for the south, but I doubt not God will raise up other great spirits to aid us with their counsels and to fight our battles for us."[107] In facing their greatest challenge at Gettysburg, the Texas Brigade's survivors perhaps now recalled the complimentary words from "Stonewall" Jackson himself, after the splendid performance of Hood's men, including the "Bloody Fifth" Texas, at Gaines's Mill: "These men that carried that place were soldiers indeed."[108]

Knowing that the Texans, especially the 4th Texas, had been most responsible in breaking through the lengthy formations of blue, General Jackson was not guilty of exaggeration in his praise, because the Texans had smashed through three Union lines, captured a row of artillery pieces, and then repulsed the attack of the 5th United States Cavalry.[109]

Decisive Afternoon of Destiny

Meanwhile, under the hot cannonade of the four New York artillery pieces of Captain James E. Smith's Battery perched atop Houck's Ridge and other guns of the Third Corps that so cruelly stole members from the ranks seemingly with seemingly each shot, the Texas Brigade soldiers situated on the open crest of Warfield Ridge along the dusty Emmitsburg Road continued to await word to move forward across the open ground before them that dropped gently toward the two small watercourse to the east. Already reliable Texas skirmishers, experienced fighting men who could move fast with agility and shoot with deadly accurately, had been sent ahead to feel for any advanced enemy parties that might be lurking before the main line.

The skirmishers in gray and butternut advanced at a good pace down the gradually sloping ground and through the open fields that led straight down into the slight valley of Rose Run on the left and Plum Run on the right, moving onward with fixed bayonets and the ease of veterans. With the ever-aggressive Lee intent on exploiting his gains of the previous two days that has been won by such hard fighting and high sacrifice of some of his best fighting men, no more doubts on either side existed about what exactly was coming next on this afternoon, when the fate of the nation might well be decided. Quite literally, this was a rendezvous with destiny at the southern end of the sprawling battle-line, because it was now or never for the Army of Northern Virginia.

Now during the war's third summer that was more blood-soaked than the previous two, one realization was now beyond all dispute or debate by this time: traditional frontal assaults of infantry—essentially the time-honored Napoleonic linear tactics, as long taught at West Point, of a bygone age—against well-defended by well-armed veterans in fortified high-ground positions were little more than suicidal wastages of lives, because of improved weaponry. The rifled-musket was more accurate and deadly at longer range than during the Mexican-American War days of the smoothbore musket.[110]

Now the Texans faced a deadly triumvirate that had long proved unbeatable in this war: hundreds of veterans, armed with modern weaponry and bolstered by well-served artillery, situated in dominant fashion on the high ground of Houck's Ridge and the Devil's Den. Five of Brigadier General John Henry Hobart Ward's veteran regiments held the crest of Houck's Ridge with a tight grip, which they were determined not to relinquish. These highly-motivated bluecoats were now ready and waiting for Major General John Bell Hood's onslaught with a firm resolve to hold Sickles' and the army's left flank at all costs.

Nevertheless, Hood's men were not daunted by the formidable challenge looming before them. Instead, they fully accepted the stiff challenge of launching a desperate attempt to carry the high ground, before the afternoon ended. Lee's finest soldiers felt that they could overcome any odds once unleashed by Hood, whose crack division was to initiate Longstreet's assault *en echelon* on the army's extreme right, or south: no accident because Lee now depended on his finest division commander and best troops to win the day, when everything was at stake for the future destinies of both republics.

As if knowing as much, thousands of battle-hardened veterans on both sides were determined to fight to the bitter end if necessary for the great goal of winning a decisive victory. In a letter, a determined Lieutenant Robert Hugh Gaston, Company "H," 1st Texas, emphasized to his parents, especially his mother who had been "in very low spirits since we [he and brother Captain William Henry Gaston who was killed at Antietam] left" Texas, that "I think that it will be a great deal better for us to toil through a long war or even to die on the battlefield than to stay at home [as we now] contend for [our] rights."[111]

Gaston's never-say-die words were echoed by Private John Camden West, Company "E," 4th Texas. The proud owner of a modest farm that consisted of fertile land situated along a creek bottom near the frontier town of Waco (an Indian word) located on the Brazos River, West emphasized in a letter how he had suffered almost unimaginable hardships for "the good of my country and the cause of liberty."[112]

Equally defiant, Sergeant David Henry Hamilton, who also stood with a heightened sense of determination in the ranks of Company "M" (Sumter Light Infantry), 1st Texas, promised the girls back home in Trinity County during the May 1862 sendoff, including festive balls and dancing to the fiddles played by popular black and white musicians far into the night, to far-away Virginia that he would "never dance again until independence of the Confederacy was declared" and won.[113]

Ironically, these veterans, who now wanted to once again "see Texas [and] ramble about in green woods," in Lieutenant Gaston's heartfelt words, were about instead to descend into the hell of the eerie and prehistoric-looking landscape of the Devil's Den at the southern end of Houck's Ridge. Here, on a total of 10 acres in what was the most bizarre-looking geological anomaly in the Gettysburg battlefield, there was no trees or much vegetation growing amid this unearthly-looking jumbled pile of giant boulders and ledges: the antithesis of the bountiful and fertile land that they had left behind on the southwest frontier that so many of these young men and boys would never see again.[114]

Hardly appearing like members of Lee's finest combat brigade, the 1st Texas men were described by one Texan as consisting of the most "'wild and woolly' young fellows" of the army.[115] In a May 1863 letter, the erudite Private John Camden Smith, born in Camden, South Carolina, and possessing personal connections to the upper-class political and military elite of South Carolina, described the representative attitude of the Texas Brigade's ranks by the time of the showdown at Gettysburg. He wrote how these hardened veterans "sometimes talk almost like bullies at a street corner, except with a mild, calm air of determination and no swagger. The usual feeling seems to be, 'We can't be whipped, but we may all be killed'" in this war.[116]

The alignment of the veteran Texas Brigade soldiers represented something that transcended place and time. Ironically, just like at the battle of the Alamo, the so-called "Cradle of Texas Liberty" (the Texas creation story that became not only a legend but also a myth) so the Texas Brigade soldiers now hoped to be the key players the creation story of a new Southern republic by winning the victory at the southern end of the battle-line to ensure its long life far into the future. After all, if they could roll-up General Meade's vulnerable left flank, then the Texans could all but guarantee a new day in the sun for the Confederacy, and a bright future among the nations of the world.

Just as the struggle at the Alamo on the early morning of March 6, 1836 had served as a "regeneration through violence" of the new-born Texas republic that led to the winning of the Texas Revolution, so the Gettysburg challenge (like during the climactic showdown at Yorktown, Virginia, in October 1781 during the American Revolution) now offered the ragged Texas soldiers the same golden opportunity to rejuvenate the dying Confederacy and resurrect the loftiest of Southern dreams that included a Manifest Destiny that called for future expansion into the Caribbean and Central America. Just as the Alamo and its fatal consequences had inspired a generation of Texians to save a failed revolution by the most surprising of successes of San Jacinto, so a Confederate victory at Gettysburg would also result in a dramatic rebirth of a people's republic that were now on the road to dark oblivion and the ash heap of history.[117]

Meanwhile, in the scorching afternoon heat, the patter of skirmishing grew louder, echoing over the sunbaked valley of Rose Run, whose cool waters trickled south toward the lower ground Plum Run, where the two small creeks met. Before the experienced men—now silent and serious-looking by their burden to save a nation—in the formations of their regiment aligned between the 1st Texas and the 5th Texas, the extended ranks of the Navarro Rifles, 4th Texas, the veteran skirmishers from Navarro, Ellis, Hill, and Freestone Counties, Texas, continued to advance relentlessly through the open fields of the Michael Bushman farm before Houck's Ridge under the bright sunshine.[118]

Symbolically, the Spanish name of Navarro reflected not only a rich Latino history but also the rich legacies of the Texas Revolution that remained vibrant in the hearts and the minds of these boys of the Navarro Rifles. Among the staunchest Tejano patriots of the 1835–1836 revolutionary struggle were the Navarro brothers. Jose Antonio Navarro, a proud patriot, had signed the Texas Declaration of Independence on March 2, 1836 at Washington-on-the-Brazos only four days before the Alamo's fall because of the lack of assistance from the east Texas settlements. Therefore, Navarro County had been named in Jose Navarro's honor, and the county seat, Corsicana, had been named for his father's birthplace, the island of Corsica, where Napoleon Bonaparte had been born far from the Paris and nation that he was destined to rule to change the face of Europe.[119]

Unleashing a Pent-Up Fury

The dramatic showdown for possession of the all-important high ground at the battle line's southern end was about to erupt in full fury. On the far right of the lengthy battle-line, the five Alabama regiments of Brigadier Evander McIver Law's Brigade were the first soldiers of Hood's Division to step off not long after 4 p.m., initiating the assault *en echelon* on the Union left flank. The five regiments of Alabama Rebels surged straight eastward toward where the sun had first peaked over the horizon on the day that Lee and seemingly everyone else in the Army of Northern Virginia had originally expected to bring the long-elusive decisive victory early in the morning. But for a wide variety of reasons, such was not the case, and now even harder work would have to be accomplished by Hood's men this afternoon.

Meanwhile, the assault in the Texas Brigade's sector north of Law's Alabama brigade finally took definite shape when General Hood galloped to the head of the Texas Brigade on the left-center before the ranks of the 1st Texas in a swirl of dust. Here, at the northern end of the crest of Warfield Ridge, Hood was in a frustrated, if not angry, mood at this time. Major William Henry Sellers, Hood's reliable *aide de camp* had just returned from Longstreet's headquarters with the young major general's final orders, which once again overruled Hood's ambitious plan for a stealthy flank march around the Round Tops.

Hood's dramatic appearance was a sight that the tense Texas Brigade soldiers, eager to be unleashed in the attack *en echelon* to Law's left just to the south, had long anxiously awaited, while lying prone under the shellfire from Captain Smith's New York guns on Houck's Ridge and other Third Corps artillery that blew clods of dirt and rocks over them. While the cannon of both sides roared like thunder under the clear skies of a rapidly dying summer day, Hood never looked more inspirational or dynamic than ever before on this scorching afternoon.

Although the hard-fighting division commander, who had commanded the division since early in the 1862 Peninsula Campaign, was "a better soldier than speaker," Hood was now the most eloquent when facing his greatest challenge, because he realized the supreme importance of the upcoming assault on Meade's left on July 2. Most of all, he wanted his own inspirational force of dynamic leadership and personal actions on the battlefield to speak louder than any words that he could possibly say on this day of destiny. Hood knew exactly what was at stake this afternoon at the southern end of the lengthy battle-line: it was literally a case of now or never for the Confederacy and its principal army that was responsible for winning the decisive victory to bestow a long life to the infant republic.[120]

With the 3rd Arkansas on the left flank, the 1st Texas on the left center, the 4th Texas on the right center, and the 5th Texas on the right flank and after most of July 2 had been wasted by fumbling Confederate leadership at the highest levels, the Texas Brigade was more than ready for its greatest challenge. Prudently in preparation for initiating Lee's flank assault in echelon, Hood had already ordered forth a pioneer detail "to throw down" a large section of the rail fence—a significant weakening of its overall structural integrity along a lengthy expanse to shortly allow for the advancing line to knock-down the entire fence—that spanned north–south across the open fields that descended to Rose Run and then Plum Run before the Texans, so as not to impede the momentum of the upcoming attack.

The fate of the most important battle of the war might well be determined by the Texans' upcoming assault, and these veterans fully realized as much. The Texas Brigade had not been unleashed on the tactical offensive since the attack through the Miller Cornfield of Antietam more than nine months before, but the memories of the sparkling success at Second Manassas remained alive and well among these veterans. Consequently, the men in the ranks were eager to meet the boys in blue, because they were confident of once again securing victory.

Unlike a number of Lee's division commanders who failed to measure-up to lofty standards, Hood was more than every inch of a fighter. In fact, he was the most aggressive and best fighting division commander in the Army of Northern Virginia Hood, consequently, was determined to accompany his troops into the heart of the tempest with his customary dramatic flair. If his troops broke through, then he needed to be in the forefront to exploit the tactical advantage as soon as possible to exploit Lee's tactical concept of an assault in echelon: one secret of Major General Hood's success as a commander on previous battlefields.

Along the open expanse of Warfield Ridge, Major General John Bell Hood galloped down the lengthy row of Brigadier General Jerome Bonaparte Robertson's anxious troops. Robertson's middle name reflected the name of the dynamic military man who had dominated not only Europe, but also an age, the Age of Napoleon. Proud of the fact that he commanded the Confederacy's elite soldiers who had never failed him in the past, the native Kentuckian stood up in his iron stirrups of his war horse, and then yelled, "Fix bayonets, my brave Texans." Eager for the opportunity to turn the Army of the Potomac's left that lacked the necessary amount of protection, the Texans instantly answered with a resounding cheer—a "regular Texas war whoop." These veterans instantly leaped to their feet "as if at a game of ball" that was about to be played back. A metallic ringing of bayonets attached to the ends of around 1,400 muskets, the trusty Enfield rifles, echoed over the fields of summer.

On the brigade left-center, Lieutenant Colonel Philip Alexander Work never forgot how the "order to 'Forward' was given by Genl Hood himself; he, with his staff, being then with the 1st Tx.—and only a few steps in front."[121] Out in front, Hood then screamed at the top of his voice, "Forward and take those heights!"[122] In a letter, James Henry Hendrick, Company "E," 1st Texas, described: "General Hood gave the command forward [and the crack] division moved forward at a double quick step with a yell."[123]

At long last, the much-belated assault to turn Meade's left finally began to gain steam and momentum. Knowing that the high ground had to be carried by storm and at all costs despite his repeated strong objections to even launching the desperate attempt, Hood's view of the heights of Little Round Top told him that the cost to his Texas Brigade would be frightfully high, if Union troops gained the strategic crest. But the men of the 1st Texas focused their eyes on their immediate objective, which was the first high ground before Little Round Top—Houck's Ridge. At this point, Hood and his men could not see what lay in store for them at the southern end of John Houck's ridge, the Devil's Den.

Before the thinned ranks of the 1st Texas, Lieutenant Colonel Work screamed, "Follow the Lone Star Flag to the top of the mountain!"[124] Officers along the line shouted, "Forward-Guide Right-March!"[125] While the other troops of Hood's Division, except for some of Law's Alabamians who likewise raised a chorus of high-pitched shouts to the southeast since they had advanced just before the Texas Brigade had been unleashed as part of the assault in echelon, remained silent, hundreds of Texans again raised "such a wild indescribable battle yell that no one having heard ever forgot": a certain guarantee that they were about to once again perform at an unparalleled high level on the battlefield.[126]

However, already everything was different from previous battlefields on which the Texans had won their fame. As Corporal Polley explained the tactical situation of assaulting high ground in striking contrast to past battlefields, especially on the Virginia Peninsula: "Hitherto, the Texans had fought on ground over which they could move rapidly in line, and where the enemy was accessible—where the terror caused by their daring rush and swift on-coming counted large" on the battlefield.[127]

Hood now had all nine regiments of his two front-line brigades on the attack and rolling forward like a well-oiled machine. With trusty .577-caliber Enfield rifles at right shoulder shift, the confident Texans had surged off the crest of the northern end of Warfield Ridge, steam-rolling down the slope that flowed gently toward Rose Run and then Plum Run.

With colorful battle-flags flying and bayonets flashing under the bright sunshine, the Texans advanced as one down the ridge's eastern slope that gently descended all the way into the shallow creek (Plum Run) valley to the east. When the left of the 1st Texas neared a rail fence along the Emmitsburg Road, Lieutenant Colonel Work shouted "Grab it by the bottom rail and heave," which was a strong arm directive that proved most effective, because the fence rails went flying in every direction.[128] Private Albert Cuthbert Sims, in the 1st Texas's ranks, described how "the whole column moved forward and with one united effort threw down the fence to the ground [and then] we emerged into the skirt of the [thin] belt of timber," before the expanse of open fields blessed by the summer sun.[129]

With their usual *élan*, the Texans advanced with their typical spirit and discipline down the gentle slope that gradually descended toward Rose Run that ran north–south and paralleled Houck's Ridge, before the little creek continued to flow south to eventually enter Plum Run that ran through the valley at the base of Little Round Top, to the north, and Big Round Top, to the south. The unnerving sight of the cheering Texans moving forward with fixed bayonets made the troops of Ward's brigade (the Army of the Potomac's largest brigade that had been assigned by Dan Sickles to anchor his left flank), and Captain James E. Smith and his New York gunners were more determined to hold firm against the surging tide of Rebels. Besides a sense of pride, Smith felt the heavy burden of responsibility because his New York artillery now served the guardians of the left flank of the entire Army of the Potomac.

With his four lethal 10-pounder Parrott rifles booming from their "excellent" elevated perch atop Houck's Ridge—or actually the top of the Devil's Den that extended to the north–and with New York gunners directing their long-range fire at the Texans' surging ranks, now exposed in the open fields of summer, with case shot, Smith was determined to hold the high ground at costs. He was now motivated by a single desire that had become an all-consuming and desperate obsession that seemed to stem from some kind of ancient primeval survival of the fittest instinct on this afternoon of destiny: to do whatever it took to "cripple this attack and check it as much as possible."[130]

Fate Intervenes and General Hood Goes Down

Nevertheless, at this time and like on July 1, the stars seemed to have once again lined-up for General Lee for the reaping of success, especially in regard to having his finest combat brigade, under General Jerome Bonaparte Robertson, in the key position to deal a death blow to Meade's Army by turning its left flank. Quite simply, the right men were in the right place at the right time, because Lee depended so heavily on General Hood and his hard-hitting troops. The odds were still good that a decisive victory could be reaped before the sun dropped over the heavily-forested Cumberland Mountains to the west. However, a cruel fate suddenly intervened as hardly had the attack begun to early sabotage the overall chances for a successful assault on a day when seemingly nothing was going right for the Army of Northern Virginia.

After he rode through the open gap earlier torn into the lengthy rail fence by the detail of gray-uniformed pioneers, who had been earlier sent forth before the rail fence was knocked-down by the onrushing ranks, and after having proceeded not far down the sloping ground leading to Rose Run laying before the surging ranks of the 1st Texas, Major General Hood was now extremely vulnerable on the open ground. Standing out prominently in a fine gray uniform and on horseback before his advancing troops, the former United States cavalrymen was quickly sighted by Captain James E. Smith's sharp-eyed gunners, who knew a good target when they saw one.

Consequently, the New York gunners turned their fire on the tall, majestic Confederate leader who was completely exposed out in the open on horseback. But even these veteran artillerymen from the Empire State had no idea that their new target was a highly-respected division commander with unlimited promise, because such high-ranking officers usually remained in the rear and safely out of harm's way. But as usual, Hood was in the foremost to exploit any tactical opportunity that might suddenly appear before his attackers. He, therefore, was determined to orchestrate, if not micromanage as much as possible, his division's movements from the front and not the rear: a quality that endeared him to his men, and significantly increased the chances for success.

Suddenly, as directed by Hood, young Major John Cheves Haskell, a well-educated former attorney from South Carolina of second in command of Major Mathias Winston Henry's divisional (Hood's) artillery battalion, brought up two additional batteries to support Hood's attack in a vital role as flying artillery. Only in his early twenties, Major Haskell, educated at South Carolina (University of South Carolina) College, was a highly-capable artillery officer like his immediate superior Major Henry, despite having lost an arm to the blast of a Union cannon at close range during the Battle of Gaines's Mill.

Most importantly, the insightful Hood fully understood that close artillery support was crucial for achieving success on this afternoon, when everything was at stake. But before Hood could give precise instructions about exactly where he wanted the artillery to advance close behind his surging infantrymen, a cruel fate suddenly intervened. One of Captain Smith's shells from a 10-pounder Parrott exploded above this advanced party of mounted Confederate officers, who were stationary and ideal targets on the open ground among small trees of an orchard on the eastern slope of Warfield Ridge. Unfortunately for Southern fortunes on the far south of the army's battle-line, iron fragments broke Hood's left arm, slicing down from above the elbow to the hand.[131]

Lieutenant Colonel Philip Alexander Work described the shocking tragedy that horrified the advancing men of the 1st Texas, when pouring forth over the descending ground just north of the Michael Bushman farm situated amid the fertile farmlands: General Hood "had ridden forward only a short distance when he received a wound [in the left arm] from a spherical case shot which exploded some twenty or thirty feet above him—and immediately falling from his horse—but was caught and eased down by his aides who instantly dismounted him. I saw the whole occurrence," while leading the 1st Texas forward into the raging storm in the all-important struggle to turn the Union left.[132] About to lose his left arm to amputation and fortunate to survive the nightmarish operation in primitive and unsanitary conditions, Hood was taken rearward in a hurry before he bled to death.[133]

In his own words, Hood described:

> As I was borne off on a litter to the rear, I could but experience deep distress of mind and heart at the thought of the inevitable fate of my brave fellow-soldiers, who formed one of the grandest divisions of that world-renowned army; and I shall ever believe that had I been permitted to turn-Round Top Mountain, we would not only have gained that position, but have been able finally to rout the enemy.[134]

As one of Lee's hardest fighting generals and certainly his best division commander, Hood's fall from his horse, which was not the one that had been presented to him by his 4th Texas boys, could not have come at a worse time for Confederate fortunes in the struggle to turn Meade's left flank. Quite simply, half of Lieutenant General James Longstreet's First Corps—assigned by Lee to deliver the most decisive blow of the second day—was suddenly and effectively minus its most dynamic and capable leader during what was shaping up to be the most important attack of the war.

A Class of 1853 graduate of West Point and with ample experience from years of prewar service in the United States Army and, unfortunately, for the overall offensive effort, Hood was destined to not give another order on the most important afternoon of the war. And, of course, he never saw what was shortly to become Gettysburg's most hellish battleground, the Devil's Den. As an unfortunate fate would have it just as the assault had begun, the tall, native Kentuckian of almost limitless ability as a leader was out-action for the rest of July 2, the day of decision when the Army of Northern Virginia possessed the best chance to win it all, as opposed to the popular and stereotypical view that July 3 was the most decisive day at Gettysburg.

Ironically, Captain Smith's ambition "to cripple" the attack of Hood's Division had been partly fulfilled with a single shot from a Parrott rifle hardly before the battle had begun on the second day, because Hood's Division was now without its leader, and controlling and guiding force for the remainder of the most important battle of the war. All in all, perhaps no single artillery shot of the Battle of Gettysburg was more effective in sabotaging overall chances for the success of turning Meade's left flank.[135] With some understatement, gifted historian Stephen Sears correctly emphasized the inevitable results of Hood's fall, because "the striking power of this crack division would be divided and diluted over the course of the fighting."[136]

As subsequent events fully demonstrated, Hood's leadership skills in carefully coordinating the assault of his crack division were desperately needed for this all-important assault on Meade's left flank, because of the stiff tactical challenges that lay ahead. Perhaps the astute Private James M. Polk, Company "I" (Navarro Rifles), 4th Texas, said it best. He lauded one of Hood's principal strengths as a battlefield commander that could no longer be utilized in the most confused and seemingly ill-fated of battles: "Gen. Hood could get order out of confusion on a battlefield in less time and apparently with less trouble than any one I ever saw."[137]

At Gettysburg, this invaluable quality of a talented and experienced leader was shortly needed for the attacking Texas Brigade when undertaking its most formidable challenge of the war. But since time immemorial, the universal truth now applied at the southern end of the battle-line on the afternoon of July 2: Hood's veterans fought more for each other than for General Hood, who no doubt would have been somewhat shocked by this realization. Nevertheless, Hood's fall from horse so near the beginning of the assault was a disaster of immeasurable consequences that profoundly affected the overall outcome of the struggle to turn Meade's left flank in the hours ahead.

Ironically, some enlisted men in the ranks had already expected the worst, before Hood was cut down with serious injuries. They had noticed that General Hood was not riding his usual war horse, a beautiful and high-spirited roan that was considered lucky by the men in the ranks. Because Hood had been so successful in directing battle, especially the tactical offensive, on what was seen as his lucky roan, the horse's notable absence had been immediately seen as an extremely bad omen for events to come. Hood had never been harmed while riding his favorite roan, and the animal had not been touched by Yankee bullets and shells. The men in the ranks were convinced that their beloved general would always be safe while riding on the back of his roan, even during the fiercest battle.

Therefore, when Hood was suddenly cut down and symbolically fell off the new horse that his men feared was not lucky like the roan, the worst fears of the most superstitious Texans, who knew that success on the battlefield often depended on luck, or the fortunes of war, were entirely confirmed. Consequently, some Texans, thinking almost like ancient Greeks and Romans, now eyed the high ground before them with even greater dread than before, believing that a missing roan had ordained them to an unfair and a cruel fate.

Young General Evander McIver Law's Quandary

As the senior brigade commander and brigadier general of Hood's Division, after John Bell Hood was felled from his horse as if by a lightning bolt from a Rebel-hating Yankee God, young General Evander McIver Law was now the division commander on the most important afternoon of the war. Earning his promotion to brigadier general only last October less than nine months before, the South Carolina-born Law was one of the shining stars of the Army of Northern Virginia.

But he was young at only age twenty-six, and worst of all, Law had never commanded a division before in combat. The ultimate challenge of Gettysburg was certainly no place to learn on the job. Having been appointed to a brigadier general's rank last autumn by way of the combination of his leadership ability and ample political support of leaders in high places, General Law was not quite able to measure up to the formidable tactical and leadership requirements, which now called for maintaining the assault's momentum and organizational cohesion in Hood's absence: a very tall order for a young man, especially on a crucial field of strife where developments, especially the division's charge, were moving at a fast pace and gaining momentum. Even more, no one yet knew the exact strength and locations of Union troops, except for the row Captain Smith's booming guns atop Houck's Ridge and silhouetted against the immediate eastern skyline, and Law would have to ascertain as much as possible about the overall tactical situation to maximum the assault's striking power to effectively turn Meade's left flank.

In part because of the excessive amount of time it took to notify Law that he was now in command of the division, he was bound to fail to provide proper guidance to any brigade of the four brigades of Hood's Division. In fact, Law was unable to even inform his senior regimental commander, Colonel James Lawrence Sheffield, who led the 48th Alabama, that he now commanded the Alabama Brigade. An experienced commander, Sheffield, born in 1819 in Huntsville, Alabama, and a Marshall County politician, had served as a deputy sheriff from 1844 to 1847.

Of course, such a timely notification of Law's new responsibility—command of Hood's Division—was absolutely crucial because the Alabama Brigade was the "brigade of direction" for Hood's Division during this echelon assault. But no such notification was forthcoming until late in the day and, by then, it was already too late. Therefore, no Confederate commander penned in his official report of having received any orders from Law until the battle had already been all but decided. Coinciding with the overall inferior performances of Confederate leaders at the highest levels and despite his own personal courage and determination, Law's leadership failures on a tactical level played a role in altering the fate of the Texas Brigade's attack on July 2.

At this time, Law certainly looked the part of promising and dashing leader, who was entirely ready for the Gettysburg challenge. He was intelligent and a proud graduate of the Citadel in Charleston, South Carolina. However, Law was simply no match (nor were a good many other leading officers, including Lee and Longstreet for that matter) for the confusing situation commonly known as the fog of war that befuddled so many other Southern leaders on the afternoon July 2. Quite simply, Law now faced his greatest leadership and battlefield challenge, and he was in over his head. All in all, this vexing situation was simply too much for Law's leadership capabilities, especially in the most confusing of battles. But to be fair to Law, the overall situation was already beyond his control.

Without adequate leadership or direction and despite the best division in Lee's Army, Hood's unleashed division was about to become like a runaway freight train without brakes, with two brigades dividing during the assault. Then these separate components were destined to push onward in three parts without coordination or proper unity. While the advancing Texas Brigade shortly split in two because of the impossibility of keeping the brigade's left on the Emmitsburg Road and the brigade's right on the left of Law's Brigade as directed by Hood, the Alabama Brigade also soon became even more splintered and divided. Therefore, the excellent Alabama Brigade would fight today in three separate groups to considerably diminish its overall strength and striking power, when a concentration in force was most needed for success.[138]

Leadership Failures from Deep Within

Even worse for the Texas Brigade after "Texas [was] turned loose," in Private James O. Bradfield's words, Brigadier General Jerome Bonaparte Robertson's exact whereabouts became somewhat of a mystery because of contradictory statements from his officers and enlisted men. Robertson's notable absence compounded the leadership void after Hood's fall and before Law was notified that he was now in charge of the division, while the troops continued to move swiftly on the attack.

But, according to Lieutenant Colonel Philip Alexander Work who certainly knew a good deal about the exact situation, the Kentucky-born Robertson, the son of a Scottish immigrant and a former St. Louis, Missouri, hatter (apprenticed at age eight after his immigrant father's death and forced to fend for himself at an early age on the streets of the largest city west of the Mississippi River), before migrating to Texas in 1836, remained entirely absent on the left of his brigade, especially after it shortly splintered off on its own upon breaking away from Law's left.

In the no-holds-barred words of Colonel Work, a true fighting man who was later shocked to learn that Robertson had not ever written an official report about the battle, although he was required to do so as brigade commander: "As I was unaware that Genl R[obertson] had reported that battle (and this was because no regimental commander of the brigade either saw or received an order from him at any time after the advance began—and he was not an eye witness of anything that occurred)" in the battle.[139]

Work held no personal grudge, only truly reported what happened on this afternoon in hell, as he had seen first-hand and learned from personal experience. For the most part, Work's incriminating words were right on target, because ample evidence has revealed that Robertson was lacking in his ability to demonstrate essential leadership qualities and in not providing proper guidance to his advancing regiments, which mirrored Law's own equally lackluster performance during this attack. However, near the end of the day's fighting, Robertson belatedly sent an order to Lieutenant Colonel Work to take command of the hard-hit 3rd Arkansas, after its commander (the feisty Colonel Vannoy "Van" Hartrog Manning) was destined to be hit in the bloodletting. At nearly age fifty, Robertson was older than most regimental and brigade commanders, and evidently the wisdom bestowed with age resulted in him not exposing himself unnecessarily or recklessly on the battlefield this afternoon. He was formally charged with the lack of aggressiveness in a following campaign, but not at Gettysburg where blame for failure was widespread among Confederate leadership at all levels.[140]

Problems also existed in the past. After Robertson had departed his old company, the Marshall Guards of Company "E," 1st Texas to take command of the Texas Brigade, most Harrison County men of his experienced unit were "very willing to get rid of him," in the words of Private Rufus Felder, because of the lack of leadership abilities that caused them to be "very much disappointed in him."[141].

Having survived the Texas Revolution and previous battles, including with mounted Native Americans who roamed the Texas frontier, Colonel Robertson was also a savvy politician by instinct and experience. In consequence, he was not a popular commander—from company to brigade leader—in part because, unlike Hood who had occasionally intervened to temper Robertson's martinet ways, Robertson made the mistake to attempting to too tightly control his men's behavior in camp. He prohibited gambling, which, of course, was a favorite pastime of the common soldiers with women and alcohol not absent. After suffering nasty wounds in assaults during the Peninsula Campaign at Gaines's Mill in the shoulder and then in the groin at Second Manassas, the former Texas legislator had commanded the Texas Brigade since the autumn of 1862.

Because the Texas Brigade was not engaged at Fredericksburg or Chancellorsville and to compliment Law's lack of experience in commanding a division, Robertson possessed limited experience in leading a full brigade in action. Due to exhaustion and his nagging groin injury that had caused him to collapse on the grueling march north in the Army of Northern Virginia's first northern invasion, Robertson had absented himself from the first great clash of arms at Antietam on September 17, 1862. He was now in the process of doing the same in the next major battle on northern soil, when even more was at stake for his brigade, the army, and the nation.

By this time, a large rift had developed between the colonel and his feisty 1st Texas soldiers, perhaps because he had been once a penniless orphan and then a lowly hatter. Robertson, therefore, felt now felt that he needed to distance himself from a past that he considered an embarrassment. But much of the problem stemmed from the fact that he was also a smooth-talking politician of a self-serving, if not Machiavellian, nature, a former Texas state senator. During a dress parade, an amused Hood had once joked in fun at the "dark, beetle-browed" Robertson for his meticulous fussing about the most obscure details of the complex mechanics of drill, saying that the colonel "reminded him of his 'Old Aunt Polly.'" Unfortunately for Robertson who proudly wore a silver Texas star insignia on his hat, Hood's cutting remark was heard by the men in the ranks. Then, in the words of Private Albert Cuthbert Sims, 1st Texas, "all of the soldiers got to calling him Aunt Polly, to the great annoyance of Gen. Robertson."[142]

During a lengthy march on a past campaign, one exhausted 1st Texas soldier, who badly needed a break along with his worn comrades, yelled out when Robertson and his staff rode past, "Rest, Polly." An infuriated Robertson reigned up his horse and demanded, "Who was that who called me Polly?" Of course, the men in the ranks remained perfectly silent. Then, the angry general turned to a young officer of his staff and asked, "Captain, who was that called me Polly?" Unable to refuse a direct order, the captain pointed out the outspoken culprit, and the incensed Robertson had the man punished by carrying half a dozen muskets for the march's remainder that continued until nightfall.[143]

Additionally, Robertson had recently placed the popular Captain Samuel A. Willson, who led Company "F" (Woodville Rifles, 1st Texas) as Work's successor although only in his mid-twenties, unfairly under arrest for a minor, almost silly, infraction that was a mistake. But to his credit, Robertson then released him in time for the great showdown at Gettysburg.[144]

Then, Work later suspected that his official report about the Battle of Gettysburg had been tampered with in order to present Robertson, who wore his hair long in Texas frontier fashion, in a more favorable light, especially in regard to being active on the field and giving direct orders to Work, who never saw the brigade commander or received a single directive from Robertson once the assault was launched. If this was the case, then Robertson was indeed truly Machiavellian and devious enough to order someone else to do the dirty work. He concluded: "I suspect a part of my Gettysburg report as published as being bogus and containing interpolations, and that this was done for a purpose. Jno. G. Scott [former Company 'G,' 1st Texas, private who had been appointed *aide de camp* to Robertson on November 12, 1862] of Gen R's staff was entirely capable of such practices."[145]

As fate would have it, with both divisional and brigade leadership having early fallen apart and as often in the past, it was now left largely to the veteran common soldiers, including teenagers yet to shave or make love to a woman, in the Texas Brigade's ranks to win the day. They would have to compensate not only for the absent leadership at the division and brigade levels, but also for the many failures of the army's top leadership, especially Lee and Longstreet, when their young nation's destiny hung in the balance. Therefore, despite the fact that divisional and brigade leadership failed to rise to the challenge, it was a stirring testament to the combat prowess of the common soldiers that what was unleashed, in the words of a Texas soldier from a letter, was in fact "one of the most gallant charges ever made by the" Texans.[146]

However, as seen on previous fields, this previously seen development of the common soldiers taking the initiative was not surprising because the Texas Brigade boys were still fundamentally free-thinking individualists and resourceful frontiersmen, who were self-reliant, flexible, and opportunistic on the battlefield. William "Bill" Andrew Fletcher, Company "F," 5th Texas, was one such soldier who rose to the fore. He grew up on the east Texas frontier, where "I have fished and hunted a great deal, from a small boy up; I have had the association and advice of both the white man and the Indian in Woodcraft" and how to fight with skill.[147]

Another natural soldier whose skill at killing Yankees by well-aimed shots or a steel bayonet had been well-honed by the frontier experience, Private Albert Cuthbert Sims described in regard to him and his twin brother, Albert Hubert Sims, who died in April

1863: "We were brought up in the wild forest of east Texas where the scream of the panther, the howl of the wolf and the squeal of the razor-back" boar were heard.[148]

These were the kind of rawboned and can-do frontier types who were now at the heart of the sweeping Texas charge toward the high ground that had to be taken for the loftiest Confederate dreams to become reality. Private Albert Cuthbert Sims, in the 1st Texas's ranks on the brigade's left-center, described how unity of purpose had been demonstrated early in the assault, when "the whole column moved forward and with one united effort threw down the fence to the ground [and] we emerged into the skirt of the timber."[149]

After having emerged from the thin "skirt of the timber" on Warfield Ridge, Lieutenant Colonel Work continued to lead his 1st Texas troops onward down the slight slope that grew steeper as they drew ever nearer to the belt of timber and underbrush along Rose Run that filled the bottom of the little valley only recently peaceful and the epitome of natural serenity. Ironically, Work gained some comfort in the fact that his father, Dr. John Work, now served as the assistant surgeon of the 1st Texas since October 1862, and brought a familial quality to his war far from home.

Although open fields along the slope on the west side of Rose Run lay before the 1st Texas's surging ranks, the land was covered with well-constructed stone fences that had long marked farmers' boundary lines and kept cattle and other livestock safely confined on the owners' property. These stone walls, low but sturdy, made excellent defensive positions, where a relative handful of boys in blue could make a determined stand against attackers surging through the open fields.

Meanwhile, the alignment between the Texas Brigade's right and the left of the Alabama Brigade began to fall apart almost from the beginning of its sweeping advance toward Plum Run, below where Rose Run entered the larger watercourse that flowed at the base of Little Round Top. The Texans' eagerness to once again come to grips with the boys in blue and to strike a devastating blow fueled them onward at a faster pace than the 4th Alabama Rebels on the far left of Law's brigade. Consequently, on Robertson's far right, the 5th Texas, like the rest of the Texas Brigade on the move to the north, pushed onward at right shoulder shift at a faster rate than the nearby 4th Alabama, which now advanced on the left flank of Law's Brigade.

Revealing that a healthy rivalry existed between the Texas and Alabama Brigades, one 4th Alabama soldier named Rufus King, who was about to be killed in the assault, issued an impromptu challenge, when he yelled to his comrades, "'Come on, boys; come on!' The Fifth Texas will get there before the Fourth! Come on boys; come on!" However, this renewed rush of Alabamians, who were determined not to be showed up or embarrassed by the Texas Rebels, caused their line to lose its neat alignment. An angry Alabama adjutant shouted to his troops to advance in a much more straight alignment like the 5th Texas men. Worst of all, this race eastward played a role in additionally separating the 5th Texas (also the 4th Texas whose right was next to the 5th Texas' left) from the brigade's right wing to the north.[150]

Like the 5th Texas and its companies such as the Milam County Greys (Company "G"), the Dixie Blues (Company "E"), and the Texas Polk Rifles (Company "H"), the onrushing 4th Texas, led by handsome Lieutenant Colonel Benjamin Franklin Carter, who was "one of the finest officers in the division" and yet in his early thirties, also advanced at a rapid rate. The popular Tennessee-born Carter, a graduate of Jackson College and successful politician who possessed sufficient eloquence to have previously impressed a good many homespun voters, and the former mayor of Austin, Texas, was about to receive his death stroke.[151] As written in a letter, Private John Camden West described how "we moved forward as fast as we could" over the open ground and farmer's fields that descended to the meandering waters of Rose Run.[152]

All the while, the wide, open fields before Rose Run were swept by the fire of the booming New York guns atop Houck's Ridge that continued to roar like there was no tomorrow. In their eagerness to punish the Texas attackers, who continued to surge across the open ground with discipline at right shoulder shift and "as if on parade," in the words of one of Ward's soldiers, Smith's four 10-pounder Parrott rifles unleashed their first concentrated fire in unison.

Hurriedly in their eagerness, the New York gunners quickly reloaded and readjusted by lowering barrels for the next salvo of shell-fire that also sailed too high and over the lengthy formations surging across the open ground. But then the third try of the overly-anxious cannoneers was right on target, with round shot hitting before the ranks. These projectiles wreaked havoc in the Texas Brigade's formations as hoped and prayed by the sweating bluecoat artillerymen, who laid down a deadly ricochet fire.

One solid shot that hit immediately in front of the lengthy formation bounced up to inflict damage, "knocking off one soldier's head and cutting another in two, bespattering us with blood," penned one horrified survivor of a close call. Carrying the 1st Texas's colors, light-hearted Private Rodney "Rod" Meekins, Company "B," 1st Texas, was one of the first soldiers killed by this concentrated artillery fire. Prophetically, the usually merry "Rod" Meekings had only recently predicted his own death in the next battle at a time when his comrades expected an easy victory in upcoming days on Pennsylvania soil, where so many Texans were destined to find final resting places this afternoon. Likewise, because General McLaws' Division had not yet attacked to the north because of Lee's assault in echelon concept, Sickles' Third Corps' batteries aligned along Wheatfield Road, which ran southeast toward Little Round Top, blasted away into the Texas Brigade's left flank.[153]

Facing the Union Army's Most Lethal Marksmen

Adding to the severe punishment delivered by the booming 10-pounder Parrott rifles and unfortunately for the attackers was the accurate fire of the Union Army's finest marksmen, Colonel Hiram Berdan's Sharpshooters of two specialized regiments. Officially designated as 2nd United States Sharpshooters, Ward's Brigade, these experienced sharpshooters were the most lethal fighting men in the Union Army.

Berdan's Sharpshooters were known as the "Green Coats," because of their distinctive green uniforms that blended in well with the natural surroundings in spring and summer, especially the dense woodlands. Along with the accurately-firing marksmen of the 1st United States Sharpshooters, these expert killers of the 2nd United States Sharpshooters had been earlier and smartly hurled forward by General Ward before Houck's Ridge for the express purpose of slowing Hood's advance.

After taking a lengthy north–south position behind a white-colored (limestone) stone wall situated along a slight rise before the Slyder House located about half-way between Warfield Ridge's crest and Rose Run, which flowed south before the waters of Plum Run and roughly parallel to that larger watercourse, Berdan's marksmen were in an ideal position to significantly reduce the number of attackers and impede the advance.

With deadly effectiveness in blasting away at a massed array of targets exposed on an entirely open field of fire, they reaped a grim harvest from the surging ranks of both Robertson's and Law's Brigades. Firing rapidly and with deadly affect, Berdan's soldiers now fulfilled their well-deserved lethal reputation of having killed more Confederates than any other regiment of the Army of the Potomac.

What these famed sharpshooters, armed with fast-firing Sharps rifles (breech-loaders that fired around ten shots per minute) that made them General Meade's most deadly soldiers, demonstrated before Ward's Brigade was that they were not only the army's best marksmen, but also the finest sharpshooting men in all the North. After all, exacting standards had been established for volunteers to join this elite corps of sharpshooters. Firing at a rate far faster than their the average Union infantrymen armed with the standard .58 Springfield rifled-muskets and an ample abundance of rounds (more than sixty) for just such a crucial mission of protecting the army's vulnerable left flank, Berdan's Sharpshooters were now in the right place at the right time. From the good cover of the stone wall, they delivered an accurate fire upon Hood's men, who were caught in the open in the midst of a leaden storm, while surging across ground that had become a grim killing field.[154]

Born in January 1844 of Alabama parents who migrated to Texas, Private John Marquis "Mark" Smither, 5th Texas, described the horror in a letter, writing how "our men tumbl[ed] out of ranks at every step, knocked over by the Enemy's sharpshooters..."[155]

But the greatest damage to the onrushing ranks was inflicted by Smith's 10-pounders, especially when the Texas Brigade boys surged closer to Berdan's Sharpshooters blazing away from behind the stone wall situated in the open fields west of Rose Run and Plum Run. The four Parrott rifles of the New Yorkers unleashed not only a hail of shell, with fuses cut to perfection and burning at five and six seconds, and solid shot, but also the ultimate nightmare of infantrymen, canister. With ammunition running low and the attackers closing-in, a frantic Captain James E. Smith roared to his fast-working gunners, "Give them shell! Give them solid shot! Damn them, give them anything." Because the crest of Houck's Ridge was no narrow and boulder-strewn and as mentioned, only four New York field pieces could be placed in good firing positions atop the barren crest now shrouded in rising palls of whitish smoke.

Meanwhile, the other two guns and all of the Empire State battery's caissons and ammunition limbers were placed in the gorge of Plum Run at the eastern base of Houck's Ridge in guardian fashion, just in case any Rebels surged northeast up the valley of Plum Run between Houck's Ridge, to the west, and Little Round Top, to the east. Well-placed in anticipation of the struggle for possession of General Meade's left, these two New York guns protected the rear of the defenders, who continued to gamely hold firm with courage on Houck's Ridge.

Because of the placement of Captain Smith's guns based upon unfavorable geography that was too rugged because the artillerymen had no choice since it was the best high ground just west of Plum Run, all artillery ammunition had to be brought by hand by the New York artillerymen for more than 50 yards up the rugged, boulder-studded eastern slope of Houck's Ridge. This logistical nightmare in the heat of battle not only took a great deal of time, but also ensured a lack of ample available ammunition for the four fast-firing artillery pieces atop the commanding crest now wreathed in layers of smoke that hung heavy in the intense heat.

Casualties from the fire of Rebel skirmishers were kept low by savvy New York artillerymen smartly taking cover behind boulders after performing their assigned duties in preparation for firing the 10-pounder Parrott rifles. Blasting away from the unique geographical setting of Houck's Ridge and near its southern end—the 10 acres of giant boulders (a geological anomaly) of the Devil's Den—the New York gunners steadily hurled a mixture of deadly munitions at the onrushing Texans to cause extensive damage.

Indeed, this rather unorthodox mixture of artillery munitions resulted in a most "destructive fire," which cut down additional men from the swiftly-advancing ranks, littering the open fields with bodies splashed in red.[156] Meanwhile, farther away from Warfield Ridge, the open slope became slightly steeper for the Texas attackers during the gradual descent toward Rose Run. As the assault gained momentum partly because of Lieutenant Colonel Work's ability to resist the temptation to stop the attack and unleash a volley at their tormentors, Private James O. Bradfield, Company "E," 1st Texas, described: "We moved quietly forward down the steep decline, gaining impetus as we reached the more level ground below [and] The enemy had already opened on us, but we did not stop to return it."[157]

A veteran New York infantryman in support of Smith's Battery never forgot how the fiery blasts from the four New York field pieces, positioned north–south along the narrow crest, "tore gap after gap through the ranks of the advancing" troops of Hood's Division, especially the Texas Brigade that was exposed in the open fields.[158] Knocking General Hood out of the battle and so early removing the dynamic leader of Lee's hardest-fighting division and leaving it without a directive head early in the assault while inflicting damage on the attackers, Captain Smith and his New York artillerymen were already enjoying their finest day from the beginning of Longstreet's desperate effort to turn Meade's left flank.

Maintaining a rapid and lethal fire with case shot, the sweaty work of Captain Smith's gunners brought an artillery hell to the Texas Brigade, raking the advancing ranks with a deadly hail of canister. So many iron canister balls hit the soil around the soldiers' feet that they kicked up sprits of dust and engendered fear to the average soldier in the ranks, while creating a death rhythm of sorts. Nothing was more lethal than these awful salvoes of canisters that tore swaths out of the surging formations, cutting down "many of [the] gallant officers and men."[159]

Meanwhile and despite the severe punishment inflicted, the Texas Brigade's assault formations continued to steam-roll onward across the open fields, gaining momentum and keeping up a fast-pace. In fact by this time, Robertson's attack was already out-of-control in surging ever-eastward over a wide stretch of open ground, especially in regard to the 5th Texas on the far right. The 5th Texas had early—within the first 200 yards of the advance to the east—began to lose contact with the Alabamians to the south. But the greatest trouble developed on the north of the Texas Brigade's line. As directed by Lee's orders, Robertson had attempted in vain to keep his extreme left, Colonel Vannoy Hartrog Manning's 3rd Arkansas (the Texas Brigade's left) on the Emmitsburg Road and moving northeastward, according to Lee's orders.

However, this strict but tactically impractical compliance with Lee's orders resulted first in a halt in the assault for a hasty realignment of the 3rd Arkansas and 1st Texas, from left to right, parallel, or northeastward, to the northeast running road. Therefore, the Texas Brigade's left veered northeastward during the advance. This movement sent the 3rd Arkansas, including veteran companies like the Hot Springs Hornets (Company "F"), onto property of the George Rose farm and into the dense expanse of greenery known as the Rose Woods (northwest of the Devil's Den), where the little, meandering creek known as Rose Run flowed north–south through the center of this timbered area, located just south of the Wheatfield. Meanwhile, with their targeted objective of overrunning the high ground directly before them, the 1st Texas troops continued to head straight east toward the blue formations of Ward's brigade and Smith's four blazing artillery pieces atop Houck's Ridge, where whitish smoke lifted slowly in the hot and humid air.

Meanwhile and ominously, Robertson's two right regiments, the 4th and 5th Texas gradually veered more to the right, or southeastward, across the open ground below where Rose Run intersected the larger Plum Run. This situation caused a gap to grow between the Texas Brigade's two wings, now separating in its widening middle, during the advance. To the right of the 1st Texas, the troops of the 4th and 5th Texas, from north to south, swarmed onward with a momentum all of their own, increasing the growing width of the gap between the left of the 4th Texas, under Colonel John C. G. Key, who had been born in 1809, that had broken away from the 1st Texas's right.

All the while, this gap only steadily widened as the attackers continued to pour ever-eastward with flags flapping and bayonets sparkling in the July sunlight. Quite simply, during the sweeping advance over a wide area and one that steadily picked-up steam, General Robertson had early lost control of his brigade and from almost the beginning. Therefore, the Texas Brigade's regimental commanders were left on their own to do the best they could under disadvantageous circumstances, and with no effective leadership or communication from Robertson. Of course, Robertson had especially lost control of the two attacking wings, which also were now on their own and, therefore, would fight independently on this afternoon.[160]

Although General Robertson did not realize it at the time in another example of leadership dysfunction because Law, now commanding the division in place of the wounded Hood and entirely unable to fill the native Kentuckian's big shoes, Lieutenant Colonel Work was now in charge by rights of seniority of the Texas Brigade's surging left wing, consisting of his 1st Texas and the 3rd Arkansas, whose northernmost troops were surging through the hardwood trees, scattered boulders, and the thick underbrush of the Rose Woods. In Work's words, the 1st Texas and 3rd Arkansas were fighting as a separate and independent "minor brigade" on the north.[161]

As Work wrote: "... at about 5 P.M. on the 2nd I was by Genl Law (Division Commander since Hood [was] wounded and whom I saw wounded at the very onset of the advance) placed in command of the 1st Tx and 3rd Ark. as a minor brigade."[162] On such a hellish day under the blazing sun and a hot fire, Lieutenant Colonel Work's consuming passion to destroy "the damnd Yankees" wherever he found them had reached a new high by this time, especially after having lost so many good men in advancing across the open ground.[163]

Meanwhile, unable to do anything to remedy the rapidly-dissolving tactical situation of his Lone Star State brigade having been pulled farther apart in its very middle (a guarantee of disaster in almost any assault), and now advancing in two wings that were coming even more separated by the minute, Robertson sent a mounted courier off in a hurry to General Law to inform him to take control of the 4th and 5th Texas and unite these two regiments with the Alabama Brigade's left, while he tried to join the advance of his left wing (the 1st Texas and 3rd Arkansas), which he was unable to accomplish, despite his determined efforts.[164]

Arkansas Boys Fight in the Rose Woods and More Dysfunction in Hood's Division

A good fighting commander and an inspirational leader, Colonel "Van" Manning, born near Raleigh, North Carolina, in 1839 and married to Mary Zikphro Manning, led his Arkansas soldiers with an aggressive style that revealed his pride in commanding the only Arkansas regiment of the Army of Northern Virginia. On the left, or north, of the 1st Texas that continued to surge over the open fields before the small watercourse known as Rose Run, meanwhile, the Arkansas boys encountered stubborn bluecoats in the tangled thickets of the Rose Woods.

Fortunately, the heavy cover and tall trees of the Rose Woods at least protected them from the fire of Sickles' Third Corps batteries aligned along the Wheatfield Road to the north. In the words of Private Albert Cuthbert Sims, "presently random firing began [to erupt] along the line, but I could see no enemy [line but then] a full volley from the 3rd Arkansas Regiment [just south of the Wheatfield in the Rose Woods and northwest of the Devil's Den] on our left proclaimed the enemy in sight."[165]

Here, in the thick, summer-like foliage of the Rose Woods that bordered the fields to the south now full of charging Texas and Alabama soldiers, fewer than 500 Arkansas Rebels tangled with the veteran troops of General Ward's Brigade, the 86th New York Volunteer Infantry and the 20th Indiana Volunteer Infantry, from north to south, and aligned in the dense woodlands below the Wheatfield. These were very good fighting men, and they fully demonstrated as much. But the greatest shock came suddenly from the north, where the 17th Maine Volunteer Infantry, which had been sent from General David B. Birney's First Division, Third Corps, as a most timely reinforcement, unleashed a volley that crashed through the humid woodlands of tall timber and into Manning's stunned Rebels from the far-away Trans-Mississippi State.

In firing southward to inflict considerable damage, the Maine boys, hardy outdoor types from a northern frontier region, possessed the advantage of a stone wall running east–west along the southern edge of the Wheatfield and perpendicular to the vulnerable left flank of the 3rd Arkansas, because the troops of McLaws' Division to the north had not yet advanced in echelon to protect the northern end of the Arkansas battle-line. Hard-hit from fires streaming from two directions and with his Arkansas boys badly-outnumbered in the dark woodlands that was seemingly becoming a deathtrap, dark-haired Colonel Vannoy "Van" Hartrog Manning, a handsome, dapper man, prudently called a halt. He then hurriedly and wisely refused his left flank to face the serious 17th Maine threat, because his left flank dangled dangerously "in mid-air." Fortunately, for the 3rd Arkansas, Manning made his smart tactical adjustment just in time, before falling with a concussion from a bursting shell.[166]

With the 3rd Arkansas battling for its life in the smoke-filled shadows of the Rose Woods, it was now up to the 1st Texas, which continued to advance across the open fields while the outmatched Arkansas soldiers fought in the thickets, alone to overrun the most formidable high ground in their front, Houck's Ridge. With the outbreak of heavy firing to the north, or left, and after surging "a distance exceeding half a mile," in Lieutenant Colonel Work's estimation that was actually an exaggerated distance, the colonel saw that he needed more protection in front.

The lengthy line of green-uniformed skirmishers, Berdan's Sharpshooters who continued to fire rapidly with the Sharps rifles from behind the stone wall along the rise situated in the open fields, had to be pushed back as soon as possible to minimize losses among Work's surging formations. Therefore, after having advanced in the attempt over a good distance from the relative shelter of the timber on Warfield Ridge, "Company 'I' [Crockett Southrons named after Alamo martyr David Crockett of Tennessee], commanded by Lieut. J[ohn]. H. Wooters [was] thrown out, as skirmishers [and] engaged the skirmishers of the enemy, driving them back upon a regiment supporting the enemy's battery."[167]

But Lieutenant Colonel Work and his regiment, the "Ragged First," on the brigade's lonely left wing, advancing through the open fields situated below the Rose Woods, now possessed a greater concern, which was not addressed because it was impossible to do so at this time: both flanks, the right of the 1st Texas—like the left of the 3rd Arkansas before having been swept by the volleys from the 17th Maine—hung precariously in mid-air.[168] In the colonel's words, "the Third Arkansas Regiment on my left, became hotly engaged with a strong force of the enemy upon its front and left, thus leaving my left flank uncovered and exposed" to an excessive degree.[169]

By this time and boding ill for Confederate fortunes on the far right in regard to the all-out bid to turn Meade's left flank, not only had the Texas Brigade separated into a widely-divided left and right wing (each consisting of two regiments fighting independently), but also the Alabama troops of Law's Brigade, which continued to advance east straight toward the Round Tops. Therefore, at a time when unity was the key to success in order to deliver a powerful knock-out blow, not only the Texas Brigade, but also the Alabama Brigade had been divided and continued to widen that self-destructive divide, while surging forward on a day when seemingly nothing was going right for Confederate leadership. On Law's far left, the 4th Alabama split off from the Alabama Brigade and stayed in line with the advancing troops of the 4th and 5th Texas that had already become widely separated from the 1st Texas' right.

Therefore, the 1st Texas was the primary unit of the entire Texas Brigade to now charge straight east over the open field and directly toward not only Houck's Ridge and Captain Smith's booming guns, but also toward the Devil's Den from the front or west, while the 3rd Arkansas fought in the smoke-filled Rose Woods that seemed to have swallowed up Manning's Razorback regiment. Indeed, the entire 3rd Arkansas seemed to have disappeared into the lush greenery. To the south, meanwhile, the 4th Alabama initially advanced toward the southern end of the Devil's Den, but then gradually slipped farther south and headed toward Big Round Top. To the right of the 4th Alabama, the 47th Alabama and the 15th Alabama, from left to right (or north to south), also veered to the right, or south, pushing toward the heavily-timbered, western base of Big Round Top.

Without the necessary time to gain any kind of decent grip on the increasingly complex and confusing situation, General Law was unable to coordinate the advance of the division's reserves, which surged ahead on their own but only belatedly. In fact, Law had not even been notified that he was now in command of the division, before the reserves behind the front-line troops finally moved out. General Henry Lewis Benning had been ordered to follow Law's advance on the south, but he somehow lost sight of the Alabamians' swift surge eastward. Instead, Benning, a former lawyer instead of a professional soldier, somehow mistook the Texas Brigade for Law's Alabamians, and hurled his reserves forward behind the wrong troops who were advancing much farther to the north! Clearly, General Hood's guiding hand was badly needed at this crucial time.

Behind the advance of these front-line troops, therefore, Hood's second wave assault formations, General Benning's Georgia Brigade of four regiments and General George

"Tige" Anderson's Georgia Brigade of five regiments, from north to south, went off course like most of Hood's brigades on this seemingly ill-fated day. After having begun to advance after Benning had started forward, Anderson's five regiments of Georgians also veered to the left and headed toward the escalating tempest roaring over Rose Woods and the golden stalks of the Wheatfield, while the advancing Benning's Georgians slid northeastward to advance behind the Texas Brigade instead of behind Law's Alabama Brigade, after veering southeastward, as ordered.

Unlike General Benning who was destined to have anything but his finest day on July 2, "Tige" Anderson possessed good reasons for his movement. He had quickly responded to an urgent call from General Robertson for assistance on the north, advancing northeast to support the Texas Brigade's left wing on the north. For Southern fortunes, "Old Rock" Benning's tactical blundering from the beginning was actually a fortunate tactical development, because of the strength of his "Old Rock" Brigade of around 1,400 men (greater by more than double the number of Union reinforcements destined to be hurled into the escalating fight) would be urgently needed to assist the 1st Texas in the bitter struggle for possession of Houck's Ridge, and especially the Devil's Den. However, General Benning's belated support of the wrong troops—the Texas Brigade (or specifically the 1st Texas in this case) instead of the Alabama Brigade to the south—greatly reduced the chances of capturing Little Round Top, making young Law's task of turning Meade's left flank far more difficult, if not impossible.[170]

Meanwhile, before directly assaulting Houck's Ridge, the 1st Texas had first to overrun to stone wall that stood west of Rose Run, where the most deadly marksmen of the Army of the Potomac made their defiant stand, firing rapidly and inflicting more damage on Work's surging ranks pouring through the open fields just south of the smoke-filled Rose Woods. Descending upon the Berdan's sharpshooters with fixed bayonets and pushing them from behind their stone wall with a cheer, meanwhile, the onrushing 1st Texas soldiers continued to surge ever-eastward and ever-closer to the four blazing guns of Smith's New York guns that continued to roar from the barren crest of Houck's Ridge.

Demonstrating more leadership skill and insight, Captain Smith had made the smart decision to direct his fire on the onrushing Texas infantry and not the roaring Confederate artillery pieces along Warfield Ridge that offered tempting targets: a smart decision that cost a good many Texas lives, because these attackers were the greatest and "the true threat" to the Union left flank. With steel bayonets glistening under the July sunlight while moving at "a brisk gait," the howling Texas continuing onward without halting and resting, after hurling the green-uniformed sharpshooters from the stone wall.

Escaping just in time before being overrun by a tide of veteran Rebels, these elite Union soldiers fell back with discipline, after having inflicted considerable damage with their fast-firing Sharps rifles in taking out and eliminating some of the finest men and officers from Hood's advancing ranks. Likewise to the south below the surging

Texians, the Alabamians also pushed the lethal sharpshooters in green rearward from their fence of stone to the south.[171]

Upon nearing Rose Run, Private James O. Bradfield described how the attack's momentum continued to increase when shouts of "Forward-double quick,' [that now] rang out."[172] By this time, one 4th Texas soldier described the attack as nothing more than "a wild, frantic and desperate run, yelling, screaming, and shouting" that warned the boys in blue of even more hot work that lay ahead.[173]

Then, the onrushing 1st Texas soldiers finally reached something not seen in their Texas homeland in the low-lying gulf coastal region, a low, but sturdy, fence of stone that industrious farmers for generations had collected from the fields and utilized to mark off property boundaries and keep stock, mostly cattle, on their property. Berdan's Sharpshooters had made this open field a hell on earth for the Texans, who had been caught between "hell and high water": the blazing fire of the lethal Sharps rifles at closer range and Captain Smith's 10-pounder Parrotts. Private Albert Cuthbert Sims, Company "F," 1st Texas, described:

> We pressed forward to a stone fence, where I gladly would have remained for the remainder of the evening for the protection it afforded us, but no[t] so; we just go forward, and I leaped upon the fence, the rocks giving way and I went head forward down a little slant on the side of a branch [Rose Run was a small, north–south flowing tributary of Plum Run, just to the east, and that met this larger creek to the south]. My file leader, seeing my fall, turned back to ask if I was badly hurt, to which I replied that I was not, and arose and soon regained by place in the advancing line.[174]

The cold waters of Rose Run offered no serious obstacle to Work's fast-moving soldiers now advancing on the double-quick with steel bayonets at the fore. Private James O. Bradfield explained:

> Across the valley and over the little stream that ran through it, they swept, every man for himself. The first man down was my right file man, [Private] William [L.] Langley, a noble brave boy [of Company "E," Marshall Guards, 1st Texas], with a minie ball straight through the brain. I caught him as he fell against me, and laid him down, dead. As I straightened up to move on, that same familiar "spat" which always means something, sounded near, and looking around, I saw Bose Perry [Private Sidney Franklin Perry, Company "E," 1st Texas, who lost two brothers killed at Antietam] double over and catch on his gun. He did not fall, however, but came on, dragging his wounded leg, and firing as he advanced.[175]

Already, some of the best and brightest of the Texas Brigade had been cut down, even before coming to grips with the enemy. In a sad letter, James Henry Hendrick lamented the long "list of casualties in our company ["E" and] Bill Langley [listed first] killed" early in the attack.[176]

But the mounting losses were not sufficient to slow the 1st Texas' attack, which steam-rolled onward and never lost momentum. By this time and bolstered by skirmishers of the 124th New York, Berdan's Sharpshooters had taken a second defensive position behind still another stone wall, running parallel to General Ward's battle-line atop Houck's Ridge, at the base of the "Triangular Field" immediately on the east side of Rose Run. Berdan's Sharpshooters in green and skirmishers in blue of the 124th New York Volunteer Infantry, in Private Bradfield's words, "stood their ground bravely, until we were close on them, but did not await the bayonet [and] They broke away from the rock fence as we closed in with a rush and a wild rebel yell, and fell back to the top of [Houck's] ridge, where they halted and formed on their second line."[177]

While the 1st Texas soldiers continued to charge straight toward Houck's Ridge and the Devil's Den on the ridge's southern end in battling the tenacious 2nd United States Sharpshooters and 124th New York skirmishers, which meant that the gap between Work's right and the other Texas regiments—which continued to advance southeastward—only additionally widened, the Texas Brigade continued to widen its already extensive gap, with the 4th and 5th Texas, from left to right or north to south, continuing to veer father south and even farther away from the 1st Texas' right. When the onrushing troops of the 5th Texas neared a rail fence, one captain yelled out a challenge. He offered ten dollars for the first soldier to scale the obstacle and the Texans quickly swarmed over the barrier.

All the while, a good distance north of the 5th Texas, the 1st Texas troops continued to pour ever-eastward over the open ground as if nothing could stop them. As noted, the Rose Woods, in full summer foliage and engulfed in a cloud of sulfurous smoke, widely separated the 1st Texas for its sister regiment, the 3rd Arkansas to the north, on the wayward left wing, nearly as much as the Mississippi River separated their home regions.

A proud member of Company "F" (the Woodville Rifles, which was Work's old company), of the 1st Texas, Private Albert Cuthbert Sims wrote how after swarming across the small branch of cold spring water called Rose Run, "we [then] pushed forward through a field of Timothy [grass] through which the minie balls were hissing."[178]

After having endured the murderous fire of the 2nd United States Sharpshooters and the 124th New York skirmish line and suffering severely from the punishment, the onrushing 1st Texas soldiers continued toward Houck's Ridge, which was lined with hundreds of bluecoat veterans of the Third Corps, with silk flags waving. Smartly, General Ward ordered the left of his brigade, the 4th Maine and the 124th New York, from north to south and occupying the highest portions of the barren crest, to hold their fire until they "could plainly see the enemy [and] not to fire at a longer distance than 200 yards."[179]

Therefore, on the rocky crest, the disciplined Maine and New York soldiers held their fire with a disciplined patience before opening up with their first volley on the

1st Texas vulnerable in the open fields of summer. These Federals took careful aim upon the onrushing Texans, who seemed to have been released from the depths of hell. Then, all of a sudden, a close-range volley erupted from the crest of Houck's Ridge, exploding from the high ground and lighting up the open crest with a sheet of flame. Clumps of Work's Texans fell in the hail of lead from the close-range volley that was described as nothing short of "horrendous."[180]

In a letter to his "Mother, Sister and Family," Private H. Watters Berryman described the losses among the attackers of Company "I" (Crockett Southrons), 1st Texas: "Poor Mort[imer Martin] Murphy was killed in making one of the most gallant charges ever made by the First Texas.... Lieut. H[enry]. N. Jones and Wiley [A.] House [both of Crockett, Texas] fell at the same place."[181] Of Irish descent and in his mid-twenties, Private Murphy had just married a pretty Irish girl Elizabeth H. Mallory on October 4, 1860, and the couple had rejoiced at the birth of their first son, William Henry Murphy, on January 1, 1861, just before the war erupted and cruelly changed their lives forever.[182]

Despite the torrent of bullets that swept through the ranks of Company "I," brothers Privates H. Watters Berryman, a teenager, and Newton, "Newt," M. Berryman survived the tempest. Thankfully, H. Watters Berryman penned in his letter: "It is the will of God that Newt and myself" came out of the "gallant" charge alive.[183] To the teenager, it seemed like a miracle that his older brother survived the hail of lead. As he wrote in his letter: "Newt was wounded in the head. He was right by my side. It knocked him down. I thought he was killed, but he jumped up and kept to fighting harder than ever. I tried to persuade him to leave the field, but he would not leave. He told me if every man left for a slight wound we would never gain a battle. He was struck a gashing blow on the forehead by a minnie ball."[184]

Out in front as usual in leading the way toward the blazing New York guns of Houck's Ridge, Lieutenant Colonel Work also somehow escaped the hail of bullets. Ironically, if he suffered a wound, the Cloverport, Breckinridge County, Kentucky-born colonel knew that he would be very well treated by his own father, the highly-capable Dr. John Work, who served as the assistant surgeon of the 1st Texas.[185]

Now within relatively close range of the New York artillerymen and Ward's infantrymen who were blasting away from the high ground, with his men needing to catch their breath and recover from the recent "horrendous" volley, and upon encountering the first rough ground and timber along the creek's east side, Work knew that he had to call a halt. He, therefore, ordered his troops to stop their progress in the lowest part of the brush-covered environs of Rose Run (described by one soldier as a "marshy branch"), before the imposing, rocky ridge of John Houck. Here, the exhausted Texas soldiers, drenched in sweat and panting heavily in the scorching heat and high humidity, were ordered to align and unleash their first volley of the day. Private Albert Cuthbert Sims, a faithful follower of Lieutenant Colonel Work, described how in the little, brushy valley "we halted, loaded and fired, the front rank on their knees and the rear standing."[186]

Clearly, at this point in the fight, Work had made a smart tactical decision. This underbrush-covered low spot offered not only some protection but also an added advantage, because the over-eager New York gunners on the dominant ground of Houck's Ridge overshot the Texans' lower position in their eagerness to kill Rebels, causing the blasts of canister to pass "over us with the noise of partridges in flight," in the words of one attacker. Clearly, the New Yorkers could not sufficiently depressed the barrels of their 10-pounder Parrott guns to hit the Texans, who had found a sweet spot and natural shelter from the leaden storm. Here, on the low ground before Houck's Ridge, the 1st Texas boys caught their breath under the searing sun, while preparing for the hard fighting that lay ahead. They now prepared for the final sprint up Houck's Ridge, which glowed with rifle- and cannon-fire, that was now wreathed in thick palls of sulfurous, whitish smoke that hung in the windless air.[187]

After suffering severe punishment from a slight rise now held by the 99th Pennsylvania Volunteer Infantry, the 20th Indiana, and the 86th New York, from left to right (or south to north), after General Ward had ordered these three regiments to advance around 75 yards from the original Houck's Ridge Line and taking the brutal enfilade fire from the 17th Maine, Manning's Arkansas boys withdrew around 75 yards out of urgent necessity. Taking their wounded comrades with them and hurriedly reloading their muskets, the hard-hit Arkansans retired through the hell of the smoke-filled Rose Woods littered with bodies. A cruel destiny had led these young men and boys from Arkansas to a final grave in the soil of the George Rose farm.

At the front, the perceptive Lieutenant Colonel Work saw clear and disturbing signs of a significant repulse occurring on his left flank that spelled disaster for the Texas attackers, leaving their northern, or left, flank dangling dangerously in mid-air. An old Indian fighter with well-honed tactical instincts, Work was now concerned that the left flank of his 1st Texas was now entirely "uncovered and exposed" and as never before, because of the withdrawal of the 3rd Arkansas: the recipe for disaster. He, therefore, proceeded to race to the north in person with reinforcements of the ever-reliable veterans of Company "G" (Reagan Guards). With clattering gear that caused a metallic sound to echo louder than the zip-zip of lead bullets, Lieutenant Benjamin A. Campbell led around forty soldiers from Anderson County northward on the run.[188]

Displaying tactical skill in a crisis situation as in the past, Lieutenant Colonel Work explained how in order "to protect [his left flank was] threw out upon my left and rear Company 'G' [which] soon engaged the enemy and drove them from their threatening position to the left and the front of the Third Arkansas [but] It was while in the execution of this order that Lieutenant Campbell, a brave and gallant officer, fell, pierce through the heart."[189]

Work still continued to face a most vexing tactical quandary, however. As commander of the brigade's left wing, Work found himself in a desperate situation. The northern flank of the left wing was exposed because McLaws' troops (a division of four brigades under Brigadier Generals Joseph B. Kershaw, William Barksdale, Paul Jones Semmes, and William Tatum Wofford) to the north had not still advanced (a decided disadvantage of attacking in echelon, if the successive assaults were launched without proper time and coordination, especially if unleashed too late to maximize opportunities) to protect his vulnerable left flank, because of Lee's decision to advance *en echelon.* As he explained the dangerous tactical situation: "Owing to the failure [of McLaws' Division to advance] neither this nor the Third Arkansas was able to advance, without advancing against a vastly superior force, and with the left flank of the Third Arkansas (protecting my left) exposed to attack."[190]

Lieutenant Work hoped that either McLaws would advance in time to protect his left or that Benning's Georgia brigade, part of the second, or reserve, line of Hood's Division, to the rear would then move forward on his left to provide protection. However, in both cases, Lieutenant Colonel Philip Alexander Work was fated to be sadly disappointed.[191]

Meanwhile, attempting to maintain order and control his far-flung units in an attempt to maximize his ever-dwindling numbers by delivering a concentrated blow before losses reached unacceptable levels, Law resorted to drastic action in what was his best known decision in regard to the struggle for possession of the Devil's Den. Most of all, he realized that he needed to silence the New York guns, that had been steadily knocking clumps of Alabama boys out of the ranks with a brutal impunity, as soon as possible. On the open ground of the Slyder Farm, consequently, Law hastily shifted the veterans of the 44th and 48th Alabama from the Alabama brigade's right to a location in the brigade's rear and marched them by the left flank in order to maneuver these two regiments into a position for an advance north toward the jumbled pile of boulders, Devil's Den.

General Law, the young man who had been born in Darlington, South Carolina, and had co-founded the Tuskegee Military School in Tuskegee, Alabama, in 1860, was determined to gain the left flank of Smith's New York guns that continued to bellow in defiance from the top of Houck's Ridge. However, in a tactical decision that significantly reduced the possibility of turning Meade's left flank on the far south at Little Round Top, Law had ordered these two regiments from his right flank and away from the offensive effort of the 15th Alabama, which continued to push east at a good pace on the far south, along with the 4th and 47th Alabama. The 15th Alabama was shortly to confront the 20th Maine Volunteer Infantry of Colonel Strong Vincent's brigade, Fifth Corps, which was destined to gain the summit of Little Round Top to set the stage for the tenacious struggle for the new Union left flank, after the struggle for possession of Houck's Ridge and the Devil's Den—the current left flank of the Army of the Potomac.

However, to address another one of Law's pressing tactical concerns, the two Alabama regiments were formed on the left of the 4th and 5th Texas to partially plug the sizeable gap that existed between the Texas and Alabama Brigades, while aligned perpendicular to the Devil's Den and the southern end of Houck's Ridge. However, these last-minute tactical readjustments left the 15th Alabama, under Colonel William Calvin Oates, entirely on its own on the Alabama Brigade's right flank and the southernmost regiment of the Army of Northern Virginia.

Attempting to sort out some of the escalating confusion, Law directed his assistant adjutant general, Captain Leigh Richmond Terrell, who had been born in New Kent County, Virginia, in 1835 and a former lawyer from Uniontown, Alabama, to ride rapidly south to the far right. A bright and capable officer, Terrell possessed considerable promise, but his career ended in a sad death in Richmond, Virginia, during October 1864. In a remarkable feat under the circumstances that included navigating his favorite horse through the boulders of the Devil's Den on his mission south, he eventually enlightened Colonel Oates about the recent tactical developments and the disturbing news that Hood had been cut down hardly before the assault had begun.

Colonel Oates's orders from General Law were to "hug the base of Great Round Top and go up the valley between the two mountains [to find] the left of the Union line, turn it and do all the damage I could," setting the stage for the showdown between the much-celebrated 15th Alabama and the 20th Maine in the bloody struggle for possession of the strategic high ground of Little Round Top on Colonel Strong Vincent's left, or southern, flank.

However, Oates and his diminutive 15th Alabama were largely on their own in the upcoming confrontation with the 20th Maine, after the 44th and 48th Alabama had been pulled away from the right, leaving the young colonel and his depleted, weary command the job of seizing the vital ground of the Round Tops.[192] But more importantly on the other side of Plum Run opposite Little Round Top, Houck's Ridge had to be secured first because it was now the existing Union left flank, before any hope of gaining permanent possession of Little Round Top—shortly to be the new Federal left flank—became a reality.

Captain James E. Smith's Defiant New York Battery

After unleashing a rolling volley from the low, brushy ground of the shallow valley before the daunting sight of Houck's Ridge held by hundreds of General Ward's veterans, the sweat-drenched men of the 1st Texas caught their breath, after their long sprint over the open fields of death now littered with the bodies of fallen comrades. They then prepared for the final rush up the ascending west side of Rose Run, after hurriedly reloading .577-caliber muskets and making sure that steel bayonets were properly fixed to the business end of their trusty Enfield rifles. In the words of Private Albert Cuthbert Sims, "We only remained in this [valley] for a few minutes when we again went forward" and rushed all the way to near the foot of Houck's Ridge with a cheer.[193]

Once again, Lieutenant Colonel Work ordered his troops to attack in a determined bid to overrun not only Houck's Ridge but also the Devil's Den at the southern end of the jumbled pile of boulders that seemingly had been indiscriminately thrown together by some ancient God. Now positioned just beyond the brushy environs of Rose Run and with a resounding cheer, the 1st Texas soldiers continued their assault east and up the gently ascending ground. They then gained the north–south running stone wall at the western base of the "Triangular Field," owned by German farmer George W. Weikert. This open field of high grass was so designated because of the shape of the three stone fences that came to an apex in pointing straight east like a dagger toward Houck's Ridge and the fast-firing New York guns along the rocky crest.

Meanwhile, the steadily-advanced Texans now benefitted from another key advantage at this lower point below the barren ridge-top, because Smith's four guns could not be sufficiently depressed by the artillery at a low angle to cut the attackers to pieces on the lower ground at the foot of Houck's Ridge. Then, one of Smith's 10-pounder Parrott rifles was knocked-out by a well-placed shot from an artillery piece (perhaps a direct hit by one of the guns of Captain Reilly's North Carolina battery—before switching to canister and case shot—which had advanced closer to Houck's Ridge to play a key flying artillery role like so often seen during the Mexican-American War), reducing the amount of firepower streaming from the crest of Houck's Ridge, lying above the giant boulders of Devil's Den, and thereby saving 1st Texas lives. Captain Reilly, who still dreamed fondly of his native Emerald Isle so far away, and veteran North Carolina gunners provided an invaluable support fire for the attackers on this day of destiny.[194]

Revealing the feisty fighting spirit that consumed the elite fighting men of the Army of Northern Virginia, a number of wounded men remained in the ranks instead of retiring rearward as ordered, enhancing the chances of overrunning Houck's Ridge and the Devil's Den. These individualists realized that every man was needed in the ranks if decisive victory was to be won this afternoon. While advancing with his comrades of Company "E," 1st Texas, James Henry Hendrick wrote: "I was struck twice with a piece of shell but did not hurt me. Both were spent that struck me."[195] Therefore, Hendrick gamely continued onward and toward the very vortex of the storm, refusing to let his comrades down by retiring rearward.

All the while, success seemed to be well within the grasp of the attackers. However, a problem almost immediately developed in Work's assault that seemed on the verge of overrunning the strategic high ground. When the troops of the 1st Texas finally gained the foot of Houck's Ridge and not long after the beginning of the final sprint up the ridge's western slope to the fiery crest of Houck's Ridge, confusion swept through the ranks along with the deadly hail of bullets from Ward's veterans—the 4th Maine and the 124th New York, from left to right (or south to north), who blasted away with .58-caliber Springfield rifles, Austrian muskets, and, most ironically, Enfield rifles. Here, the 1st Texas suffered severely from the murderous musketry sweeping down the slope, and this carnage now combined with the fog of war.

When the command was seemingly on the verge of sweeping over the strategic crest of Houck's Ridge, Private Albert Cuthbert Sims, Company "F," described how when "we came to the foot of the hill on which the battery stood there was a momentary confusion. Someone ordered a retreat and we began to fall back, but the order was quickly countermanded and another forward movement" was made.[196]

A perplexed Private James O. Bradfield described how in regard to the mysterious order to suddenly halt: "Having passed the rock fence, and as we were moving on up the hill, an order came to halt. No one seemed to know whence it came, nor from whom [and] It cost us dearly, for as we lay in close range of their now double lines, the enemy poured a hail of bullets on us, and in a few minutes a number of our men were killed and wounded."[197]

With Lieutenant Colonel Philip Alexander Work still paying necessary attention to the problems stemming from his still unsupported left flank in the 3rd Arkansas sector to the north, the regiment's senior officer after Work, Major R. J. Harding, rose to the fore in Robertson's absence. At this crucial moment, he filled the leadership void in splendid fashion in a crisis situation. In front of the line and taking the initiative, Harding then ordered the 1st Texas forward up the western slope of Houck's Ridge, waving his saber and shouting at the top of his voice.

But in fact and despite his heroics, Captain Harding's efforts were not the decisive catalyst that ensured that the assault of the 1st Texas continued up the slope with renewed vigor. Instead and in a repeat of the over-eager Texan citizen-soldiers who had convinced a reluctant, overly-cautious General Houston to attack Santa Anna's encampment on the hot afternoon of April 21, 1836, the common soldiers of Work's regiment had once again played the key role before the looming heights of Houck's Ridge. Quite simply, in true democratic and frontier fashion, the common soldiers in the ranks of the 1st Texas had made up their own minds to forge ahead on their own and straight toward the bellowing New York artillery in a spontaneous advance to gain the high ground at any cost.[198]

In continuing the attack beyond the stone wall at the western base of the "Triangular Field" and up the rocky, open western slope of Houck's Ridge, the Texans loaded and fired on the run in expert fashion, as if hunting white-tailed deer along the bayous and woodlands back home. As they charged closer to the flaming crest, the accurate firing of the 1st Texans swept through the New York battery with a vengeance, cutting down gunners with the ease of veterans who seldom missed at close range.

Indeed, never before had these veteran New York artillerymen been hit with such a devastating fire, while Captain Smith watched in horror as additional cannoneers went down with well-aimed shots at close range. New York gunners in blue dropped in clumps, while others promptly fled down the rocky eastern slope of Houck's Ridge to escape the murderous musketry and save themselves from these long-haired and screaming men from the southwestern frontier. Most importantly, thanks to the charge initiated by the common soldiers of the 1st Texas, the New York "battery had been silenced [because] our aim was too accurate for the gunners," wrote Private Albert Cuthbert Sims of the sparkling triumph with a pride in the devastating work of a lethal marksmanship.[199]

By this time after the lengthy charge over the open fields, the ranks of the 1st Texas had been hard-hit by the New Yorker's artillery wrath, because the punishment had been severe and merciless. A good many young men and boys from the grassy plains of west Texas to the Brazos River Valley were now strewn in grotesque fashion across the open ground, before the looming heights of Houck's Ridge. Only the determination and elite qualities of the survivors had kept these veterans moving forward in the face of the devastating fire.

As a cruel fate would have it and with the 3rd Arkansas having long battled tenaciously against seemingly too many of General Ward's Yankees to count in the body-strewn Rose Woods just to the north, no attackers had endured a more deadly fire than the hard-hit 1st Texas. The four New York artillery pieces had been murderously effective, having reaped a grim total in short order. Captain James E. Smith had seen his finest day.

Fortunately, by this time, Confederate assistance was forthcoming to apply pressure on the stubborn bluecoat defenders of the Devil's Den at the southern end of Houck's Ridge, now covered in a blanket of sulfurous cloud of smoke that hung heavy in the humid air of July. After having passed behind the advancing ranks of the 4th and 5th Texas that were headed east toward Little Round Top, the 44th and 48th Alabama, which had been shifted by General Law from the brigade's right, now faced north during an advance toward the New York guns from the south and left flank. Leading the 44th Alabama, therefore, Colonel William Flake Perry's Alabama Rebels had surged north with a spirited "bound [and] a rush" with fixed bayonets toward the Devil's Den, which was a heaven-made for defenders.[200]

But while the four New York guns along the rocky crest of Houck's Ridge had been silenced because of the devastating fire of the 1st Texas, Ward's veteran infantrymen remained firmly in place on the strategic high ground with disciplined obedience to orders. From their vantage point of the rocky, barren crest of Houck's Ridge and as fast as possible, they blazed away at the onrushing men of the 1st Texas, that, of course, was no longer advancing beside the 3rd Arkansas, which had been long engaged in battling gamely against overwhelming odds (four Union regiments) in the smoke-laden Rose Woods to the north, after having retired around 75 yards to reground, realign and count the high cost of valor: in overall terms, a disastrous tactical setback that continued to leave Work's left entirely exposed and detached from the reeling Arkansas regiment, which had been severely punished. Most importantly for the 1st Texas attackers, however, the valor and sacrifice of the Arkansas boys had been successful in having drawn hundreds of Yankees away from the more crucial mission of defending Houck's Ridge.

Ironically, in this sense, General Lee's echelon concept had worked, but accidentally because the 1st Texas and the 3rd Arkansas had initially advanced together and at the same time. However, the confusion of battle and mistakes of Confederate leadership had caused the 3rd Arkansas to fight on its own and serve as a magnet for Unionists, leaving the most strategic position—Houck's Ridge that was the left of the Army of the Potomac—with less protection and more vulnerable to the 1st Texas attackers.

Therefore, after Captain Smith's guns had been silenced by the hail of accurate Texas rifle-fire, what evolved was a high stakes and dramatic showdown between the

1st Texas and the best infantry regiments of Ward's Brigade poised along the high ground. All the while, the howling tide of 1st Texas soldiers continued to swarm up the rocky western slope, reaching a point to within only around 50 yards of the four silenced New York field pieces that they had so desperately sought to possess at all costs.

Fortunately, the lack of fire from Captain Smith's murderous guns had granted a reprieve, and Lieutenant Colonel Work's men were determined to exploit the advantage to the fullest. At this time when the onrushing Texans were very close to their ultimate target—not only the crest but also the four New York guns—and the great goal of turning Meade's left flank anchored on Houck's Ridge and the Devil's Den, the most concentrated and deadly Union volley of the day in this sector was suddenly unleashed by Ward's troops, who lined the smoke-shrouded crest of Houck's Ridge.

This scorching pouring downhill from Ward's men considerably "thinned their ranks," wrote one soldier of the 124th New York Volunteer Infantry. The explosion of lead projectiles hurled forth from the volley staggered the Texans at this close range of only around 50 yards, almost as if hit by a thunderbolt from the sky. However, ignoring the carnage and deaths of additional comrades, including relatives and best friends, Work's veterans nevertheless steeled themselves for the final sprint to gain the rocky crest in one final desperate effort to overrun the strategic high ground.

Knowing that a decisive success was still well within their grasp, desperate Texas officers (except for the still absent Lieutenant Colonel Work), stained in sweat and black powder, screamed orders for their men to attack once again up the western slope of the ridge and take what was rightfully their own (the four silenced New York cannon standing alone atop the crest and there for the taking), if they only could push Ward's more numerous infantrymen, although relatively fresh and having suffered few losses, off the blazing crest of Houck's Ridge.[201]

With the tenacious struggle for possession of Houck's Ridge and the Devil's Den reaching a crescendo in the vortex of the storm that now consumed General Sickles' left flank, where the Army of the Potomac's left flank seemed about to be turned at last, a frantic Captain Smith yelled in desperation to the nearby infantrymen of the 124th New York "For God's sake, men, don't let them take my guns away!"[202]

5

Bloody Struggle for the New York Cannon of Houck's Ridge

With a life of its own and as fate would have it, the bloody struggle for the possession of Captain Smith's guns of Houck's Ridge had only begun under a blazing July 2 sun in a cloudless sky. All of a sudden, the enemy did exactly what was least expected by the veteran Texans at this crucial moment. Sensing a golden tactical opportunity now that the attack of the 1st Texas had lost momentum after so many good men and officers had been cut down, dark-haired Colonel John Augustus Van Horne Ellis, commanding the 124th Volunteer Infantry, now played a most distinguished role in taking advantage of the opportunity.

A man of action with extensive worldly experiences and a former sea captain who had sailed the Pacific's waters, he was receptive to the audacious tactical idea of Major James Cromwell, who commanded the regiment's left that extended along the open crest of Houck's Ridge to the barren top of the massive array of boulders, the Devil's Den. To Colonel Ellis, who had been born the son of a respected physician in New York City on May 1, 1827, Cromwell advocated the immediate launching a counterattack down the ridge and into the "Triangular Field."

Colonel Ellis, a graduate of Columbia University (Class of 1844), nodded his approval because he knew that the existing tactical opportunity should be exploited to the fullest, sensing that the best defense was a bold offense at this crucial juncture of the struggle to turn Meade's left flank. Then, a mounted Cromwell rode over to the front of the regiment's left. He ordered his New Yorkers (known as the "Orange Blossoms" because these 124th New York men were mostly from Orange County, which was located north of New York City in the Hudson River country) to charge. With fixed bayonets, the "gallant men of Orange" attacked down the barren western slope of Houck's Ridge with a rousing cheer in a bold "spoiling attack" in a desperate bid to save Smith's battery—four artillery pieces abandoned on the ridge top—that lay there for the taking. Most of all, the dead New York gunners lying around the silent cannon also revealed that Captain Smith's battery was ripe for capture.

The accurate gun-fire of the 1st Texans had either cut down or intimated every gunner of Smith's battery, leaving the four Parrott field pieces unmanned and silhouetted atop the barren crest like some mystical, dreamy vision that caused Lieutenant Colonel Philip Alexander Work's surviving men to fairly lust at the astonishing sight. At this time, the only Empire State artillerymen left along the open crest of Houck's Ridge were lying wounded, dead, or dying around their field pieces: an intoxicating sight to the Texans. Clearly, at this key moment, a spirited counterattack by the relatively-fresh troops of the 124th New York against the looming threat of the 1st Texas soldiers under scanty cover in the "Triangular Field" was necessary to save the guns.

Under the circumstances, Colonel Ellis' bold counterattack could not have been better-timed. Stunned by the New York counterattack when least expected and delivering the greatest pressure on the 1st Texas' left flank, the breathless Texans, exhausted from their lengthy charge across the open fields under a blazing sun, were at a supreme disadvantage at this time. They already had suffered serious losses and were low on cartridges unlike the New Yorkers, who possessed eighty rounds (double the usual number of cartridges). In fact, some of General Ward's men even possessed as many as 100–200 cartridges, as if knowing that they would be needed before this day of destiny in Adams County finally came to an end.

Therefore, the surprised Texans, covered in sweat and streaks of dirt and powder, had no choice but to fall back before the New York onslaught down the slope, retiring into the "Triangular Field." But this necessary withdrawal was not a disorganized retrograde movement, because the most veteran 1st Texas men, including the noncommissioned and junior officers, provided a degree of stability in a crisis situation: another case of lower level leadership rising to the fore among the ranks of the veteran common soldiers. All in all, however, Colonel Van Horne's attack down the slope was too audacious in overall tactical terms, because Ward's brigade was now isolated and without support on the far left flank of the Army of the Potomac.

However, recovering from the stunning shock like veterans who had known previous crisis situations in Virginia and Maryland, the Texans once again quickly rallied behind the split-rail fence in the brushy valley of Rose Run about 100 yards to the rear. Here, behind the reassuring cover of the rails, they steadied themselves for meeting the New York attackers, who were cheering on their heels.

Then, after having taken good firing positions and despite the rising dust, the Texans then returned a devastating volley that swept through one of the most desperate Union charges seen at Gettysburg. Dozens of boys in blue were cut down by the volley, and "Orange Blossoms," now splashed in red, littered the ground in sickening clumps. Indeed, this concentrated Texas volley that had been unleashed at close range "seemed in an instant to bring down a full quarter" of the 124th New York attackers. Young Major Cromwell was shot off his horse and he tumbled hard to the ground, when a Texas bullet slammed into his heart. After the inspirational leader of the audacious counterattack dropped lifeless from the saddle, his war horse continued to gallop another twenty yards down the slope.

Filling the leadership void in timely fashion, Colonel Ellis, also mounted before his men to inspire his troops during the counterattack, was shortly cut down when a .577 bullet tore through his head. He was killed instantly at this obscure place in Adams County far from the oceans that he loved and had sailed as a younger man when overwhelmed with a sense of wanderlust that seemed to have no end. Symbolically, Colonel Ellis's frightened war horse, without its unfortunate rider, galloped through the thin line of surviving 1st Texas men.

Without support on either side and with both flanks hanging in mid-air, it was the 124th New York's turn to retire, after having made the mistake of assuming that these tough western fighting men before them had been merely ordinary Rebel troops, despite the unmilitary appearances of the boys of the "Ragged First:" a big mistake and tactical error. To their shock, the once-confident "Orange Blossoms" had discovered an extremely harsh reality that ensured a lengthy casualty list at the hands of a deadly opponent during a close-range combat in which "it would have been the work of but a few minutes to have annihilated the 124th N.Y."[1]

Once again, the Texans' aggressive fighting spirit was demonstrated in not only repulsing the counterattack, but also in quickly once again going on the offensive to exploit their advantage, after the severely-punished "Orange Blossoms" retired back toward body-strewn Houck's Ridge. The rejuvenated soldiers of the 1st Texas once again charged up the slope with fixed bayonets and ear-piercing yells that split the air. The high-pitched war cries echoed over smoke-wreathed Houck's Ridge to serve notice that these dust-covered and ragged men had not been defeated, and were once again taken the offensive. Work's soldiers were even determined the hurl their "Orange Blossoms" tormentors of the 124th New York back to where they had come at the point of the bayonet.

In the onrushing ranks of Company "E" (Marshall Guards), Private James O. Bradfield never forgot how this bloody contest for possession of Houck's Ridge had evolved into very much of a fight that was fueled by the Texas common soldiers, who simply refused to admit defeat. This tenacious struggle would be either won or lost by these veteran men—the humble privates—in the enlisted ranks. In Bradfield's words that described how the battle-hardened veterans of the Marshall Guards (Company "E"), 1st Texas, once again now rose splendidly to the challenge in still another crisis situation, when everything was at stake, especially in regard to turning the left flank of the Army of the Potomac: "Without waiting orders [to charge], every man became his own commander and sprang forward toward the top of the hill at full speed."[2]

Indeed, during this bloody afternoon in hell in which so many young lives were lost, and Colonel Ellis was only the latest victim, what now happened in this vicious struggle to turn the Union Army's left was going to be determined by the common soldiers in gray and butternut themselves, and what they could accomplish on their own with sharp bayonets, the accuracy of their fire from trusty Enfield rifles, and the swinging of musket-butts to smash Yankee heads like pumpkins. No longer in this savage contest on Meade's left flank were professional, finely-uniformed military men, educated at the finest military academies in America, riding muscular war horses—

often prized thoroughbreds—like the legendary chivalric knights of old, and leading troops with inspiring words now the key determinants to ensure a successful assault and decisive victory on the southern end of the battle-line.

Most of all, it was now left to the average Texas fighting man, mostly ex-farmers who had known nothing little more than how to plow a straight row in the cornfield or to silently stalk game along the east Texas bayous now knew enough as veterans that what they accomplished on this afternoon would go a long way to winning the war. While charging up the open, western slope of Houck's Ridge with flags waving, the Texans seemed to instinctively realize as much, and acted accordingly on their own initiative.

Indeed, these elite fighting men no longer needed to be told by any officer exactly when to open fire with their Enfield rifled-muskets to inflict maximum damage or when to charge to exploit a golden tactical opportunity, because everything was now all instinctive and second nature for these veterans, especially when so much was at stake. Therefore, it no longer mattered who was in command or giving orders on the afternoon of July 2, because these battle-hardened men knew that the very life of their infant republic now hung in the balance. Therefore, the yelling Texans, with bayonets flashing in the July sunlight and ragging clothing flapping during their final sprint, charged up the ridge and unleashed a murderous small arms fire. As usual, these Texas marksmen especially targeted New York officers, and cut down a disproportionate number of fine leaders of the 124th New York, which had been hurled back all the way from the "Triangular Field" to Houck's Ridge.

Deadly Fratricide

This time nothing could stop the Texans surging up the western slope of Houck's Ridge and all the way to the embattled crest, where battle-smoke hung heavy in the heat and humidity like a whitish-colored blanket, or so it seemed. After sensing the kill and reinvigorated by the sweet taste of victory in the sulfurous air, the 1st Texas boys were now beyond all control by this time, knowing that they were on the verge of a dramatic victory. However, and most importantly, they were now in the process of making the most dramatic gains of any Texas Brigade troops at this time during the most important battle to date.

Ironically, on the verge of overrunning the four New York artillery pieces standing alone atop Houck's Ridge like silent guardians that overlooked the smoke-filled valley of Rose Run and just when it seemed as if nothing in the world could stop them from sweeping over the crest in triumph, Work's Texans were suddenly hit by a scorching fire from the rear. Incredibly, in Private Albert Cuthert Sims's words that revealed the greatest surprise in the 1st Texas' history: "At this critical moment General Benning's Brigade [the 2nd, 15th, 17th, and 20th Georgia Infantry Regiments] came upon the field, after having begun their assault from a higher point of Warfield Ridge south of the Texas Brigade [and] The 20th Georgia, not knowing that they were coming to our support, supposing us to be the enemy, opened fire on us."[3]

Besides causing the nightmare of fratricide when least expected, the arrival of General Benning's Georgians came at a severe disappointment to Lieutenant Colonel Work's his men, coming at exactly the wrong time and place. Work had received no help from Benning's four Georgia regiments to bolster his weak left flank because of the much-delayed advance of the four veteran brigades of McLaws' Division to the north, which was all part of the staggered plan of attacking in echelon.

Instead, these four seasoned Georgia regiments, consisting of excellent fighting men, had veered to the right or south, and the bulk of Benning's brigade advanced far from the left of the 1st Texas. Instead of protecting the left flank hanging in mid-air, Work's troops were now being fired upon from the rear by the men of the 20th Georgia (mirroring the earlier mistake of General Benning in having followed the Texas Brigade by mistake—an incorrect assumption—instead of Law's Alabama Brigade, now far to the south, as ordered) that was now too far south to provide any support on the vulnerable left flank.

By this time, Lieutenant Colonel Work had returned from the north in assisting in the desperate effort to restore the situation in the 3rd Arkansas' sector. In Work's words that described the confusion and disastrous tactical situation that had suddenly developed just when his onrushing men were about to overrun Houck's Ridge: "Benning's brigade made its appearance, but instead of occupying the ground to the left of Robertson's brigade, so as to enable the latter to move forward with its left flank secure from attack, it occupied the ground still occupied, by a portion at least, of this brigade."[4]

However, this blistering fratricidal fire from the Peach State regiment, advancing behind and to the right-rear of the 1st Texas, of the brigade of Colonel Henry Lewis "Old Rock" Benning was not only accurate, but also deadly. Providing earlier good support to the 1st Texas, the 20th Georgia veterans had already blasted away at the 124th New York men, helping to ensure the hasty retreat of the "Orange Blossoms" back up the slope and to the crest of Houck's Ridge.

Ironically, before this afternoon, the Texans had possessed a distinct fondness for the Georgia boys, who they affectionately called "goobers," because of their earlier close relationship with the hard-fighting 18th Georgia soldiers, who had served with distinction in the Texas Brigade until November 1862. The confusion that resulted in an ugly example of fratricide in a key situation was partly caused when the 20th Georgia's commander, the popular Colonel John "Jack" A. Jones, was killed by a bursting shell that tore away "half of his head" during the assault up the western slope of Houck's Ridge. The colonel's fall horrified his men, and left the Georgians without one of their finest leaders.

Despite the fratricide of Georgia boys shooting down men of the 1st Texas, the only positive development that somewhat compensated for the loss of General Hood but also Robertson, who remained absent from the brigade's left wing, was the timely arrival Benning's veteran Georgians of the "Old Rock Brigade" in its rear as a reinforcement, but only if they stopped firing into the Texans' rear. As this case of fratricide demonstrated, Benning's 20th Georgia soldiers were better at the tactical defensive than at the tactical offensive, as they had demonstrated during their spirited defense of the stately Rohrbach, or lower, bridge (later known as Burnside's Bridge) over Antietam Creek during the Battle of Antietam on September 17, 1862.

In thwarting the repeated assaults of General Ambrose Burnside's Ninth Corps, Army of the Potomac, for most of that summer-like morning that were calculated to storm the strategic bridge of stone on Lee's far right flank, they had bought precious time to ensure the survival of Lee's Army on the southern end of the thin defensive line.

The accurate fire of these 20th Georgia veterans, along with the 2nd Georgia Regiment now led by a mounted Colonel William Terrill Harris, who was haunted by a dark premonition of death (a nagging feeling that did absolutely nothing to diminish his dynamic leadership role and heroics on this afternoon, however), was deadly. With Colonel Harris out in front and encouraging everyone onward, the 2nd Georgia, on the right of General Benning's brigade, headed toward the Devil's Den with fixed bayonets and high-pitched Rebel Yells, following the right of the 1st Texas.[5]

Color Sergeant George A. Branard Leads the Way

Clearly, the firing into the 1st Texas's rear was a most unusual turning point of the struggle for possession of Houck's Ridge. Clearly, something had to be done and soon to get the Georgians, with their fighting blood up, to stop firing at a time when the Texans realized that it was better to be killed by Yankees in front rather than by fellow Rebels in the rear. Formerly a lowly corporal of the Lone Star Rifles (Company "L," 1st Texas) but who had gained promotion from private for his heroism first demonstrated during the attack at Eltham Plantation in carrying the flag of the 1st Texas, one man took the initiative in this critical situation, when so much was at stake. Still only a teenager and a former mechanic of the middle class before the war erupted, Color Sergeant George A. Branard had been promoted to his coveted and highly-respected position of color bearer on May 11, 1862.

Branard was lucky and seemingly indestructible in somehow having survived the terrific bloodletting at Antietam that had cost the 1st Texas more than 80 percent casualties. During the nightmarish struggle that had raged fiercely through the Miller Cornfield north of Sharpsburg (Antietam), nine color bearers of the 1st Texas were cut down on that fatal September 17 morning. Branard himself had suffered a wound at Antietam, but lived to tell the tale.

Color Sergeant Branard now brought the same courage and resourcefulness from the great killing field of Antietam to Gettysburg. To halt the blistering fire of the 20th Georgia and ignoring the Peach State bullets streaming by from the rear, Branard hurriedly "stepped out in an open space and waved our state flag to and fro, who, they saw, ceased firing" into the rear of the 1st Texas.[6]

Ironically, the 15th Georgia had initially advanced too rapidly, but had been slowed not only once, but twice by Benning's orders to allow the slower-moving regiments of his

Peach State brigade to catch-up during the attack. By all indications, the 15th Georgia, on the brigade's left flank, was lacking in effective leadership at this time to significantly reduce discipline and overall control. Clearly, the absence of these essential qualities cost Texas lives in this crucial situation. Not knowing that the 1st Texas was before them because of the thick pall of smoke hovering low over the field and holding their fire, the four regiments of the Georgia brigade pushed forward to assist Work's attackers.

To the left-rear of the 1st Texas and on the left flank of Benning's Brigade, the 368-man 15th Georgia, under Colonel Dudley DuBose and on the 20th Georgia's left, then advanced to gain the rear of Lieutenant Colonel Work's larger regiment of more than 425 soldiers, However, the two regiments—the 1st Texas and the 15th Georgia—became mixed and intertwined in the smoky confusion and noise, despite the best efforts of Work, who had returned from the left after restoring the 3rd Arkansas's battered flank position to the north, and the 15th Georgia's commander.

In Work's words that described the situation around 100 yards before the crest of Houck's Ridge, "The Fifteenth Georgia Regiment [the left of Benning's Georgia Brigade] falling in and remaining with the First Texas Regiment [and] After several ineffectual efforts upon the part of both the commanders of the Fifteenth Georgia and myself to separate the men of the two regiments, we gave the order to move forward when both regiments, thus co[-]mingled, moved forward" up the western slope in a final bid to overwhelm Houck's Ridge and haphazardly concentrated jumble of diabase boulders, from where well-positioned Yankees blasted away at the right of the 1st Texas, of the Devil's Den.[7]

In the surging ranks of Company "E" (Marshall Guards), 1st Texas, Private James O. Bradfield described how, "By this time, Benning's brigade, which had been held in reserve, joined us and together we swept on to where the Blue Coats stood behind the sheltering rocks [of the Devil's Den] to receive us," while charging up the western slope of Houck's Ridge.[8]

As usual before the howling 1st Texas soldiers, Color Sergeant Branard led the way up the rocky, barren western slope of Houck's Ridge. Meanwhile, other men of Work's regiment eased to the south in an attempt to outflank the defenders of the Devil's Den, while simultaneously attacked from the west by the right of the 1st Texas. Near the regiment's center Branard sprinted ahead to inspire the boys forward in the face of the hot fire unleashed by the 86th New York's and the 124th New York's veterans. Even while bullets whizzed around him, Branard almost certainly no longer thought about how nine 1st Texas color bearers had been shot down like fish in a barrel in Antietam's Miller Cornfield, because all that mattered now to the Texans was to gain the strategic crest of Houck's Ridge—the left flank of the Army of the Potomac.

Racing up the western slope of Houck's Ridge ahead of the 1st Texas' onrushing soldiers who unleashed Texas war-cries, with Benning's 15th Georgia men, who were now both intermixed with the Texans and followed close behind the Lone Star State attackers, Branard was a sight to see. The color bearer's solo dash for the crest of the embattled ridge ahead of Work's regiment brought a sense of admiration among soldiers on both sides. Among the New Yorkers' ranks, some awed veterans in blue began to shout, "Don't shoot that color bearer—he is too brave."[9]

The sight of Lee's most fierce warriors descending upon them with fixed bayonets flashing in the sunlight was simply too much for the remaining New Yorkers still left on the high ground, if any felt like still reaping revenge for the repulse of their daring counterattack down the ridge's western slope, now covered with fallen "Orange Blossoms." A large number of unfortunate "Orange Blossoms" littered the rocky ground as thickly as pink cherry tree blossoms, after a windstorm in the spring. With the Texans drawing ever-nearer in a headlong charge that steamrolled up the high ground, the first panicked Empire State men of the 86th and 124th New York soldiers headed down through the big rocks along the eastern slope of Houck's Ridge to gain the relative safety of the valley of Plum Run.

Still leading the way for the 1st Texas that could no longer be slowed-down or stopped, the nineteen-year-old Color Sergeant Branard continued to race up the western slope with the colors of silk. He was the first member of Work's regiment to gain the smoke-covered crest of Houck's Ridge, which was still defended by 86th and 124th New Yorkers, and before any Georgians, who followed behind him with fixed bayonets. Meanwhile, in the swirling dust, the Texas soldiers gained the highest ground, and engaged in hand-to-hand combat with the defenders, including the men who defended outlining sectors of the Devil's Den. Private James O. Bradfield described the fighting on both Houck's Ridge and in the Devil's Den as "one of the wildest, fiercest struggles of the war—a struggle such as it is given to few men to pass through and live" to see the red sunset of July 2 hovering over the heavily-forested Cumberland Mountains to the west.

After having led the wild charge up the rocky western slope of farmer Houck's ridge, what Color Sergeant Branard now saw before him almost certainly took his breath away. The open crest of Houck's Ridge was thin and narrow, but it presented a panoramic view of the open valley of Plum Run just below the parallel elevation (Little Round Top) to the east. Branard also saw the barren western slope of Little Round Top, rising up like a boulder-strewn tower to dwarf Houck's Ridge.

A modest, quiet young man who "was always inconspicious in camp and disliked ostentation," Branard had been now transformed into the most dynamic member of the 1st Texas when caught amid the heated passions of the raging battle, especially in leading the way for his fellow attackers, which included Georgians. He now surpassed all past performances on the battlefield, which was quite a remarkable achievement in itself.

Upon gaining the narrow ridge-top that overlooked the western slope of Little Round Top to the east and on the other side of Plum Run, Color Bearer Branard immediately crawled up the largest boulder on the crest near the Devil's Den. Here, at the ridge's southern end and beyond the southernmost gun of the row of New York field pieces, which were aligned the body-covered crest that descended south to the boulders at the top of the Devil's Den, that spanned from south to north, Branard was about to lay his claim. Not far from the southernmost the New York artillery piece that had already killed and wounded a good many Texas boys and atop the granite-like boulder at the northern end of the around 10 acres of the Devil's Den, after somehow surviving his exposed role in leading the way uphill for the attackers, Branard "planted the adored standard of the Texans, adorned with the Lone Star, shining far off to friend and foe, with the effulgence of its glory."[10]

The Capture of the Devil's Den

All across the field, large numbers of soldiers in blue and gray now looked up and saw the "Lone Star State" flag of the 1st Texas flying proudly from the top of Houck's Ridge and just above the dark boulders of Devil's Den, demonstrating to one and all that the Texans had gained the most formidable high ground lying before Little Round Top and the Army of the Potomac's left flank. Shredded by bullets and held proudly aloft in the smoky air by Color Sergeant Branard, the colorful silk battle-flag now represented far more than a key victory that had been won by valor and sacrifice in swarming over the high ground that anchored Meade's left flank, but also represented communities, families, religion, and Texas itself.

Meanwhile, the strategic crest of Houck's Ridge—the key to the bloody struggle on Meade's left flank because this was the high ground anchor point of Sickles' Third Corps—was overrun by the larger-sized 1st Texas, whose screaming members had led the way up the slope, and also attackers of the smaller and late-arriving 15th Georgia. Private Bradfield described how the desperate struggle for possession of the crest "continued for some time," with the last stubborn Yankees proving especially tenacious in fighting to the bitter end, until hurled back. A feisty New York artilleryman named Private Michael Broderick, who was now blasting away with a musket in a futile defense of the high ground, was taken prisoner before he could slip away down the ridge's boulder-studded eastern slope. Private Bradfield never forgot the decisive turning point of the bloody struggle: "… our fire grew so hot that brave as they were, the Federals could no longer endure it, but gave way and fled down the flow, leaving us in possession of the field": Meade's left flank had been captured to fulfill Lee's tactical objective with the fall of strategic Houck's Ridge and the Devil's Den.

An animated Private John C. Stinson, Company "G" (Reagan Guards), 1st Texas, mounted a New York field piece and shouted "Victory!" But the cost for this sparkling success was not cheap, because nearly 100 men of the 1st Texas had been left behind killed or wounded before the crest of Houck's Ridge, where the 86th and 124th New York had been vanquished and hurled aside by well-placed shots and jabbing bayonets. Nearly 150 New Yorkers had been cut down in the tempest, and a larger number, perhaps as many as 375 Empire State men, were captured by the Texans and Georgians in overrunning Houck's Ridge. But more importantly, the "Lone Star State flag crowned the hill, and Texas was there to stay," crowed Private Bradfield, who rejoiced in the sparkling success.

On the right of the 1st Texas, the southern most companies, especially Company "E" (Marshall Guards) of Work's regiment belatedly overran the most eerie geological spot on the entire Gettysburg battlefield from the west and southwest, the Devil's Den. The struggle for Devil's Den lasted longer than the fight for Houck's Ridge, because the around 10 acres of boulders were filled with bluecoat marksmen, who were still blasting away from good firing positions among the big rocks and boulders.

The young, handsome Private William "Bill" L. Langley, Company "E," 1st Texas, and who charged up the western side of the Devil's Den beside his brother Private Thomas H. Langley, was killed near the granite-like boulders of the Devil's Den according to some historians. If so, then it might have been "Bill" L. Langley whose body was moved on July 6 by photographers for placement behind the manmade stone barricade that was created by Confederates after the assault on the Devil's Den. According to some historians who have been incorrect in their analysis, young Private Langley's body has been long misidentified as a Virginia soldier, Andrew Hoge, and supposedly a sharpshooter, which was certainly not the case. In one of the most famous photographs of the Civil War, the body of this fallen Rebel "sharpshooter" has been shown among his barricade of stacked rocks, after his remains were deliberately moved by photographers for what was rightly considered a better photograph.

This fallen young Confederate—most likely a member of the 1st Texas—was destined to become the primary subject of Timothy O' Sullivan's camera on July 6, 1863. But in truth and although his company (Marshall Guards) overran the Devil's Den, Private Langley had been killed much earlier in the assault, and never reached this point at the southern end of Houck's Ridge. He had not fallen beside a large boulder on the western slope of the Devil's Den, before his body, stiffened after four days, was carried from the western side of the Devils' Den for its final placement behind the stone barricade. This photo taken by the Alexander Gardner team of photographers—Timothy O'Sullivan—can be seen on the cover of this current book.

Fierce Combat Continues Unabated

Meanwhile, after some of the war's most bitter combat, the last-surviving defenders of Ward's brigade, isolated and now on their own with victorious Rebels swarming over the strategic crest, were driven off the high ground that served as Meade's left flank and down the eastern slope of Houck's Ridge. However, a good many remaining bluecoats continued to hold firm and fight among the boulders of the Devil's Den.

To escape the Texas and Georgia onslaught that gained the most strategic high ground at the southern end of the battle-line, hundreds of bluecoats steadily retired down through the ledges and boulders and into the open valley of Plum Run at the ridge's eastern base that was largely devoid of timber. The three New York cannon, which had been silenced by the intense fire of the Texans (along with a fourth gun that had become disabled and pushed off the crest by the Empire State artillerymen to keep it out of the Rebels' hands) before their final sprint up the western slope, were claimed by the victorious Texas soldiers. To secure their prizes atop the crest and as mentioned, the lethal fire of these veterans had either cut down all of the remaining New York artillerymen, or forced them to retire down the eastern slope of Houck's Ridge in short order.[11]

But ironically, the sparkling success in overrunning the strategic crest of Houck's Ridge brought greater danger, because the Texans were now exposed on the open, barren ridge-top, and scattered groups of Yankees situated among the massive array of boulders of the Devil's Den continued to resist for some time. Private Albert Cuthbert Sims, 1st Texas, nearly lost his life upon gaining the crest: "As we came to the brow of the hill, that overlooks the [Plum Run] valley at the foot of Little Round Top my gun [a trusty .577 Enfield Rifle] was knocked from my hand and ten or twelve feet to the rear; I did not turn back to get it, but picked up another" from a dead or wounded attacker.[12]

Leading Company "A" (Marion Rifles), Captain George T. Todd and Private E. P. Derrick, who had been wounded at Antietam, took cover behind a boulder, amid the jumble of boulders of the Devil's Den, to escape the hot incoming fire. Private Derrick was pressing his luck, having already tempted fate numerous during the sweeping assaults at Second Manassas and Antietam. A well-placed shot hit Derrick squarely in the head, killing him instantly and splattering his blood and brains all over the captain's gray uniform. The Devil's Den was still hell on earth for men on both sides, because the contest lingered longer at the southern base of Houck's Ridge.[13]

In the ranks of the Marshall Guards, Company "E," on the right of the 1st Texas, Private James O. Bradfield summarized the tenacious struggle for possession of the Devil's Den and the bloody process of eliminating the last diehard defenders among the ledges and crevices:

> Just here, and to our right, in a little cove called the "Devil's Den," [where] occurred one of the wildest, fiercest struggles of the war [because] the opposing lines stood with only the sheltering rocks between them—breast to breast, and so close that the clothing of many of the enemy was set on fire by the blaze from the Confederate rifles.... Not alone, however, for just to our right [and to the right of the 15th Georgia] stood Benning [and his 20th, 17th, and 2nd Georgia, from left to right, or north to south].[14]

Without exaggeration, Private Bradfield concluded how "a storm from the Infernal regions was spending its fury in and around a spot so fitly named, 'The Devil's Den.' [and] Had it not been for the protection afforded us by the large rocks and boulders which lay scattered over the hill-top, no living thing could have remained on its summit."[15]

Had the attackers of the Devil's Den known that this ominous name applied to the jumble of huge boulders, Irish soldiers of the Texas Brigade might have recalled that the clear waters of picturesque River Nore, in southeast Ireland, rose from the high ground known for generations to the Irish people as Devil's Bit Mountain.[16]

Costly Prizes, New York Cannon

Meanwhile, above and just to the north of the Devil's Den, the coveted prizes consisting of only three field pieces were captured by the 1st Texas. The Empire State cannoneers had hurled the fourth field piece—earlier disabled evidently from the fire of Captain Reilly's "Old North State" guns—off the crest and down the eastern slope of Houck's Ridge and "among some large rocks" to prevent its capture, before prudently retiring down the ridge.[17]

As noted, the 1st Texas men were the most advanced attackers who had been the first gained the strategic crest of Houck's Ridge, that dominated the valley of Plum Run to the east, and in larger numbers than the 15th Georgia troops, whose numbers were smaller than Work's regiment. As Lieutenant Colonel Work wrote in his report how his advanced skirmishers led the way, "and then, aided by volunteers from this (First Texas) regiment, engaging the [Union] regiment and artillery, succeeded in driving back the regiment and silencing the enemy's guns—taking and holding possession of the latter"—the three artillery pieces of Captain James E. Smith's New York Battery.[18]

Work's accurate description of events, especially in regard to the Texans' capture of the artillery, was verified by Private James O. Bradfield, Company "E," 1st Texas. He wrote how the New York guns "were captured and [later] pulled off the hill by the 1st Texas regiment."[19] Likewise, in a July 8, 1863 letter to his mother, James Henry Hendrick, Company "E," 1st Texas, penned with pride: "Our regiment drove the Yankees some distance and taken three pieces of artillery."[20]

However, General Benning thought and believed differently, because he possessed a biased personal and state agenda that extended well into the postwar period. Benning had ample good reason to depict events at Houck's Ridge at the Texans' expense and in favor of his own Georgia troops: not unlike leaders and members of the 44th Alabama, who later claimed more than they had actually achieved at Houck's Ridge and the Devil's Den in the never-ending war of words long after the war. Indeed, both Alabama and Georgia veterans sought to claim more than they had actually accomplished at Houck's Ridge and the Devil's Den, while minimizing the Texans' achievements that were superior to the men of these two other states.

As mentioned and like so many other self-serving generals on both sides at Gettysburg, Benning possessed ample good reason to distort the historical record to serve his purposes and that of his men. First and foremost, General Benning had brought his brigade—2nd, 15th, 17th, and 20th Georgia—into the battle behind the wrong troops (having mistaken the advancing Texas Brigade for Law's Alabama Brigade farther to the south!) to enter into action on the wrong part of the battlefield, and then he later refused to issue an order for his veteran troops to cross Plum Run and attack Little Round Top, where they were badly needed to assist the Texas and Alabama men during the showdown for possession of the second Union left flank that developed after the struggle to turn Meade's left on the west side of Plum Run. Unlike their former judge of the Georgia Supreme Court commander, Benning's soldiers, tenacious fighting men in their own right, were covetous of winning greater laurels, even though their last volley of musketry of the day had been directed at the backs of the 1st Texas rather instead of at the Federals.

In the words of Private Albert Cuthbert Sims, who had reached the crest of Houck's Ridge in triumph with his elated comrades: "When the firing ceased the Georgians began to lay claim to the honor of capturing the battery, which the Texans disputed; but Benning, a hero of the defense of Burnside's Bridge and Antietam, quieted the dispute by saying, 'Ah, boys, those Texans had captured this battery [by their accurate fire] before you were a quarter of a mile of here."[21]

Later under heavy pressure from his leading officers who were concerned about how future historians would describe the performance of the Georgia troops in the assault on Houck's Ridge that anchored the left of the Third Corps, they convinced "Old Rock," but he evidently did not need much convincing, to massage the historical record. Naturally desiring to give his fellow home staters a larger measure of recognition and determined to do his best to prompt the glory of his Georgia boys, Benning bestowed greater credit for the guns capture by his men. In this regard, Benning was just being a good commander and a faithful Georgian, but it came at the expense of Lieutenant Colonel Work and his 1st Texas soldiers. Again, perhaps "Old Rock," who also had his own lofty reputation to protect especially when he was guilty of making crucial errors on July 2, was using his self-serving version of the New York gun's capture by the Georgians—and not Texans—in part to justify his decision to refuse orders to attack Little Round Top, and assist in that crucial struggle for the new left flank of the Army of the Potomac.

The seasoned commander of the 20th Georgia, Colonel James Daniel Waddell, a University of Georgia (then known as Franklin College) graduate (Class of 1853), former attorney, and a hero of the Georgians' magnificent defense of Burnside's Bridge against the legions of the Ninth Corps, at Antietam, gave even more credit to the men of his regiment for having captured the four field pieces of Captain Smith's battery: a natural, if not inevitable, development for a proud officer and Georgian.

Colonel Waddell was a courageous commander, and one of the best leaders in the Georgia Brigade. Likewise, another one of Benning's regimental commanders, Colonel Dudley McIver DuBose, the capable Scotch-Irish colonel of the 15th Georgia, also seconded Waddell's claim. DuBose's claim was actually more valid (although not sufficiently so) than Waddell's claim, because the 15th Georgia charged up the slope with the Texans. As could be expected, he grossly minimized the leading role and more significant contributions, from beginning to end, of the 1st Texas in capturing the New York artillery atop Houck's Ridge.

In a gross understatement, he only wrote how the Texan attackers had merely "behaved well" in leading the attack: a gross understatement and distorted commentary that minimized the long-proven combat prowess of the army's elite soldiers, who had once again not only proved, but also enhanced their reputations for superior combat prowess on the decisive afternoon of July 2. Of course, adding insult to injury, Waddell forgot to mention in his official report that the fire of his troops had swept the rear of the 1st Texas, inflicting damage among the foremost attackers in the worst case of Confederate fratricide in a key situation at Gettysburg.[22]

In regard to the post-war writings of the Georgians, including influential "Old Rock" Benning, whose name was bestowed upon the revered "home" of the United

States Infantry at Fort Benning, Georgia, in the early twentieth century, who continued to maintain that the Peach Staters had captured the New York guns, Work placed less blame on the self-serving General Benning for the transgression. In the end and with a smooth diplomatic touch, he calmly reasoned that Benning had merely "adopt[ed] the reports the regimental commanders," Waddell (20th Georgia) and Dubose (15th Georgia) in regard to the capture of Smith's three cannon by the Georgians instead of the 1st Texas soldiers, who were most responsible for taking the New York guns.[23]

Indeed, the Texans were the first and foremost troops to secure possession of the prized Empire State cannon (and Houck's Ridge and the Devil's Den), and taking possession of all three field pieces aligned among the body-strewn crest. According to army protocol, they had correctly laid the most legitimate claim to the three pieces of Captain Smith's New York Battery, because the Texas soldiers were in the forefront of the attack and were the first to reach the field pieces.

But ironically, the first soldiers to have reached the three cannon were not privates and corporals of Work's 1st Texas or Benning's Georgians from the west, after Sergeant Branard gained the strategic crest on his own audacious initiative. Instead, the first two ragged privates, James M. Polk, who had recovered from a nasty shoulder wound suffered during the sweeping assault at Gaines's Mill, and J. Q. Harris, a schoolteacher, to reach the thin, reddish soil on the crest. These were the first Texans to reach the high ground, where bodies of dead New York gunners and infantrymen lay along the narrow ridge-top, and the three field pieces. They were veteran members of South Carolina-born Lieutenant James Rogers Loughridge's Company "I," 4th Texas.

Private Harris gained the crest just before Polk, but they basked in the remarkable success together. These two men were the most advanced Navarro County skirmishers of the Navarro Rifles. They had become separated from the 4th Texas after the regiment had veered south and unknown to them, leaving them on their own. Consequently, out of necessity, these skirmishers of Company "I" had then joined the 1st Texas to bestow a most timely reinforcement to Work's command immediately before the final surge up the western slope of Houck's Ridge.

Since these seasoned fighting men were already out in front and because they were experts in the skirmisher's art, Work had likewise employed them as skirmishers, who led the way up the western slope of Houck's Ridge along with the skirmishers of Captain Wooter's Company "I," 1st Texas. After his wild dash up the slope of Houck's Ridge to gain the smoke-lined crest, Private Harris had been struck with an extreme violent blow upon placing his hand on one of the captured field pieces, when a shell burst nearby and iron pieces of shell tore through his chest. Growing pale from the loss of blood and the traumatic shock of the fatal wound, Harris "turned around and tried to walk ... but fell over and was dead in less than five minutes." Private Harris' days of teaching school were over. Private Polk was stunned by the horrific sight of the gaping hole left by the wound, which he believed "he could put his arm through."[24]

But of course, the most exposed soldier was the first Texan to have gained the crest, Color Sergeant Branard. Defying fate, he was still atop the large boulder on the embattled crest of Houck's Ridge and near the northern end of Devil's Den, standing tall behind the bullet-tattered colors that announced an amazing triumph. Suddenly, a shell burst overhead with a loud bang. A hail of iron shell fragments rained down, splintering the wooden flagstaff, knocking the feisty, teenage color out-of-action. A jagged piece of iron tore into Branard's forehead and inflicted a bloody gash. This hard blow left the 1st Texas' flag-bearer unconscious and with lasting physical damage, eliminating the sight of his left eye and impairing hearing in his left ear for the rest of his life. Like a limp rag doll splashed with red, Color Sergeant Branard tumbled from the top of the granite-like boulder, and then was "hurled ... unconscious down the slope of the mountain" known as Houck's Ridge.[25]

As mentioned, it was not in regard to capturing the three New York guns that the Georgians were at the forefront. In truth, the most significant contribution of Benning's Georgians was still to come, and that was in defense of Houck's Ridge, after the crest was first overrun by the Texans led by Color Sergeant Branard. According to Private Albert Cuthbert Sims, the Georgians "rendered good service in aiding us to hold what we had gained" with so much blood and sacrifice.[26] However, in truth, the words of a 4th Texas soldier, John C. West, were right on target: the "First Texas suffered the brunt of the battle" to turn Meade's left flank.[27]

In the end, the role played by the Georgians, a full brigade of four regiments as opposed to a single Texas regiment (1st Texas) naturally had a larger impact on the overall battle's final outcome on the afternoon of July 2 in this vital sector. Overrunning and capturing the crest of Houck's Ridge and the Devil's Den was only the beginning of the struggle before the higher ground of Little Round Top, because the resurgent Yankees were determined to regain possession of the high ground. Indeed, only beginning to fight this afternoon in hell, Colonel Elijah Walker, a dynamic leader who hailed from the town of Rockland (a most symbolic name in regard to the struggle for the Devil's Den), Maine, on the coast, gamely ordered his 4th Maine soldiers to fix bayonets and to prepare to attack up the eastern slope of Houck's Ridge and to the right (north) of the Devil's Den to stop the hail of Georgia and Texas gunfire pouring down the slope. This elevated fire was vicious, hitting the right flank of the newly-arrived 40th New York Volunteer Infantry, Colonel Philippe Regis de Trobriand's Third Brigade, First Division, Third Corps, when advancing through the Plum Run Valley in a belated attempt to reinforce Ward's hard-hit brigade.

The combined counterattack of the 4th Maine, a contingent of the 124th New York, and later the 99th Pennsylvania launched a furious counterattack in a desperate bid to regain the strategic high ground. To meet the assault and like Benning's Georgians, the sweat-stained men on the right of the 1st Texas in the Devil's Den hurried gathered as many muskets and rounds from cartridge-boxes as possible from the clumps of dead and wounded men.

Determined not to relinquish an inch of high ground at any cost, some of Work's survivors now prepared to rely on bayonets and musket-butts, because they had already expended all their rounds. It was clear to the victorious Texans that the Federals were determined "to make one more grand effort to regain the ground they had lost," in

Private James O. Bradfield's words. The attacking Maine, New York, and Pennsylvania soldiers met the Texans and Georgians on the crest, where officers fired revolvers at close range and bayonets crossed that a metallic clang that rang over Houck's Ridge.

Hard as nails and a feisty leader with an iron will, Colonel Walker was cut down with a wound in the left leg, but he continued to bravely encourage his Maine boys, who were in the process of winning recognition for hard fighting before the 20th Maine went into action on Little Round Top, to even greater exertions. These Maine men proved as tough as their rocky land along the Atlantic. Every color guard member of the 99th Pennsylvania was cut down in the attack. With more than a dozen bullet holes having been made through his uniform in battling for possession of the Devil's Den, now held by the right companies of the 1st Texas and assisted by the 2nd Georgia on the far right of Benning's brigade, even the brave 99th Pennsylvania color sergeant was "frightened almost to death," by the combat's ferocity. The resurgent Yankees from Maine, New York, and Pennsylvania gained what seemed like a secure toe hold on Houck's Ridge, after more intense combat that littered the high ground with additional bodies.

But shortly, the interlopers in blue were once again pushed off the high ground by General Benning's resurgent Georgians, the Texans, and Law's 44th Alabama, which had attacked north from the thin belt of woods, across the open ground, and into the maze of the massive boulders of the Devil's Den and Houck's Ridge from the south. After the 4th Maine gained Houck's Ridge, the way had become unblocked for the Alabamians to advance northeast up the valley of Plum Run between Houck's Ridge and Little Round Top, and strike a blow.

An animated General Benning encouraged his troops, yelling "Give them Hell!" Under severe pressure from front and flank and despite reinforced with the 6th New Jersey Volunteer Infantry and the 40th New York Volunteer Infantry, which had been dispatched by Major Genera David Bell Birney who commanded the First Division, Third Corps, General Ward finally ordered his badly-outnumbered troop to relinquish their toehold on the high ground (the southern end of Houck's Ridge) and retire northward up Houck's Ridge, which spanned north–south, toward the embattled Wheatfield.

The brutal killing ground of the Wheatfield, where the Irish Brigade, Army of the Potomac fought with distinction, lay directly north of Houck's Ridge. During the retreat and despite nearly 50 percent losses, the ever-reliable 4th Maine, whose battle-flag was carried by young Color Sergeant Henry O. Ripley, protected the rear of the reeling brigade and especially the decimated New York "Orange Blossoms," whose left flank had been earlier swept by fire from the 44th Alabama.

Once again, Houck's Ridge was now all-Confederate, with the cheering Rebels, including troops of the 1st Texas and Benning's Georgians overrunning the final pockets of stubborn resistance among the mass of giant boulders that presented such excellent cover among the ledges and crevices of Gettysburg's most eerie landscape. Once again atop the strategic crest of Houck's Ridge and the Devil's Den and exploiting the high ground advantage, the Texans and Georgians blasted away down the ridge's east slope, raking the withdrawing Yankees and Captain Smith's New York cannoneers of the last remaining two field pieces, which had earlier kept the attacking Alabamians at bay, in the valley of Plum Run.

The resurgent Confederates gobbled up around 200 prisoners of Ward's hard-hit brigade, which had paid a stiff price (around 800 men in total) for the determined bid of defending Houck's Ridge and the Devil's Den to the bitter end and then attempting to regain the high ground. All in all, these tactical gains achieved by the troops of Hood's Division on Meade's left flank were significant, possessing potential decisive results. The combined hard-hitting capabilities of the Texans, Georgians, and Alabamians had succeeded in overrunning a key high ground position at the southern end of the Union battle-line for the final time. And the victors would not relinquish their grip on July 2.

Most importantly, not only the left flank of Sickles' Third Corps but also the Army of the Potomac now "was gone" at this time. Therefore, all that remained for the achieving of a final decisive victory to achieve a success was for the victors to turn north and then roll up the units of the Army of the Potomac, positioned along Cemetery Ridge (just to the northeast and directly north of Little Round Top), from south to north like an old carpet, or so it seemed to the winners of the struggle for the Devil's Den and Houck's Ridge.

A Reluctant General "Old Rock" Benning

However, the situation on Meade's left flank proved to be a most fluid, because the struggle itself was fluid and still evolving with a will of its own. Everything suddenly changed for Southern fortunes when sizeable numbers of Union troops—Colonel Strong Vincent's Third Brigade, First Division, of Major General George Sykes' Fifth Corps, of the army's reserve—suddenly arrived atop Little Round Top to create a new left flank of the Union Army. Meade had earlier made a crucial decision that saved the day when he had ordered his only available reserves, the Fifth Corps, hurried to the left flank in a desperate bid to reinforce the Third Corps, before it was too late.

After once again regaining permanent possession of Houck's Ridge, General Benning, as the highest ranking overall commander, the victors on Houck's Ridge failed to exploit the advantage of having gained of the strategic high ground before the western slope of Little Round Top. Even though the Texans and Alabamians had lost more men than the Georgians, Benning decided not to continue the assault to exploit the gains of capturing all of the high ground west of Plum Run, despite ordered to do so.

A good tactical opportunity still existed to achieve greater gains, especially if Confederate guns of Major Mathias Winston Henry's divisional artillery battalion (like Captain Reilly's battery that had already advanced to provide timely support that played a role in the capture of Houck's Ridge and the Devils' Den) moved forward (as General Hood had planned) in a support role to rake Little Round Top's defenders, while protecting the left flank of troops advancing from Houck's Ridge to Little Round Top to link with the attackers, including two Texas regiments, to the east on the other side of Plum Run.

Unfortunately, some of the fight had gone out of the usually hard-hitting General Benning since the war's bloodiest day in mid-September of the previous year. After defending the majestic stone structure, with three arches, known Burnside's Bridge at Antietam, with great skill, "Old Rock" Benning had shortly afterward then played a key role in launching the spirited counterattack on the powerful Ninth Corps to buy precious time and save the day on Lee's collapsed right flank, before the arrival of Ambrose Powell Hill's Division from Harpers Ferry. But that same aggressive spirit that had risen to the fore at Antietam was not rekindled by Benning after the capture of Houck's Ridge nearly ten months later.

Unfortunately, the three captured New York cannon positioned in commanding fashion atop the crest of Houck's Ridge were not turned around to face east and fire on the crest of Little Round Top, even though ammunition was available, especially after the caissons and ammunition limbers of Smith's Battery were captured in the valley of Plum Run. Although the retreating Union artillerymen had taken their cannoneers' equipment for loading and firing with them, the Confederate artillery of Major Henry's battalion of Hood's Division should have been ordered forward (as General Hood had planned and would have ordered if not wounded) with the necessary tools to work the guns to inflict greater damage.

At almost the last minute before Robertson's Texans and Law's Alabamians struck, the sudden arrival of hundreds of Colonel Strong Vincent's Brigade on the crest of Little Round Top set the stage for a new struggle for possession of the recently-created Union left flank on a higher elevation east of Houck's Ridge and on the other side of Plum Run Valley. Instead of pushing east across the narrow valley of Plum Run to join and assist in the assault on the western slope of Little Round, where Texas and Alabama troops fought and died on their own in repeated assaults up the rocky slope, General Benning remained stationary with his four veteran Georgia regiments on his high-ground perch. He simply decided to stay put with an ironclad determination that had often mirrored his decisions as a justice on the Georgia Supreme Court, allowing the all-important struggle for possession of Little Round Top to proceed with renewed fury on its own and without any assistance from the west: a tactical mistake of significant proportions.

Here, beyond the first high ground of Houck's Ridge and the Devil's Den, every Confederate soldier was needed for the overwhelming Little Round Top, where the attackers of the 4th and 5th Texas were now seen toiling up the western slope and following their Lone Star State flags, while nearing the rocky heights, held by Colonel Vincent's well-positioned troops, lined with flame and smoke.

However, General Benning refused to send not only any of his four Georgia regiments forward to assist in the fierce struggle east of Plum Run, but also the 1st Texas or the 3rd Arkansas, which also remained stationary. But with General Longstreet absent, Hood wounded, and Law, who had replaced Hood and attempted to do the best he could, but was too inexperienced to capably command his division in the midst of a raging battle, especially after it had splintered and fought separately, Benning now acted on his own.

Therefore, when he was ordered to advance, Benning refused to do so. But to be fair, this was not entirely Benning's fault. For whatever reason, Law failed to ride up to Houck's Ridge to organize an offensive effort to assist Little Round Top's attackers in the primary mission: turning Meade's left flank that was now located on the higher ground of Little Round Top. In the end, consequently, the Confederate offensive effort that should have continued east from Houck's Ridge and the Devil's Den was never resumed this afternoon.

Therefore, not only were the Alabama and Texas attackers of Little Round Top on their own in regard to the lack of infantry support, but also the lack of artillery support from west of Plum Run. Unfortunately, for Hood's veterans who were fighting and dying on Little Round Top's rocky slopes on their own east of Plum Run, Major Mathias Winston Henry's artillery battalion, of Hood's Division, had failed to advance to provide close-fire support that would have caused the blue defenders of Little Round Top considerable trouble. For whatever reason on a day of many mysteries in regard to a malfunctioning Confederate leadership at the highest levels, Law failed to order the division's artillery forward to provide close support, which would have greatly assisted the hard-fighting foot-soldiers of the 4th, 15th, 47th, 48th Alabama and the 4th and 5th Texas, in their hour of need. Clearly, on this afternoon of destiny, the wheels of fate had turned against Hood's men, and these wheels continued to turn at an even faster pace before the sun dropped over the horizon to the west.

Like General Law, Benning, a senior general officer, was having his worst day as a brigade commander who had won considerable distinction in the past. First, he had followed the wrong brigade (Robertson's Texas Brigade—and then its left wing after separating—instead of Law's Alabama Brigade, which advanced farther south) from the very beginning of the attack. The former attorney was now acting more like the prudish, inflexible Georgia Supreme Court justice that he had been before the war, rather than going forward to assist in the assault on Little Round Top in the determined bid to turn Meade's left flank to yet win the day. Benning's idle Georgia regiments east of Plum Run could have turned the tide either on Colonel Vincent's weak right, held by the 16th Michigan on the north end of the thin battle-line, or the left flank, held by the 20th Maine Volunteer Infantry on the southern end of the brigade's line, if rushed to assist the relatively few attackers, including the 4th Texas and 5th Texas, of Little Round Top. Therefore, in the end, the valor and high sacrifice of the 1st Texas in leading the way in the capture the strategic crest of Houck's Ridge and the Devil's Den was in vain, and a wasted effort in large part because of the lack of support given to the attackers of Little Round Top.[28]

However, the 1st Texas soldiers had mostly fought New York soldiers from beginning to end in the bitter struggle for possession of Houck's Ridge and the Devil's Den. As mentioned, Philip Alexander Work's men had then played a key role in holding firm while defending their hard-earned ground on Houck's Ridge and the Devil's Den against repeated counterattacks, including from the 40th New York (the "Mozart Regiment" from New York City). In the words of Lieutenant Colonel Work, who briefly described the most forgotten phase of the bitter struggle for the high ground west of Plum Run: "... an incessant fire was kept up by this regiment, and the enemy was several times repulsed in their efforts to retake the hill."[29]

With General Benning not ordering an advance to assist the men fighting and dying on the western slope of Little Round Top, the Texas busied themselves with sharpshooting with the Federals on the high ground to the east. One of the most distinguished examples of this kind of heroism was exhibited by teenage Private Wilson J. Barbee, 1st Texas. At age twenty-three, he had enlisted in Galveston in August 1, and evidently was a resident of the largest port city in Texas. Known as "a jolly, whole-souled lad," in one comrade's words, the young man was usually calm and placid until transformed in the heat of combat, when "he went wild, seemed to have no sense of fear whatever, and was a reckless dare-devil."[30]

This young man had been one of Hood's trusty scouts, who had been noted for his frontier savvy and skills that were often put to good use. Barbee had returned to his regiment from the key scouting mission ordered by Hood to ascertain tactical opportunities and the exact location of the Federal Army's left flank. He had been freed of his usual mounted courier duties for General Hood, after that gifted officer's fall from his horse in the attack's beginning. Therefore, Private Barbee had left his "little sorrel horse," which he rode like the wind, behind in order to grab an Enfield rifled-musket and to take advantage of a long-awaited opportunity to fight beside the boys in the ranks and to inflict damage among the Federals. He had made the most of the opportunity, leading the way for his comrades of the Lone Star Rifles of Company "L," 1st Texas, during the attack on Houck's Ridge and the Devil's Den.

During the defense of the Devil's Den before the surging blue ranks during the counterattack and after a difficult climb, the agile and lithe Private Barbee took a commanding position atop a diabase "rock upon the highest pinnacle of the hill, and there, exposed to a raking, deadly fire from artillery and musketry, stood until he had fired twenty-five shots" at the Yankees. In such an exposed and conspicuous position atop a dominant boulder of the Devil's Den, it was only a matter of time before the fast-firing Private Barbee "received a Minie ball wounded in the right thigh, and fell wounded."[31]

Private James O. Bradfield never forgot the display of courage exhibited by the daring young man: "Barbee was knocked off the rock by a ball that struck him in the right leg. Climbing instantly back, he again commenced shooting. In less than two minutes, he was tumbled off the rock by a ball in the other leg. Still unsatisfied, he crawled back a second time, but was not there more than a minute before, being wounded in the body, he again fell, this time dropping on his back between the rock that had been his perch, and that which was my shelter. Too seriously wounded this time to extricate himself from the narrow passageway, he called for help, and the last time I saw him that day, he was lying there, crying and cursing because the boys would not come to his relief and help him back on to the rock."[32]

Private Barbee survived his wounds received on July 2, but not the campaigning in early 1864. Far from where he had reaped glory at the Devil's Den, he fell to rise no more during a hot skirmish near the small town of Dandridge, Tennessee, on January 18,

1864. Only in his mid-twenties, the irrepressible Private Barbee was just another young Texas soldier of promise who found shallow graves far from the Lone Star State.[33]

But even in having repulsed the repeated Union assaults and then applying their sharpshooting skills in methodically shooting down Yankees to the east brought no end to the blood-letting for the 1st Texas soldiers. As Lieutenant Colonel Work explained how the surreal horrors of war continued unabated for his men on a day that had been most ill-fated and bloody: "Late in the evening a terrific fire of artillery was concentrated against the hill occupied by this (the First) regiment, many were killed and wounded, some [literally] losing their heads, and others so horribly mutilated and mangled that their identity could hardly be established, but notwithstanding this, all the men continued heroically and unflinchingly to maintain their position" atop the commanding perch of Houck's Ridge and the Devil's Den.[34]

Even though the bullet-shredded Lone Star State flag still waved in triumph and defiance from the embattled crest of Houck's Ridge, the fighting in this bloodied sector was still far from over. When pressure increased to the north in the absence of his left flank regiment, the 3rd Arkansas which had fallen back under tremendous pressure, that should have provided protection, Colonel Work turned and advanced the left of the 1st Texas to near the southern border of the Wheatfield to meet the escalating Federal threat. Here, in Work's words: "My position was such that I was enabled to pour a deadly enfilading fire into the enemy as they advanced through a wheat field to attack the troops in position on my left, and I have no doubt that this fire contributed greatly to the repulse of the enemy attacking our forces some 300 to 400 yards on my left."[35]

Private Albert Cuthbert Sims described an incident that hastily dispersed his company ("F") of the 1st Texas in this sector: "As we came down a slant by the side of a wood [Rose Woods] a shell cut off a white Oak Tree [below the Wheat Field], which made us scatter to keep it from falling on us, but we soon closed up the gap and went forward" into the fray.[36]

But Work's timely maneuvers and aggressiveness to the north only stirred up a hornet's nest, resulting in an escalation of the combat in this sector north of Houck's Ridge and the Devil's Den. Therefore, Work explained the crisis situation when "the troops on my left were driven back, and my left was exposed" once again.[37]

In consequence and with this bloody day finally drawing to an end and while Little Round Top remained in Union hands, Lieutenant Colonel Work presented Lieutenant Henry Epps Moss, who commanded Company "D" (Star Rifles) and the dependable soldiers of Marion and Jefferson Counties, with a key assignment. Captain Moss was directed "to take charge of the colors, and retaining them there with a few men to hold the hill until the regiment could safely retire [and then] I ordered the regiment to fall back to a stone fence about 100 yards in my rear":

> The major part of the regiment and the Fifteenth Georgia fell back as ordered, but quite a large number, having noticed that the colors were not moving to the rear, refused to withdraw, and remaining upon the crest of the hill, succeeded in holding the enemy in

> check in their immediate front, and obliquely upon their front and left, until the troops upon my left had been re-formed and were again advancing, when I directed Major F[rederick]. S. Bass to return to the crest of the hill with the body of the regiment, and, with Captain D[avid]. K. Rice, of Company "C" [Palmer Rifles from Harris County], proceeded himself to collect together all fugitives, slightly wounded, and exhausted men, and placed them so as to protect my right and rear from an attack in that quarter, one of my advanced scouts in that direction having reported to me that a column of the enemy was moving down a ravine or hollow and threatening me in that quarter.[38]

As throughout this bloody day of destiny on the south of the Army of Northern Virginia's battle-line, Lieutenant Colonel Work continued to rise to the challenge of facing fast-paced new developments on the battlefield. In his own words: "Having made every disposition to guard my right and rear, I placed Captain D. K. Rice in charge of such defense, and proceeded to the Third Arkansas Regiment, of which General Robertson had ordered me to take charge" of the hard-hit command.[39]

Therefore, demonstrating considerable tactical flexibility and insight almost as if battling the fast-riding Comanche on the Texas plains as he had demonstrated with skill in 1854, Work was a most capable replacement for Brigadier General Jerome Bonaparte Robertson, who had taken a wound in the leg late in the day and after he ordered the Kentucky-born colonel to take command of what remained of the 3rd Arkansas, after Colonel "Van" Manning had been wounded.[40]

After a dark veil of the humid night of July 2 finally closed the curtain on the day's surreal horrors and the scene of dramatic Confederate successes in capturing Houck's Ridge and the Devil's Den west of Plum Run, Captain Samuel A. Willson wanted to make sure that the gains of the 1st Texas were not wasted. Willson, who commanded Company "F" (Woodville Rifles), 1st Texas, and who had succeeded Work as a delegate (the only native-born Texan among the delegates) to the Texas Secession Convention of March 2, 1861, "requested of Col. Work that he, with the help of others be allowed to move the canon [*sic.*] off the field which we had captured that evening, which they did, except one which the enemy, seeing they would have to abandon, pushed off a precipice down among some large rocks, so that they could not get it."[41]

As Work explained in his official report how to gain permanent possession of the trophies, just in case the Federals once again counterattacked:

> [He] detailed Companies "E" and "I" for the purpose, I sent three pieces of the artillery captured to the rear. There were three other pieces—two at one point and one at the other—that I was unable to remove, for the reason that they were located between the lines of the enemy and our own, and were so much exposed that they could not be approached except under a murderous fire. While they could not be removed by us, neither could they be approached by the enemy, for the same fire that drove the [New York] artillerists from their guns and the infantry from their support, was ever in readiness to keep them in check and drive them back.[42]

6

The Savage Contest for Possession of the Crucial High Ground

Meanwhile, the bloody struggle for possession of Little Round Top, higher and rockier than any hill seen in east Texas by Texas Brigade members, had only fairly begun. Although long viewed as separate, the fight for Houck's Ridge (the first left flank of General Sickles' Third Corps and Meade's Army) was closely interrelated from the beginning to the escalating contest on Little Round Top (the newly-created Union left flank of an ever-fluid battle on the far south) just to the east.

Indeed, Houck's Ridge had to have been first secured by the Confederates for any realistic possibility of capturing Little Round Top. If Houck's Ridge was not permanently secured first by Hood's men, then the Yankees, especially veteran gunners manning the three New York field pieces of Captain James E. Smith's Battery, atop the high ground along the crest could have blasted the 4th and 5th Texas attackers, who attacked up the open western slope of Little Round Top, along with Law's Alabama boys just to their south, or on the Texans' right, from the rear.

After the 1st Texas captured the three guns of Smith's Battery and after Work's right overran the Devil's Den and as mentioned, therefore, the fight had continued with renewed intensity for the dust-covered men of Hood's Division: a time-consuming process that played a role in sabotaging an offensive effort on the opposite side, east, of Plum Run. Alabama troops west of Plum Run also deserved credit for excellent fighting that also contributed to success. For instance, helping to overrun the Devil's Den for the second time after the 1st Texas had first achieved this goal during the initial assault, the 44th Alabama had pushed through the Devil's Den from the south: a one-two punch that had overpowered the last bluecoat resistance, and hurled the troops of the 4th Maine Volunteer Infantry (First Division, Second Brigade), which brought up the rear of Ward's reeling brigade, back north.

In addition, the 48th Alabama, positioned just southeast of the 44th Alabama, had surged slightly northeast through the killing ground of the boulder-strewn and underbrush-covered valley (later named the "Slaughter Pen" located between the

Devil's Den and Big Round Top just southeast of the Devil's Den) of Plum Run, consisting of shallow water only around 1–2 feet in width, while applying additional pressure on Walker's 4th Maine that had gamely protected the withdrawing rear of Ward's battered command. As noted, all of these successes had been achieved by the combined fighting of the Texas, Georgia, and Alabama troops. For an extended period of time, the Devil's Den was described as "a smoking crater," having become truly a hell on earth for combatants on both sides.[1]

Meanwhile, with Houck's Ridge, the Devil's Den, and the three cannon of Smith's New York battery securely in Texas and Georgia hands, the assault on Little Round Top to the east continued unabated. Unfortunately for Confederate fortunes, General Gouverneur K. Warren, a capable West Pointer (Class of 1850) and respected member of Meade's staff—chief engineer of the Army of the Potomac—had helped to save the Union with his early timing warming (along with sharp-eyed Federal signalmen atop Little Round Top who had already earlier spied Longstreet's threat) of Longstreet's approaching storm. Of course, General Meade also deserved great credit, because he had dispatched Warren to the south for the express purpose of making sure that the high ground of Little Round Top was secured. Once Warren saw that thousands of Longstreet's First Corps were "sweeping from the woods [and] far outflanking the left of the Third Corps line, where Smith's battery, in air and almost unsupported on the rocks of the Devil's Den, gallantly waited their doom," Warren's desperate call for reinforcements to defend Little Round Top, now the key to the battlefield on the south, paid high dividends in the end.

Clearly, not long after the fall of Houck's Ridge and the Devil's Den, the Army of the Potomac had been most fortunate, because of the timely arrival on the powerful Sixth Corps (the last corps of the army to reach the field), after a forced march of more than 30 miles, in the early afternoon, which had released the army's reserve, the Fifth Corps, to be redeployed, after having been smartly ordered by Meade to march south to protect the army's vulnerable left flank.

Therefore, the Fifth Corps found itself suddenly in the right place and the right time, when the Army of the Potomac "was tottering on the brink of an enormous disaster" not yet seen in this war, after the fall of Houck's Ridge and the Devil's Den—the first left flank of the Potomac. Just in the nick of time, a Fifth Corps brigade of four regiments, under Harvard graduate (Class of 1859) from Erie, Pennsylvania, Colonel Strong Vincent, hurried his New York, Michigan, Pennsylvania, and Maine troops up an old logging road that cut through the dense timber and led up the south side of Little Round Top around 4:30 p.m. Some jealous older officers, who lacked compared talent, considered the handsome Vincent little more than a showy, bombastic "dude." But young Vincent, age twenty-six, was as tough as nails and every inch of a fighter: the antithesis of a dandy. Even more, he was a true gentleman and a scholar, having graduated from Trinity College and Harvard University.

Additionally, the Parrott rifles of Battery "D," 5th United States Artillery, Fifth Corps, under Lieutenant Charles Edward Hazlett, were brought up by hand by the hard-working gunners and positioned to face west along the rocky crest of Little Round Top. This strategic crest overlooked a vast expanse of the battlefield as far as the eye could see to the west toward Seminary Ridge and north to Cemetery Ridge. Ironically, the Texan Brigade had encountered Hazlett's Battery and Vincent's 44th New York Volunteer Infantry, during the fighting at Second Manassas on another hot summer day.[2]

Therefore, by the time that the 4th Texas, which surged up the slope under a blazing fire near Little Round Top's northern end to attack the far right of Vincent's line, and 5th Texas and 4th Alabama and the 47th Alabama—from north–south, or left to right—struck its blow, the rocky crest of Little Round Top was already well-defended by an entire brigade of less than 1,000 men under Colonel Vincent's capable command. These determined veterans in blue proved experts at shooting down attacking Rebels who struggled uphill on a hot day with business-like efficiency, blasting downhill to reap a grim harvest.

Once again, with so many officers cut down by the hail of projectiles and from heat exhaustion (the fate of three of five of Hood's Alabama regimental commanders fell by the wayside to leave their men, already without more leadership, even more on their own) because of the combined effect of the afternoon's intense heat and lack of water during the assault on one of the year's hottest days, it was once again left largely to the common soldiers—and not finely-uniformed generals (Hood was down and Law was mostly absent) or colonels—to overrun Little Round Top from the west.[3]

Fortunately, the hard-fighting 5th Texas soldiers had been recently issued shoes, which assisted in their arduous climb up the western slope during the desperate attempt to storm the formidable height of Little Round Top.[4] Private John Mark Smither, 5th Texas, described the early phase of the assault to the left of the 4th Alabama and Law's other two Alabama regiments in a letter:

> ... we advanced through a field about half a mile before we reached the timber at the foot of the mountain [Big Round Top], our men tumbling out of ranks at every step, knocked over by the Enemy's sharpshooters who lined the side of the mountain, on arriving within 250 yds of the timber their Batteries opened on us with grape and canester [*sic.*] mowing down the grass all around my feet but the distance being most too great [and therefore] they did us little damage, after getting within the timber we incountered [*sic.*] the skirmishers & Sharpshooters posted behind a stonewall, but we soon had them flying up the side of the mountain."[5]

Yelling all the way up the bullet-swept slope, the Texans had followed in pursuit of Berdan's Sharpshooters at a rapid pace, sensing decisive victory on the horizon, before delivering their assault on Colonel Vincent's defensive line.

Serving as an inspirational color bearer, William A. Fletcher, Company "F," 5th Texas, described the tactical dilemma of battling for a lengthy period without reinforcements from Houck's Ridge and at the Devil's Den, because these victors provided no support to the attackers of Little Round Top: "We had but poor chance to retaliate with much effect [while] Our men commenced falling rapidly and especially color bearer.... I saw the colors fall five times" in the tumult.[6]

As penned by Major Jefferson C. Rogers, 5th Texas:

> ... the heroic conduct of [Color Sergeant] T. W. Fitzgerald, of Company "A" [5th Texas], who was the color bearer. He pressed gallantly forward, and was badly wounded far in front [and later captured]. J. A. Howard, of Company "B," color corporal, then took the flag, and remained firmly at his post. He was almost instantly killed. The colors were then taken by Sergeant W. Evans, of Company "F," who planted them defiantly in the face of the foe during the remainder of the fight...[7]

Leading the 5th Texas, Colonel Robert Micajah Powell, a former attorney at age thirty-seven, described the stern challenge posed by the high ground of Little Round Top—higher and more boulder-strewn than Houck's Ridge—in even more stark terms, writing how the "ascent was so difficult as to forbid the use of arms."[8] Born in Montgomery County, Alabama, in 1826 and migrating to Texas to embark upon a new life in 1849, Powell was a popular commander, who had been an attorney—like Colonel Strong Vincent—and state legislator before the nightmare of the so-called brothers' war. While leading his 5th Texas troops onward into the leaden storm, he was cut down. The former captain of the Waverly Confederates (Company "D") then watched the savage struggle intensifying to new furies until it seemed "like a devil's carnival."[9]

Advancing in the 4th Texas' surging ranks on the far left, or north, of the Texas line and targeting the vulnerable 16th Michigan Volunteer Infantry that held the right flank of Vincent's Brigade, Van C. Giles described how the open western side of Little Round Top was "covered with great boulders that had tumbled from the cliffs above years before [and] These afforded great protection to the men. Every tree, rock and stump that gave any protection from the rain of Minie balls that were poured down upon us from the crest above us, was soon appropriated. John Griffith and myself pre-empted a moss-covered old boulder about the size of a 500-pound cotton bale."[10]

During the 5th Texas' assault just to the right, or south, of the 4th Texas, Private John Mark Smither penned in a letter about the nightmare of assaulting Little Round Top and Colonel Vincent's tenacious defenders:

> After a time we succeeded in working our way up the steep side of the mountain [Little Round Top] and arrived within sight of the formidable works our Enemies had prepared for us, nothing daunted ... our boys pushed on through the brush over the rocks until they arrived within 25 steps of the works [and] on finding that the plan of scaling the heights was impossible, for we could hardly have gone over them if there had been no Yankees there, our side immediately took shelter, Indian fashion, behind rocks & trees and commenced popping away at the Yankees whenever they showed their heads, the

> Yankees seeing that we had stopped commenced firing as fast as they could, pouring volley after volley down on us with frightful effect.[11]

A proud member of Company "F" (Company Invincibles), 5th Texas, and from the town of Beaumont, Texas, Fletcher also described how these seasoned Texans utilized Indian fighting skills during the determined push up the rocky western face of Little Round Top, with individual courage and combat prowess rising to the fore:

> We stopped advancing, without orders a far as I was concerned, as I had heard none. Another man and I were well to the front, behind rock; the enemy was only a short distance up and so near over us that with good aim we could have near been shot in the top of the head, either standing or kneeling [and] We did not attempt to scale the hill for it would have been a good job on some parts for one used to mountain climbing stripped for the business.[12]

With so many fine officers cut down, the Texas Brigade's resilient common soldiers continued to bring to Confederacy ever-closer to a decisive success, or so it seemed in the day's second all-out offensive bid to turn the Army of the Potomac's left flank, but this time east of Plum Run. In the words of Van C. Giles: "Nearly all our field officers were gone [and therefore] order and discipline were gone. Every fellow as his own general. Private soldiers gave commands as loud as the officers. Nobody paid any attention to either."[13]

Bloody Repulse

The strategic high-ground position held by Colonel Strong Vincent's veterans, who benefitted immensely from the boulder-strewn western slope before Little Round Top's crest, served not only as a natural breastwork but also as an impregnable fortress. Located about one-third of the way down the western slope, Vincent's defenses, both natural and created by hand in piling up rocks, were simply too powerful to overcome by too few attackers. Fletcher described: "We did not hold this [advanced] position long before the order was passed on the line to 'fall back,' [at a time when] all parts of our line were as badly butchered as at [this] point … I learned some time afterward that the peak was called 'Roundtop' or 'Heights.'"[14]

But incredibly, the veterans of the 5th Texas and 4th Texas, from north to south, were far from finished in regard to their fanatical attempts to carry the high ground. Despite initially frustrated and the loss of a good many comrades, including relatives, the never-say-die Texans once again attacked up the slope with fixed bayonets. Seemingly doing the impossible against the odds, the most determined Texas soldiers, dodging from rock to rock while bullets whizzed by, surged all the way to the fiery crest. In the ranks of the 5th Texas, two Leon County twins of Company "C" (Leon Hunters) were cut down, Privates Henry T. Driscoll and J. P. Driscoll.

Obsessed with a single tactical objective while pushing forward well in advance of his comrades, one ragged Rebel from the Lone Star State neared the smoke-shrouded crest of Little Round Top. He had targeted a colorful, Union battle-flag for capture. This lowly enlisted man would not be denied, even while the fire from Colonel Vincent's soldiers had never been hotter or more accurate. Upon finally gaining the boulders of Little Round Top's crest after much effort, this unknown Texas Brigade soldier suddenly acted on impulse, when he neared the most tempting of targets. He lunged across a boulder and stretched as far as he could to grab a handful of the smooth silk of a Union flag. Shocking the Federal color bearer who could not believe that any soldier—more mountain goat than human being—could have possibly ascended the entire length of the bullet-swept western slope of Little Round Top to actually reach the top covered in boulders, and then to have the audacity to dare attempt to capture the colors of a well-positioned Union regiment occupying the crest, where hundreds of fast-firing Yankees blazed away.

In the hands of a Yankee captain who had earlier taken the flag, evidently from a fallen color bearer, to inspire his troops to still greater exertions, the Union officer was stunned by the Rebel's daring. He managed to retain the cherished banner, despite the Texan's best efforts in pulling the colors with all his strength. Therefore, the frustrated Rebel now relied on his steel bayonet, because his musket was unloaded, after having expended his rounds. He jabbed repeated with his bayonet, cutting the captain's arms and hands until they were "stuck full of holes" during this savage private contest near the strategic crest of smoke-shrouded Little Round Top.[15]

Himself amazed by the never-say-die spirit of his 5th Texas boys, after the first repulse and withdrawing around 200 yards down the body-strewn slope, Private John Mark Smither described in a letter to his mother:

> After a desperate battle of 2 or 3 hours we perceiving ourselves flanked on the right for Law's Brigade [the 4th Alabama, 47th Alabama, and 15th Alabama, from left to right, or north to south] on the right of our Regt [5th Texas] had fallen back, received orders [*sic.*] to fall back which we did in good order[,] retreating about 200 yds where we halted and formed our line. Genl Law [belatedly] coming up at the time, Hood being wounded, gave orders to advance on the place. Now it was expected that our men would have refused to have gone in again, but no they tried it a second and third time.[16]

In the words of a 4th Texas soldier who could hardly believe the extent of the carnage and bloodletting: "There seemed to be a viciousness in the very air we breathed."[17] Colonel Powell, leading the 5th Texas, described how the bloody "scene was strikingly like a devil's carnival."[18]What made the savage combat even more surreal was the fact that one young "Irish lad" in blue defending Little Round Top had a Son of Erin relative, who fought with distinction in the 5th Texas's ranks: still another reminder that the Irish in blue and gray were involved in their own civil war during the bitter struggle for possession of Little Round Top like in other sectors at Gettysburg.[19]

Almost incredibly and against the odds, the most significant penetration and gains were achieved by the 4th Texas on the far left to the north during its last and most determined assault to gain the crest. Symbolically, in almost turning the right flank of Vincent's brigade, which was held by the veterans of the 16th Michigan, it was appropriate that Hood's old regiment came closer to achieving a decisive success in capturing Little Round Top than any other regiment of Hood's Division: a fact that certainly would have made the badly-wounded General Hood extremely proud had he known of what his old command was achieving during some of the most vicious combat of the war.

Veterans of such crack companies as the Lone Star Guards (Company "E"), the Robertson Five Shooters (Company "C"), and the Mustang Grays (Company "F") overcame the odds and came extremely close to carrying the day by turning Vincent's flank from the north. In fact, at one point, decisive victory seemed to have been won. After somehow scaling the steep northwestern side of Little Round Top, the 4th Texas boys actually succeeded in turning the right flank of the 16th Michigan, hurling many Michiganers to the crest and even down the eastern slope of Little Round Top.

For a few precious minutes around 5:30 p.m. and after Colonels Vincent, age twenty-six, and Hazlett were fatally cut down and his hard-hit brigade of Maine, Pennsylvania, New York, and Michigan troops was never more vulnerable on the northern flank, the Texans had achieved one of the most impressive successes yet seen at Gettysburg. Incredibly, the 4th Texas soldiers were on the verge of turning the right flank of Colonel Vincent's brigade, and perhaps even capturing Little Round Top, if an enfilade fire could be turned south upon Vincent's other defenders on lower ground along the hill's defenses situated along the western slope below the crest.

But when a decisive success for the 4th Texas seemed inevitable and thanks to General Warren's earlier timely initiatives made on his own and without orders, additional Fifth Corps reinforcements advanced up the northern face of Little Round Top and arrived atop the smoke-filled crest in just the nick of time: the troops of the 140th New York Volunteer Infantry, which was capably led by Irishman Colonel Patrick Henry O'Rorke, who had been born in County Cavan, Ireland. The exhausted 4th Texas boys, stained in sweat and streaked with black powder, recovered from their surprise in time to unleash a close-range volley upon the suddenly arriving New Yorkers.

Out in front encouraging his New Yorkers, Colonel "Paddy" O'Rorke, who was the proud son of the "Little Dublin" Irish community of Rochester, New York, was felled by a Texas bullet that pierced his neck and spine, killing him instantly. The struggle at the northern end of Little Round Top raged with increased savagery and new furies between the Texans and New Yorkers in a dramatic showdown that had seen opposing troops from these same states earlier battling for possession of Houck's Ridge and the Devil's Den on the opposite side of Plum Run. However, the repeated New York volleys streaming down the slope from the crest was simply too much, and the hard-hit Texans, low on ammunition and manpower, were forced to retire upon the body-strewn hillside, after having come ever so close to turning the right flank of Vincent's brigade on the far north.[20]

After the repulse of the most successful Texas assault up the western slope of Little Round Top, the surviving Texans once again formed their ranks for still another assault up the hill of death, if sufficient strength could be mustered. However, these repeated and almost fanatical assaults up the rocky slope of Little Round Top for the Texans ended as suddenly as they began, after more bloodletting for no gain. In a letter, Private Smither wrote how his 5th Texas was "formed to go in a 4th time when night came on [which] forced us to abondon [*sic.*] the fight."[21]

In the end, all of the Texas and Alabama assaults on Little Round Top were in vain, sputtering to an end with no decisive result. Fletcher, Company "F," 5th Texas, described how the men were disgruntled about the series of frontal assaults up the western slope that were little more than suicidal efforts to carry in the high ground: "There was quite a lot of censure for the last two forward movements by the men."[22]

Disillusioned survivors, like Rufus King Fielder, were bitter over the folly of the repeated frontal assaults against the most formidable natural position that they had ever seen. As he penned in a letter shortly after the nightmarish contest that had become a slaughter, the 5th Texas charged "up an almost perpendicular peak at the top of which the enemy had fortified to make it impossible to take had the enemy only been armed with rocks."[23]

A member of the same crack regiment, which contained such hard-fighting companies as the Leon Hunters (Company "C"), the Milam County Greys (Company "G"), and the Dixie Blues (Company "E"), that fought with uncommon valor, William A. Fletcher was especially bitter over the high sacrifice and wasted effort, asking, "Why were we fighting an impregnable position—was it ignorance?... It was a very unfortunate condition for the right of an army with true and tried men being shot down like dogs."[24]

Unleashing his venom on his corps commander instead of General Lee who had ordered the offensive effort against the Union left flank, Fletcher denounced "Old Pete" Longstreet, who "by nature was a fighter, but not a tactician."[25] Val C. Giles, 4th Texas, also blamed Longstreet, especially in regard to his lateness in reaching the field and launching the assault against the impregnable high ground on July 2, because it was so late "in the afternoon when we reached the battlefield, nearly ten and a half hours behind time [and] that delay lost the Battle of Gettysburg to the Confederates.... The loss of those ten hours gave the enemy ample time to occupy and fortify Cemetery Ride and Little Round Top. Little Round Top was the key to the Battle of Gettysburg, and when we failed to occupy it, as General Lee expected us to do, the battle was lost."[26]

Indeed, time had been of the essence, and Little Round Top had been occupied by sizeable numbers of Fifth Corps veterans virtually at the last minute. By only a matter of minutes, Hood's troops had failed to successfully turn the left flank of the Army of the Potomac at Little Round. Had the Texans been unleashed only an hour earlier that the afternoon, then the battle of Gettysburg might well have resulted in Lee's most important victory of the war. But Confederate failure at Little Round Top—Meade's second and last left flank on the far south during the decisive afternoon of July 2—has cast a shadow over the success of capturing the first Union left flank at Houck's Ridge and the Devil's Den.

Once again, the Texans had fought magnificently, and for no gain except for a glory that was badly out-of-date by this time, a lengthy casualty list, and three pieces of captured New York artillery. With the field pieces of Captain James E. Smith's New York Battery in his hands after their capture by the 1st Texas, Colonel Work, "Immediately after dark—having detailed Companies 'E' (Marshall Guards) and 'I' (Crockett Southrons) for the purpose—I sent these [three] pieces of the artillery captured to the rear."[27]

All in all, the 1st Texas had almost captured not three but half a dozen field pieces from Smith's New York Battery. As Philip Alexander Work explained: "There were three other pieces—two at one point and one at another, that I was unable to remove, for the reason that they were so much exposed [on the east side of Houck's Ridge] that they could not be approached except under a murderous fire."[28]

At Gettysburg, the young men and boys of the 1st Texas could rightly claim achievements that were not gained by the attackers of Little Round Top during some of the hardest fighting of the Civil War. They also could claim the most Union artillery pieces captured and permanently retained by Lee's troops as hard-won prizes of the Army of Northern Virginia—no small accomplishment under the most challenging and difficult circumstances posed on America's most gory battlefield during the crucial second day.[29]

Final Day of Slaughter, July 3

As a strange fate would have it, the bitter contest that consumed Hood's Division during its desperate assaults on Meade's left flank—first Houck's Ridge and the Devil's Den before the great challenge of Little Round Top—and took such a ghastly high toll from its ranks, especially among the Texas Brigade, gave General Longstreet a good excuse that he desired on July 3 in regard to not using Hood's Division in Pickett's Charge. In overrunning Houck's Ridge and the Devil's Den, the 1st Texas lost thirty killed, fifty wounded, and another forty-five captured. Nevertheless, the 1st Texas remained a formidable combat unit, maintaining its lethality and its lofty reputation.

On the morning of the third day, Longstreet successfully convinced Lee not to use Hood's Division for the last-ditch offensive effort to gain a decisive victory at Gettysburg. Therefore, the best fighters and combat troops in the Army of Northern Virginia were not employed in the most famous offensive effort of the Civil War, Pickett's Charge. Thanks to Longstreet's firm insistence that went against the tactical designs of Lee's original plan, this was a final command decision made by Lee at a crucial time on July 3 when no additional mistakes (more than enough had been made of July 2) could be afforded because everything was at stake—not only the battle, but also the Confederacy's fate—and when the strength of this last-ditch offensive effort needed to be enhanced in every possible way and by all possible means.

As he first believed before convinced otherwise by his contrarian top lieutenant, General Lee was correct in needing the army's best fighters on the afternoon of July 3. Instead of joining Pickett's Charge the surviving 1st Texas members remained in position on the far south and behind a stone wall to protect the army's right flank. Here, on the far south, they repulsed Gen. Elon Farnsworth's cavalry attack on the fatal third day at Gettysburg.[30]

Farnsworth was shot out of the saddle by a well-aimed shot from a 1st Texas Enfield rifle. In a letter, Private H. Watters Berryman, a member on the skirmish line before the 1st Texas, described:

> ... a brigade of Yankee cavalry came charging upon the gallant First Texas. As I was in front, cavalry came very near running over me, but I jumped behind a stone fence and held my position. I killed a captain and wounded a lieutenant [and] I took five or six prisoners [and then joined the regiment where] All the boys had fired off their pieces, and the Yankees would not give them time to reload, so the boys were using the butts of their guns. Moore killed one with a rock. Newt [his brother] managed to load his gun. There was a Yank cutting one of the boys over the head with a sabre, when Newt ran up and blew his brains out [and we] disposed of the regular Yankees, [after bitter hand-to-hand combat].[31]

James Henry Hendrick, Company "E," 1st Texas, described in a letter how "two regiments of cavalry charged our regiment [and] They came up to ten steps of the regiment. Some of the regiment knocked them off their horses with rocks. We killed a great many of them and captured over one-hundred prisoners. They could not break our lines."[32] Clearly, these well-equipped Union cavalrymen were unfortunate to have run into these tough and seasoned Texas soldiers, who knew how to eliminate opponents in any manner possible.[33]

Unfortunately, for the Texas Brigade's survivors, fate had not been kind on bloody July 2. In the end, the second day—and not the third day as generally assumed by most historians—was not the most decisive day during the showdown at Gettysburg. Not all the hard fighting and heroics in the world could compensate for the seemingly conspiracy of ill-fate, poor leadership decisions, and sheer bad luck that combined to sabotage the Texas Brigade's best efforts. Among the long list of factors that early went against Lee's ambitious plans on his right flank on the afternoon of July 2, perhaps none was more significant than the wounding of the best division commander of the Army of Northern Virginia, knocking him out of action for the rest of this crucial day of decision. As fate would have it, Major General John Bell Hood, the army's most aggressive and capable division commander, was cut down hardly before the assault on the Union left flank began.

Unfortunately for the Army of Northern Virginia, Hood's fall only continued the day-long process of the gradual unraveling of Lee's battle-plan to turn the left flank of the Army of the Potomac. When Hood fell from his horse when a shell from a New York cannon burst just above him, much of the chances for the Texas Brigade, and the rest of the division, to succeed in the vital mission of overwhelming the Union left went down with him. At the height on the battle for possession of Meade's left, Hood—and any other leader for that matter—was desperately needed to orchestrate the finer points of coordinating the assaults of his division and moving up artillery to adequately support the infantry (and no one could even come close to replacing him, especially in his regard) in a timely fashion in order to make the attacks successful.

However, the key factor of General Hood's fall in dooming the best efforts of his crack troops in their desperate attempt to turn the Union left has been long minimized by historians in large part because of post-war historiography. General Hood's reputation has been long sullied and blackened by personal agendas and for political reasons. This development, the systematic "destruction of John Bell Hood's historical memory," has played a role in the widespread overlooking and minimizing of the importance of the efforts of his Texas troops in spearheading the assault that overran Houck's Ridge and the Devil's Den, when it had been the true Union left flank, before the arrival of Colonel Strong Vincent's Brigade on Little Round Top.[34]

Not only General Hood's fall, but also the overall efforts of the 1st Texas soldiers in playing the leading role in capturing Houck's Ridge and the Devil's Den have been mostly ignored by historians, thanks largely to the excessive focus on the glorification of the nearby later struggle for possession of Little Round Top. While the story of the Alamo has been embellished and romanticized into an enduring legend even though it was of no true strategic importance, the far more important story of the Texas Brigade on the second day at Gettysburg has been left in the historical shadows, including because of the focus on Pickett's Charge on the last day, despite the fact that the fate of two republics hung in the balance on July 2, 1863.[35]

Epilogue

Too often minimized by historians because of the glorification on the nearby struggle of Little Round Top and leading players, especially Colonel Joshua Lawrence Chamberlain and his 20th Maine, the overrunning of Houck's Ridge and the Devil's Den, when these strategic high ground positions represented Meade's left flank, and the capture of Captain James E. Smith's New York battery, all of which were spearheaded by the attack of the 1st Texas, were some of the most notable achievements on either side during the three days of intense combat at Gettysburg.

But these stirring accomplishments were not enough to achieve a decisive success, especially after the arrival of sizeable Union reinforcements of the Fifth Corps poured onto Little Round Top and took good defensive positions just below the commanding summit. In the end, not all the valor and high sacrifice of the hard-fighting Texans, along with their Alabama comrades, were enough to capture Little Round Top.

In summarizing the struggle of the Texas soldiers, perhaps no one said it better than a feisty common soldier of the Texas Brigade. An embittered Rufus King Felder, 5th Texas, allowed his undisguised anger and disgust to bubble to the surface, which were fueled by the horror of the desperate struggle for possession of Little Round Top and because so many attackers had been cut down for nothing. In a July 9, 1863 letter, he wrote with justifiable bitterness and condemned the fumbling Confederate leadership:

> [On the] evening of the 2nd, Lee attempted to carry the heights by storm [but] It seemed like madness in Lee to have attempted to storm such a position. He came very near losing his whole army by it.... The slaughter on both sides was terrible.... We were on the extreme right & had the highest portion of the peak [of Little Round Top] to charge. We charged a mile at double quick up an almost perpendicular peak at the top of which the enemy had fortified to make it impossible to take had the enemy only been armed with rocks. Our regiment [5th Texas] suffered severely having charged up within thirty yards of the enemy four successful times & [then] having to fall back.[1]

The repeated assaults up the rocky western slope of Little Round Top haunted the survivors like no other combat of the Civil War, because of the sheer horror and lost opportunities that faded away forever. In a letter, Private John Camden West, Company "E," 4th Texas, summarized how "several desperate efforts were made to charge [up Little Round Top and] the entire ascent would have been difficult to a man entirely divested of gun and accounterments. It was a mass of rock and boulders amid which a mountain goat would, have repelled.… Our assault, with short intervals, was kept up until dark" with undiminished intensity.[2]

Nevertheless, Little Round Top could not be carried by storm, despite all of the repeated all-out efforts and high sacrifice in lives. Incredibly, this was the first time in the Texas Brigade's history that an enemy's defensive position was not carried by assault. Captured like a good many comrades in the assault on Little Round Top, Private Benjamin Simpson, 5th Texas, still defiantly boasted to his 44th New York Volunteer Infantry (Colonel Strong Vincent's Third Brigade, First Division, Fifth Corps) captors, who defended the defensive line's center along Little Round Top, of his command's past accomplishments.

As penned by one New Yorker in a letter about Simpson:

> He feels proud of his brigade to which he is attached, and says they never failed to carry any point they were ordered to. The only point they gained at Gettysburg was the point of a bayonet [and] Simpson has the satisfaction of knowing that his own schoolmates [from his native Rochester, New York, where Ireland-born Colonel Patrick Henry O'Rorke hailed] and former companions assisted in giving these vaunted heroes such a sound thrashing.[3]

Ironically, before the war, Simpson had migrated west and relocated from Rochester, New York, to the port of Galveston, Texas. As fate would have it, he met his old friends and classmates, who now in blue uniforms and stood firm in heroic fashion on Little Round Top, from Rochester at Little Round Top on the bloody afternoon of July 2.[4]

But of all the regiments of the Texas Brigade, none was more successful in achieving its key tactical objectives than the 1st Texas, which led the way in the capture of Houck's Ridge and the Devil's Den. Indeed, they had captured the highest ground position—the left flank of not only Sickles' Third Corps but also that of the Army of the Potomac—won by Hood's Division during the three days of combat, Houck's Ridge and the Devil's Den, at the ridge's southern base, during what one Texan appropriately described as "one of the wildest, fiercest struggles of the war."[5]

In striking contrast, a seemingly endless amount of courage and hard fighting had not been enough for the veterans of the 4th and 5th Texas, along with their hard-fighting Alabama comrades of Brigadier Evander McIver Law's Brigade, to carry the highest defensive position at Gettysburg, Little Round Top. In the words of Private John Camden West, 4th Texas, from a letter that described the repeated assaults to capture the strategic crest of Little Round Top: all of the "courage and even desperation was useless" against such a formidable high ground position and quite unlike any encountered on every previous battlefield in this war.[6]

In the end, the Texas Brigade's best offensive efforts were doomed by seemingly a conspiracy stemming from an unusual set of circumstances and unforeseen developments, especially leadership failures at the highest levels, which severely hampered the Texans' much-touted combat capabilities and chances for success from the very beginning. In a letter to his brother that revealed a correct assessment, a strategic-minded Private John Camden West, Company "E," 4th Texas, concluded:

> I believe the wounding of General Hood early in the action was the greatest misfortune of the day [and] if a considerable force had been thrown around the mountain [Big Round Top] to our right the enemy would have been routed in half an hour [and then] Baltimore would have been ours and the New York [draft] riots would have been as famous as the battle of Bunker Hill.[7]

Clearly, West viewed the struggle at the southern end of the battle-line as the war's great lost opportunity, and one that would never come again for General Lee and his hard-luck Army of Northern Virginia, when the life of an infant nation was at stake.[8]

In another letter, the God-fearing private concluded with typical commonsense of the enlisted ranks and on-target analysis about the Army of Northern Virginia's second invasion of the North:

> Our move in Pennsylvania was a failure, and I think General Lee never would have attacked the enemy in their position on the mountain side except for the splendid condition of his army, and his confidence in its ability to accomplish anything he chose to attempt [including the effort of the Texas Brigade to carry] one of the strongest positions of the enemy, which was on a high mountain and defended by batteries on mountains still higher. We took and held the lower heights [Houck's Ridge] long enough to capture the batteries, but were unable after several charges to scale the higher ones, being subjected to a fire on our left flank and in front while attempting to climb over rocks and gorges, which would have delighted a mountain goat.[9]

However, Private James O. Bradfield, Company "E" (Marshall Guards), 1st Texas, perhaps said it best. He laid the Texas Brigade's failure to capture Little Round Top on not some ill-fated destiny, but because of the handiwork of an angry Yankee-hating God, who had been responsible for thwarting the loftiest Confederate ambitions and most fanatical offensive efforts: "The best blood of Texas was there [on the afternoon of July 2] But God must have ordained our defeat [because the elite Texas Brigade soldiers] bore their country's flag to victory on every field, until God stopped them at Little Round Top."[10]

Despite the Army of Northern Virginia's defeat and high losses not easily replaced in the hard days of continued struggle that lay ahead for an infant nation's survival, confidence continued to remain high in the decimated ranks of the Texas Brigade that regained its old fighting spirit in the months after Gettysburg. Not long after the three-day battle and as written in a letter, Private John Camden West penned of the renewed faith in the war's successful outcome in part because he and his comrades were convinced that God, destiny, and history were still on their side, as these ill-fated men hoped and prayed: "I do not believe the combined Yankee army can subjugate the Texas brigade, though they may all be killed."[11]

But in truth, the Texas Brigade was never quite the same after making its all-out offensive effort to overrun not only Houck's Ridge and the Devil's Den, which proved successful, but also Little Round Top that was unsuccessful. Of all the troops in the Army of Northern Virginia, no fighting men in dirty gray and butternut had faced greater obstacles or had been assigned a more difficult challenge at Gettysburg than the Texas soldiers. The two parallel, high-ground positions represented the most daunting defense in depth based on two high ground defensive positions posed to any troops at Gettysburg, first Houck's Ridge and the Devil's Den and then Little Round Top (from west to east): the most formidable combined high ground objectives faced by any troops on either side during the three days at Gettysburg.

All in all, the Texas troops overcame the odds and slim chances for success by capturing not only Houck's Ridge and the Devil's Den (both of which were Meade's—actually Dan Sickles—first left flank), but also very nearly capturing strategic Little Round Top, especially after much of the 16th Michigan (Colonel Strong Vincent's right flank) was pushed aside, which was then the left flank (second) of the Army of the Potomac.

Symbolically, only a few weeks after the supreme offensive effort of the Texas soldiers on July 2, the once-revered "father of Texas," Sam Houston, who was now an object of intense scorn among Texas Confederates (including Texas Brigade members) for having turned "traitor" by supporting an unpopular Unionism and anti-secessionism, died on July 25, 1863. A lover of the Union and a true American patriot forever, Houston had early warned Texas secessionists that the idea of going to war against their country "is madness," but relatively few Texans paid heed to the old San Jacinto hero, who still carried scars from the bloody battle of Horseshoe Bend (during the Creek War) on March 27, 1814. On his deathbed at his modest home in Huntsville, Texas, and most appropriately, Houston's last dying words (the truest "detector of the heart") were voiced for his family to hear, emphasizing what lay foremost in his heart to the very end, "Texas—Texas!"[12]

During the same decisive month of July 1863, two eras were in the process of passing away forever in America. In this fateful July, the dynamic North Carolina-born leader and faithful follower of his former commander "Irish Andy" Jackson died. It was ignored by most Texans that Houston had led the torturous way to the remarkable victory at San Jacinto and a new republic's salvation. Houston passed when still another people's Southern republic (that, of course, now included Texas much to his disgust) also conceived in revolution received a mortal blow from which it would never recover with decisive defeat at Gettysburg.

Here, on July 2, 1863, the Texas Brigade's soldiers discovered a manmade hell in the most eerie and nightmarish of all battlefields on the North American continent, the Devil's Den, during a key turning point of the Civil War. The Confederacy's death spiral accelerated in the years ahead after the largest battle ever fought on the North American continent was lost. Caught in the lethal vise of an unwinnable war of attrition because of the Confederacy's lack of industrialism and manpower, the slow death of the South's experiment in rebellion continued unabated to the inevitable conclusion, thanks in large part to an unprecedented death rate at gory places like Gettysburg, because the Confederacy's armies could never refill their depleted ranks that had been cut to pieces. The young men and boys of the Texas Brigade gamely fought to the very end in vain, while maintaining their lofty reputation as the army's best fighting troops.

By early 1865, during the last year of the Confederacy's short lifetime, a desperate situation called for the most extreme of measures, and no soldiers of Lee's Army appreciated that undeniable reality of the South's ultimate tragic fate and final demise than the battle-scarred veterans of the Texas Brigade. Therefore, the Texas soldiers penned an audacious petition that appealed directly the Confederate government on behalf of the most radical step that they viewed as the only remaining possible solution to the Confederacy's death spiral in a war of attrition that the infant nation could never win.

In no uncertain terms while the late winter winds of Virginia howled in the bitterly cold of February 1865, the Texans fully realized that the decimated Army of the Northern Virginia and the dying Confederacy no longer had a realistic chance for survival during America's most brutal war because of the North's superior manpower resources, including the use of tens of thousands of black troops. President Abraham Lincoln had issued the Emancipation Proclamation to open the door for the enlistment of soldiers, both free men and forever slaves, of African descent in what was a major turning point of the war.

After unanimous agreement of the Texas Brigade's survivors in the democratic tradition of the western frontier, consequently, the battle-hardened Texans of lower- and middle-class roots implored the elitist, upper-class leadership of the Confederate government in Richmond "to lay aside prejudice" against blacks to embrace the only practical solution left remaining to the Confederacy's salvation: the immediate enlistment of large numbers of African Americans to serve in black units in the ranks of their own Army of Northern Virginia.

Quite simply, for the very survival of their young republic, the remaining resilient band Texas Brigade veterans were more than ready to fight side by side with ebony soldiers (former slaves and free men like in the ranks of the 54th Massachusetts Infantry Regiment, the first black regiment of the North) in Confederate uniforms of gray. After having survived the slaughters of the Peninsula Campaign, Second Manassas, Antietam, and Gettysburg, the mostly yeoman farmers, who were primarily non-owners of slaves back home because of their lower- and middle-class status, from across Texas begged President Jefferson Davis to accept blacks as equal fighting men in a bid to yet save the day for the dying Confederacy, before it was too late.

As the veteran soldiers fully realized, this radical solution called for putting aside all racial "prejudice"—that was deeply-entrenched in the South's society and culture to an extreme degree to serve as a primary cultural foundation—for the fast-fading chances of still fulfilling the great dream of "independence and separate nationality," wrote a committee of Texas Brigade men.[13] But by this time, it was already far too late of the Army of Northern Virginia and the manpower-short Confederacy that had been bled white by nearly years of brutal conflict in a deadly war of attrition, and especially because of what had happened during the three days at Gettysburg.

General Lee's surrender at Appomattox Court House on a beautiful Palm Sunday April 9, 1865 ended the legendary career of not only the Army of Northern Virginia, but also its hardest-fighting and premier combat unit, the Texas Brigade. In the end, the obscure and previously-unknown locations situated amid the picturesque farmlands of southeastern Pennsylvania known as the Devil's Den, Houck's Ridge, and Little Round Top became just grim killing fields of lost opportunities, seemingly countless mangled bodies, broken Confederate hopes, and dying dreams of a young republic, where it had received a death stroke for all practical purposes on July 2 and July 3. Here, the final resting places were found in the rich soil of Adams County, Pennsylvania, for seemingly countless young men and boys, who died for what they believed was right.

After the war's end, all that the relatively few Texas Brigade survivors of the surreal carnage that was the nightmare of Gettysburg were left with only a stubborn sense of pride in what they had accomplished against the odds, while they fought and died for homes, families and comrades far-away. After the slaughter of America's best and brightest at Gettysburg, the Texas Brigade's survivors never sang the popular song "The Yellow Rose of Texas" with quite the same enthusiasm and lightheartedness as during the heady days of 1861 and 1862.

Ironically, these roughhewn Lone Star State soldiers who were either veterans of the Texas Revolution or their sons or grandsons now more closely identified with the unforgettable words of Isaac N. Jones, who wrote a letter to Elizabeth Patton Crockett to console the grieving Tennessee-born wife of David Crockett, who fell in the Alamo's defense on the cold morning of March 6, 1836 in the name of the establishment of another people's republic: "I cannot restrain my American smile at the recollection of the fact that he died as a United States soldier should die, covered with his slain enemy, and, even in death, presenting to them in his clenched hands, the weapons of their destruction."[14]

These same sentiments also provided some consolation of hundreds of Texas Brigade soldiers who fell on bloody July 2, 1863 in battling for their own people's republic. Of the around 1,400 soldiers of the Texas Brigade who charged the two parallel high ground defensive positions of Gettysburg's most formidable defense in depth, more than 700 men were killed, wounded, or captured.

Clearly, Texas Brigade losses were exceptionally high, revealing the savage combat at close quarters and the iron-willed determination to scale not one, but two high-ground positions in desperate bids to win the day at any cost. Once again and as on so many past battlefields, the Texas Brigade's soldiers demonstrated their unsurpassed "fighting abilities, which were the best and most legendary in Lee's Army."[15]

As written in a heartfelt letter, perhaps the July 9, 1863 words of Private H. Watter Berryman, Company "I," 1st Texas, said it best in regard to the Texas Brigade's distinguished role at Gettysburg, including what was "one of the most gallant charges ever made by the First Texas" on Houck's Ridge and the Devil's Den.[16]

In his official battlefield report, Lieutenant Colonel Philip Alexander Work had nothing by glowing praise for the splendid performance of his 1st Texas soldiers:

> Every man of the regiment proved himself a hero. Hundreds might be mentioned, each of whom with reason and propriety might point to his gallant acts and daring deeds [especially those of] Privates W. Y. Salter, Company "I"; J. N. Kirkey and G. Barfield, of Company "B," and W[ilson]. J. Barbee, of Company "L," for great and striking gallantry.... Private Barbee, though a mounted courier, acting for Mahor-General Hood, entered the ranks of his company, "L," and fought through the engagement. At one time, he mounted a rock on the highest pinnacle of the hill, and there, exposing to a raking, deadly fire of artillery and musketry, stood until he had fired twenty-fire shots, when he received a minie-ball wound in the right thigh, and fell. Having exhausted their original supply of ammunition, the men supplied themselves from the cartridge boxes of their dead and disabled comrades, and from the dead and wounded of the enemy, frequently going in front of the hill to secure a cartridge box. Many of the officers threw aside their swords, seized a rifle, and going into the ranks, fought bravely and nobly. The regiment lost in killed 25, in wounded 48, and missing 20 [on the bloody afternoon of July 2].[17]

In explaining what had made his common soldiers the finest combat troops of the Army of Northern Virginia in its prime and when it was considered invincible, Lieutenant Colonel Work summarized the close connection between the Texas Brigade and the Texas Revolution that had fueled the Texans' fighting resolve to overcome any odds and any battlefield objective no matter how formidable, including overwhelming of Houck's Ridge and coming ever so close to capturing Little Round Top:

> The success of the Texan regiments was not due to the training of Hood or any other commander, but that they were composed of the very pick and flower of an intelligent, educated, adventurous and high spirited people. Infused with the spirit of chivalry, the Texans on every battlefield displayed the sublime, fearless, exalted courage of the heroes of the Alamo and San Jacinto, adoring their Lone Star flag and guarding it with the unsullied record as a dutiful son [in] the name of an honored father.[18]

Consequently, and as repeated demonstrated when unleashed with fixed bayonets and flags flying on the decisive afternoon of July 2, the Texans were most of all the "favorite shock-troops" of General Lee and the Army of Northern Virginia.[19]

One postwar tribute to Major General John Bell Hood and his hard-fighting men from Southern veterans who well knew of the Texas Brigade's combat prowess emphasized the significance when Hood was "placed in command of that devoted band of Texans than whom heroic leader never had more worthy followers. As brigade and as division commander upon fields made glorious by the 'incomparable infantry' of the Army of Northern Virginia, Hood shone as one of the most brilliant soldiers" of Lee's Army.[20]

In essence, what the insightful Lieutenant Colonel Work explained in regard to the never-say-die attitude of the Texas Brigade's fighting men were the qualities that made this command General Lee's "Grenadier Guard." This determination of the 1st Texas soldiers to succeed at all costs on the afternoon of July 2, 1863 was evident in the case of Private Newton "Newt" M. Berryman. More than willing to pay the ultimate price for his country conceived in the heady idealism of revolution, the young man continued to fight against the seemingly countless Federals, despite bloodied by a bullet that had ripped across the forehead. He defiantly refused to go to the infirmary, because, as he told his brother Private H. Watters Berryman of Company "I" (Crockett Southrons), 1st Texas, "if every man left for a slight wound we would never gain a battle."[21] Likewise during the fierce assault of the 1st Texas on Houck's Ridge and the Devil's Den, Private Sidney Franklin Perry who was known as "Bose," Company "E," (Marshall Guards), 1st Texas, was hit the leg, but he gamely continued to attack with all his remaining physical strength and will power, while "dragging his wounded leg, and firing as he advanced."[22]

However, the Texas Brigade's fighting spirit was perhaps best seen in the words of Private John Camden West, which were written in a summer 1863 letter to his beloved wife. Penned not long after the terrible slaughter at Gettysburg, he wrote of his unfailing determination to fight year after year if necessary in order to win his nation's independence at any cost:

> I have no desire to return home while the war lasts [and] You must not be uneasy if you hear of me [falling in battle and] it is almost impracticable and hopeless to attempt to recover the body of a private soldier [who were usually thrown into burial pits without individual markers unlike many officers, especially those of high rank] killed in battle, so don't think about this; I can rest [in] one place as well as another.[23]

For a good many young men and boys from across the South, Gettysburg became that final resting place far from home and family in a remote, far-away land, where a great dream had died an ugly death. Most of these tragic deaths of the brave common soldiers resulted from the long list of mistakes and sheer folly of top Confederate leadership, including General Lee, and their extremely-poor decisions and misguided performances on July 2, dooming the best efforts and superior fighting of the common soldiers in the ranks. Quite simply, the top leadership of the Army of Northern Virginia, from Lee to many of his top lieutenants, especially Lieutenant General James Longstreet, saw its worst day to date on July 2, which paved the way to disastrous defeat, when on the verge of what seemed like a decisive success. The lengthy list of missed opportunities on the second day at Gettysburg led to not only defeat, but also became a nail in the coffin of the Confederate nation.

The overall thesis of this current book, that has honored and paid tribute to the common soldiers in the ranks, has verified the undeniable truth of the words from a letter written by Charles William Trueheart, Army of Northern Virginia, in February 1863—less than five months before the dramatic showdown at Gettysburg. In his letter, Trueheart emphasized the seldom-mentioned ugly truths, including about General Lee and in regard to the future struggle for possession of the Union left flank, that led to Confederate defeat not only on July 2 but also in regard to the war in general:

> Our Texas troops serving in this state [Virginia], have on all occasions shown themselves unflinchingly brave, steady, and dashing.... Speaking of Gen'ls, I for my part ... can't help being half of the opinion that we haven't any military geniuses among our Generals; that is, any comparable to Marlborough, Wellington, Napoleon Bonaparte, or even our Gen'l Washington. I am rather inclined to the opinion that our [common] soldiers are better than our Gen'ls in their respective spheres; and deserving of more credit for the victories won than they—tho' the praise all goes to the Generals. I believe that with such *soldiers* as we have composing our Southern army, and a truly great military head to direct them, that we should have conquered a peace months ago [long before the fatal and ill-fated Gettysburg Campaign]; that instead of the almost barren victories of Manassas, No. 1 and No. 2, Sharpsburg, and Fredericksburg, etc., [we should] have utterly routed and demoralized, making large captures from, if not annihilating the Yankees.[24]

Indeed, Charles William Trueheart, a well-educated and highly-capable assistant surgeon of the Army of Northern Virginia, was right on target in this insightful analysis that correctly pointed a well-deserved accusatory finger mostly at General Lee and his top lieutenants for the dismal failure at Gettysburg. Such was indeed the case in regard to the bloody struggle for possession of the Devil's Den and Houck's Ridge, where the common soldiers had performed magnificently, but their high sacrifice was once again wasted and in vain by the folly of the army's top leadership.

But Major John Cheves Haskell, who was second in command of the artillery battalion of Hood's Division, Longstreet's First Corp, on the afternoon of July 2 said it best. He laid blame squarely for defeat at Gettysburg on the top levels of the army's leadership, including General Lee. In no uncertain terms, he emphasized:

> ... we were handicapped by West Point [which] gave us some dummies, who were grievous stumbling blocks in our way [and at Gettysburg] I think we were weighted by first, a

> demoralized army, and for this I hold General Lee largely responsible [partly because] he had an utterly undue regard for the value of the elementary teaching of West Point [but most of all, defeat stemmed from the fatal delays on July 2 because] Hood's Division was almost destroyed, trying to capture that position [Little Round Top] we could have occupied without a shot two hours earlier.[25]

After the wasting of so many opportunities and so many lives of some of the best and brightest men from across America, the fortunate survivors of the vicious combat that raged in and around the Devil's Den, situated at the southern base of Houck's Ridge, never forgot the pile of jumbled boulders, crevices, and ledges for which they fought like madmen on a hot afternoon in southeastern Pennsylvania. Perhaps decades after America's bloodiest war had ended, when surviving veterans thought about the fierce combat that had raged furiously at the Devil's Den, they felt the urge or need to cleanse their troubled minds and souls of the haunting memories of the nightmarish afternoon of July 2, 1863 by telling their children or grandchildren about what had been experienced by them at this rocky den of death.

But if tempted to do so, then these fortunate survivors of some of the bloodiest combat in America's bloodiest war might well have suddenly ceased their thoughts and changed their minds, knowing that they would never be able to truly describe the horrors of the Devil's Den, because it simply might not be believed by anyone who had never seen this eerie-looking place. Quite simply, no words could adequately describe this strange 10 acres of death called the Devil's Den to convey to others, especially family members, what it really looked like or the surreal horrors that had occurred there on the bloody afternoon of July 2, 1863, when men in both blue and gray fought like devils from the lower regions of hell.

As long as they survivors lived with the omnipresent ghosts and traumas of the war years, they never forgot what they had witnessed on Gettysburg's most hellish battleground—truly Satan's bloody playground and his own home turf on the most decisive afternoon of the Civil War—during the most terrible day of the three days of savage combat. For such reasons, the survivors never forgot the Devil's Den as long as they lived.

Endnotes

Chapter 1

1. Richard M. McMurry, *John Bell Hood and the War for Southern Independence* (Lexington: The University Press of Kentucky, 1982), p. 42.
2. Douglas Southall Freeman, *Lee's Lieutenants, Manassas to Malvern Hill* (3 vols., New York: Charles Scribner's Sons, 1942), vol. 1, p. 197; Joseph B. Mitchell, *Military Leaders in the Civil War* (McLean: EPM Publications, Inc., 1972), pp. 194–195.
3. Hood, *John Bell Hood, The Rise, Fall, and Resurrection of a Confederate General* (El Dorado Hills: Savas Beatie, LLC, 2013), p. xxiii.
4. Mitchell, *Military Leaders in the Civil War*, pp. 194–195.
5. Stiles, *Four Years under Marse Robert* (Marietta: R. Bemis Publishing Company, 1995), p. 76.
6. Polley, *Hood's Texas Brigade, Its Marches, Its Battles, Its Achievements* (New York: Neale Publishing Company, 1910), p. 287.
7. McMurry, *John Bell Hood*, p. 28.
8. *War of the Rebellion: Official Records of the Union and Confederate Armies* (128 vols., Washington, D.C.: United States Government Printing Office, 1880–1901), vol. 19, ser. 1, pt. 1, p. 1022.
9. Hassler (ed.), "Civil War Letters of William Dorsey Pender to His Wife," *Georgia Review*, vol. 17 (Spring 1963), p. 65.
10. Polley, *A Soldier's Letters to Charming Nellie* (New York: Neale Publishing Company, 1908), p. 69; Polley, *Hood's Texas Brigade*, p. 231.
11. Carson, "Hampton's Legion and Hood's Brigade," *Confederate Veteran*, vol. xvi, no. 7 (July 1908), p. 342.
12. Hunter, "The Rebel Yell," *Confederate Veteran*, vol. 21, no. 5 (May 1913), p. 219.
13. Polley, *Hood's Texas Brigade*, pp. 13–292; Robertson, *The Stonewall Brigade* (Baton Rouge: Louisiana State University Press, 1963), pp. vi–vii; Connelly and Bellows, *God and General Longstreet, The Lost Cause and the Southern Mind* (Baton Rouge: Louisiana State University Press, 1982), pp. 1–148.
14. Polley, *Hood's Texas Brigade*, pp. 13–282.
15. Tucker, *The South's Finest*, pp. vii–viii.
16. Polley, *Hood's Texas Brigade*, p. 59.
17. Nevin, *The Texans* (Alexandra: Time-Life Books, 1975), pp. 15–41; Hardin, *Texian Illiad, The Military History of the Texas Revolution* (Austin: University of Texas Press, 1994), pp. 5–6.

18. Nevin, *The Texans*, p. 15.
19. Hardin, *Texian Illiad*, p. 5.
20. Smithwick, *The Evolution of a State, Recollections of Old Texas Days* (Austin: University of Texas Press, 1983), pp. ix and 72.
21. Hardin (ed.), *Lone Star: The Republic of Texas, 1836–1846* (Carlisle: Discovery Enterprises, Ltd., 1998), p. 45.
22. Oates (ed.), *Rip Ford's Texas* (Austin: University of Texas Press, 1987), p. 15; DePalo, Jr., *The Mexican National Army, 1822–1852* (College Station: Texas A & M University Press, 1997), pp. 24–65; Fehrenbach, *Texas, A Salute from Above* (New York: Portland House, 1988), p. 16; Hardin (ed.), *Lone Star*, 5, note 2.
23. Fehrenhach, *Lone Star, A History of Texas and the Texans, From Prehistory to the Present* (New York: Da Capa Press, 2000), p. xiii.
24. Fehrenbach, *Texas*, p. 15.
25. Roberts and Olson, *A Line in The Sand, The Alamo In Blood and Memory* (New York: The Free Press, 2001), pp. 48–49.
26. Fehrenbach, *Lone Star*, pp. 81–109.
27. *Ibid.*, 597.
28. McMurry, *John Bell Hood and the War for Southern Independence*, p. 28; Everett, *Chaplain Davis and Hood's Texas Brigade* (Baton Rouge: The Louisiana State University Press, 1999), p. 18; Fehrenbach, *Lone Star*, pp. 81–109, 174–215, and 445–506; Fehrenbach, *Texas*, p. 16.
29. Fletcher, *Rebel Private: Front and Rear* (New York: Meridian Books, 1995), p. 9.
30. West, *A Texan in Search of a Fight, Being the Diary and Letters of a Private Soldier in Hood's Texas Brigade* (Memphis: General Books, LLC, 2012), pp. 1, 6–7, and 19.
31. Polley, Hood's Texas Brigade, p. 182.
32. McMurry, *John Bell Hood and the War for Southern Independence*, p. 28.
33. Hardin and Hook, *The Texas Rangers* (London: Osprey Books, 1996), p. 3; Fehrenbach, *Lone Star*, pp. 445–506; Nevins, *The Texans*, pp. 15–40
34. Smithwick, *The Evolution of a State*, p. 99.
35. Polley, *Hood's Texas Brigade*, p. 22; Compiled Service Records of Confederate Soldiers Who Served in Organizations from the State of Texas, Record Group 109, National Archives, Washington, D.C.; Simpson, *Gaines' Mill to Appomattox, Waco and McLennan County in Hood's Texas Brigade* (Waco: Texian Press, 1988), pp. 2–28 and 54; Fehrenbach, *Lone Star*, pp. 152–278 and 445–506.
36. Polley, *Papers, 1852–1879, Daughters of the Republic of Texas Library*, San Antonio, Texas; The Handbook of Texas Online.
37. Polley, *Hood's Texas Brigade*, p. 210.
38. Simpson, *Gaines' Mill to Appomattox*, p. 39
39. *Morning Courier and New York Enquirer*, July 9, 1836; Williams, *Hood's Texas Brigade in the Civil War* (Fayetteville: McFarland and Company Publishers, 2012), p. 19.
40. McMurry, *John Bell Hood*, p. 42.
41. Polley, *A Soldier's Letters to Charming Nellie*, p. 33.
42. McMurry, *John Bell Hood*, p. 227.
43. Hardin and Hook, *The Texas Rangers*, pp. 3–7; Roberts and Olson, *A Line In The Sand*, p. 141; CTSR, NA; Simpson, *From Gaines' Mill to Appomattox*, pp. 2–28; Nevin, *The Texans*, p. 212; Fehrenbach, *Lone Star*, pp. 152–278 and 445–506; Moore, *Savage Frontier, Rangers, Riflemen, and Indian Wars in Texas, 1835–1837*, vol. 1 (2 vols: Denton: The University of North Texas Press, 2002), pp. 1–92 and 97–100.
44. Polley, *A Soldier's Letters to Charming Nellie*, p. 18; CTSR, NA; Simpson, *Gaines' Mill to Appomattox*, pp. 2–28; Fehrenbach, *Lone Star*, pp. 174–215 and 445–506.
45. McMurry, *John Bell Hood*, p. 28; CTSR, NA; Simpson, *Gaines' Mill to Appomattox*, pp. 2–28; Fehrenbach, *Lone Star*, pp. xiii, 174–215, and 445–506.

46. Oates (ed.), *Rip Ford's Texas*, p. 15; CTSR, NA; Simpson, *Gaines' Mill to Appomattox*, pp. 2–28 and 32; Fehrenbach, *Lone Star*, pp. 445–506.
47. Williams, *Hood's Texas Brigade in the Civil War*, p. 43.
48. McMurry, *John Bell Hood*, p. 73; Fehrenbach, *Lone Star*, pp. 445–506.
49. Polley, *Hood's Texas Brigade*, pp. 14–275.
50. Evault Boswell, *Texas, Boys in Gray* (Plano: Republic of Texas Press, 2000), p. 200.
51. Polley, *Hood's Texas Brigade*, p. 17.
52. *Ibid.*, p. 54.
53. *Ibid.*, p. 58.
54. *Ibid.*, p. 54.
55. CTSR, NA; Everett (ed.), *Chaplain Davis and Hood's Texas Brigade* (Baton Rouge: Louisiana State University Press, 1999), pp. 22 and 35; CTSR, NA; Simpson, *Gaines' Mill to Appomattox*, pp. vii–viii, 1; E. M. Halliday, *Understanding Thomas Jefferson* (New York: HarperCollins Publishers, 2001), pp. 128–129.
56. Everett (ed.), *Chaplain Davis and Hood's Texas Brigade*, pp. 35–36; Fletcher, *Rebel Private*, p. 9; CTSR, NA; Granville H. Crozier, "A Private with General Hood," *Confederate Veteran*, vol. xxv, no. 12 (Dec. 1917), pp. 556 and 558; Fehrenbach, *Fire and Blood, History of Mexico* (New York: Da Capo Press, 1995), pp. 392–393; Williams, *Hood's Texas Brigade in the Civil War*, pp. 7–13.
57. Simpson, *Hood's Texas Brigade, Lee's Grenadier Guard* (Fort Worth: Landmark Publishing, 1999), p. 25; Polley, *Hood's Texas Brigade*, p. 31.
58. Williams, *Hood's Texas Brigade in the Civil War*, p. 21.
59. Polley, *Hood's Texas Brigade*, p. 22.
60. Smith, "One of The Most Daring of Men," The Life of Confederate General William Tatum Wofford," *The Journal of Confederate History Series*, vol. xvi (Murfreesboro: Southern Heritage Press, 1997), p. 29.
61. Robert Campbell, "A Lone Star in Virginia," *Civil War Times Illustrated*, p. 90; Simpson, *Hood's Texas Brigade*, pp. 85–86; Polley, *Hood's Texas Brigade*, p. 16; CTSR, NA; Tucker, *George Washington's Surprise Attack, A New Look at the Battle that Decided the Fate of America* (New York: Skyhorse Publishing, 2014), pp. 1–56.
62. Polley, *Hood's Texas Brigade*, p. 68.
63. Patterson, "John Bell Hood," *CWTI*, p. 17.
64. CTSR, NA.
65. Polley, *Hood's Texas Brigade*, p. 38.
66. *Ibid.*, p. 239.
67. *Ibid.*
68. Everett (ed.), *Chaplain Davis and Hood's Texas Brigade*, p. 178.
69. Simpson, *Hood's Texas Brigade*, p. 17; Everett (ed.), *Chaplain Davis and Hood's Texas Brigade*, p. 45; Todd, *First Texas Regiment* (Waco: Texian Press, 1964), p. ix; CRSR, NA; Tucker, *The South's Finest*, p. 11; Williams, *Hood's Texas Brigade in the Civil War*, p. 71.
70. Polley, *Hood's Texas Brigade*, p. 181.
71. Simpson, *Hood's Texas Brigade*, p. 30; Williams, *Hood's Texas Brigade in the Civil War*, pp. 29–30; Martin, William Harrison, The Handbook of Texas Online.
72. Simpson, *Hood's Texas Brigade*, p. 19; CTSR, NA; Everett, *Chaplain Davis and Hood's Texas Brigade*, p. 49; Simpson, *Gaines' Mill to Appomattox*, p. 54; Katcher, *The Army of Robert E. Lee* (London: Arms and Armour Press, 1994), pp. 243–244; Polley, *Hood's Texas Brigade*, p. 329; *New York Times*, June 29, 1836; *The Liberator*, Boston, Massachusetts, June 11, 1836; Identified Knife, Lt. M. C. Noble, 1st Texas, Number 2271, Historical Shop, Metairie, Louisiana; Walter Prescott Webb, *The Texas Rangers, A Century of Frontier Defense* (Austin: University of Texas Press, 1991), pp. 84–86; Smithwick, *The Evolution of a State*, p. 72.

73. Fletcher, *Rebel Private*, p. 3.
74. Fletcher, *Rebel Private*, p. 3; Simpson, *Hood's Texas Brigade*, pp. 25, 104, and 142; CTSR, NA; Polley, *Hood's Texas Brigade*, pp. 22 and 89; Tucker, *Burnside's Bridge, The Climactic Struggle of the 2nd and 20th Georgia at Antietam Creek* (Mechanicsburg: Stackpole Books, 2000), p. 68.
75. Everett, *Chaplain Davis and Hood's Texas Brigade*, pp. 60 and 83; Polley, *Hood's Texas Brigade*, p. 106.
76. Polley, *Hood's Texas Brigade*, p. 100.
77. Simpson, *Hood's Texas Brigade*, pp. 23 and 67; Tucker, *Exodus from the Alamo, The Anatomy of the Last Stand Myth* (Philadelphia: Casemate Publishers, 2011), p. 129.
78. Simpson, *Hood's Texas Brigade*, p. 67.
79. Fletcher, *Rebel Private*, pp. 1–3, and 27; Campbell, "A Lone Star in Virginia," *CWTI*, p. 90; CTSR, NA.
80. Campbell, "A Lone Star in Virginia," *CWTI*, p. 88; Everett, *Chaplain Davis and Hood's Texas Brigade*, p. 61.
81. Everett (ed.), *Chaplain Davis and Hood's Texas Brigade*, p. 123.
82. Fletcher, *Rebel Private*, p. 36.
83. Everett (ed.), *Chaplain Davis and Hood's Texas Brigade*, p. 119.
84. Hardin, *Texian Illiad*, p. 214; Fehrenbach, *Lone Star*, pp. 231–233; William C. Davis, *Three Road to the Alamo, The Lives and Fortunes of David Crockett, James Bowie, and William Barret Travis* (New York: Harper Collins Publishers, 1998), pp. 572–573.
85. Hood, *John Bell Hood*, pp. 6–7; Freeman, *Lee's Lieutenants*, vol. 1, pp. 198–199; Fehrenbach, *Lone Star*, pp. 81–109, 174–233, and 445–605; Fletcher, *Rebel Private*, p. 36; Faust, *This Republic of Suffering, Death and the American Civil War* (New York: Vintage Books, 2008), p. 3.
86. Hood, *John Bell Hood*, p. 7; Freeman, *Lee's Lieutenants*, vol. 1, pp. 198–199; CRSR, NA; Palmer, Jr., *The Dead of Eltham's Landing*, Historical Society of West Point, West Point, Virginia.
87. Hood, *John Bell Hood*, p. 7; Curtis, *From Bull Run to Chancellorsville, The Story of the Sixteenth New York Infantry together with Personal Reminiscences* (New York: G.P. Putnam's Sons, 1906), pp. 96–101, and 350; Simpson, *Hood's Texas Brigade*, pp. 102–103; Roberts and Olson, *A Line in The Sand*, pp. 10, 95, 109, 143–144, 161, 180, and 190; Fehrenbach, *Lone Star*, pp. 67–68; Hardin, *Texian Illiad*, pp. 213–215; Pruett and Cole, Jr., *Goliad Massacre* (Austin: Eakin Press, 1985), pp. 109–120; Faust, *This Republic of Suffering*, pp. 6–9 and 32–33; Palmer, Jr., *The Dead of Eltham's Landing*, HSWP.
88. Faust, *This Republic of Suffering*, p. 38.
89. Hood, *John Bell Hood*, p. 7.
90. *Ibid.*, pp. 36–38; Fletcher, *Rebel Private*, pp. xii–xiv and 49; CTSR, NA; Williams, *Hood's Texas Brigade in the Civil War*, p. 56.
91. Faust, *The Republic of Suffering*, p. 37.
92. Matt Dale to Brother, June 7, 1862, Confederate Research Center, Hillsboro, Texas; Hardin, *Texian Illiad*, p. 209; Moore, *Savage Frontier*, vol. 1, pp. ix–x, 47, 59, and 97–98; Lozano, *Viva Tejas, The Story of the Tejanos, the Mexican-born Patriots of the Texas Revolution* (San Antonio: The Alamo Press, 1985), pp. 1–2 and 33–47; Dale, Matthew, The Handbook of Texas Online.
93. Fletcher, *Rebel Private*, pp. xii, 1–3, and 30.
94. *Ibid.*, p. 33.
95. *Ibid.*, p. 35.
96. *Ibid.*, p. 57.
97. Hassler (ed.), "Civil War Letters of William Dorsey Pender to His Wife," *GR*, p. 65.
98. *Ibid.*, p. 244; CTSR, NA.

99. Hanks, "History of Captain B. F. Benton's Company 1861–1865," Confederate Research Center, Hillsboro, Texas.
100. *Ibid*., p. 173.
101. Simpson, *Hood's Texas Brigade*, p. 76, note no. 5; Everett (ed.), *Chaplain Davis and Hood's Texas Brigade*, pp. 69 and 95; CTSR, NA; Williams, *Hood's Texas Brigade in the Civil War*, p. 154.
102. Simpson, *Hood's Texas Brigade*, p. 76; TCSR, NA; Burke, John, The Handbook of Texas Online.
103. Fletcher, *Rebel Private*, p. 28.
104. Campbell, "A Lone Star in Virginia," *CWTI*, p. 86; Hardin, *Texian Illiad*, pp. 173–174.
105. Polley, *Hood's Texas Brigade*, p. 14.
106. Polley, A *Soldier's Letters to Charming Nellie*, pp. 17–18; Simpson, *Hood's Texas Brigade*, pp. 61–63; Glover (ed.), *"Tyler to Sharpsburg"* (Waco: W. M. Morrison, 1960), p. 6; Williams, *Hood's Texas Brigade in the Civil War*, p. 35.
107. Hood, *John Bell Hood*, pp. 1–5; McMurry, *John Bell Hood*, pp. 1–35; Gerald A. Patterson, "John Bell Hood," *Civil War Times Illustrated* (February 1971), pp. 12–15.
108. Glover (ed.), *"Tyler to Sharpsburg,"* p. 7.
109. McMurry, *John Bell Hood*, p. 34.
110. Oates, *The War Between the Union and The Confederacy and Its Lost Opportunities*, p. 400.
111. Hood, John Bell Hood, p. x.
112. McMurry, *John Bell Hood*, p. 32.
113. Polley, *Hood's Texas Brigade*, p. 129; Mitchell, *Military Leaders of the Civil War*, pp. 194–195; West, *A Texan in Search of a Fight, Being the Diary and Letters of a Private Soldier in Hood's Texas Brigade* (Memphis: General Books, LLC, 2012), p. 20.
114. Polley, *Hood's Texas Brigade*, p. 291.
115. *Ibid*.; Simpson, *Hood's Texas Brigade*, p. 468; CTSR, NA.

Chapter 2

1. Polley, *Hood's Texas Brigade*, p. 54; Mitchell, *Military Leaders of the Civil War*, pp. 194–195.
2. Polley, *Hood's Texas Brigade*, p. 54.
3. CTSR, NA; Polley, *A Soldier's Letters To Charming Nellie*, p. 32; CTSR, NA; Gregory A. Coco, *Confederates Killed In Action at Gettysburg* (Gettysburg: Thomas Publications, 2001), p. 43; *Sentinel*, Gettysburg, Pennsylvania, August 4, 1863; Nevins, *The Texans*, 206; Main, George Washington, The Handbook of Texas Online; West, *A Texan in Search of a Fight*, 17, p. 23; Higgins, *The Swamp Fox, Francis Marion's Campaign in the Carolinas 1780* (Oxford: Osprey Publishing, 2013), pp. 12–75.
4. Winik, *April 1865* (New York: HarperCollins, 2001), pp. 5 and 25.
5. Tucker, "Motivations of United States Volunteers During the Texas Revolution," *East Texas Historical Journal*, vol. 29, no. 1 (1991), pp. 25–26; Everett, *Chaplain Davis and Hood's Texas Brigade*, pp. 55–56; *National Banner and Nashville Whig*, Nashville, Tennessee, March 18, 1836; *Telegraph and Texas Register*, San Felipe de Austin, Texas, December 2, 1835.
6. Oates, *Rip Ford's Texas*, p. 9; Hanks, History of Captain B. F. Benton's Company 1861–1865," CRC; Polley, *Hood's Texas Brigade*, pp. 14 and 54; CTSR, NA; *National Banner and Nashville Whig*, May 30, 1836; *New York American*, New York City, New York, November 25, 1836.
7. *Bangor Commercial Advertiser*, Bangor, Maine, March 19, 1836.
8. *Nashville Banner and Nashville Whig*, March 18, 1836.

9. Sam Houston to Sam Houston, Jr., May 22, 1861, Texas State Library and Archives Commission, Austin, Texas; Samuel Houston, Jr., Biographical Sketch, Samuel Houston, Jr., Papers, 1862–1886, Briscoe Center for American History, The University of Texas at Austin, Austin, Texas.
10. Samuel Houston Jr., Biographical Sketch, Samuel Houston, Jr., Papers, 1862–1886, Briscoe Center for American History, UT.
11. West, *A Texan in Search of a Fight*, pp. 2–3.
12. Hardin, *Texian Illiad*, pp. 9 and 91; Roberts and Olson, *A Line in The Sand*, p. 93; Williams, *Hood's Texas Brigade in the Civil War*, p. 33.
13. CTSR, NA; James M. McCaffrey, *Only A Private, A Texan Remembers the Civil War, The Memoirs of William J. Oliphant* (Houston: Halcyon Press, Ltd., 2004), pp. 2 and 11; Fisher, John, Handbook of Texas Online; *Frankfort Commonwealth*, Frankfort Kentucky, May 25, 1836.
14. Simpson, *Hood's Texas Brigade*, pp. 27 and 91, note no. 4; Roberts and Olson, *A Line in The Sand*, pp. 126–129; CTSR, NA.
15. Simpson, *Hood's Texas Brigade*, p. 40; CTSR, NA.
16. Simpson, *Hood's Texas Brigade*, p. 59.
17. Everett (ed.), *Chaplain Davis and Hood's Texas Brigade*, pp. 33 and 112; Roberts and Olson, *A Line in The Sand*, p. 93.
18. *Valor*, The Biennial Publication of Hood's Texas Brigade Association, Number 2 (1973), p. 25.
19. Robert Campbell, "A Lone Star in Virginia," *Civil War Times Illustrated* (December 2000), p. 88.
20. Polley, *Hood's Texas Brigade*, introduction; pp. 14 and 54; Hardin, *Texian Illiad*, pp. 5–91.
21. Polley, *Hood's Texas Brigade*, p. 199; Roberts and Olson, *A Line in The Sand*, p. 124.
22. Simpson, *Hood's Texas Brigade*, pp. 45, 47, and 51; Hardin, *Texas Illiad*, pp. 85 and 148–149; *Southern Patriot*, Charleston, South Carolina, November 21, 1835; *New Orleans Bee*, New Orleans, Louisiana, January 4, 1836.
23. *Baltimore Gazette and Daily Advertiser*, Baltimore, Maryland, August 14, 1832.
24. Everett (ed.), *Chaplain Davis and Hood's Texas Brigade*, p. 103; Mitchell, *Military Leaders of the Civil War*, pp. 194–195; Polley, *Hood's Texas Brigade*, p. 284.
25. Polley, *Hood's Texas Brigade*, p. 108; Everett (ed.), *Chaplain Davis and Hood's Texas Brigade*, p. 164.
26. Everett (ed.), *Chaplain Davis and Hood's Texas Brigade*, p. 155.
27. Darden, Stephen Heard, The Handbook of Texas Online.
28. Simpson, *Gaines' Mill to Appomattox*, p. 33; Campbell, *An Empire for Slavery*, 43, note no. 13; Albert A. Nofi, *The Alamo and the Texas War for Independence* (Conshohocken: Combined Books, 1992), p. 154.
29. West, *A Texan in Search of a Fight*, p. 1.
30. *Valor*, p. 26.
31. *Ibid.*, p. 7.
32. West, *A Texan in Search of a Fight*, p. 3.
33. *Ibid.*, pp. 1, 3, and 9–11.
34. *Valor*, p. 26.
35. Mitchell, *Military Leaders in the Civil War*, pp. 194–195; CTSR, NA.
36. *The Daily Dispatch*, Richmond, Virginia, February 6, 1862.

Chapter 3

1. Polley, *Hood's Texas Brigade*, pp. 13, 16, and 238; Simpson, *Hood's Texas Brigade*, pp. 21, note 51 and 72–74; "Col. F. S. Bass," CRC; Williams, *Hood's Texas Brigade in the Civil War*, pp. 25–26.

2. Katcher, *The Army of Northern Virginia* (London: Osprey Publishing Ltd., 1975), p. 16.
3. *Valor,* p. 13.
4. Williams, *Hood's Texas Brigade in the Civil War*, p. 49.
5. Fletcher, *Rebel Private*, p. 216; CTSR, NA.
6. Hamilton, *History of Company M, First Texas Volunteer Infantry, Hood's Brigade* (Waco: W. M. Morrison, 1962), p. 85; Fehrenbach, *Lone Star*, pp. 81–92 and 220–233; Nofi, *The Alamo*, pp. 149–159.
7. Simpson, *Hood's Texas Brigade*, pp. 14–15; CTSR, NA; Hanks, History of Captain B. F. Benton's Company 1861–1865," CRC; First Texas File, Antietam National Military Park Archives, Sharpsburg, Maryland.
8. CTSR, NA; Fletcher, *Rebel Private*, pp. 17 and 51; Simpson, *Hood's Texas Brigade*, p. 100, note 46; Everett (ed.), *Chaplain Davis and Hood's Texas Brigade*, pp. 61–62.
9. Zaboly, *American Colonial Ranger, The Northern Colonies 1724–64* (Oxford: Osphrey Publishing, 2004), pp. 4, 22, 28–30, and 46.
10. Cubbison, "Petite Guerre: Saratoga's Small War," *Patriots of the American Revolution*, vol. 4, issue 5 (September–October 2011), pp. 28–33.
11. Simpson, *Hood's Texas Brigade*, pp. 16–17; Hanks, "History of Captain B. F. Benton's Company 1861–1865," CRC; TCSR, NA.
12. *Valor*, p. 23.
13. Hanks, "History of Captain B. F. Benton's Company 1861–1865," CRC.
14. "Col. F. S. Bass," Biographical Sketch, Confederate Research Center, Hillsboro, Texas; First Texas File, ANMPA.
15. Simpson, *Hood's Texas Brigade*, pp. 17 and 23; Matt Dale to Brother, June 7, 1862, CRC; First Texas File, ANMPA.
16. Simpson, *Hood's Texas Brigade*, pp. 25 and 42; CTSR, NA; Everett (ed.), *Chaplain Davis and Hood's Texas Brigade*, p. 37; Hamilton, History of Company M, First Texas Volunteer Infantry, Hood's Brigade," pp. 10 and 21–22; First Texas File, ANMPA.
17. Simpson, *Hood's Texas Brigade*, pp. 73–74, 90; CTSR, NA; Everett (ed.), *Chaplain Davis and Hood's Texas Brigade*, p. 78.
18. CTSR, NA; Simpson, *Hood's Texas Brigade*, p. 22; Todd, *First Texas Regiment*, p. 2; First Texas File, ANMPA.
19. First Texas File, ANMPA; CTSR, NA.
20. Susannah F. Ural, 'A Little Body of Malcontents,' *Civil War Times* (June 2014), pp. 66–68.
21. First Texas File, ANMPA; *Tyler Courier–Times Telegraph*, Tyler, Texas, April 16, 1972; *Anthens Daily Review*, Athens, Texas, April 12, 1972; CTSR, NA.
22. *Palestine Herald-Press*, Palestine, Texas, October 18, 1967; CTSR, NA.
23. CTSR, NA; Hamilton, History of Company M, First Texas Volunteer Infantry, Hood's Brigade, pp. 19 and 40; Fehrenbach, *Lone Star*, pp. 81–92; Matovina, *The Alamo Remembered, Tejano Accounts and Perspectives* (Austin: University of Texas Press, 1995), pp. 1–124; Guerra, *Heroes of the Alamo and Goliad, Revolutionaries on the Road to San Jacinto and Texas Independence* (San Antonio: The Alamo Press, 1987), pp. 3, 5, 18, 24–25, and 44; Fehrenbach, *Lone Star*, p. 231.
24. *Valor*, p. 9.
25. *Ibid*., p. 10.
26. CTSR, NA.
27. Roberts, *Confederate Military History*, Texas, vol. 15 (Wilmington: Broadfoot Publishing, 1989), p. 510; CTSR, NA.
28. CTSR, NA; Mary Lasswell, compiled and edited, *Rags and Hope, The Memoirs of Val C. Giles, Four Years with Hood's Texas Brigade, Fourth Texas Infantry, 1861–1865* (New York: Coward-McCann, Inc., 1961), pp. 57 and 145.
29. Lasswell (ed.), *Rags and Hope*, p. 74.

30. "Texan at War, The Letters of Private James Henry Hendrick, Army of Northern Virginia," 1964 typescript by Hugh Irvin Power, Jr., First Texas File, ANMPA; CTSR, NA.
31. Everett (ed.), *Chaplain Davis and Hood's Texas Brigade*, p. 62.
32. CTSR, NA; Simpson, *Hood's Texas Brigade*, pp. 71–72, 83–84; Todd, *First Texas Regiment*, p. 2; Fehrenbach, *Lone Star*, pp. 81–92; McLeod, Hugh, The Handbook of Texas Online; Williams, *Hood's Texas Brigade in the Civil War*, pp. 28 and 34.
33. Simpson, *Hood's Texas Brigade*, pp. 67 and 189; CTSR, NA; Everett (ed.), *Chaplain Davis and Hood's Texas Brigade*, p. 62.
34. "Texan At War," First Texas File, ANMPA; Fehrenbach, *Lone Star*, p. 246.
35. Pohanka, *Don Troiani's Civil War* (Mechancisburg: Stackpole Books, 1995), pp. 42–44; Giles, "The Flag of First Texas. A.N. Virginia," *Confederate Veteran*, vol. 15, no. 9 (Sept. 1907), p. 417; Otott, "Clash in the Cornfield: The 1st Texas Volunteer Infantry in the Maryland Campaign," *Civil War Regiments*, vol. 5, no. 3 (1997), pp. 77–78; Fehrenbach, *Lone Star*, p. 246.
36. *Valor*, 12.
37. W. D. Pritchard, "Hood's Brigade," typescript, First Texas File, ANMPA.
38. *Ibid.*; Smithwick, *The Evolution of a State*, 72; Polley, *Hood's Texas Brigade*, pp. 14 and 108.
39. Polley, *Hood's Texas Brigade*, pp. 14 and 108.
40. *Ibid.*, pp. 110–111.
41. Simpson, *Hood's Texas Brigade*, p. 22; CTSR, NA; "Col. F. S. Bass," CRC; Williams, *Hood's Texas Brigade in the Civil War*, pp. 40–41; Frederick S. Bass, Jefferson, Texas, to Scoto Shipp, Virginia Military Academy, Lexington, May 13, 1893, Confederate Research Center, Hillsboro, Texas; First Texas File, ANMPA; First Texas File, ANMPA.
42. Williams, *Hood's Texas Brigade in the Civil War*, pp. 34 and 40.
43. CTSR, NA; Todd, *First Texas Regiment*, 5; "Col F. S. Bass," CRC.
44. Simpson, *Hood's Texas Brigade*, p. 44; CTSR, NA; Williams, *Hood's Texas Brigade in the Civil War*, pp. 26–27.
45. Simpson, *Hood's Texas Brigade*, pp. 76–78; Todd, *First Texas Regiment*, pp. 3–4; "Col. F. S. Bass," CRC; CTSR, NA.
46. Everett (ed.), *Chaplain Davis and Hood's Texas Brigade*, pp. 49–50.
47. Everett (ed.), *Chaplain Davis and Hood's Texas Brigade*, pp. 13 and 47.
48. *Ibid.*, pp. 52–53; CTSR, NA.
49. Everett (ed.), *Chaplain Davis and Hood's Texas Brigade*, p. 58; "Col. F. S. Bass," CRC.
50. CTSR, NA; Everett (ed.), *Chaplain Davis and Hood's Texas Brigade*,165; McLeod, Hugh, The Handbook of Texas Online.
51. Simpson, *Hood's Texas Brigade*, pp. 94–95; McMurry, *John Bell Hood*, p. 36; CTSR, NA.
52. Simpson, *Hood's Texas Brigade*, pp. 96–103.
53. *Ibid.*; Everett (ed.), *Chaplain Davis and Hood's Texas Brigade*, p. 61; McMurry, *John Bell Hood*, p. 39; Todd, *First Texas Regiment*, p. 4; Pritchard, "Hood's Brigade," First Texas File, ANMPA; CTSR, NA; Glover (ed.), *"Tyler to Sharpsburg,"* pp. 15–16.
54. *Western Sentinel*, Winston, North Carolina, June 6, 1862.
55. *Ibid.*
56. Everett (ed.), *Chaplain Davis and Hood's Texas Brigade*, p. 63.
57. *Ibid.*
58. *Western Sentinel*, June 6, 1862; Freeman, *Lee's Lieutenants*, vol. 1, 197.
59. *Valor*, p. 15.
60. *Western Sentinel*, June 6, 1862.
61. Everett (ed.), *Chaplain Davis and Hood's Texas Brigade*, pp. 103–104.
62. *Ibid.*, pp. 104–107; Everett (ed.), *Chaplain Davis and Hood's Texas Brigade*, p. 69; CTSR, NA.

63. Everett (ed.), *Chaplain Davis and Hood's Texas Brigade*, pp. 75 and 79; Robert Campbell, "A Lone Star in Virginia," *CWTI*, p. 40; McMurry, *John Bell Hood*, pp. 45–46; Simpson, *Hood's Texas Brigade*, pp. 114–115.
64. Everett (ed.), *Chaplain Davis and Hood's Texas Brigade*, pp. 82–91; McMurry, *John Bell Hood*, pp. 47–49; Polley, *A Soldier's Letters to Charming Nellie*, p. 57; Simpson, *Hood's Texas Brigade*, pp.120–121.
65. McMurry, *John Bell Hood*, pp. 47–49; Simpson, *Hood's Texas Brigade*, pp. 120–121.
66. CTSR, NA.
67. Polley, *Hood's Texas Brigade*, p. 71; First Texas File, ANMPA; Higgins, *The Swamp Fox*, pp. 20, 34, 36 and 68.
68. Everett (ed.), *Chaplain Davis and Hood's Texas Brigade*, p. 103; Simpson, *Hood's Texas Brigade*, pp. 125–128 and 134.
69. "Texan at War," ANMPA.
70. Everett (ed.), *Chaplain Davis and Hood's Texas Brigade*, p. 165; Polley, *Hood's Texas Brigade*, p. 70; Todd, *First Texas Regiment*, p. 9; Williams, *Hood's Texas Brigade in the Civil War*, pp. 26–27.
71. Everett (ed.), *Chaplain Davis and Hood's Texas Brigade*, 113; Simpson, *Hood's Texas Brigade*, p. 144; Polley, *Hood's Texas Brigade*, pp. 81–82; Todd, *First Texas Regiment*, p. 9; Smith, "One of the Most Daring of Men," pp. 42–45; Pritchard, "Hood's Brigade," First Texas File, ANMPA.
72. Everett (ed.), *Chaplain Davis and Hood's Texas Brigade*, p. 116; McMurry, *John Bell Hood*, p. 55; Simpson, *Hood's Texas Brigade*, pp. 144–152; Polley, *Hood's Texas Brigade*, p. 103; Polley, *A Soldier's Letters to Charming Nellie*, pp. 76–77; John J. Hennessy, *Return to Bull Run, The Campaign and Battle of Second Manassas* (New York: Simon and Schuster, 1993), pp. 362–373; Todd, *First Texas Regiment*, p. 9; Smith, "One of The Most Daring of Men," pp. 43–48; Hardin, *Texian Illiad*, pp. 211–217.
73. Everett (ed.), *Chaplain Davis and Hood's Texas Brigade*, p. 116; Polley, *Hood's Texas Brigade*, p. 89; Polley, *A Soldier's Letters to Charming Nellie*, pp. 76–77; Mark Mayo Boatner, *The Civil War Dictionary* (New York: David McKay Company, Inc., 1959), p. 593; Hennessy, Return to Bull Run, pp. 372–378; Smith, "One of the Most Daring of Men," pp. 48–49.
74. Evault Boswell, *Texas Boys in Gray* (Plano: Republic of Texas Press, 2000), p. 80.
75. McMurry, *John Bell Hood*, 55–56; Everett (ed.), *Chaplain Davis and Hood's Texas Brigade*, p. 121; Simpson, *Hood's Texas Brigade*, pp. 156–157; CTSR, NA.
76. Everett (ed.), *Chaplain Davis and Hood's Texas Brigade*, p. 116.
77. *Ibid.*, p. 117; Polley, *Hood's Texas Brigade*, p. 96.
78. Everett (ed.), *Chaplain Davis and Hood's Texas Brigade*, pp. 165–166; CTSR, NA; Matt Dale to Brother, June 7, 1862, CRC.
79. Matt Dale to Brother, June 7, 1862, CRC.
80. CTSR, NA; Polley, *Hood's Texas Brigade*, p. 132.
81. Lance J. Herdegern, *The Iron Brigade in the Civil War and Memory* (El Dorado Hills: Savas Beatie, 2012), p. 279 and note 22.
82. CTSR, NA; Lasswell (ed.), *Rags and Hope*, pp. 89–90.
83. Lasswell (ed.), *Rags and Hope*, p. 119.
84. West, *A Texan in Search of a Fight*, pp. 16 and 19.
85. *Ibid.*, p. 21.

Chapter 4

1. Stephen Sears, *Gettysburg* (Boston: Houghton Mifflin Company, 2003), pp. 1–17.
2. J. Mark Smither to Mother, June 28, 1863, Texas Heritage Museum, Historical Research Center, Hillsboro, Texas.

3. West, *A Texan in Search of a Fight*, p. 20.
4. Williams, *Hood's Texas Brigade in the Civil War*, p. 148.
5. Lasswell (ed.), *Rags and Hope*, p. 178.
6. Polk, *The North and South American Review* (Austin: Von Boeckmann-Jones, 1912, p. 15.
7. West, *A Texan in Search of a Fight*, p. 20.
8. Smithers to Mother, June 28, 1863, THM.
9. *Ibid.*
10. *Ibid.*
11. Sears, *Gettysburg*, pp. 92–93.
12. Guelzo, *Gettysburg*, p. 78.
13. West, *A Texan in Search of a Fight*, p. 21.
14. Sears, *Gettysburg*, p. 107.
15. Hennessy, *Return to Bull Run*, pp. 362–363; Wert, *A Glorious Army*, pp. 75–107, 189–205, and 235–243; Sears, *Gettysburg*, pp. 226–239, 254–256.
16. Gottfried, *Brigades of Gettysburg, The Union and Confederate Brigades at the Battle of Gettysburg* (New York: Skyhorse Publishing, 2012), p. 427; Wert, *A Glorious Army*, pp. 75–107; Polley, *Hood's Texas Brigade*, p. 160; Sears, *Gettysburg*, pp. 255–262; Hennessy, *Return to Bull Run*, pp. 362–363; Oeffinger (ed.), *A Soldier's General, The Civil War Letters of Major General Lafayette McLaws* (Chapel Hill: University of North Carolina Press, 2002), pp. 196–197; Sims, "Recollection of the Civil War," THM; Guelzo, *Gettysburg*, p. 235; Adelman and Smith, *Devil's Den, A History and Guide* (Gettysburg: Thomas Publications, 1997), p. 22.
17. West, *A Texan in Search of a Fight*, p. 19.
18. CTSR, NA; *Valor*, p. 22.
19. J. Mark Smither to Mother, July 29, 1863, Texas Heritage Museum, Historical Research Center, Hillsboro, Texas.
20. Sears, *Gettysburg*, pp. 236 and 247.
21. *Ibid.*, p. 252.
22. James A. Kegel, *North with Lee and Jackson, The Lost Story of Gettysburg* (Mechanicsburg: Stackpole Books, 1996), pp. 11–261.
23. Polley, *Hood's Texas Brigade*, pp. 160–161; Wert, *A Glorious Army*, pp. 256–260; Penny and Laine, *Struggle for the Round Tops, Law's Alabama Brigade at the Battle of Gettysburg* (Shippensburg: White Mane Publishing Company, 1999), p. 30; Guelzo, *Gettysburg*, pp. 235–252; Gottfried, *Brigades of Gettysburg*, pp. 427–429; Williams, *Hood's Texas Brigade in the Civil War*, pp. 50 and 154; Sears, *Gettysburg*, pp. 249–262.
24. Cowell, *Tactics at Gettysburg* (Gaithersburg: Olde Soldier Books, 1987), p. 49; Sears, *Gettysburg*, p. 262.
25. Sears, *Gettysburg*, p. 254; Polley, *Hood's Texas Brigade*, pp. 160–161.
26. Polley, *Hood's Texas Brigade*, pp. 160–162; Piston, *Lee's Tarnished Lieutenant, James Longstreet and His Place in Southern History* (Athens: University of Georgia Press, 1987), pp. 57–58; Wert, *A Glorious Army*, pp. 256–258; Gettysburg Foundation, Devil's Den Trail, p. 5; Penny and Laine, *Struggle for the Round Tops*, pp. 30–32; Guelzo, *Gettysburg*, pp. 243–253 and 262–263; Adelman and Smith, *Devil's Den*, pp. 19–20 and 23; Sears, *Gettysburg*, pp. 264–265; Reardon and Vossler, *A Field Guide to Gettysburg, Experiencing the Battlefield through Its History, Places, and People* (Chapel Hill: University of North Carolina Press, 2013), p. 221.
27. Smither to Mother, July 29, 1863, THM.
28. West, *A Texan in Search of a Fight*, p. 21.
29. Guelzo, *Gettysburg*, p. 250.
30. *Ibid.*, pp. 252 and 257–258.

31. Polley, *Hood's Texas Brigade*, pp. 161–162; Scott, *Unveiling and Dedication of Monument to Hood's Texas Brigade* (Houston: F. B. Chilton, 1911), p. 311; Penny and Laine, *Struggle for the Round Tops*, pp. 31–32; Wert, *A Glorious Army*, p. 258; Guelzo, *Gettysburg*, pp. 262–263; Gottfried, *The Artillery of Gettysburg* (Nashville: Cumberland House, 2008), pp. 104–105; Adelman and Smith, *Devil's Den*, pp. 21–22.
32. Sears, *Gettysburg*, p. 265.
33. Piston, *Lee's Tarnished Lieutenant*, pp. 57–58.
34. Guelzo, *Gettysburg*, pp. 262–263.
35. West, *A Texan in Search of a Fight*, p. 21.
36. Penny and Laine, *Struggle for the Round Tops*, p. 32; Sears, *Gettysburg*, p. 365; Wert, *A Glorious Army*, p. 258.
37. Williams, *Hood's Texas Brigade in the Civil War*, pp. 33–34; Adelman and Smith, *Devil's Den*, pp. 21–23; Polley's *Hood's Texas Brigade*, pp. 74 and 160; Penny and Laine, *Struggle for the Round Tops*, pp. 30–32; Sims, "Recollection of the Civil War," THM; Guelzo, *Gettysburg*, p. 253; CTSR, NA; Black Jack Travis, *Men of God, Angels of Death, History of the Rowan Artillery* (private printing, 2008), pp. 11–14 and 117–118; O'Grady, *Clear the Way!, The Irish in the Army of Northern Virginia* (Mason City: Savas Publishing Company, 2000), pp. 190–193; Lasswell (ed.), *Rags and Hope*, p. 132; Gottfried, *Brigades of Gettysburg*, p. 430; West, *A Texan in Search of a Fight*, p. 19.
38. Fletcher, *Rebel Private*, p. 78.
39. Lasswell (ed.), *Rags and Hope*, pp. 57 and 75; CTSR, NA.
40. West, *A Texan in Search of a Fight*, p. 15.
41. *Valor*, p. 17.
42. Lasswell (ed.), *Rags and Hope*, p. 131.
43. Penny and Laine, *Struggle for the Round Tops*, pp. 31–32 and 34.
44. Wert, *A Glorious Army*, p. 258.
45. Fletcher, *Rebel Private*, p. 78.
46. A. C. Sims, Recollection of the Civil War, Texas Heritage Museum, Historical Research Center, Hillsboro, Texas.
47. Work to Langley, May 28, 1908, HRC; Guelzo, *Gettysburg*, p. 255.
48. Fletcher, *Rebel Private*, p. 80.
49. Rufus King Felder to Family, July 9, 1863, Texas Heritage Museum, Historical Research Center, Hillsboro, Texas.
50. Wert, *A Glorious Army*, p. 260.
51. Smither to Mother, July 29, 1863, THM.
52. Guelzo, *Gettysburg*, p. 241.
53. *Ibid.*, 263; Sims, "Recollection of the Civil War," THM.
54. West, *A Texan in Search of a Fight*, p. 19.
55. R. Henderson Shuffler, editor, *The Adventures of a Prisoner of War 1863–1864* (Austin: University of Texas Press, 1964), pp. 6–7. 12–13, 19–20, 26, and 44.
56. Shuffler (ed.), *The Adventures of a Prisoner of War 1863–1864*, p. 39.
57. *Ibid.*, p. 44.
58. Fletcher, *Rebel Private*, p. 78.
59. Sims, "Recollection of the Civil War," THM; Gottfried, *The Artillery of Gettysburg*, 105; Guelzo, *Gettysburg*, p. 263.
60. Shuffler (ed.), *The Adventures of a Prisoner of War 1863–1864*, 44; Gottfried, *The Artillery of Gettysburg*, p. 105.
61. Thomas Bates to Elizabeth, December 6, 1862, Chappell Hill Historical Society, Chappell Hill, Texas; Sims, "Recollection of the Civil War," THM.
62. Guelzo, *Gettysburg*, p. 240; Katcher, *The Army of Robert E. Lee*, p. 243; Kerby, *Kirby Smith's Confederacy, 1863–1865* (Tuscaloosa: University of Alabama Press, 1972), pp.

67–68; Third Texas Infantry, The Handbook of Texas Online; Sims, "Recollection of the Civil War," THM; Lasswell (ed.), Rags and Hope, p. 109.

63. Williams, *Hood's Texas Brigade in the Civil War*, p. 135.
64. Gregory A. Coco, *Confederates Killed in Action at Gettysburg* (Gettysburg: Thomas Publications, 2001), pp. 36–37.
65. Sims, "Recollection of the Civil War," THM.
66. Lasswell (ed.), *Rags and Hope*, p. 128.
67. West, *A Texan in Search of a Fight*, pp. 13 and 19.
68. Iron Stirrup found in Texas Camp in Virginia, Ebay Dealer, Ormond Beach, Florida, April 2014.
69. James Henry Hendricks to Mother, July 8, 1863, United States Military History Institute, Carlisle, Pennsylvania.
70. Philip Katcher, *American Civil War Armies, State Troops* (London: Osprey Publishing, 1989), pp. 39–40 and 45; Williams, *Hood's Texas Brigade in the Civil War*, p. 73; Philip Katcher, *American Civil War Armies, Confederate Artillery, Cavalry and Infantry* (London: Osprey Publishing, 1987), p. 36; Editors of Time-Life Books, *Echoes of Glory, Arms and Equipment of the Confederacy* (Alexandria: Time-Life Books, 1991), pp. 52–53, 70–71, 95, 97, 130, 166–167, 188–189 and 201; Photography of Lieutenant Eli N. Baxter, Lawrence T. Jones, III, Texas Photographs, Southern Methodist University, Central University Libraries, De Golyer Library, Dallas, Texas; Polley, Hood's Texas Brigade, pp. 26 and 35; Guelzo, *Gettysburg*, p. 263; Bruce Catton, *Glory Road, The Bloody Route from Fredericksburg to Gettysburg* (Garden City: Doubleday and Company, Inc., 1952), p. 286.
71. *Ibid.*, 40; Kerby, *Kerby Smith's Confederacy*, pp. 74–75; Katcher, *American Civil War Armies, Confederate Artillery, Cavalry and Infantry*, p. 38; Editors of Time-Life Books, *Echoes of Glory*, pp. 7, 36–37 and 40–41.
72. West, *A Texan in Search of a Fight*, 17.
73. CTSR, NA; Polley, *Hood's Texas Brigade*,169; Williams, *Hood's Teas Brigade in the Civil War*, 26.
74. Glover (ed.), "Tyler to Sharpsburg," p. 5; Fletcher, *Rebel Private*, p. 44.
75. West, *A Texans in Search of a Fight*, p. 12.
76. Hale, *The Third Texas Cavalry in the Civil War* (Norman: The University of Oklahoma Press, 1993), pp. 9–17; Hunt, *Haiti's Influence on Antebellum America, Slumbering Volcano in the Caribbean* (Baton Rouge: Louisiana State University Press, 1988), pp. 1–190
77. Katcher, *The Army of Robert E. Lee*, 243–244; CTSR, NA; Williams, *Hood's Texas Brigade in the Civil War*, pp. 111 and 113.
78. CTSR, NA; Robert N. Rosen, *The Jewish Confederates* (Columbia: University of South Carolina Press, 2000), 30–31, 203; Polley, *Hood's Texas Brigade*, p. 49.
79. Jackson, *Alamo Legacy, Alamo Descendants, Remember the Alamo* (Austin: Eakin Press, 1997), pp. 52–53.
80. *Ibid.*, pp. 85–88; Walker, Jacob, Handbook of Texas Online; M. A. Dunham letter to Sarah A. Walker, October 20, 1864, Daughters of Republic of Texas Library, The Alamo, San Antonio, Texas.
81. Polley, *The Texas Brigade*, p. 134.
82. CTSR, NA; Katcher, *The Army of Robert E. Lee*, pp. 120 and 243; Glover (ed.), *"Tyler to Sharpsburg,"* p. 9.
83. Hardin (ed.), *Lone Star*, p. 61.
84. Polley, *Hood's Texas Brigade*, p. 13; McLeod, Hugh, The Handbook of Texas Online; Bailey's Prairie, Tx., The Handbook of Texas Online.
85. Winik, *April 1865*, p. 44; Polly, *The Texas Brigade*, p. 135; Piston, *Lee's Tarnished Lieutenant*, p. 40.

86. Glover (ed.), "*Tyler to Sharpsburg,*" p. 9.
87. Kerby, *Kirby Smith's Confederacy*, pp. 51–67 and 431–434; Hale, *The Third Texas Cavalry in the Civil War*, pp. 192–193; James Marten, "On the Road with Thomas H. DuVal: A Texas Unionist's Travel Diary, 1863, *Journal of Confederate History*, vol. 6, p. 76.
88. Glover (ed.), "*Tyler to Sharpsburg,*" p. 7; Hale, *The Third Texas Cavalry in the Civil War*, pp. 192–194
89. Glover (ed.), "*Tyler to Sharpsburg,*" p. 6.
90. Williams, *Hood's Texas Brigade in the Civil War*, p. 56.
91. Glover (ed.), "*Tyler to Sharpsburg,*" p. 7; Hale, *The Third Texas Cavalry in the Civil War*, pp. 192–194; Kerby, *Kirby Smith's Confederacy*, pp. 1–434.
92. Williams, *Hood's Texas Brigade in the Civil War*, p. 152.
93. Smither to Mother, June 28, 1863, THM.
94. J. Mark Smither to Mother, July 29, 1863, Texas Heritage Museum, Historical Research Center, Hillsboro, Texas.
95. Lasswell (ed.), *Rags and Hope*, p. 93.
96. Bowden and Ward, *Last Chance for Victory, Robert E. Lee and the Gettysburg Campaign* (New York: Da Capo Press, 2001), p. 284.
97. Kerby, *Kirby Smith's Confederacy*, p. 74; Twin Sisters, Handbook of Texas Online; Giles, Rags and Hope, pp. 27–34; Lasswell (ed.), *Rags and Hope*, pp. 27–32; Williams, *Hood's Texas Brigade in the Civil War*, p. 17.
98. Twin Sisters, Hand of Texas Online.
99. Glover (ed.), "*Tyler to Sharpsburg,*" pp. 1–2; CTSR, NA
100. Polley, *The Texas Brigade*, pp. 134–135; Twin Sisters, Handbook of Texas Online.
101. Glover (ed.), "*Tyler to Sharpsburg,*" pp. 1 and 6; Hale, *The Third Texas Cavalry in the Civil* War, p. 13; Polley, The Texas Brigade, pp. 134–135.
102. Polley, *The Texas Brigade*, p. 135.
103. *Ibid*., p. 284.
104. McCaffrey, *Only A Private*, pp. 9–10 and 15–16; Third Texas Infantry, Handbook of Texas Online.
105. Polley, *Hood's Texas Brigade*, p. 284.
106. Joseph B. Polley letter to father, May 12, 1863, Museum Quality America, Division of Cal Packard, LLC.
107. West, *A Texan in Search of a Fight*, p. 8.
108. Boswell, *Texas Boys in Gray*, p. 200.
109. Williams, *Hood's Texas Brigade in the Civil War*, pp. 67–72.
110. Grady McWhiney and Perry D. Jamieson, *Attack and Die, Civil War Military Tactics and the Southern Heritage* (Tuscaloosa: University of Alabama Press, 1982), pp. 3–125; Sims, "Recollection of the Civil War," THM.
111. Glover (ed.), "*Tyler to Sharpsburg,*" p. 10; Guelzo, *Gettysburg*, pp. 255 and 263–264.
112. West, *A Texan in Search of a Fight*, pp. 9 and 16.
113. Williams, *Hood's Texas Brigade in the Civil War*, p. 16.
114. Glover (ed.), "*Tyler to Sharpsburg,*" p. 9; Sears, *Gettysburg*, p. 265
115. Polley, *The Texas Brigade*, p. 288.
116. West, *A Texan in Search of a Fight*, pp. 1 and 14–15.
117. Brear, *Inherit the Alamo, Myth and Ritual at an American Shrine* (Austin: University of Texas Press, 1995), pp. 1–2; Guelzo, *Gettysburg*, pp. 257–267.
118. TCSR, NA; Spencer, *From Coriscana to Appomattox, The Story of the Corsicana Invincibles and the Navarro Rifles* (Coriscana: The Texas Press, 1984), pp. 59 and 61.
119. Navarro, Jose Antonio, The Hand of Texas Online.
120. Glover (ed.), "*Tyler to Sharpsburg,*" p. 19; Work to Langley, May 28, 1908, THM; Sims, "Recollection of the Civil *War," THM; Penny and Laine,* Struggle for the Round

Tops, pp. 30–31; *Gottfried, Brigades* of Gettysburg, 438; Guelzo, *Gettysburg*, pp. 262–264.

121. Work to Langley, May 28, 1908, THM; Sims, "Recollection of the Civil War," THM; Guelzo, *Gettysburg*, pp. 255–256 and 263; West, *A Texan in Search of a Fight*, p. 12; Adelman and Smith, *Devil's Den*, p. 25.
122. Sears, *Gettysburg*, p. 268.
123. James Henry Hendrick to mother, July 8, 1863, USAMHI.
124. Guelzo, *Gettysburg*, p. 256.
125. Gottfried, *Brigades of Gettysburg*, p. 438.
126. Guelzo, *Gettysburg*, p. 256; Adelman and Smith, *Devil's Den*, p. 25; Gottfried, *Brigades of Gettysburg*, pp. 430, 435, and 438.
127. Polley, *Hood's Texas Brigade*, 166.
128. Sears, *Gettysburg*, 268; Gottfried, *Brigades of Gettysburg*, 438.
129. Sims, "Recollection of the Civil War," THM.
130. Guelzo, *Gettysburg*, p. 263; Gottfried, *The Artillery of Gettysburg*, p. 106; Adelman and Smith, *Devil's Den*, pp. 22–23.
131. Guelzo, *Gettysburg*, pp. 263–264; John Cheves Papers, 1857–1941, Southern Historical Collection, University of North Carolina, Chapel Hill, North Carolina; Scott Bowden and Bill Ward, *Last Chance for Victory, Robert E. Lee and the Gettysburg Campaign* (New York: Da Capo Press, 2001), p. 284.
132. Work to Langley, May 28, 1908, THM; Sims, "Recollection of the Civil War," THM; Adelman and Smith, *Devil's Den*, pp. 27–28.
133. Sears, *Gettysburg*, p. 268.
134. Polley, *Hood's Texas Brigade*, p. 162.
135. Guelzo, *Gettysburg*, pp. 263–264; Bowden and Ward, *Last Chance for Victory*, p. 280; Williams, *Hood's Texas Brigade in the Civil War*, pp. 36–37, 54; Adelman and Smith, *Devil's Den*, p. 28; Sears, *Gettysburg*, pp. 265 and 268.
136. Sears, *Gettysburg*, p. 268.
137. Adelman and Smith, *Devil's Den*, p. 28; Williams, *Hood's Texas Brigade in the Civil War*, pp. 37–38.
138. Bowden and Ward, *Last Chance for Victory*, pp. 280 and 284–285; Freeman, *Lee's Lieutenants, Gettysburg to Appomattox* (4 vols., New York: Charles Scribner's Sons, 1944), vol. 3, p. 122; Gottfried, *Brigades of Gettysburg*, pp. 428–430, 435, and 438; Adelman and Smith, *Devil's Den*, p. 28; Sears, *Gettysburg*, p. 268.
139. Work to Langley, May 28, 1908, THM; Robertson, Jerome Bonaparte, The Handbook of Texas Online; Gottfried, *Brigades of Gettysburg*, p. 438; Bowden and Ward, *Last Chance for Victory*, pp. 284–285; Williams, *Hood's Texas Brigade in the Civil War*, p. 39; Reardon and Vossler, *A Field Guide to Gettysburg*, p. 222.
140. Latschar, "My brave Texans, forward and take those heights!," GNMP; Gottfried, *Brigades of Gettysburg*, pp. 428–429; Williams, *Hood's Texas Brigade in the Civil War*, pp. 31 and 39; CTSR, NA; Reardon and Vossler, *A Field Guide to Gettysburg*, p. 219; Sears, *Gettysburg*, p. 268.
141. Williams, *Hood's Texas Brigade in the Civil War*, p. 31; Polley, *Hood's Texas Brigade*, p. 183.
142. Sims, "Recollection of the Civil War," THM; CTSR, NA;. Latschar, "My brave Texans, forward and take those heights!," GNMP; Guelzo, *Gettysburg*, p. 256; Williams, *Hood's Texas Brigade in the Civil War*, pp. 31, 39, and 118.
143. Sims, "Recollection of the Civil War," THM.
144. *Ibid.*; Williams, *Hood's Texas Brigade in the Civil War*, p. 27.
145. Sims, "Recollection of the Civil War," THM
146. Freeman, *Lee's Lieutenants*, vol. 3, p. 122; New York Times, July 3, 1913; Polley, *Hood's Texas Brigade*, pp. 169–170; Adelman and Smith, *Devil's Den*, p. 28.

147. Fletcher, *Rebel Private*, pp. 15 and 215–216.
148. Sims, "Recollection of the Civil War," THM.
149. *Ibid.*; Gottfried, *Brigades of Gettysburg*, p. 439.
150. Polley, *Hood's Texas Brigade*, 168; Bowden and Ward, *Last Chance for Victory*, 284; Adelman and Smith, *Devil's Den*, pp. 21 and 26; Gottfried, *Brigades of Gettysburg*, 430; Work, Philip Alexander, The Handbook of Texas Online.
151. Coco, *Confederates Killed in Action at Gettysburg*, pp. 43–45.
152. West, *A Texan in Search of a Fight*, pp. 12 and 19.
153. Sims, "Recollection of the Civil War," THM; Guelzo, *Gettysburg*, pp. 263–264; *National Tribune*, New York, New York, February 4, 1886; Williams, *Hood's Texas Brigade in the Civil War*, p. 152; Adelman and Smith, *Devil's Den*, p. 25.
154. Wiley Sword, *Sharpshooter: Hiram Berdan, his famous Sharpshooters and their Sharps rifles* (Lincoln: Andrew Mowbray Incorporated Publishers, 1988), pp. 55–62; *National Tribune*, February 4, 1886; Guelzo, *Gettysburg*, p. 264; Adelman and Smith, *Devil's Den*, pp. 21 and 28.
155. J. Mark Smither to Mother, July 29, 1863, THM.
156. Guelzo, *Gettysburg*, p. 264; *National Tribune*, February 4, 1886; Adelman and Smith, *Devil's Den*, p. 25.
157. Polley, *Hood's Texas Brigade*, p. 168; Adelman and Smith, *Devil's Den*, p. 24.
158. *National Tribune*, February 4, 1886; Gottfried, *The Artillery of Gettysburg*, p. 106.
159. Guelzo, *Gettysburg*, p. 264; Gottfried, *The Artillery of Gettysburg*, p. 106; Adelman and Smith, *Devil's Den*, p. 31.
160. Work to Langley, May 28, 1908, THM; Guelzo, *Gettysburg*, pp. 264–265; Sears, *Gettysburg*, p. 268; Reardon and Vossler, *A Field Guide to Gettysburg*, p. 222; Gottfried, *Brigades of Gettysburg*, p. 438; Bowden and Ward, *Last Chance for Victory*, p. 283; Williams, *Hood's Texas Brigade in the Civil War*, pp. 16 and 157–158; CTSR, NA.
161. Work to Langley, May 28, 1908, THM; Sears, Gettysburg, p. 268; Adelman and Smith, *Devil's Den*, p. 28.
162. Work to Langley, May 28, 1908, THM
163. Sims, "Recollection of the Civil War," THM.
164. Work to Langley, May 28, 1908, THM; Gottfried, *Brigades of Gettysburg*, p. 439.
165. Sims, "Recollection of the Civil War," THM; Adelman and Smith, *Devil's Den*, p. 25; Gottfried, *Brigades of Gettysburg*, p. 438.
166. Williams, *Hood's Texas Brigade in the Civil War*, p. 157; Gottfried, *Brigades of Gettysburg*, p. 429; Adelman and Smith, *Devil's Den*, p. 31.
167. Work to Langley, May 28, 1908, THM; Guelzo, *Gettysburg*, p. 264; Adelman and Smith, *Devil's Den*, pp. 28 and 31; Polly, *Hood's Texas Brigade*, p. 181.
168. Gottfried, *Brigades of Gettysburg*, p. 439.
169. Polly, *Hood's Texas Brigade*, p. 181.
170. Guelzo, *Gettysburg*, pp. 264–265; Bowden and Ward, *Last Chance for Victory*, pp. 285–286; Adelman and Smith, *Devil's Den*, pp. 24 and 43; Gottfried, *Brigades of Gettysburg*, p. 438.
171. Guelzo, *Gettysburg*, pp. 264 and 266; Sword, *Sharpshooter*, pp. 8 and 57; Adelman and Smith, *Devil's Den*, p. 29.
172. Polley, *Hood's Texas Brigade*, p. 168.
173. Sears, *Gettysburg*, p. 268.
174. Sims, "Recollection of the Civil War," THM; Guelzo, *Gettysburg*, pp. 264 and 266; Sword, *Sharpshooter*, pp. 8 and 57.
175. CTSR, NA; Polley, *Hood's Texas Brigade*, pp. 168–169.
176. James Henry Hendrick, to Mother, July 8, 1863, USAMHI.
177. Polley, *Hood's Texas Brigade*, p. 169; Reardon and Vossler, *A Field Guide to Gettysburg*, p. 222.

178. Sims, "Recollection of the Civil War," THM; Guelzo, *Gettysburg*, p. 266; Adelman and Smith, *Devil's Den*, p. 28; Reardon and Vossler, *A Field Guide to Gettysburg*, p. 222.
179. Adelman and Smith, *Devil's Den*, p. 29; Reardon and Vossler, *A Field Guide to Gettysburg*, p. 222.
180. Adelman and Smith, *Devil's Den*, p. 29.
181. *New York Times*, July 3, 1913; CTSR, NA.
182. CTSR, NA; Pvt. Mortimer Martin Murphy (1840–1863)–Find A Grave Memorial," internet.
183. *New York Times*, July 3, 1913.
184. *Ibid.*
185. Work, Philip Alexander, The Handbook of Texas Online.
186. Sims, "Recollection of the Civil War," West, *A Texan in Search of a Fight*, p. 19.
187. Guelzo, *Gettysburg*, pp. 263–264.
188. Sims, "Recollection of the Civil War," THM; Polly, *Hood's Texas Brigade*, p. 181; Adelman and Smith, *Devil's Den*, pp. 31–32.
189. Polley, *Hood's Texas Brigade*, p. 181; Work, Philip Alexander, The Handbook of Texas Online.
190. Polley, *Hood's Texas Brigade*, p. 181
191. *Ibid.*
192. Tucker, *Storming Little Round Top, The 15th Alabama and Their Fight for the High Ground, July 2, 1863* (New York: DaCapo Books, 2002), pp. 125–312; Gottfried, *Brigades of Gettysburg*, p. 430; Adelman and Smith, *Devil's Den*, p. 28.
193. Sims, "Recollection of the Civil War," THM; Bowden and Ward, *Last Chance for Victory*, p. 286.
194. Bowden and Ward, *Last Chance for Victory*, pp. 289–290; Adelman and Smith, *Devil's Den*, pp. 25 and 119; Gottfried, *Brigades of Gettysburg*, p. 439.
195. Hendrick, July 8, 1863, USAMHI.
196. Sims, "Recollection of the Civil War," THM; Adelman and Smith, *Devil's Den*, p. 22.
197. Polley, *Hood's Texas Brigade*, p. 169; Gottfried, *Brigades of Gettysburg*, p. 439.
198. Polley, *Hood's Texas Brigade*, pp. 169 and 181.
199. Sims, "Recollection of the Civil War," THM; Gottfried, *Brigades of Gettysburg*, p. 429.
200. Sims, "Recollection of the Civil War," THM; Gottfried, *Brigades of Gettysburg*, p. 432.
201. Adelman and Smith, *Devil's Den*, p. 31; Gottfried, *Brigades of Gettysburg*, p. 439.
202. Adelman and Smith, *Devil's Den*, p. 31.

Chapter 5

1. Guelzo, *Gettysburg*, p. 366; Gottfried, *Brigades of Gettysburg*, pp. 439–440; Williams, *Hood's Texas Brigade in the Civil War*, p. 158; Adelman and Smith, *Devil's Den*, pp. 20, 33 and 35–36.
2. Williams, *Hood's Texas Brigade in the Civil War*, p. 158; Gottfried, *Brigades of Gettysburg*, p. 440.
3. Sims, "Recollection of the Civil War," THM; Gottfried, *Brigades of Gettysburg*, p. 440.
4. Sims, "Recollection of the Civil War," THM; Polley, *Hood's Texas Brigade*, p. 181.
5. Sims, "Recollection of the Civil War," THM; Tucker, *Burnside's Bridge, The Climactic Struggle of the 2nd and 20th Georgia at Antietam Creek* (Mechanisburg: Stackpole Books, 2000), pp. 83–152; Adelman and Smith, *Devil's Den*, pp. 29 and 52; Gottfried, *Brigades of Gettysburg*, p. 440; Sims, "Recollection of the Civil War," THM; Dreese, *This Flag Never Goes Down* (Gettysburg: Thomas Publications, 2004), pp. 62–64; Adelman and Smith, *Devil's Den*, pp. 43–46; Williams, Hood's *Texas Brigade in the Civil War*, p. 33.
6. Sims, "Recollection of the Civil War," THM.

7. *Ibid.*; *O.R.*, vol. 27, ser. 1, pt. 2, p. 409; Adelman and Smith, *Devil's Den*, pp. 29 and 134.
8. Polley, *Hood's Texas Brigade*, p. 169.
9. Dreese, *This Flag Never Goes Down*, pp. 62–64; Bowden and Ward, *Last Chance for Victory*, p. 290; Adelman and Smith, *Devil's Den*, p. 31.
10. Bowden and Ward, *Last Chance for Victory*, p. 290; Reardon and Vossler, *A Field Guide to Gettysburg*, p. 223; Dreese, *This Flag Never Goes Down*, pp. 62–64.
11. James Henry Hendrick to Mother, July 8, 1863, USAMHI; *O.R.*, vol. 27, ser. 1, pt. 2, p. 409; Sims, "Recollection of the Civil War," THM; Adelman and Smith, *Devil's Den*, pp. 31, 40, and 134; CTSR, NA; Work to Langley, May 28, THM; Spencer, *From Corsicana To Appomattox*, pp. 62–63; Bowden and Ward, *Last Chance for Victory*, pp. 290–291; Coco, *On the Bloodstained Field*, I & II, 262 *Human Interest Stories of the Campaign and Battle of Gettysburg* (La Vergne: Ingram Book Company, 2013), pp. 87–88; Hoge, "The Tragedy of Devil's Den," *Confederate Veteran*, vol. 33 (1925), p. 20; Frassanito, *Gettysburg, Then & Now, Touring the Battlefield With Old Pictures, 1863–1889* (Gettysburg: Thomas Publications, 1996), pp. 25–26; Gettysburg Foundation, Devil's Den Trail, p. 17; Dreese, *This Flag Never Goes Down*, pp. 15 and 64; Williams, *Hood's Texas Brigade in the Civil War*, p. 157; Polley, *Hood's Texas Brigade*, pp. 168–169; Reardon and Vossler, *A Field Guide to Gettysburg*, p. 223.
12. Sims, "Recollection of the Civil War," THM.
13. Adelman and Smith, *Devil's Den*, p. 31; CTSR, NA.
14. Polley, *Hood's Texas Brigade*, p. 169.
15. *Ibid.*, p. 170.
16. River Nore, internet.
17. Sims, "Recollection of the Civil War," THM; Adelman and Smith, *Devil's Den*, p. 25.
18. Work to Langley, May 28, 1908, THM; Polley, *Hood's Texas Brigade*, p. 169; CTSR, NA.
19. Polley, *Hood's Texas Brigade*, p. 168.
20. James Henry Hendrick to Mother, July 8, 1863, USAMHI.
21. Sims, "Recollection of the Civil War," THM; Tucker, *Burnside's Bridge*, pp. 83–152; Rozier (ed.), *The Granite Farm Letters, The Civil War Correspondence of Edgeworth and Sallie Bird* (Athens: The University of Georgia Press, 1988), p. 118; Reardon and Vossler, *A Field Guide to Gettysburg*, p. 222.
22. Sims, "Recollection of the Civil War," THM; O.R., vol. 27, ser. 1, pt. 2, p. 408; Tucker, *Burnside's Bridge*, pp. 17–18, 50, 57, and 83–152; Rozier (ed.), *The Granite Farm Letters*, p. 118; Work to Langley, May 28, 1908, THM.
23. Work to Langley, May 28, 1908, THM.
24. CRSR, NA; Spencer, *From Corsicana To Appomattox*, pp. 62–63; Work to Langley, May 28, 1908, THM; Williams, *Hood's Texas Brigade in the Civil War*, p. 158; Polley, *Hood's Texas Brigade*, p. 169.
25. Dreese, *This Flag Never Goes Down*, p. 64.
26. Sims, "Recollection of the Civil War," THM.
27. Polley, *Hood's Texas Brigade*, p. 177.
28. Guelzo, *Gettysburg*, p. 267; Rozier (ed.), *The Granite Farm Letters*, p. 118; Tucker, *Burnside's Bridge*, pp. 130–151; Bowden and Ward, *Last Chance for Victory*, pp. 284, 290, and 293–294; Sears, *Gettysburg*, p. 269; Gottfried, *Brigades of Gettysburg*, pp. 428–451; Dreese, *This Flag Never Goes Down*, pp. 65 and 71; Polley, *Hood's Texas Brigade*, pp. 169–170; Sears, *Gettysburg*, p. 275; Adelman and Smith, *Devil's Den*, pp. 40–43 and 45–46.
29. Sears, *Gettysburg*, pp. 275–276; Polley, *Hood's Texas Brigade*, p. 182; Bowden and Ward, *Last Chance for Victory*, p. 290.
30. Polley, *Hood's Texas Brigade*, pp. 171–172.

31. *Ibid.*; Williams, *Hood's Texas Brigade in the Civil War*, pp. 157–158.
32. Polly, *Hood's Texas Brigade*, p. 172.
33. CTSR, NA.
34. Polley, *Hood's Texas Brigade*, p. 183.
35. *Ibid.*, 182; Williams, *Hood's Texas Brigade in the Civil War*, pp. 157–158.
36. Sims, "Recollection of the Civil War," THM.
37. Polley, *Hood's Texas Brigade*, p. 182.
38. *Ibid.*
39. *Ibid.*, pp. 182–183.
40. *Ibid.*, p. 183; Williams, *Hood's Texas Brigade in the Civil War*, p. 163; Work, Philip Alexander, The Handbook of Texas Online.
41. Sims, "Recollection of the Civil War," THM; Williams, *Hood's Texas Brigade in the Civil War*, 27.
42. Polley, *Hood's Texas Brigade*, p. 183.

Chapter 6

1. Gottfried, *Brigades of Gettysburg*, pp. 432–433; Guelzo, *Gettysburg*, pp. 267–270; Dreese, *This Flag never Goes Down*, pp. 65 and 71.
2. Guelzo, *Gettysburg*, pp. 257–262 and 267–370; Sword, *Sharpshooter*, p. 27; Williams, *Hood's Texas Brigade in the Civil War*, pp. 87 and 90.
3. Sears, *Gettysburg*, pp. 276 and 278–279; Gottfried, *Brigades of Gettysburg*, pp. 431–435.
4. West, *A Texan in Search of a Fight*, p. 16.
5. Smither to Mother, July 29, 1863, THM.
6. Fletcher, *Rebel Private*, p. 79.
7. Coco, *Recollections of a Texas Colonel at Gettysburg* (Gettysburg: Thomas Publications, 1990), p. 39.
8. Powell, "With Hood at Gettysburg," *Weekly Times*, December 13, 1884, Philadelphia, Pennsylvania.
9. *Ibid.*; Williams, *Hood's Texas Brigade in the Civil War*, p. 41.
10. Lasswell (ed.), *Rags and Hope*, pp. 179–180.
11. Smither to Mother, July 29, 1863, THM.
12. Fletcher, *Rebel Private*, pp. 79–80.
13. Lasswell (ed.), *Rags and Hope*, pp. 179–180.
14. Fletcher, *Rebel Private*, p. 80.
15. Powell, "With Hood at Gettysburg," *Weekly Times*, December 13, 1884; Williams, *Hood's Texas Brigade in the Civil War*, 160; CRSR, NA.
16. Smither to Mother, July 29, 1863.
17. Lasswell (ed.), *Rags and Hope*, p. 181.
18. Powell, "With Hood at Gettysburg," *Weekly Times*, December 13 1884.
19. *Ibid.*
20. Guelzo, *Gettysburg*, pp. 268–274.
21. Smither to Mother, July 29, 1863.
22. Fletcher, *Rebel Private*, p. 80.
23. Rufus R. King to Family, July 9, 1863, Texas Heritage Museum, Historical Research Center, Hillsboro, Texas.
24. Fletcher, *Rebel Private*, p. 84; Rozier (ed.), *The Granite Farm Letters*, p. 118.
25. Fletcher, *Rebel Private*, p. 83.
26. Lasswell (ed.), *Rags and Hope*, pp. 178–179.
27. Work to Langley, May 28, 1908, THM.
28. *Ibid.*

29. *Ibid.*
30. Williams, *Hood's Texas Brigade in the Civil War*, pp. 163–166 and 304.
31. *Ibid.*, pp. 165–166; *New York Times*, July 3, 1913.
32. James Henry Hendrick to Mother, July 8, 1863, USAMI.
33. *Ibid.*
34. Hood, *John Bell Hood*, pp. x–292; Bowden and Ward, *Last Chance for Victory*, p. 284.
35. Roberts and Olson, *A Line in the Sand, The Alamo in Blood and Memory* (New York: The Free Press, 2001), pp. 172–293.

Epilogue

1. Rufus R. King to Famly, July 9, 1863, THM.
2. West, *A Texan in Search of a Fight*, p. 21.
3. Murry, *"Nothing Could Exceed Their Bravery"* (Wolcott: Benedum Books, 1999), p. 51.
4. *Ibid.*, pp. 50–51.
5. Sears, *Gettysburg*, p. 276.
6. West, *A Texan in Search of a Fight*, 21.
7. *Ibid.*
8. *Ibid.*
9. *Ibid.*, p. 22.
10. Polley, *Hood's Texas Brigade*, p. 172.
11. West, *A Texan in Search of a Fight*, p. 23.
12. Faust, *The Republic of Suffering*, p. 10; Williams, *Hood's Texas Brigade in the Civil War*, pp. 12–13; Nevins, *The Texans*, pp. 222–223.
13. *Richmond Daily Dispatch*, Richmond, Virginia, February 27, 1865; Winik, *April 1865*, p. 57; CTSR, NA.
14. *Jamesown Journal*, Jamestown, New York, September 7, 1836; Hood, *John Bell Hood*, pp. 281–285.
15. Williams, *Hood's Texas Brigade in the Civil War*, p. 304; Gottfrield, *Brigades of Gettysburg*, pp. 435–436.
16. *New York Times*, July 3, 1913.
17. Polley, *Hood's Texas Brigade*, p. 185.
18. Adelman and Smith, *Devil's Den*, pp. 118–119.
19. Williams, *Hood's Texas Brigade in the Civil War*, p. 118.
20. Hood, *John Bell Hood*, p. 301.
21. *New York Times*, July 3, 1913.
22. Polley, *Hood's Texas Brigade*, p. 169.
23. West, *A Texan in Search of a Fight*, p. 23.

24 Williams, E. B. (ed.), *Rebel Brothers: The Civil War Letters of the Truehearts* (College Station: Texas A&M Oress, 1995), p. 75.

25 Govan, G. E. and Livingood, J. W. (eds.), *The Haskell Memoirs: The Personal Narrative of a Confederate Officer* (New York: G. P. Putnam's Sons, 1960), pp. 19, 55, 58.

Bibliography

Books and Articles

Adelman G. E. and Smith, T. H., *Devil's Den, A History and Guide* (Gettysburg: Thomas Publications, 1997)

Bass, F. S., Jefferson, Texas, to Scoto Shipp, Virginia Military Academy, Lexington, May 13, 1893, Confederate Research Center, Hillsboro, Texas

Bates, T., Letter to Elizabeth, December 6, 1862, Chappell Hill Historical Society, Chappell Hill, Texas

Boatner, M. M., *The Civil War Dictionary* (New York: David McKay Company, Inc., 1959)

Boswell, E., *Texas Boys in Gray* (Plano: Republic of Texas Press, 2000)

Bowden S. and Ward, B., *Last Chance for Victory, Robert E. Lee and the Gettysburg Campaign* (New York: Da Capo Press, 2001)

Brear, H. B., *Inherit the Alamo, Myth and Ritual at an American Shrine* (Austin: University of Texas Press, 1995)

Burke, J., The Handbook of Texas Online.

Campbell, R. B., "A Lone Star in Virginia," *Civil War Times Illustrated*; *An Empire for Slavery* (LSU Press, 1989)

Carson, E. S., "Hampton's Legion and Hood's Brigade," *Confederate Veteran*, vol. xvi, no. 7 (July 1908)

Catton, B., *Glory Road, The Bloody Route from Fredericksburg to Gettysburg* (Garden City: Doubleday and Company, Inc., 1952)

Coco, G. A., *Confederates Killed in Action at Gettysburg* (Gettysburg: Thomas Publications, 2001); *On the Bloodstained Field*, I & II, 262 *Human Interest Stories of the Campaign and Battle of Gettysburg* (La Vergne: Ingram Book Company, 2013); *Recollections of a Texas Colonel at Gettysburg* (Gettysburg: Thomas Publications, 1990)

Compiled Service Records of Confederate Soldiers Who Served in Organizations from the State of Texas, Record Group 109, National Archives, Washington, D.C.

Connelly T. L., and Bellows, B. L., *God and General Longstreet, The Lost Cause and the Southern Mind*, (Baton Rouge: Louisiana State University Press, 1982)

Cowell, A. T., *Tactics at Gettysburg*, (Gaithersburg: Olde Soldier Books, 1987)

Crozier, G. H., "A Private with General Hood," *Confederate Veteran*, vol. xxv, no. 12 (Dec 1917)

Cubbison, D. R., "Petite Guerre: Saratoga's Small War," *Patriots of the American Revolution*, vol. 4, issue 5 (September–October 2011)

Curtis, N. M., *From Bull Run to Chancellorsville, The Story of the Sixteenth New York Infantry together with Personal Reminiscences* (New York: G.P. Putnam's Sons, 1906)

Dale, M., Letter to Brother, June 7, 1862, Confederate Research Center, Hillsboro, Texas

Darden, S. H., The Handbook of Texas Online.

Davis, W. C., *Three Road to the Alamo, The Lives and Fortunes of David Crockett, James Bowie, and William Barret Travis* (New York: Harper Collins Publishers, 1998)

DePalo, Jr., W. A., *The Mexican National Army, 1822–1852* (College Station: Texas A & M University Press, 1997)

Dreese, M., *This Flag Never Goes Down* (Gettysburg: Thomas Publications, 2004)

Dunham M. A., Letter to Sarah A. Walker, October 20, 1864, Daughters of Republic of Texas Library, The Alamo, San Antonio, Texas.

Editors of Time-Life Books, *Echoes of Glory, Arms and Equipment of the Confederacy* (Alexandria: Time-Life Books, 1991)

Everett, D. E., *Chaplain Davis and Hood's Texas Brigade* (Baton Rouge: The Louisiana State University Press, 1999)

Faust, D. G., *This Republic of Suffering, Death and the American Civil War* (New York: Vintage Books, 2008)

Fehrenbach, T. R., *Fire and Blood, History of Mexico* (New York: Da Capo Press, 1995); *Texas, A Salute from Above* (New York: Portland House, 1988); *Lone Star, A History of Texas and the Texans, From Prehistory to the Present* (New York: Da Capa Press, 2000)

First Texas File, Antietam National Military Park Archives, Sharpsburg, Maryland.

Fisher, J., Handbook of Texas Online

Fletcher, W. A., *Rebel Private: Front and Rear* (New York: Meridian Books, 1995)

Frassanito, W. A., *Gettysburg, Then & Now, Touring the Battlefield with Old Pictures, 1863–1889* (Gettysburg: Thomas Publications, 1996)

Freeman, D. S., *Lee's Lieutenants, Manassas to Malvern Hill* (3 vols., New York: Charles Scribner's Sons, 1942), vol. 1; *Lee's Lieutenants, Gettysburg to Appomattox*, (4 vols., New York: Charles Scribner's Sons, 1944), vol. 3

Gettysburg Foundation, Devil's Den Trail

Giles, V. C., "The Flag of First Texas, A.N. Virginia," *Confederate Veteran*, vol. 15, no. 9 (Sept. 1907)

Glover, R. W. (ed.), *"Tyler to Sharpsburg,"* (Waco: W. M. Morrison, 1960)

Gottfried, B. M., *Brigades of Gettysburg, The Union and Confederate Brigades at the Battle of Gettysburg* (New York: Skyhorse Publishing, 2012); *The Artillery of Gettysburg* (Nashville: Cumberland House, 2008)

Guelzo, *Gettysburg*

Guerra, M. A. N., *Heroes of the Alamo and Goliad, Revolutionaries on the Road to San Jacinto and Texas Independence* (San Antonio: The Alamo Press, 1987)

Hale, D., *The Third Texas Cavalry in the Civil War* (Norman: The University of Oklahoma Press, 1993)

Halliday, E. M., *Understanding Thomas Jefferson* (New York: HarperCollins Publishers, 2001)

Hamilton, D. H., *History of Company M, First Texas Volunteer Infantry, Hood's Brigade* (Waco: W. M. Morrison, 1962)

Hanks, O. T., "History of Captain B. F. Benton's Company 1861–1865," Confederate Research Center, Hillsboro, Texas.

Hardin S. and Hook, R., *The Texas Rangers*, (London: Osprey Books, 1996)

Hardin S. L., *Texian Illiad, The Military History of the Texas Revolution*, (Austin: University of Texas Press, 1994); (ed.), *Lone Star: The Republic of Texas, 1836–1846* (Carlisle: Discovery Enterprises, Ltd., 1998)

Hassler, W. S. (ed.), "Civil War Letters of William Dorsey Pender to His Wife," *Georgia Review*, vol. 17 (Spring 1963)

Hennessy, J. J., *Return to Bull Run, The Campaign and Battle of Second Manassas* (New York: Simon and Schuster, 1993)

Herdegern, L. J., *The Iron Brigade in the Civil War and Memory* (El Dorado Hills: Savas Beatie, 2012)

Higgins, D. R., *The Swamp Fox, Francis Marion's Campaign in the Carolinas 1780* (Oxford: Osprey Publishing, 2013)

Hoge, J. N., "The Tragedy of Devil's Den," *Confederate Veteran*, vol. 33 (1925)

Hood, S. M., *John Bell Hood, The Rise, Fall, and Resurrection of a Confederate General* (El Dorado Hills: Savas Beatie, LLC, 2013)

Houston, Jr., S., Biographical Sketch, Samuel Houston, Jr., Papers, 1862–1886, Briscoe Center for American History, The University of Texas at Austin, Austin, Texas.

Houston, S., Letter to Sam Houston, Jr., May 22, 1861, Texas State Library and Archives Commission, Austin, Texas

Hunt, A. N., *Haiti's Influence on Antebellum America, Slumbering Volcano in the Caribbean* (Baton Rouge: Louisiana State University Press, 1988)

Hunter, A., "The Rebel Yell," *Confederate Veteran*, vol. 21, no. 5 (May 1913)

Jackson, R., *Alamo Legacy, Alamo Descendants, Remember the Alamo* (Austin: Eakin Press, 1997)

Katcher, P. R. N., *The Army of Northern Virginia* (London: Osprey Publishing Ltd., 1975); *American Civil War Armies, Confederate Artillery, Cavalry and Infantry* (London: Osprey Publishing, 1987); *American Civil War Armies, State Troops* (London: Osprey Publishing, 1989); *The Army of Robert E. Lee* (London: Arms and Armour Press, 1994)

Kegel, J. A., *North with Lee and Jackson, The Lost Story of Gettysburg*, (Mechanicsburg: Stackpole Books, 1996)

Kerby, R. L., *Kirby Smith's Confederacy, 1863–1865* (Tuscaloosa: University of Alabama Press, 1972)

King, R. R., Letter to Family, July 9, 1863, Texas Heritage Museum, Historical Research Center, Hillsboro, Texas

Lasswell, M. (ed.), *Rags and Hope, The Memoirs of Val C. Giles, Four Years with Hood's Texas Brigade, Fourth Texas Infantry, 1861–1865* (New York: Coward-McCann, Inc., 1961)

Lozano, R. R., *Viva Tejas, The Story of the Tejanos, the Mexican-born Patriots of the Texas Revolution* (San Antonio: The Alamo Press, 1985)

Marten, J., "On the Road with Thomas H. DuVal: A Texas Unionist's Travel Diary, 1863, *Journal of Confederate History*, vol. 6

Matovina, T. M., *The Alamo Remembered, Tejano Accounts and Perspectives* (Austin: University of Texas Press, 1995)

McCaffrey, J. M., *Only A Private, A Texan Remembers the Civil War, The Memoirs of William J. Oliphant* (Houston: Halcyon Press, Ltd., 2004)

McLeod, H., The Handbook of Texas Online

McMurry, R. M., *John Bell Hood and the War for Southern Independence* (Lexington: The University Press of Kentucky, 1982)

McWhiney, G. and Jamieson, P. D., *Attack and Die, Civil War Military Tactics and the Southern Heritage* (Tuscaloosa: University of Alabama Press, 1982)

Mitchell, J. B., *Military Leaders in the Civil War* (McLean: EPM Publications, Inc., 1972)

Moore, S. L., *Savage Frontier, Rangers, Riflemen, and Indian Wars in Texas, 1835–1837*, vol. 1, (2 vols: Denton: The University of North Texas Press, 2002)

Murry, R. I., *"Nothing Could Exceed Their Bravery"* (Wolcott: Benedum Books, 1999)

Navarro, J. A., The Hand of Texas Online

Nevin, D., *The Texans*, (Alexandra: Time-Life Books, 1975)

Nofi, A. A., *The Alamo and the Texas War for Independence* (Conshohocken: Combined Books, 1992)

O'Grady, K. J., *Clear the Way!, The Irish in the Army of Northern Virginia* (Mason City: Savas Publishing Company, 2000)

Oates, S. (ed.), *Rip Ford's Texas*, (Austin: University of Texas Press, 1987)

Oates, W. C., *The War Between the Union and The Confederacy and Its Lost Opportunities* (Neale Publishing Company, 1905)

Oeffinger, J. C. (ed.), *A Soldier's General, The Civil War Letters of Major General Lafayette McLaws* (Chapel Hill: University of North Carolina Press, 2002)

Otott, G. E., "Clash in the Cornfield: The 1st Texas Volunteer Infantry in the Maryland Campaign," *Civil War Regiments*, vol. 5, no. 3 (1997)

Palmer, Jr., W. A., "The Dead of Eltham's Landing," Historical Society of West Point, West Point, Virginia

Patterson, G. A., "John Bell Hood," *Civil War Times Illustrated* (February 1971).

Penny, M. M. and Laine, J. G., *Struggle for the Round Tops, Law's Alabama Brigade at the Battle of Gettysburg* (Shippensburg: White Mane Publishing Company, 1999)

Piston, W. G., *Lee's Tarnished Lieutenant, James Longstreet and His Place in Southern History* (Athens: University of Georgia Press, 1987)

Pohanka, B. C., *Don Troiani's Civil War* (Mechancisburg: Stackpole Books, 1995)

Polk, J. M., *The North and South American Review* (Austin: Von Boeckmann-Jones, 1912)

Polley, J. B., *A Soldier's Letters to Charming Nellie*, (New York: Neale Publishing Company, 1908); *Hood's Texas Brigade, Its Marches, Its Battles, Its Achievements*, (New York: Neale Publishing Company, 1910); Letter to father, May 12, 1863, Museum Quality America, Division of Cal Packard, LLC; *Papers, 1852–1879, Daughters of the Republic of Texas Library* (San Antonio, Texas, The Handbook of Texas Online)

Powell, "With Hood at Gettysburg," *Weekly Times*, December 13, 1884, Philadelphia, Pennsylvania

Pritchard, W. D., "Hood's Brigade," typescript, First Texas File, ANMPA.

Pruett J. L. and Cole, Jr., E. B., *Goliad Massacre* (Austin: Eakin Press, 1985)

Reardon, C. and Vossler, T., *A Field Guide to Gettysburg, Experiencing the Battlefield through Its History, Places, and People* (Chapel Hill: University of North Carolina Press, 2013)

Roberts R. and Olson, J. S., *A Line in the Sand, The Alamo In Blood and Memory* (New York: The Free Press, 2001)

Roberts, O. M., *Confederate Military History*, Texas, vol. 15 (Wilmington: Broadfoot Publishing, 1989)

Robertson, J. B., The Handbook of Texas Online

Robertson, J. I., *The Stonewall Brigade*, (Baton Rouge: Louisiana State University Press, 1963)

Rosen, R. N., *The Jewish Confederates* (Columbia: University of South Carolina Press, 2000)

Rozier, J. (ed.), *The Granite Farm Letters, The Civil War Correspondence of Edgeworth and Sallie Bird* (Athens: The University of Georgia Press, 1988)

Scott, J. O., *Unveiling and Dedication of Monument to Hood's Texas Brigade* (Houston: F. B. Chilton, 1911)

Sears, S., *Gettysburg* (Boston: Houghton Mifflin Company, 2003)

Shuffler, R. H. (ed.), *The Adventures of a Prisoner of War 1863–1864* (Austin: University of Texas Press, 1964)

Simpson, H. B., *Gaines' Mill to Appomattox, Waco and McLennan County in Hood's Texas Brigade*, (Waco: Texian Press, 1988); *Hood's Texas Brigade, Lee's Grenadier Guard*, (Fort Worth: Landmark Publishing, 1999)

Sims, A. C., "Recollection of the Civil War," Texas Heritage Museum, Historical Research Center, Hillsboro, Texas

Smith, G. J., "'One of the Most Daring of Men,' The Life of Confederate General William Tatum Wofford," *The Journal of Confederate History Series*, vol. xvi (Murfreesboro: Southern Heritage Press, 1997)

Smithers J. M., Letter to Mother, June 28, 1863, Texas Heritage Museum, Historical Research Center, Hillsboro, Texas.

Smithwick, N., *The Evolution of a State, Recollections of Old Texas Days*, (Austin: University of Texas Press, 1983)

Spencer, J., *From Coriscana to Appomattox, The Story of the Corsicana Invincibles and the Navarro Rifles* (Coriscana: The Texas Press, 1984)

Stiles, R., *Four Years under Marse Robert* (Marietta: R. Bemis Publishing Company, 1995)

Sword, W., *Sharpshooter: Hiram Berdan, his famous Sharpshooters and their Sharps rifles* (Lincoln: Andrew Mowbray Incorporated Publishers, 1988)

"Texan at War, The Letters of Private James Henry Hendrick, Army of Northern Virginia," 1964 typescript by Hugh Irvin Power, Jr., First Texas File, ANMPA

Third Texas Infantry, The Handbook of Texas Online

Todd, G. T., *First Texas Regiment* (Waco: Texian Press, 1964)

Travis, B. J., *Men of God, Angels of Death, History of the Rowan Artillery* (private printing, 2008)

Tucker, P. T., "Motivations of United States Volunteers During the Texas Revolution," *East Texas Historical Journal*, vol. 29, no. 1 (1991); *Burnside's Bridge, The Climactic Struggle of the 2nd and 20th Georgia at Antietam Creek* (Mechanicsburg: Stackpole Books, 2000); *Exodus from the Alamo, The Anatomy of the Last Stand Myth* (Philadelphia: Casemate Publishers, 2011); *George Washington's Surprise Attack, A New Look at the Battle that Decided the Fate of America* (New York: Skyhorse Publishing, 2014); *Storming Little Round Top, The 15th Alabama and Their Fight for the High Ground, July 2, 1863* (New York: DaCapo Books, 2002); *The South's Finest* (White Man Pub., 1993)

Ural, S. F., 'A Little Body of Malcontents,' *Civil War Times* (June 2014)

Valor, The Biennial Publication of Hood's Texas Brigade Association, No. 2 (1973)

Walker, J., Handbook of Texas Online

War of the Rebellion: Official Records of the Union and Confederate Armies, (128 vols., Washington, D.C.: United States Government Printing Office, 1880-1901), vol. 19, ser. 1, pt. 1

Webb, W. P., *The Texas Rangers, A Century of Frontier Defense* (Austin: University of Texas Press, 1991)

Wert, J. D., *A Glorious Army* (Simon and Schuster, 2011)

West, J. C., *A Texan in Search of a Fight, Being the Diary and Letters of a Private Soldier in Hood's Texas Brigade* (Memphis: General Books, LLC, 2012)

Williams, E. B., *Hood's Texas Brigade in the Civil War* (Fayetteville: McFarland and Company Publishers, 2012)

Winik, J., *April 1865* (New York: HarperCollins, 2001)

Work, P. A., The Handbook of Texas Online.

Zaboly, G., *American Colonial Ranger, The Northern Colonies 1724–64* (Oxford: Osphrey Publishing, 2004)

Newspapers

Anthens Daily Review, Athens, Texas, April 12, 1972

Baltimore Gazette and Daily Advertiser, Baltimore, Maryland, August 14, 1832.

Bangor Commercial Advertiser, Bangor, Maine, March 19, 1836.

Frankfort Commonwealth, Frankfort Kentucky, May 25, 1836.

Jamesown Journal, September 7, 1836

Morning Courier and New York Enquirer, July 9, 1836

National Banner and Nashville Whig, March 18, 1836; May 30, 1836

National Tribune, New York, February 4, 1886

New Orleans Bee, New Orleans, Louisiana, January 4, 1836.

New York American, November 25, 1836.
New York Times, June 29, 1836; July 3, 1913
Palestine Herald-Press, Palestine, Texas, October 18, 1967
Richmond Daily Dispatch, Richmond, Virginia, February 27, 1865
Sentinel, Gettysburg, Pennsylvania, August 4, 1863
Southern Patriot, Charleston, South Carolina, November 21, 1835
Telegraph and Texas Register, San Felipe de Austin, Texas, December 2, 1835.
The Daily Dispatch, Richmond, Virginia, February 6, 1862.
The Liberator, Boston, Massachusetts, June 11, 1836
Tyler Courier-Times Telegraph, Tyler, Texas, April 16, 1972
Western Sentinel, Winston, North Carolina, June 6, 1862